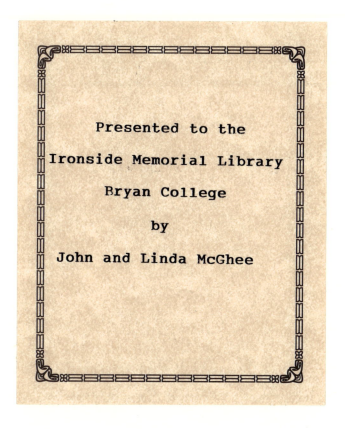

Beating the Unbeatable Foe

Beating the Unbeatable Foe

One Man's Victory Over Communism, Leviathan, and the Last Enemy*

Frederick Schwarz, M.D.

Regnery Publishing, Inc.
Washington, D.C.

** The last enemy that shall be destroyed is death.
St. Paul (1 Corinthians 15:26)*

134481

Library of Congress Cataloging-in-Publication Data

Schwarz, Frederick Charles.
    Beating the unbeatable foe : One man's victory over communism,
leviathan, and the last enemy / by Frederick Schwarz.
       p. cm.
    ISBN 0-89526-437-4 (alk. paper)
    1. Schwarz, Frederick Charles.   2. Christian Anti-Communist
Crusade—Biography.   3. Right-wing extremists—United States—
Biography.   4. Anti-communist movements—United States—
History—20th century.   5. Communism and Christianity.
6. Political persecution—United States—Case studies.   I. Title.
E748.S38445A3   1996
261.2'1'092—dc20
[B]   96-8369
                                                                             CIP

Published in the United States by
Regnery Publishing, Inc.
An Eagle Publishing Company
422 First Street, SE, Suite 300
Washington, DC 20003

Distributed to the trade by
National Book Network
4720-A Boston Way
Lanham, MD 20706

Printed on acid-free paper.
Manufactured in the United States of America

10 9 8 7 6 5 4 3 2 1

Books are available in quantity for promotional or premium use. Write to
Director of Special Sales, Regnery Publishing, Inc., 422 First Street, SE, Suite
300, Washington, DC 20003, for information on discounts and terms or call
(202) 546-5005.

With unlimited affection and gratitude, I dedicate this book to my wife Lillian and our children—Rosemary, David, and the Johns—and their growing families, who grace our lives with radiant joy.

Contents

....

Acknowledgments

....

WITHOUT THE CONTRIBUTION OF MANY people, the triumphs recorded in this book would not have been possible. I venture to select a few, with apologies to the many omitted who merit inclusion.

The Honorable Maxwell Bushby, O.B.E., for many years Speaker of the Parliament of the Australian State, Tasmania, and a lifelong personal friend was a loving husband and father, a devout Christian, and a fervent anti-Communist. He was valued as a member of the Crusade's Board. It was his dying wish that this book be written to provide an accurate account of the nature and history of the Crusade in order to dispel prevailing delusions.

The Reverend Donald Crowhurst served with distinction as a research director, editorial advisor, and limitless laborer during the production of the manuscript. Since we both have strong opinions, an onlooker could have thought some of our debates about content and syntax to be fierce rather than the friendly and challenging exchanges that they were. Our friendship of forty years survived intact and undiminished.

Miss Ella Doorn. The name Ella has become a synonym for efficient and unlimited secretarial service. My psychiatrist daughter says, "Every good man deserves an Ella." For forty-three years Ella has served as my personal secretary and secretary of the Crusade. She has been ready to work twenty-four hours each day, seven days a week, fifty-two weeks each year. So much more than a job, she saw her work as God's calling for her life. Her astonishing devotion reached beyond the immediate tasks of the Crusade, and she lovingly embraced my wife Lillian and the entire Schwarz family.

Clark Bowers has astonished and embarrassed many top Communist leaders by his knowledge and understanding of their philosophy. He angered Mikhail Gorbachev at a conference with his pertinent questions, and during a visit to China astonished theoreticians of the Chinese Communist Party, who reported, "We have never been asked such intelligent, pertinent questions like those he asked."

The Reverend James D. Colbert served the Crusade with exemplary loyalty and devotion for forty-three years. The Crusade suffered a major loss with the recent death of this saintly man. Thousands in many countries mourn his passing. He was a fount of memory and vital information, and an active and humble participant in most of the events recorded in this book. Jim was also vice president and chairman of our Crusade's board of directors.

Senator Thomas J. Dodd, a featured speaker at our Schools of Anti-Communism, remained loyal and strong in his support (along with people like William F. Buckley, Jr.), even when the storm of slander exploded. He expressed the highest respect for my message and was himself a most articulate and devoted anti-Communist. He was an outstanding democratic senator for the state of Connecticut, and father of Christopher Dodd, Connecticut's present liberal senator and president of the federal Democratic Party.

Congressman Walter Judd had personal experience with Communism when he was a Christian missionary to China. He spoke at most of our Schools of Anti-Communism, and his superb oratory always held the student audience spell-bound. He would often say during his address to our students that he would sooner be speaking to them than to the Congress of the United States. He served ten superb terms as a member of the U.S. House of Representatives.

Reed Irvine is now nationally known as the founder and chairman of the watchdog organization, Accuracy in Media. He has been a dear friend and colleague for many years. Prior to the formation of Accuracy in Media, we held many anti-Communism rallies and anti-subversive seminars in Washington, D.C.

Tom Phillips is living proof that America remains the land of unsurpassed opportunity. From a humble beginning out of his garage, he has built a remarkable publishing empire based in Washington, D.C. Early in his career he distributed my book *You Can Trust the Communists (to be Communists)* and published *Three Faces of Revolution.* He is completely devoted to freedom and has been a very close personal friend for many years. He and his wife Jan have spent many happy hours together with Lillian and me in Australia and the United States.

The poet says, "Old friends are like diamonds, precious and rare." Like Tom Phillips, Elton Wilson, Ph.D., is truly a diamond. Our friendship began nearly fifty years ago. We share a mutual love of poetry and quote it to each other with zest. He has a deep understanding of Communist philosophy, and he served as director of the Australian Crusade with distinction. He amazes me with his skill at solving cryptic crossword puzzles.

At an age when most men are content to retire, he enrolled in the University of New South Wales, Australia, and earned his doctorate in political science. I salute him and his wife Marjorie.

Lillian and I are proud to think of Dr. John Whitehall as our son. His career has been remarkable. He is a pediatric physician who is armed with a remarkable understanding of Communist philosophy and the rare ability to make it understandable to others. He has faced and exposed Communism in many countries, including Australia, Vietnam, South Africa, Timor, Mexico, Canada, the Philippines, and the United States of America. He has faced danger with serenity and faith. The Communist New Peoples Army of the Philippines listed him for assassination.

Fame is fleeting, but Herbert Philbrick was nationally known for many years. His story was told in his book *I Led Three Lives,* and in the television series with the same title.

As a young married man he joined a Baptist church in the Boston area, where he became active in a peace group that functioned in the church. After being elected its president he learned to his surprise and consternation that the group was controlled by the U.S. Communist Party. On reporting this to the FBI, he was asked to continue as its president and to join the Communist Party and report on its activity. He did as advised and rose in the Communist ranks until he was elected to the national politburo. He surprised the party leaders when he became the star witness against them in the Smith Act trials.

Proofreaders play a vital role in the creation of a book, and *Beating the Unbeatable Foe* has been fortunate to have the services of several most competent volunteers. They are Barbara Morgan, Harry and Dodie Andersen, and Philip (Pip) Wilson of Australia. They love and respect the English language, and their enthusiasm was surpassed only by their competence.

Following our mass rallies of the late fifties and early sixties, I took the message from city to city, a role comparable to that of the early circuit riders. It was a network of freedom-loving friends who made this possible. When I wished to conduct a meeting in a city I would call a friend who would select a location and organize a rally. These friends are numerous, and I name some, with apologies to those whose names are omitted. Maxine and Walter Graham held the fort in Milwaukee, Wisconsin, for many years, and Ruth and Floyd Burroughs were directors of a Crusade office in Indianapolis, Indiana. Reed Irvine operated in Washington, D.C., and Bill and Elizabeth Strube in Houston, Texas. In Dallas there are Marty Lynch, Ed and Genie Farrow, and Jean and George Jones. Ophthalmologist Dr. Fred Kapetansky and his wife Audrey were host and hostess in Columbus, Ohio, and anesthetist Harry Sammons and his wife Lee filled that role in St. Louis, Missouri, where they were aided by George and Barbara Hixon, Menlo and Mary Jean Smith, Fred and Phyllis Schlafly, and Eleanor Schlafly. In Portland Dr. Roger Congdon performed miracles. To these and scores of others an eternal debt of gratitude is owing. Their selfless service and friendship has enriched my life and work. They represent the true heart of America.

Finally, I pay tribute to the wholehearted support of my wife Lillian, my children, and my grandchildren. I have been encompassed with understanding and love and consider myself the richest man in the world.

Foreword

....

ON JANUARY 1, 1990 AT THE Beverly Wilshire Hotel in Beverly Hills, California, over five hundred distinguished guests gathered to pay tribute to Dr. and Mrs. Fred Schwarz for their inspirational lives and great contributions to the freedom of America. The following pages are excerpts from some of those testimonials given.

MRS. ELEANOR SCHLAFLY, CO-FOUNDER OF THE CARDINAL MINDSZENTY FOUNDATION

In 1958 Dr. Fred Schwarz held a School for Anti-Communism in St. Louis, Missouri. My brother Fred, [his wife] Phyllis, and I attended, [and] it was excellent. But there was a special and significant happening: Dr. Fred Schwarz suggested to us that we form an organization for Catholics so that they might learn of the evils of Communism. Three months later, the Cardinal Mindszenty Foundation was launched. We honor . . . Dr. Fred Schwarz for his outstanding leadership in the whole field of opposing communism and upholding faith, family and freedom. We . . . thank him for his brilliant analysis of communism, making it understandable for all of us.

MR. REED IRVINE, CHAIRMAN OF ACCURACY IN MEDIA

People like Dr. Fred Schwarz, who [has] for forty and more years been fighting the evil that is now virtually crumbling before our eyes . . . are the people who really deserve to be honored.

MIKE ANTONOVITCH, LOS ANGELES SUPERVISOR

It has been said that eagles don't flock, we have to find them one at a time. As we all know the eagle stands for self-reliance, for liberty and independence. Tonight we are honoring an eagle and his wife. Dr. Fred Schwarz . . . has been [a] strong and independent . . . voice for freedom and liberty at a time when people said that there was no need for such a voice. By using the intellect [and] education, and not emotion, he has been able to reach all parts of the world with a simple little book, *You Can Trust the Communists to Be Communists*.

THE OFFICIAL PLAQUE FROM THE CITY OF LOS ANGELES READS IN PART:

Dr. Schwarz has earned the title, 'Father of Anti-Communism. . . . Therefore, I, Ernie Kell, mayor of the city of Long Beach, commend Dr. Fred Schwarz for his forty years of dedicated service and congratulate him as he celebrates his 77th birthday and the 50th anniversary of his marriage to Lillian, his beloved wife. Let the great seal of the city of Long Beach be affixed hereto. Adopted this 9th day of January, 1990.

MR. JACK KEMP, SECRETARY OF HOUSING AND URBAN DEVELOPMENT

What a pleasure it is to have an opportunity to join Dr. Schwarz, Lillian and their family and friends on this occasion that is, if not the end of history, certainly the end of communism. . . . As an old pro-football player with the San Diego Chargers and later the Buffalo Bills, I was deeply moved and indeed educated, by the tapes, movies, [and] books of Fred Schwarz. . . . I personally appreciate the fact that [people such as] President Reagan, President Bush and Pope John Paul have been involved in the struggle against totalitarian communism for so many years [and] deserve as much credit as anybody of this piece of the Berlin Wall being cracked off by East Germans. Dr. Schwarz, above anyone else, has had the opportunity to educate literally thousands, if not hundreds of thousands, of young men and women all over the world in the struggle for democracy and freedom and the struggle against the tyranny of communism. I want to say to all your family and friends, "God bless you, God bless America and thank you for your incredible leadership."

MR. WILLIAM F. BUCKLEY, JR., FOUNDER OF THE *NATIONAL REVIEW* MAGAZINE

Dr. Fred Schwarz . . . has been a great teacher, holding spellbound hundreds of thousands of Americans. [He taught] them the elementary truths about communist practices during the era when temptation was high to ignore communism on the assumption that that was the way to make it go away. The Marxist dogmas are all but dead.

DALE EVANS

I can remember when [Dr. Schwarz] first started here. The first time I ever met Dr. S. was in the Shrine Auditorium; [it was] his first big seminar. . . . I was so excited at this man's dedication and at his sincerity and his fearlessness. This was the day when it wasn't too popular to announce yourself as a Christian—particularly in fighting communism in Hollywood. This man believed in what he said, he knew what he was talking about and he was fearless in proclaiming it. . . . Dr. Schwarz preaches that 'where the Spirit of the Lord is, there is liberty.' We have so much liberty in our country that we sometimes take it for granted, and the other side of that coin of freedom is responsibility. He (an Australian) has taken our responsibility on himself in this country. We should be eternally grateful. . . .

U.S. CONGRESSMAN DANA ROHRBACHER

I am so pleased . . . to acknowledge the wonderful things that Dr. Schwarz has meant to me as an individual, what he has meant to our country and what he has meant to the cause of human freedom. . . . When I was a young person I went through my ups and downs in life, [and] Dr. Schwarz was there to help me personally, with guidance, with love and affection. . . . I wouldn't be here today without that. . . . [He gave me direction] politically, [in] the understanding he gave me of Marxism and Leninism. . . . Through those people that he converted, his effect on our country and on the world is going to go on and on and on. Dr. Schwarz taught us that ideas have consequences. . . . I happen to believe that it was ideas that put up the Berlin Wall. I think it is the understanding of ideas that is going to bring down and is bringing down the Berlin Wall. . . .

U.S. CONGRESSMAN BOB DORNAN

My mother told me when I came home on my first leave [from the Air Force] that she had discovered somebody who was going to change history. She gave me one of [Dr. Schwarz's] pamphlets. . . . When you . . . think of these great anniversaries in your life, what you have done

with your career and not just in saving people's bodies as
a doctor, but in saving their souls, you have really fulfilled
those . . . ideals of every man and woman who want to
amount to something in this short passage of time that
God gives up on this delicate little planet. Faith, family
and freedom—God, family, country. . . . Thank you for
teaching me, as a Christian, that the greatest evil in this
century and maybe in all time was the evil of communism.
It has far outshone in 72 years the evil of the 12-year
Third Reich. . . . God bless you, Dr. Schwarz, for showing
us the way to battle, as decent men and women. For
Christianity, for Jesus and for the countries that we love.

FRED ROGERS, M.D., FOUNDER AND PRESIDENT OF THE NATIONAL COORDINATING COUNCIL

I want to personally add my unlimited gratitude to
Dr. Fred Schwarz and the magnificence of his work. The
vital greatness and the accomplishments of the Christian
Anti-Communist Crusade will probably never be measured but certainly at this very moment, their work is
going on all over the world. . . . I think we are seeing
privatization sweeping abroad and I think in this country we are perhaps behind in looking to freedom and liberty and we need to take cognizance of what is going on
in all these other countries. As we give honor tonight,
we clearly want to recognize the countless hours and
years of the many, many people who have supported
and been part of the crusade, the staff, individuals often
unknown, unseen, unnamed who have nurtured and
have with devotion maintained this truly great work.
The purpose of life is not to be happy, though we all
seek happiness; the purpose of life is to matter—to be
productive—to have it make some difference that we
have lived at all. . . . Happiness lies in stretching to the
furthest boundaries that with which we are capable,
with the resources of our mind and our hearts. Perhaps

there is no one who has exemplified that concept of meaning and of mattering and of being important than our Dr. Fred Schwarz. The entire Senate of the State of California agrees with me, and it is my unique privilege to present, for those forty leaders . . . this plaque . . . as a commemorative for your work.

JOHN STORMER, AUTHOR OF *NONE DARE CALL IT TREASON*

Back about thirty years ago . . . I was first awakened to the fact that there were some troubles in the world, [and] one of the truths that I was exposed to was the book *You Can Trust the Communists to Be Communists*. A whole lot of other truths were in your anti-communism crusade [and] they certainly provided a foundation for most of what I have done in the years since then. Today they are showing themselves, particularly your explanation of dialectal materialism, and the way the communists proceed to advance through retreating. It gives us the only real understanding of what is happening in Western Europe, Eastern Europe and the Soviet Union today.

DR. JIM DOBSON, FOUNDER OF FOCUS ON THE FAMILY

Dr. Fred Schwarz came to speak at my college when I was an undergraduate in 1957. The school was Pasadena College, Pasadena, California. He made quite an impression on me. I still recall he things he said, thirty years later, and they continue to influence my life.

U.S. SENATOR STEVE SIMMS

At the very time the United States was reeling from the ultra-liberal and left-wing nonsense about McCarthyism, Dr. Schwarz took the lead in showing the

American people that the real communists were devotedly working to overthrow this country. The Christian Anti-Communism Crusade has provided the education this nation needs to survive.

CONGRESSMAN LARRY MCDONALD (DECEASED)

Your understanding of the dialectics of communism as expressed in *You Can Trust the Communists to Be Communists* is greatly admired as is your great dedication. Keep up the wonderful work.

AMBASSADOR FAITH WHITTLESEY—FORMER AMBASSADOR TO SWITZERLAND

Bravo to Dr. Schwarz for his lifelong selfless dedication to the cause of anti-communism and the difference he has made.

DR. D. JAMES KENNEDY, PASTOR OF CORRAL RIDGE PRESBYTERIAN CHURCH

About 20 years ago I came across a large fold-out sheet which was a detailed explanation of the beliefs and practices of communism. This was during my first year or so in the ministry, and that particular piece made the most significant impact on my understanding of communism.

PRESIDENT RONALD REAGAN

Dear Fred and Lillian, Nancy and I send our heartfelt congratulations on your golden wedding anniversary and on Fred's 37th anniversary of his 39th birthday. Our thoughts and good wishes are with you as you gather with family and friends to celebrate. Fred, you are to be commended for your tireless dedication, dedication in trying to ensure the protection of freedom and human rights, and I know you join me in special satisfaction for

being supportive of your lifetime efforts. May the joy
you have shared over the years be a reflection of the
years to come. Happy anniversary, happy birthday, Fred,
and God bless you both. Sincerely, Ronald Reagan.

RONALD REAGAN

January 4, 1990

Dear Fred and Lillian:

Nancy and I send our heartfelt congratulations on
your Golden Wedding Anniversary and on Fred's 37th
Anniversary of his 39th Birthday. Our thoughts and
good wishes are with you as you gather with family
and friends to celebrate.

Fred, you're to be commended for your tireless
dedication in trying to ensure the protection of
freedom and human rights, and I know you join me in
special satisfaction in the recent events in Eastern
Europe. Of course, Lillian is also to be commended
for being supportive of your lifelong efforts.

May the joy you have shared over the years be a
reflection of the years to come.

Happy Anniversary, Happy Birthday, Fred, and
God bless you both.

                    Sincerely,

                    Ronald Reagan

Mr. and Mrs. Fred Schwarz
c/o Mr. James Colbert
Post Office Box 890
Long Beach, California 90801

Beating the Unbeatable Foe

1

....

The Miracle

And if I had the chance to fall below
Demosthenes or Cicero,
Don't view me with a critic's eye,
But pass my imperfections by,
Large streams from little fountains flow,
Tall oaks from little acorns grow.
—DAVID EVERETT, 1791

LAWRENCE E. SPIVAK, THE FOUNDER and moderator of the television series "Meet the Press," asked the first question:

> Dr. Schwarz, I'd like to ask you about some of the literature you've sent out, and some of the claims you've made in that literature. In letters you have sent out under your signature recently, you've said this: "A successful school can achieve a miracle for freedom." Now, is that just advertising talk or do you believe you can achieve a miracle for freedom?

The occasion was my appearance as the guest on this program on August 26, 1962. I replied:

3

I do believe a miracle for freedom can be achieved if accurate knowledge of the nature of Communism enters into the minds of the people of the United States and the free world. Ignorance of the pathology of Communist doctrines is one of the greatest assets that the Communists have, and if we can make a major contribution to understanding in that field, we can achieve a miracle.

Using hindsight I could have said:

"Mr. Spivak, your humility is admirable, but surprising. You are doubtlessly aware of the importance and prestige of your television program, the most prestigious program in the United States and therefore in the entire world. Guests are usually individuals of great power or renown such as heads of state, leaders of industry, prominent politicians, or great artists. It is usually a great honor to be invited to be your guest, and that honor has been bestowed upon me even though I am a citizen of a foreign country, without special status. I am an Australian citizen who came to this country a few years ago at the invitation of a humble U.S. citizen, Dr. W. E. Pietsch of Waterloo, Iowa. I paid my own fare and arrived with approximately twenty dollars. Shortly thereafter I formed a small organization called the Christian Anti-Communism Crusade. I am now your guest— surely unusual, if not miraculous.

"Nor is my appearance here an isolated event. I have been receiving great, if unfavorable, attention from the major news media of the United States, including *The New York Times; Newsweek, Life,* and *Look* magazines; and CBS television, as well as from representatives of other powerful organizations such as the Anti-Defamation League, the United Automobile Worker Union, and the United States Congress.

"To my great astonishment I am being subjected to a campaign of misrepresentation and vilification which appears to be motivated by a witch's brew of ignorance, fear, bigotry, and intolerance. So I am grateful for this opportunity to try and set the record straight."

The other members of the examining panel were James Wechsler of the *New York Post,* William Rusher of *National Review,* and Richard Clurman of *Time* magazine.
James Wechsler continued the questioning.

Dr. Schwarz, it's the declared position of the Kennedy administration, as it was of the Eisenhower regime, that we seek honorable agreements with the Communists throughout the world, however difficult and harassing the quest for such agreements may be. Is it the objective of your movement to disrupt the efforts to obtain such agreements?

SCHWARZ: Not for a minute. The objective of our movement is to give education concerning the philosophy, morality, organizational structure, techniques, and objectives of Communism, so that the value and outcome of such agreements may be realized and so that the democratic process may be more effective.

WECHSLER: I think you've answered my question. You talk a good deal about the function of your movement in educating the country. Is it your view that the leadership of this country is inadequate to that role? It seems to me that when you talk of setting up printing in India and other places, then, in effect, you've set yourself up as an adjunct to our government, or perhaps, superseding it. Is it your view that the government is inadequate to the task of resisting the Communist challenge?

SCHWARZ: Yes, I believe that the government of the United States is a constitutional government which grants liberty to its citizens. It is not a totalitarian government. It has a monopoly in military areas, but it does not have a monopoly in many other areas. The government has always encouraged people-to-people contacts and encourages individuals to operate in the field of education. We are acting in the area which the government encourages. On the evidence, it's quite clear that past programs, whoever's responsible for them, have been inadequate.

WECHSLER: But isn't the educational program you're carrying on actually at variance with the stated position and objectives of the United States government? You've said that your objective is to show that agreements, in effect, are necessarily useless. At the time of the summit meeting, which Mr. Eisenhower participated in, you hailed the collapse of the summit meeting.

SCHWARZ: You have accused me of saying what I have not said. I did not say that agreements are useless. What I have said is that we should understand the philosophy of the Communists, and the moral code that derives from it, so that we'll know the significance of agreements that are entered into; so that we'll be able to predict with a measure of accuracy how they will be interpreted and applied. With regard to your statement that the government considers itself in conflict with us, various agencies of government are using our educational material in many areas of the world.

More than thirty years have passed since this interview, and it is difficult for the old, and impossible for the young, to remember the emotional ideological climate of that time. A hysterical fear of the John Birch Society excited many in the news media and the academy, and created paradoxical situations. Devoted defenders of the right to freedom of association sought to demonize anyone who dared to associate with acknowledged or suspected members of the John Birch Society. Saying Grace before meals might well have been, "Dear God, if such there be, bless this food and curse the John Birch Society."

I was not then, and I have never been, a member of the John Birch Society, and I never met its founder, Robert Welch. Nevertheless, I was frequently accused of being an effective recruiter for it. It was commonly remarked that "Schwarz stirs them up, and Welch signs them up."

Consequently, I was anticipating questions about my relationship to that society and one soon came.

> WECHSLER: Would you tell us, Dr. Schwarz, in this situation, in this city, what your view of the John Birch Society is? I've read your comments in many places and they seem to vary, depending on what city you're in.
>
> SCHWARZ: My view has been consistent. I have established a policy that I specialize in Communist philosophy, morality, and activity, and provide education on these subjects. I do not sit in judgment on other organizations. I am willing to criticize individual actions and statements as they relate to Communist purposes, but I don't feel competent to give a categorical judgment on the John Birch Society because, frankly, my knowledge is limited. I am not a member, I have never been a member, and I have never met Robert Welch. If as many inaccuracies have been printed about the Birch Society as have been printed about the Crusade, what information I do have must be biased and partial.
>
> WECHSLER: You wouldn't consider that your educational function includes getting some knowledge about it?
>
> SCHWARZ: No, I would not. Our educational function is a very limited one and we limit it to the philosophy, morality, and nature of the Communist process and we do not claim to be experts on every subject.

At that time the expanding Communist empire wielded enormous military, economic, and educational power. It controlled thousands of nuclear warheads, vast armies, and numerous espionage and sabotage agents, and waged the most effective propaganda campaign the world has ever seen. In contrast, Mr. Welch was a retired candy manufacturer with minuscule resources.

Comparing the extent of any hypothetical danger to U.S. freedom from the John Birch Society to the magnitude of the real danger from Communist doctrines and military might was like comparing a candle with the sun.

Unsurprisingly, despite my answer, questions about the Birch Society kept coming. Mr. Clurman took it up: "Dr. Schwarz, as a teacher of anti-Communism in the United States, are you at all concerned about excesses on the Right?"

SCHWARZ: I am not greatly concerned. I think that the exaggerated concern about danger on the Right is an escape mechanism for people who are not prepared to accept the magnitude of the Communist danger. If this right wing that they berate possessed a foreign base; if Hitler were still in power in Germany and had conquered half of Europe; if the Right had multiple megaton thermonuclear bombs, ocean-ranging submarines, and the economic product of one billion people, then I would be more concerned. But, since no external base exists for this alleged right-wing threat, I don't believe it comparable to the malignancy and reality of the Communist danger.

CLURMAN: Can we talk for moment about the John Birch Society to which you alluded a minute ago? The John Birch Society and its founder, Robert Welch, have been denounced by President Kennedy, by the attorney general, by President Eisenhower, and by former Vice President Nixon. Robert Welch himself said that former President Eisenhower was himself a Communist dupe, and that Alan Dulles and the secretary of state, John Foster Dulles, were tools of the Communist conspiracy. Mr. Rusher's magazine, the *National Review*, has denounced the John Birch Society. Surely as a teacher of how to effectively fight Communism, you must have a clearer view of whether the John Birch Society is effective or not.

SCHWARZ: My function is not to act as judge of all organizations and individuals. If you ask me whether I agree with statements made by the John Birch Society,

I'm quite prepared to answer them, but I find that many profess to agree with my principle that it is inappropriate to sit in judgment on other organizations or individuals, but urge me to make an exception in their area of concern. I try to make few, if any, exceptions and to refrain from condemning organizations out of hand. If you choose to ask me if I think President Eisenhower is a Communist, I willingly reply that I consider that statement inaccurate, ridiculous, and slanderous.

CLURMAN: But don't you quite properly sit in judgment on organizations you feel are Communist organizations?

SCHWARZ: We specialize in the field of Communism. When people get out of their field their influence is thereby weakened.

CLURMAN: Mr. Welch says that Dr. Schwarz is doing a grand job of awakening people to the menace of Communism and freely acknowledges that they do their best to recruit into the John Birch Society people who have been stirred up, awakened, and armed by him, to serve as action groups to do something about it. Do you welcome that or not?

SCHWARZ: This is his privilege. I have never been associated with him, but we live in a democratic society where every group has the freedom to try to recruit whom they choose. I do not pronounce judgment on every organization that has members attending our schools.

CLURMAN: No, we're not asking you to adjudicate every organization. The John Birch Society has virtually been drummed out of respectable political conversation and has been denounced and renounced by the most distinguished Americans yet you equivocate—

SCHWARZ: I am not in the "drumming-out" business. I have enunciated a principle, and I propose to stand by that principle. I think it's important.

SPIVAK: Dr. Schwarz, you say you don't sit in judgment and yet you have sat in judgment on the John

Birch Society. Are you moving away from that judgment? On the New York Forum, July 1, in answer to a question, you said, "I don't welcome the support of the Birch Society." Now, why did you say that? And what did that mean?

SCHWARZ: I was expressing our position on individuality. We do not seek the support of any organization as such; we accept support on an individual basis.

SPIVAK: Would you say that you don't work up people so that extreme groups come in and pick up memberships?

SCHWARZ: I would say that we inform people concerning the philosophy and nature of Communism. We have reeducated many people whom you would classify as extreme. I have frequently challenged those who accuse me and the Christian Anti-Communism Crusade of being extreme to say how, when, and where this has been demonstrated. They usually reply, "You don't do it, but other people around you do." This is an example of guilt by association, and the people who engage in this practice are enemies of the democratic process, which permits freedom of speech, freedom of discussion, freedom of organization, and freedom of association.

WECHSLER: It used to be said that a political candidate who ran for office, and was asked whether he accepted the support of a Communist, and declined to answer, in some way compromised his position. Wouldn't you suggest that there was some analogy between that and your stand on the John Birch Society?

SCHWARZ: I would not. We are not political, and we have a written policy that we do not sit in judgment on other organizations and individuals. When people ask me about such organizations as Americans for Democratic Action, I make no statement on them whatsoever. I make no judgment on such organizations because I don't consider myself competent to do so. Communism is my field of expertise.

Lawrence Spivak intervened. "I don't like to press you too hard on the John Birch Society, but you are considered one of the world's experts on Communism, and you ought to know something about others who are fighting Communism and whether or not they're doing a good job. *The New York Times* quoted you as saying, 'I sometimes get the impression he,' meaning Mr. Welch, 'follows me around the country signing up people after I work them up.' "

> SCHWARZ: That was a false statement made by Cabell Phillips in an article for which I have since received an apology from *The New York Times.*
> SPIVAK: On that one, I think I've seen a statement of yours in which you praise *The New York Times* for its accuracy.

Spivak was referring to an article that had appeared in the Sunday edition of *The New York Times,* April 30, 1961, written by *Times* journalist Cabell Phillips. It was an alleged report on the St. Louis School of Anti-Communism which had been held in St. Louis, Missouri, April 24–28, 1961. I was told later that Phillips had attended one session of the school.

I learned about the article from an Australian journalist stationed in New York who phoned me. He said:

> "I see you've made *The New York Times!*"
> "Did I?"
> "Didn't you know? What's your press agent doing?"
> "We don't have a press agent."
> "What! Why haven't you?"
> "I've been too busy conducting seminars."

I picked up *The New York Times* and read the article. My immediate impression was that Cabell Phillips had written most of the article before he arrived. His article revealed far more about his own biases than about what took place at the school. Inaccurate statements abounded.

I told Spivak that I had written to *The New York Times* protesting the errors by Phillips, and that three months later I had received this letter of apology.

The New York Times
Times Square

August 22, 1961

Dear Dr. Schwarz:

The New York Times owes you an apology.
One of your friends and supporters, John W.
Wageman, 522 Valparaiso Road, Oak Ridge,
Tennessee, wrote to us recently. It was not
a very polite letter, but in the course of it
he said that we had failed to answer a letter
you had written to us about the article on the
St. Louis School of Anti-Communism by Cabell
Phillips that appeared in The New York Times on
April 30, 1961.

We made an investigation and discovered that
your letter was not, in fact, answered. This was
an oversight, because it is our policy to reply
to every reasonable letter from a reader.

We investigated the inaccuracies that you
claim were made in Mr. Phillips's article, and,
indeed, there were a few minor factual errors.
We do not feel, however, that any fundamental
mistakes have been made or that our readers
have been in any way seriously misled.

We regret the factual errors, and we shall
make every effort to see that they are not
repeated if we have occasion in the future to
write about your organization and your activities.

Sincerely,

Clifton Daniel
Clifton Daniel
Assistant Managing Editor

Dr. Fred C. Schwarz
Christian Anti-Communism Crusade
Suite 709, Heartwell Building
19 Pine Street
Long Beach, California

Thereafter, *The New York Times*' reports on the Crusade became more objective and I was no longer "the right-wing extremist, Dr. Fred Schwarz." *Times* reporters were friendly, and the paper published an unabusive profile of me.

Unfortunately, other "liberal" newspapers continued their attacks. Consider how the *St. Louis Post Dispatch* treated our St. Louis April 24–28, 1961, School of Anti-Communism. A journalist, who was assigned to the school, faithfully attended every session, submitted his report to his editor—and his editor rejected his report. The editor said to him, "This isn't at all what I wanted." The school received a column inch that merely mentioned it had been held.

Since no person's judgment is independent of the information on which it is based, editors necessarily influence, or even create, the opinions of readers by selecting partial information or disinformation. Thus editors were as much, or more, to blame than reporters for the many misjudgments about the purpose and nature of the Christian Anti-Communism Crusade.

On one occasion when I said to a reporter from a leading newspaper of Milwaukee, Wisconsin, "I continue to hope that I will read a fair and accurate report of Crusade activities in your paper one of these days," he was visibly upset and replied, "You don't understand."

Reactions to my appearance on "Meet the Press" were mixed. Lawrence Spivak told me that the program generated many more letters than usual; some were hostile, but many were favorable. I was elated when I read this column by the prestigious Walter Winchell.

TV SHOW OF THE DECADE

The way Lawrence Spivak's "Meet The Press" panel (including Mr. Spivak) were demolished from start-to-finish Sunday eve'g . . . The man-on-the-hot-seat was Red-Fighter Dr. Fred Schwarz . . . He made them all look like jerks . . . He was articulate, confident, knowledgeable and backed up everything he politely said in reply to their needling . . . He must have won over many people who call Commie detesters "witch-hunters" . . . I never met him—never was impressed by his talks—never anything! . . . but I am no knocker of his way with a fact . . . James Wechsler of the panel (once an official for The Young Communist League, which Dr. Schwarz, sportsmanlike, didn't tell the viewers) went down with dozens of hard facts on the jaw, nose, and stomach (Oooopppffff!). It was a delight to witness . . . First time I ever saw Spivak wearing a pained expression. He seemed in agony when (in reply to one of his statements) Schwarz calmly answered: "*The N.Y. Times* which ran that inaccuracy you just read apologized to me for it 3 months later" . . . Time mag's ex-press editor (Clurman), now in charge of another department, was a poor advertisement for that newsmag. Doctor! Get that tape and use it again, again, again, and again in the 50 States. Before they burn it.

Walter Winchell

This interview took place during an epidemic of irrational alarm that engulfed much of the media and the liberal intelligentsia in the United States.

For eight years I had traveled throughout the country, shining the searchlight of understanding upon the inner workings of Communism. My message had been welcomed in governmental, academic, and Christian circles. In 1961 the Southern California School of Anti-Communism had been held in Los Angeles with outstanding success. But certain circles in the ruling Democratic Party mistakenly saw this success as a threat to their political power, and a deluge of falsehood and bigotry suddenly burst upon us with the fury of a tornado. The following pages outline the steps that led to this storm and describe its characteristics and consequences.

2

....

Heritage

The lines are fallen unto me in pleasant places; yea,
I have a goodly heritage.
—PSALMS 16:6

"PAULUS" FRIEDRICH SCHWARZ WAS BORN into a Jewish family in Vienna, Austria, in 1883. He died in Rockhampton, Australia, at the age of eighty-seven. He was my father.

He was the youngest of eighteen children. Soon after his fifteenth birthday he walked to Hamburg, Germany, where he boarded a horse-boat that took him to England. He arrived in London with eleven pence and his foreign tongue. He learned the English alphabet while working in a London bakehouse and struggled with the language by reading the Bible.

While we have no record of the circumstances surrounding his conversion, it seems that he embraced Jesus as his Messiah and became a Christian while in England. He changed his name to "Paulus" and, like Paul the Apostle, he preached and he traveled.

During a quiet seventy-fifth birthday with family members, he mused on his youthful walking tour and where it eventually led him. He had preached in the open air in London's famed Hyde Park;

15

sailed to Egypt where he worked as a medical assistant; worked his passage to Australia on a cargo ship; and become a missionary and medical helper among the lepers on Peel Island Leper Colony in Moreton Bay near Brisbane, Queensland. He met and married Phoebe Smith, a Methodist Church deaconess. They raised a family of eleven children, six sons and five daughters. I was their fourth child.

A blurred photograph, taken in 1908, shows my father in the midst of a group of lepers at a burial service (please see photo section).

I was born in Brisbane on January 15, 1913, one year before the outbreak of the First World War, which raged for four dreadful years. An active ally of England and France, Australia sent many sons to serve and die in France and Gallipoli.

A patriotic fervor swept the country, and Germans were hated. Given Dad's German name and foreign accent, he was widely suspected of harboring German loyalties and had great difficulty supporting his growing family.

We were very poor. On our birthdays we received an egg as a special treat. Sunday was a special day because our regular diet of "bread and dripping" (lard) was supplemented with butter.

When I was about six years old, a great day dawned. Each member of us was given a pair of shoes, our first, the gift of a Christian benefactor.

Our material poverty was counterbalanced by an abundance of loving care by our parents. Whatever they could give us, they did. Thus I grew up in an environment of Christianity and love, for which I will always be grateful.

I suspect that my father's love of learning came from his Jewish upbringing. He sacrificed, schemed, and begged in order that each child secure the best education possible.

After primary school, I attended the Brisbane Grammar School. Although throughout my childhood I had cherished the ambition to become a medical doctor, Queensland had no medical school at that time; travel to the nearest medical school in distant Sydney was an impossible dream. In 1931 I became a science student at the University of Queensland. In 1934 I graduated with a Bachelor of Science after majoring in mathematics and physics.

Then something happened that directed the course of my future life. An American evangelist, W. E. Booth-Clibborn, a grandson of General Booth, the founder of the Salvation Army, conducted a long-running evangelistic campaign in a large tent in Brisbane. I attended, accepted Christ as my personal savior, and dedicated my life to Christian service.

At the university I plunged into evangelical Christian activity. I became a member of a small group of Christians affiliated with the "Inter-Varsity Fellowship of Evangelical Unions" (IVF) who met regularly for Bible study and witness. Wherever I went I carried a large Bible and was widely regarded as a religious fanatic. After a visit to our university, an Englishman, Howard Guinness, who represented the English IVF, reported, "I found that the leader of the Queensland Evangelical Union was a Pentecostalist, and our Union was consequently regarded as extreme and fanatical." Howard later returned to Australia and became an Anglican (Episcopalian) clergyman. Our friendship developed and we remain lifelong friends.

Poet Alexander Pope wrote that in order to really know anyone, you must search for his "ruling passion." Christian evangelism has been the ruling passion of my life. Many years later, when I formed the Christian Anti-Communism Crusade in America, its objective was defined as "Education, Evangelism, and Dedication."

My role as an aggressive Christian evangelist was illustrated by what occurred during my graduation. As I walked up to be hooded, the student audience burst into a raucous rendition of the hymn, "Onward Christian Soldiers." It was good-natured yet not meant as a compliment. But I accepted it as one. "If you are handed a lemon, make lemonade" is one of my mottoes.

I went on to spend a year in study at the Queensland Teachers' College and thereafter worked for the Education Department of the Queensland government, teaching mathematics and science at an industrial school close to the campus of the University of Queensland. I enrolled as a night student at the university to obtain a Bachelor of Arts degree.

In 1935 the Education Department appointed me to teach science at a high school in Warwick, a small town roughly one hundred miles southwest of Brisbane. I was not pleased, as it disrupted my university studies, but it led to the greatest blessing of my life.

En route to Warwick the train stopped at Clifton, where a young girl in school uniform entered my carriage. She told me her name was Lillian Morton and she was on her way to Warwick to attend high school. Neither of us could have imagined then that on January 11, 1990, we would celebrate our golden wedding anniversary, along with our children, their spouses, and eighteen grandchildren, in the ballroom of the Beverly Wilshire Hotel in Los Angeles.

Words fail me and my eyes mist over as I attempt to find words to express what a loving wife, mother, grandmother, and companion Lillian has been, and is.

As soon as I had settled as a teacher I invited the students to attend a meeting where a chapter of The Crusaders, a Christian organization that functioned in Australian secondary schools, would be formed. Lillian Morton was elected chapter secretary and we began to work together. The main activity was a Saturday night meeting for singing, Bible study, and Christian testimony.

In addition, the Crusaders organized picnics and occasional sporting contests against teams from other schools.

My weekends were busy. In addition to conducting the Crusader rallies, I participated regularly in open-air meetings in which a few of us preached the gospel to anybody who would listen. It was fortunate I had a loud voice, because we had no technical aids such as microphones and amplifiers, which were then in their infancy.

Such open-air meetings, a prominent activity of the Salvation Army, were a common feature of those days. Australian "People's Poet" Henry Lawson immortalized them in his poems "Booth's Drum" and "Bourke." In them he described his reaction and the reaction of his alcoholic friends to the meetings of the Salvation Army in Bourke, a small town famous for its isolation and its summer heat.

To illustrate the outreach of the Salvation Army open-air meetings, Lawson wrote the following stanzas.

BOOTH'S DRUM

Somewhere in the early eighties they had banged the drum
    to Bourke—
But the job of fighting Satan there was hot and dusty work.
There the local Lass was withered in the heat that bakes
    and glares,
And we sent her food and firewood, but we heeded not her
    prayers.
We were blasphemous and beery, we had neither Creed nor
    Care—
Till they sent their prettiest Lassies—and that broke our
    center there.
Often, moderately sober, we would stand to hear them
    sing,
And we'd chaff their Testifiers, but throw quids into the
    ring.
(Never less than bobs or dollars—sometimes quids—into
    the ring.)
[*a quid equals about two dollars*]

BOURKE

The "Army" on the grand old creek was mighty in those
    days gone by,
For they had sisters who could shriek, and brothers who
    could testify;
And by the muddy water holes they tackled sin till it was
    blue—
They took our bobs and damned our souls in Ninety-one
    and Ninety-two.
By shanty-bar and shearing shed they took their toil and
    did their work;
But now and then they lost their heads, and raved of hotter
    hells than Bourke;
The only message from the dead that ever came distinctly
    through

Was "Send my overcoat to hell"; it came to Bourke in
  Ninety-two.

I have never had a formal lesson in public speaking, though I have
given many. I gained a measure of skill from practical experience,
and it has served me well during a lifetime of speaking.

Something unexpected terminated my open-air speaking. I developed a hoarseness that became progressively worse. The local doctor discovered a small growth on one of my vocal cords, and I
returned to Brisbane where it was removed. It was benign. My voice
returned and has served well during the past half century.

During all this activity, a friendship developed between Lillian
and me. We visited each other's homes, to a warm and gracious
welcome.

As was usual in those days, Lillian left high school after passing the
"Junior Exam" in 1937. She returned to Clifton and worked as the
local attorney's secretary; but she traveled to Warwick frequently to
participate in our Crusader activities.

We kept the phone lines between Warwick and Clifton busy, and
before long we announced our formal engagement.

Our wedding took place in the Clifton Anglican Church on
December 26, 1939, and our glorious partnership has continued
ever since. Earth grants no greater happiness than a long and
increasingly loving marriage.

My sojourn in Warwick ended abruptly when the Department of
Education transferred me to Brisbane to teach and lecture at the
evening classes of Queensland Teachers' College.

At that time most students stopped attending high school after
passing the Statewide Junior Exam, given after three years, at the
average age of sixteen, and then sought employment. "Matricula-
tion," or the right to enroll at university, was granted after passing
specified subjects in the "Senior" exam taken after an additional
two years at high school.

Many who went to work after the "Junior" wished to go on
to pass the "Senior" and matriculate. To accommodate them the
Queensland Education Department had established a branch of the

Teachers' College to conduct night classes. I was appointed to teach science at this college and accepted gladly, as I hoped to fulfill my lifelong ambition to become a medical doctor. Happily, the University of Queensland had opened a medical school two years previously.

An Australian medical course normally requires six years of study. During the Second World War the time was shortened to five years, and since I had already passed the subjects required for the first year of the medical course, I was able to graduate in 1944.

I was not conscripted for military service since I was engaged in two occupations considered essential to the nation—science teacher and medical student.

My marriage to Lillian had taken place before my transfer to Brisbane, so we moved to Brisbane together. We rented an apartment about a mile from the college, and this enabled me to walk to school or pay a penny to ride in a streetcar, which we called a tram. Since funds were scarce, I often walked.

In the medical course, as my ruling passion dictated, I immediately became active in the Evangelical Union. This brought me into conflict with Communist students who were fervent and aggressive atheists. Their leader, Max Julius, a young law student and president of the University Student Union, came from a family of active Communists.

Early that year a debate was arranged between Max and me. The subject of the debate was, "Is Communism a Science or a Religion?" At that time the Australian Communist Party had been declared illegal by the Australian Labor Party (ALP) which was in power, even though the ALP was a self-declared socialist party. The reason was that the Australian Communists were actively supporting Adolf Hitler's Nazis.

Let us cast our minds back. The Second World War was precipitated in 1939 when Hitler and Stalin signed the Nazi-Communist Pact, and the Nazis invaded Poland. The Nazi invaders were soon joined by Soviet forces, and Hitler and Stalin divided Poland between them.

In response, England and France declared war on Germany. The German armies defeated the French and threatened to conquer

England. Under Winston Churchill's leadership, England resisted valiantly. Australia was among its allies and sent military forces to aid a beleaguered Britain.

As loyal servants of Joseph Stalin, the Australian Communists did their best to support the Nazis. They organized industrial strikes and called Australian soldiers "Six-bob-a-day murderers." In response, the Labor Socialist government took the drastic step of outlawing the Communist Party.

Though outlawed, the party did not stop its activity. For example, Stan Moran, a well-known Communist agitator, ran a Communist rally each Sunday afternoon in the Sydney Domain, similar to London's Hyde Park. Stan Moran changed the name of his rally to "The People's Rally," but he continued to proclaim the same doctrines and propaganda. When the ban was lifted he reinstated "Communist" in the name.

My debate with Max Julius took place in the university's Common Room. The audience of about one hundred consisted mostly of members and supporters of the Evangelical Union. Max arrived with one supporter.

My opposition to Communism was not based upon economics or politics but upon its false doctrines about God and man. I began by pointing out that Communism had a doctrine of God—that God did not exist but that the idea of God had been projected into human consciousness by the universal existence of the Class Struggle; that it had a doctrine of Man—that man was a collection of atoms and molecules without soul or spirit and that all human ideas and emotions were derived from experiences provided by the economic environment; that it had a doctrine of Sin—that sin resulted from the experience provided by Capitalism; that it had a doctrine of Redemption—a Communist revolution; and that it had a doctrine of the future—that the Communist victory was inevitable due to the progressive nature of being. I also pointed out that it had a Creator—Karl Marx; a Messiah—Vladimir Lenin; a Pope—Joseph Stalin; and a Devil—Leon Trotsky.

When Max spoke he ignored the subject of the debate entirely, and proceeded to launch a strong and effective attack upon capitalism. He reported that the wheat harvest in Poland had been extraor-

dinarily good that year but that this had only increased the malnu-
trition of the Polish peasants. This, he claimed, was typical of how
capitalism worked—it robbed workers of the fruits of their labors.

He made little, if any, attempt to justify Communist programs
that would allegedly correct this injustice. Rather, since Capitalism,
as he described it, was so bad, Communism must be better. His
assumption resembled the common medical fallacy—if the diagnosis
is correct, the prescribed treatment must be beneficial. He showed
no understanding of the truth that the treatment may be worse than
the disease.

An article that appeared in the Queensland Press at about that
time illustrates this. It told of a man who claimed he could cure cancer. His diagnosis of the nature of the disease was accurate, and he
promised in all sincerity to remove the cancer from a patient's back
entirely and to restore perfect health.

Many were deceived. An Australian philanthropist gave him half
a million dollars, an enormous sum in those days, to assist him in his
work. And some American victims of cancer sold their assets and
made the arduous flight to Australia in hope of a cure.

In due course an investigation revealed that his treatment was
based on a delusion and that it compounded the disease. What the
Press article didn't disclose was that he had injected a solution of
alum into the patient's back, which created a slough of healthy tissue. He had miscalled this slough the cancer and had left his victim
with a painful ulcer to add to the misery of cancer. His diagnoses
were accurate, his goal most desirable, and his sincerity appealing.
But his therapy was disastrous.

In my many debates with Communist leaders thereafter, I noted
that the Communists invariably concentrated on the injustices of
Capitalism and ignored all its positive features. I tried to present
the growing evidence that Communist therapy only increased
human suffering and death. As the years passed, that evidence has
become overwhelming, but it was already sufficiently present in
1940 for all who had eyes to see, ears to hear, and minds with
which to think.

Determined to increase my knowledge and understanding of
Communism, I embarked upon a program of study of its basic doc-

trines. Each night I read from one of the large volumes that contain the teachings of the Communist founders. Lillian, who has an impish but delightful sense of humor, would sometimes shock some of our friends by stating that she frequently had four men in bed with her—Marx, Lenin, Stalin, and myself.

THE CHRISTIAN REVELERS

My ruling passion continued unabated, as well as my desire to present the Christian gospel. Soon after relocating in Brisbane, I formed an organization called the Christian Revelers, to signify that our Christianity generated happiness and joy, not sadness and gloom. We believed in and experienced the "joy unspeakable and full of glory" that Jesus promised. I was frequently asked how I remained so cheerful despite abstaining from such human joys as alcohol, smoking, and dancing. I responded, "I have received the greatest happiness—creating joy in the world through my faith in the life and death of God's Son, Jesus Christ."

We rented a large hall in a building on Anne Street in Brisbane, and commenced Saturday night rallies. The rallies featured hearty singing and clapping. At that time clapping was frowned upon in more sedate Christian circles. If prominent Christian leaders came to town we invited them to speak, and many talented young people joined our ranks. One of our annual speakers, for example, was the secretary of the Mission to Lepers, Robert Edgar. My dad, one of the most generous persons I have ever known, always made the first donation even though money had never been plentiful in his life.

The Revelers established a "preachers' class" to train young lay preachers. Although I had no formal training, I decided to conduct this class. I have never been ordained as a minister either, but I became a lay preacher for the Methodist Church when I was eighteen and I've since polished my natural talents by constant practice.

My days were full. I would often attend classes during the day, teach during the early evening, and then rush to a church to participate in the concluding activities of a mission.

A blessed event took place on March 14, 1942, when our first child was born—a boy whom we named John Charles Morton.

At that time fathers were not allowed to attend the birth, and when I visited Lillian as soon after as I could, she was still somewhat drugged and greeted me whimsically with "blinky old son." She had wanted a girl.

That "blinky old son" has been a source of pride and joy for over fifty years. He inherited his mother's gentleness and tenderness, and in his entire life I cannot recall a single occasion of deceit.

We have been spared the worries of many, if not most, parents. Lillian once told me of a conversation she overheard. A group of women were bemoaning the conduct of their teenage children. One of them said, "You never know where they are or what they're doing." Lillian said to me, "I didn't know what they were talking about. I always know where our children are. They are where they tell me they'll be, or they're at home where they want to be."

Their home was their castle, and their friends were equally welcomed. Lillian transformed bricks and mortar into a haven of security and happiness.

John graduated in pharmacy and then in medicine. He married his first and only sweetheart, Rosalie Smith, in 1964. Rosalie is a registered nurse. John and Rosalie spent nine years in South Africa, where John served as medical superintendent of Emmaus Hospital for the Zulus in Natal State. The restoration of sight to three hundred blind South Africans was one of John's proudest achievements. Many elderly grandmothers, blinded by cataracts, danced with joy at the sight of their grandchildren; they could now take care of them in their *kraals*.

John and Rosalie have five children—Katherine, Jane, Sarah, Johnny, and Michael. Kate is a graduate in agriculture, Jane is a doctor, Sarah is a medical student, Johnny is studying acting, and Michael is in high school. Kate and her husband Sean have presented us with a bonny great-grandson, Maxwell George Harris.

John is our family physician and the personal physician for many of our friends. In addition to his medical knowledge he possesses one great talent, inherited from his mother. He is a born listener.

Rosalie and John lead an active Christian life. Rosalie's father was a Baptist minister. John is a deacon of Camden Baptist Church and teaches a Sunday School class. The essence of their home is hospitality; it overflows with warmth and life, with their children's friends roaming throughout the house, eating without restraint.

When questioned about his lifestyle, John says, "My grandfather's home was like this, my father's home was like this, and this is the way my home is going to be."

When John was a baby, Lillian and I rented a home within easy walking distance of both the Medical School building and the Brisbane General Hospital until I graduated as a medical doctor in 1944. In the interim the birth of our second child added to the joy of our lives. Rosemary Gay, the fulfillment of Lillian's dream for a girl, was born on October 22, 1944. She is now a prominent psychiatrist in Melbourne, Australia. Her husband is Murray Esler, a medical research scientist who is internationally recognized as an authority on the cause and treatment of hypertension. They have three beautiful daughters and one winsome red-haired boy: Danielle, Nicole, Simone, and Ben, short for Benjamin. Danielle is a medical student, Nicole an Arts/Law student, and Simone and Ben are still in high school.

We lived opposite Victoria Park, the headquarters of the U.S. Forces based in Brisbane at that time. Our home became the rendezvous of a number of American chaplains and Christian servicemen, some of whom became active in the Christian Revelers.

One day an American soldier played a practical joke on the commanding general of the U.S. Forces, fittingly dubbed "Iron Mike." An unnamed soldier phoned me and said he was speaking on behalf of the commanding general who wanted to bring a delegation to a Revelers rally. He gave me a phone number and asked me to firm up the arrangement. Naively and enthusiastically I phoned. A startled officer immediately realized what was up and probed, hoping to identify the prankster. The culprit was never discovered.

Another experience undermined my confidence in the anti-spy agencies. In the early days of the war, the possibility of pro-Nazi espionage in Australia was worrisome. An intelligence agency was set up to discover and expose any suspicious group. Any new organization was subject to suspicion, and the Christian Revelers was new. An intelligence agent called and asked me a series of questions and told me with considerable pride that he had tracked me down after following a trail of clues. I told him that he could have simply looked up the name "Christian Revelers" in the phone book.

3

....

A Medical Milestone

The friends of humanity cannot but wish
that in all countries,
the laboring classes should have a
taste for comforts and
enjoyments and that they should be
stimulated by all legal
means in their exertions to enjoy them.
—DAVID RICARDO, 1772–1828
(*PRINCIPLES OF POLITICAL ECONOMY*)

THE YEAR 1944 WAS SPECIAL in my life. I graduated as a Bachelor of Medicine and Bachelor of Surgery. I also devoted much time and energy in a campaign to secure economic and social justice for newly fledged doctors.

An M.D.'s first year was a period of penury and exhaustion. After graduation, each Queensland doctor spent a year as a Resident Medical Officer (RMO) at the Brisbane General Hospital, the largest hospital in the Southern Hemisphere. This is a state government institution, administered by the Brisbane and South Coast Hospital Board.

At the time the average age of new graduates was twenty-four. I was thirty-one. Most students came from middle class or poor homes scattered throughout Queensland, and their parents had sacrificed to support them.

During the year, RMOs worked long hours for a miserable pittance. It was not unusual for them to work for forty hours without sleep. Exhaustion took its toll on patients and doctors alike. I set out to change this.

Again, my Christian faith directed my motivation. To me it was unjust and morally wrong that individuals performing important work for such long hours could not afford to marry if they wished. My primary motive was not selfish. I was already married and a father, and I received a salary because I was employed by the Queensland Education Department as an evening science teacher, and pursued my medical studies in the daytime.

Since the Brisbane and South Coast Hospital Board dictated wages and conditions, any demands for justice must be made to this board.

This was further complicated because Australia was at war against the Nazis and wages were frozen. However, a government body, known as the Arbitration Court, had the power to adjust and increase wages when they were manifestly unjust. My strategy was to apply to the Arbitration Court.

Though I had previously shunned student politics, I submitted my nomination for president of the University of Queensland Medical Society and was duly elected. Henceforth I could speak and act as the representative of all medical students.

Our strategy was not secret. These were the proposed steps:

1. Prepare a memorandum that analyzed the existing situation and that included a set of economic and social demands which, if granted, would rectify existing injustices.

2. Present this memorandum and set of demands to the Brisbane and South Coast Hospital Board.

3. If the board did not consider our demands because we were not yet employees, resubmit the memorandum to the board as soon as we became so.

4. If the board refused to grant our demands, appeal to the Arbitration Court.

This strategy was executed step by step. A book, *Milestones of Australian Medicine,* published in 1994 by the University of Queensland, reports what happened. The author, Ronald Wood, one of the students at that time, describes the event in a chapter captioned "Conflict, Conciliation and Conditions of Service—A pioneering medical industrial court action in 1944." Here are a few extracts:

Frederick Charles Schwarz, a Science and Arts graduate as well as a medical student, began to take a very active role in the affairs of medical students. He was a persuasive speaker who put his case well. His oratory had considerable influence on his audience. With a strong Christian background he believed that medical graduates of twenty-four years of age should be paid enough to marry if they so wished. A subcommittee . . . was appointed to prepare a memorandum outlining a set of conditions deemed desirable for Resident Medical Officers.

In due course we appealed to the Arbitration Court.

The case was heard before a court filled with medical students. The RMOs were represented by Drs. F. C. Schwarz and H. M. Whyte and the Crown and the Board by Mr. McCracken and Dr. Pye.

Presenting his case Dr. Schwarz outlined the main points. These included: the position of RMOs in respect of age, qualification, responsibilities, costs of their course, actual or potential marital status, duties performed, hours worked, and comparative remuneration.

The decision in the case was delivered on Tuesday November 7th, 1944. Mr. Riordan stated that—

Having discussed the various arguments put to the Court, they made an award. The salary was to be 350

pounds per annum with free board and lodging. No Resident Medical Officer was to be required to work for 54 hours in any one working week averaged over a period of four weeks or more than sixteen hours in any one shift.

The article concludes:

> The wisdom and the bravery of these two men—Dr. Fred Schwarz and Dr. Mickey Whyte—and the courage of the team of young students and doctors who supported them, left a legacy of safer and better professional conditions from which patients continue to benefit today.

In June 1994, Lillian and I attended a reunion of the surviving members of our 1944 class, to celebrate the fiftieth anniversary of our graduation. Each doctor was presented with a copy of *Milestones of Australian Medicine*.

I was specially honored and was subjected to some good-natured teasing. But when one of our group shook my hand and exclaimed, "You were our savior!," I didn't know how to react.

Mickey Whyte, still looking remarkably young and handsome, was present. He had been a tower of strength as my co-advocate before the Arbitration Court. I remembered that when our opponents made false statements during the proceedings, Mickey's indignation stimulated his eloquence. Our opponents attempted to categorize RMOs as incompetent apprentices who were in the process of learning their profession, and who bore no responsibility for their patients because their work was always directed and supervised by seasoned doctors.

Mickey's own recent experiences clearly refuted this. He had been the doctor on duty from midnight till dawn, examining and prescribing treatment for every person the ambulances brought in. No senior doctor was around. He was fully responsible.

Mickey had earlier opposed our plan to approach the Arbitration Court. Paradoxically, our common motivating Christian faith led us to conflicting conclusions. Guided by such statements of Jesus as, "Whosoever would be the greatest among you, let him be your servant," and "If any man would come after me, let him deny himself," Mickey believed that the Christian's role is to be a faithful servant.

I also believed that I was acting in a Christian way by endeavoring to obey the commandment, "Do unto others as you would that they should do unto you."

Our conflict illustrated how it is possible to agree in principle yet disagree in practice. To quote an anonymous wit, "The devil is in the details."

Mickey's opposition had compelled me to find areas of agreement. We agreed that it was unfair to force doctors to work such long hours that they were too exhausted to exercise sound judgment.

During the year-long campaign I was constantly urged to "take it easy," "be reasonable," and "don't rock the boat." In reality this meant, "Accept the existing situation. Grumble about it if you like, but don't do anything to change it."

My experience during this campaign confirmed the insight of the poet Aaron Hill:

Tenderhearted stroke a nettle,
It will sting you for your pains,
Grasp it like a man of mettle,
And it soft as silk remains.

When our campaign was successful, most who had urged inactivity applauded. For example, shortly before the court appearance, a committee of the British Medical Association (BMA) urged us to stop. I refused. After the positive court verdict I received a letter of congratulations from the president of the Queensland Branch of the BMA. Often, there's a fine line between firmness and pigheadedness. I was willing to listen to our opponents, and where appropriate, change our tactics. As an example, I believed that we were required to join a union in order to be heard before the Arbitration Court and we did so. Later, Dr. W. J. Matthews brought me a copy of the court bylaws where it was stated that a group of twenty or more workers not represented by a union could approach the court directly, so we changed our tactics and made a direct application to the court.

While I am enthralled by Shakespeare's poetry, our experience taught me that his oft-quoted statements are not always true. In his play *Julius Caesar,* Mark Antony, in his famous speech following the death of Caesar, says,

> The evil that men do lives after them,
> The good is oft interred with their bones.

"Oft," but in this instance, the good we did lives on. The improved conditions we secured for Queensland doctors started a chain reaction, and hospital after hospital throughout Australia sought and were granted similar awards.

Australian Communists observed our activity, and some sent letters of congratulation. Apparently, some considered me a potential recruit. Bill Wood, a prominent professional Communist, active in attempts to infiltrate the churches, visited me and invited me to cooperate in programs to promote "peace." I was not tempted, and told him so.

If my opposition to Communism had been based upon their economic doctrines and activities alone, I might have been enticed, but my main objection was their atheism. Also, I was well aware that to them, the word "peace" was a synonym for Communist victory, and I said so. Bill made no attempt to refute this, and he appeared disappointed.

4

....

Parent, Physician, Preacher, Polemicist

He gave man speech and speech created thought.
—PERCY BYSSHE SHELLEY, 1792–1822 (*PROMETHEUS UNBOUND*)

AFTER MY TERM AS AN RMO at Brisbane General Hospital, I spent several years in medical practice. My first year as a hospital doctor was spent in Gympie, a small country town one hundred miles north of Brisbane. Lillian, John, Rosemary, and I were happy there.

We then moved to Wentworth in the southwest corner of New South Wales, a tiny town at the junction of Australia's two greatest rivers, the Darling and the Murray. Since my contract allowed me private practice, our financial condition improved.

We left Wentworth in 1946 and acquired a medical practice in North Strathfield, a suburb of Sydney, Australia's most populous city. I practiced there until 1955, when I closed it in order to devote myself full time to the work of the Crusade. The house remains our Sydney residence to this day and accommodates the office of the Australian branch of the Christian Anti-Communism Crusade.

During these years, in addition to our growing family, three major occupations filled our lives—medical practice, Christian evangelism, and the study and exposure of Communism.

34

These occupations were essentially complementary because each was devoted to the preservation and enhancement of life—medical work to sustaining physical and mental health, and evangelism to the quality of eternal life. I believed what Alfred Lord Tennyson wrote in his poem, "In Memoriam":

My own dim life should teach me this,
That life shall live for evermore,
Else earth is darkness at the core,
And dust and ashes all that is.

St. Paul, in his first epistle to the Corinthians, expressed the same sentiment. "What doth it profit me if the dead rise not? Let us eat and drink; for tomorrow we die."

But what is the relevance of Communism to health and eternal life? Communism threatens physical, mental, and spiritual life.

It was and is my conviction that Communism has the characteristics of both religion and disease. Many ex-Communists, after serving their false god for many years, have concluded that Communism is a religion. Examples abound. Whittaker Chambers expressed this eloquently in 1952 in his magnificent book *Witness*. Prominent disillusioned Communists testified similarly in the book *The God That Failed*.

Eric Aarons, former secretary of the Australian Communist Party, and who served it faithfully for forty years, is a more recent example. In his book *What's Left?*, first published in 1993, he wrote:

A political party is a bit like a church, and so it was with the Communist Party of Australia. Though now defunct, our party had a distinctive world outlook embodied in a set of beliefs, doctrines and theories. As with Communist parties throughout the world, the CPA felt that it was the agent of forces independent of and greater than itself—in its case, the forces of history. Like Churches, Communist parties protected, moulded, informed, inspired and sometimes coerced or punished their members. . . . They had their own schisms and

breakaway sects based on particular interpretations of
the founding texts. . . .

Acceptance of [Marx's] views provided a source of
great strength for Communists because, however difficult their circumstances, they saw themselves as conscious agents of historical forces that would guarantee
their final victory. In this, Communists resembled some
of those they regarded as foes, particularly the various
religious groups which drew strength from the belief
that they were agents of a force beyond themselves.
With such mutually exclusive certitudes on both sides, it
is no wonder that antipathy could become reciprocal
and often implacable.

The many millions who have been slaughtered by the Communists
during this century bear irrefutable testimony to the incontrovertible
fact that Communism is a disease.

Upon settling in Sydney, I resumed my association with the Evangelical Union (EU) at Sydney University. Speaking at one of their
meetings on the subject "Knowledge is not enough," I stressed that
faith must accompany reason and knowledge. A young Baptist pastor,
John Drakeford, was in the audience. Shortly afterward he came to
my medical office as a patient. As the need arose I surgically removed
his tonsils, gall bladder, and appendix, so I have enjoyed remarking
that I know him "inside and out." We became lifelong friends. Under
his ministry, Lillian, who had been raised as an Anglican, was bap-
tized by immersion in what is known as Believers Baptism.

John and I teamed up to conduct evangelistic missions around
Australia. In 1949 in Adelaide, the capital city of South Australia,
our mission included a debate with the secretary of South Australia's Communist Party.

I was frequently accused of being unwise to mix religion with the
exposure of Communism, a criticism that revealed a lack of understanding of the scope of both Communism and the Christian gospel.
The Communist asserts, "There is no God!" which, of course, contradicts the biblical pronouncement, "In the beginning God created
the heavens and the earth." Psalm 14 is blunt: "The fool hath said in
his heart: There is no God!"

John subsequently became youth director for the Baptist Union of New South Wales. Later, he traveled to America, and received his doctorate at Southwestern Baptist Theological Seminary in Fort Worth, Texas.

FAMILY

Two special events enlarged and enriched our family. When our son John started school, he quickly became friendly with another little boy also named John. John Whitehall became an unofficial member of the Schwarz family, like a foster son. Henceforth "the Johns," as we called them, were like twins. His own mother, a war widow, was happy about the relationship. She later remarried.

In due course both Johns became medical doctors and both served terms as missionary doctors. Both married at about the same time. John Whitehall and his wife Elsie are the parents of six children, while John Schwarz and Rosalie have five. We regard all eleven as our grandchildren.

A book should be written about John Whitehall. As a youth he preached at Christian youth missions on the beaches. He also studied the pathology of Communism and grasped the causative role of Marxist doctrine in Communist deeds. He has served the Christian Anti-Communism cause in South Africa, Vietnam, Timor, the Philippines, Mexico, Canada, and Australia. He has now moved to Townsville, Queensland, where he directs pediatrics. During their entire relationship I have never known "the two Johns" to exchange one angry word.

Our second blessed event was the birth of our son, David Frederick, on July 2, 1948. What a delightful baby and growing boy he was! His imagination fascinated us. As a toddler he enjoyed the companionship of four fictitious playmates—Dick, Charlie, Percy, and Bogeyman. He regaled us with accounts of their exploits. Dick was the favorite scapegoat for his own mischievous pranks. How often we heard, "Dick did it."

David's tendency to confuse fantasy with reality created some amusing situations. When he was four years old we owned a small Ford Prefect car. Once when its engine would start but stall almost immediately, we called a motor mechanic who soon found the problem—water was mixed with the gasoline.

Lillian looked at David. "Did you put gasoline in mummy's car?" "Yes." "Where did you get the gasoline?" He pointed to the garden hose. Lillian said, "You mustn't do that; cars won't run on water." In a puzzled voice David said, "But my car runs on water."

He was, and is, the apple of his mother's eye. Since I was absent in the United States during most of his childhood years the responsibility for his upbringing rested primarily on Lillian. She lavished love upon him, and David reciprocated. A close family friend says that if David had asked for the City Hall, Lillian would have found a way to get it for him. I sometimes feel saddened that I was unable to celebrate even one of his first twenty birthdays with him.

David left school after high school. He had no interest in becoming a doctor; he disliked the sight of blood and decided to become a professional air pilot. Eventually he became a pilot—captain for Australia's major private airline, Ansett Airways. Lillian still thinks of him as her baby boy.

David and his wife Robyn have three talented and beautiful children—Timothy, Penny (short for Penelope), and Joshua. Timothy is a journalism major, and Penny and Joshua are still in high school. Though Robyn left school at age sixteen, she continued her studies after marriage, graduated with distinction in her university courses, and has become a teacher.

Thus far I have said little about our daughter Rosemary. She, too, merits a full book.

Lillian claims that Rosemary has inherited many of my characteristics. She is eloquent and is an effective debater with strong convictions. During her university years she stood up to the bullies who taunted her about the alleged "extremist right-wing activities" of her notorious father.

Rosemary graduated as a medical doctor and soon fell in love with Murray Esler, another doctor. Shortly after their marriage they lived in Ann Arbor, Michigan. Murray was employed as a research scientist at the hypertension department of the university hospital, while Rosemary was on the staff of the state mental hospital in Ypsilanti. They eventually returned to Australia, where Rosemary qualified for a specialist degree in psychiatry. She now conducts a large private and hospital psychiatric practice.

Rosemary often teases me by charging, "You gave me no artistic genes whatsoever, and you haven't even the grace to be ashamed." While that is certainly true regarding my contribution, our children have received their fair share of such genes from their mother.

Many Sunday afternoons found me in the Sydney Domain, where I frequently met and debated Communists. Stan Moran, mentioned earlier, was an official of the Waterside Workers' Federation and a popular speaker. He attracted a large gathering. Smaller Communist meetings gave younger Communists an opportunity to hone their oratorical skills. Sometimes a leader would invite me to speak from his platform.

I remember one meeting where I mentioned "dialectical materialism." The Communist chairman challenged, "What is dialectical materialism?" I shot back, "dialectical materialism is the philosophy of Karl Marx, which he formulated by marrying the idealistic dialectic of Hegel to the materialism of Feuerbach, abstracting from it the concept of the inevitability of progress due to the conflict of opposites called the thesis and the antithesis, applying this concept to the history of economic and social progress, and deriving therefrom a doctrine of inevitable revolutionary social change." The chairman gazed at me in confused amazement, so I added, "Don't blame me; it's your philosophy, not mine; you are the one who believes it, not I."

I have frequently been asked to explain the meaning and relevance of "dialectical materialism." The late Lord Casey, when he was Australia's foreign minister, once asked "Can you explain dialectical materialism to me? I have never met anyone who could."

Later, when we conducted Schools of Anti-Communism, and Anti-Subversive Seminars, I invariably delivered a lecture entitled, "The Difficult, Devious, and Dangerous Dialectic." More on this later.

Although I was never ordained as a minister, the Baptist Union of New South Wales, Australia, appointed me its director of evangelism. Continued activities with the Inter-Varsity Fellowship of Evangelical Unions brought me into contact with leaders in many denominations. I was also widely recognized in evangelical circles as an "authority" on the doctrines of Communism. Many times I lec-

tured at Moore Theological College, where young Anglican ministers were trained, and Sydney's Archbishop Mowll regularly invited
me to address the Annual Conference of Anglican Clergy.

In 1950 two "controversial" clergymen from the United States
and Canada visited Australia, and the course of our lives changed
dramatically.

5

....

An Irresistible Invitation

O beautiful for spacious skies,
For amber waves of grain,
For purple mountain majesties
Above the fruited plain!
America! America!
God shed His grace on thee,
And crown thy good with brotherhood
From sea to shining sea.
—KATHARINE LEE BATES, 1859–1929

THE REV. CARL MCINTYRE AND the Dr. T. T. Shields visited Australia in early 1950. McIntyre was the pastor of the Bible Presbyterian Church of Camden, New Jersey, and Shields was pastor of Jarvis Street Baptist Church in Toronto, Canada. Both were eloquent and fiery preachers and leaders of Bible-believing Christians who were opposed to the domination of the mainline Protestant churches and institutions by liberal theologians and bureaucrats. They upheld the inspiration, veracity, and trustworthiness of the Bible and opposed the policies and programs of the supranational church institutions—the National Council of Churches, and the World Council of Churches.

McIntyre and Shields were leaders of the American Council of Christian Churches and the International Council of Christian Churches, organizations of Bible-believing churches and people. They were also aware of the attempts by the Communists to infiltrate, ensnare, and exploit Christian institutions and churches. Many, however, regarded them as being outside the mainstream, and therefore controversial. Had the term "extremist" been in common use at the time, their opponents would have used it to describe them.

I did not hesitate to cooperate wholeheartedly with them. They presented convincing evidence of the Communist influence in the National and World Councils of Churches and told of the proposed conference of the International Council of Churches, scheduled to be held in Geneva, Switzerland, later that year.

When they learned of my study of Communist literature, my lectures on the nature and activity of the Communists, and my debates with Communist leaders, they invited me to visit America, speak at churches affiliated with the American Council of Christian Churches, and attend the conference in Geneva. They offered to provide for my upkeep and transport from America to Geneva, but I paid my own round-trip fare between Australia and America.

I was eager to see America and the world. The care of the children and of my medical practice was manageable. Fortunately, we had Jill Everard, a devoted and competent young lady who had lived with us for six years. She loved our children, and we knew we could safely leave them in her care.

I hired a doctor to attend to my medical practice during our three-month absence. In Australia, such a temporary doctor is known as a "locum tenens." During the next few years my practice was often served by a "locum."

Early in 1950 Lillian and I set out on our first trip to America and Europe. I was thirty-seven. Up till then neither of us had been out of Australia. Clarice Inglis, one of Australia's finest sopranos, accompanied us. Her husband Bob, a well-known Sydney businessman, was immensely proud of her and her singing.

The plane that transported us was a propeller-driven DC6B. The flight was long but every traveler had a bunk and we finally reached Honolulu, Hawaii.

Upon arrival, the pastor of Kaimuki Community Church welcomed us, and we felt overwhelmed by the warm affection of the Hawaiian people.

I spoke several times at meetings in the church, and found my Australian accent both an asset and a handicap. Recalling, "If you are handed a lemon, make lemonade," I joked about my Australian accent—I claimed to speak good English and accused the Americans of speaking with an accent.

I would often begin a speech by saying, "When I say 'a' I mean 'a' and not 'i'—so if you hear 'i' when I say 'a' you are wrong and not I." Invariably this made the audience laugh, and then I would innocently ask, "Why are you laughing?" Cultural barriers soon collapsed.

At that time Communism in Hawaii was of great concern. The International Longshoremen's and Warehousemen's Union (ILWU), led by Harry Bridges and Jack Hall, wielded great power. This union represented the workers on the waterfront and in the pineapple and sugar fields. It had been expelled from the AFL-CIO because of its unvarying allegiance to every shift in policy of the Soviet Union.

In later years it was my privilege to be slandered by Harry Bridges during a debate in San Francisco.

We left Hawaii for the mainland with love in our hearts for the American people, a love that has remained and grown over the years.

On the mainland, a series of meetings had been arranged for us. We traveled across the country by plane and car in a zigzag path from west to east. Most of the meetings were in small Bible-believing churches. Occasionally, our local hosts also arranged meetings in civic clubs and schools. Clarice's singing always inspired great applause, and my message was generally greeted with more applause than mere courtesy required.

Several well-wishers gave me unsolicited advice. They told me that I must understand American psychology if I expected to be a success as a lecturer. They stressed that the American people were generous and had a strong sense of humor. But they did not have a long attention span, and I must never be long-winded. And I should never depend too much on mere logic and reason.

I interpreted this as a belief that the American people are hospitable, generous, and tenderhearted, but intellectually superficial. I did not believe this then, and experience has proved me correct.

Brevity in speech has never been my strong point because I was enthralled by my subject. And I never used notes; the results speak for themselves.

ON TO GENEVA

When we arrived in Philadelphia we connected with many of the delegates to the Geneva Conference assembled there. Soon after, in a packed charter plane, we flew to London where I addressed a crowded meeting of Evangelicals on the nature of Communism. My message may have startled many who believed that Communism was primarily political and economic, and a discussion of it was out of place at a meeting devoted to Christian evangelism. We reboarded and flew to Geneva, Switzerland.

Delegates to the Conference of the International Council of Christian Churches came from many countries—England, France, Holland, Italy, Chile, Canada, the United States, and Australia, to mention a few. Consequently, the proceedings had to be translated simultaneously into many languages.

I was scheduled to speak on "dialectical materialism."

My message was the last one of the evening. It commenced about 10 P.M., and some were already leaving. For more than an hour I attempted to present unfamiliar and complex ideas to a diminishing audience. I was not a roaring success. The reaction of one among the long-suffering listeners is illustrated by an amusing incident the following day—a story that delighted Bob Inglis whenever he heard me tell it after my return to Australia: A pastor of a church in the American Midwest, delighted by Clarice's solos, approached me and said, "Mrs. Inglis is a wonderful singer, and I would like to have her sing in my church. Could you possibly arrange that?" I said, "I'm afraid that won't be possible, as she and my wife plan to fly directly to Australia after our return to Philadelphia." But he persisted. Finally he said, "If you can arrange to have her sing in my church, I'll let you preach."

Despite my disappointment after my message, I discovered later that some had been enlightened and that the harvest was bountiful.

6

....

Dialectical Materialism

Dialectics is the soul of Marxism.
—JOSEPH STALIN

SINCE I HAVE REFERRED TO the mysterious subject of dialectical materialism several times, it seems appropriate, if somewhat premature, to present some of its major features, and show how the Communists have applied it and continue to apply it.

Lenin used it in the Brest-Litovsk Treaty of 1918 to justify his surrender to the Germans of a large area of Russia, populated by fifty-five million people. Stalin said "Dialectics is the soul of Marxism," when he sought to discredit and execute Bukharin, whom Lenin described as "the favorite of the whole Party"; and Gorbachev used it to justify the changes called *perestroika, glasnost,* and democratization, in the dying days of the Soviet Union. During a discussion with Clark Bowers in 1994, the theoreticians of the Chinese Communist Party used it to justify the current Capitalist policies of the Chinese Communists.

Karl Marx formulated this philosophy by combining the ideas of George Wilhelm Friedrich Hegel and Ludwig Feuerbach, two eminent German philosophers.

45

Hegel was the leading German philosopher of the early nineteenth century. Student intellectuals of that era would often meet in cafes and salons to discuss the meaning of the message of the master. Karl Marx was a member of a club of "Young Hegelians" during his student years in Germany.

PROGRESS

Hegel formulated his ideas into a system known as the "dialectic." The universality of "progress" is a central theme of the dialectic. This was affirmed by the statement, "Progress is inherent in being."

The conviction that "being" is progressive was widespread in intellectual circles during the nineteenth century, an era of optimism. Those who accepted it could look to the future with great expectations. However dark and depressing the present might be, the future was bright.

The theory of evolution had persuaded many that man was improving and would continue to do so, and that society would also continue to improve. Nothing could stop this progress. Evidence from human experience that sustained this belief was selected while a mass of conflicting evidence was ignored. In reality the belief was based on faith, not evidence. It is religious, not scientific, in nature.

Belief in "progress" is not so widespread today, though many of what is known as the Left continue to call themselves "progressives." Most scientific thinkers have rejected the idea. In his autobiography *Changing Patterns,* Alexander McFarlane Burnet, Australia's greatest scientist, wrote that he was aware of only one great scientist who was optimistic about the future of mankind. All the others believed that mankind was on a collision course with disaster.

Change does not always, or even usually, bring progress. Nevertheless, during dark and difficult days, the conviction of the inevitability of progress has sustained many a Communist with an inner assurance that certain victory lies ahead.

THE DYNAMIC OF PROGRESS

Universal progress required a universal cause, and Hegel taught that this cause was a universal state of conflict. In diverse situations two forces existed in conflict or "contradiction." One of them was progressive, while the other was reactionary. He called one the "thesis" and the other the "antithesis." These forces interpenetrated and formed a unity of opposites. This opposition, or "contradiction," provided the dynamic of progress. Progress was always resisted, and took place in a specific way.

One example of dialectical progress is what happens when a man tries to overturn a huge boulder with a lever. He inserts one end of the lever under the boulder and uses all his strength in order to raise the boulder. The lever exerts a progressive force on the boulder, but the weight of the boulder exerts an opposing reactionary force on the lever. This conflict results in a period of slow movement of the boulder until a critical or nodal point is reached, at which the progressive, or lifting, force overcomes the reactionary force and the boulder topples. In dialectical language, the thesis has *negated* the antithesis and a new state of conflict emerges, called the "synthesis."

In the synthesis, a new state of conflict ensues between a new thesis and a new antithesis. This leads to a succeeding stage of slow progress in a new direction until another nodal point is reached, at which slow progress is transformed into rapid, fundamental change as the new thesis negates the new antithesis and a new synthesis emerges. This synthesis may resemble the situation that originally existed, but it is invariably different in quantity and quality. This sequence is known as the "negation of the negation." Thus progress proceeds by a series of negations that cause advances and reversals.

Friedrich Engels, Marx's alter ego, illustrated dialectical progress by what happens to a seed. A seed is planted in the ground, and the ground negates it. This negation results in the emergence of the shoot, which makes steady progress by growing until it produces the fruit. The elements then negate the stalk and provide the new seed, similar to the one planted, but different in quantity and quality.

Opposed progress follows a dialectical pathway. This can also be illustrated by a hammer being used to drive a nail into a piece of hardwood. The hammer is brought down with a crashing blow, and the nail makes a little progress until the wood negates it. The hammer is then withdrawn. Watching the hammer as it is being withdrawn, an uncomprehending onlooker may conclude that the hammer is not in the process of driving the nail. A comprehending onlooker will understand that the act of withdrawal is as essential to the progress of the nail into the wood as is the downward blow.

Thus progress proceeds by a series of advances and retreats. Retreat is therefore an essential element of progress.

Lenin emphasized this repeatedly. So did his disciple Stalin. Lenin used it to justify his return to Capitalism by the New Economic Policy in 1921. Ignorant thinkers among the editorial writers for leading newspapers such as *The London Times* and *The New York Times* interpreted the Soviet return to Capitalism in 1921 as a renunciation of Communism. They did not understand that Lenin was merely withdrawing the hammer.

During a discussion with leading theoreticians of the Chinese Communist Party in Beijing in 1994, my friend Clark Bowers asked them if they considered the present situation in China to be a stage of "negation." They agreed without hesitation. He then asked, "When do you anticipate the negation of the negation?"

This seemed to cause great consternation among the Chinese. They began a long, spirited discussion among themselves in Chinese. Their spokesman then admitted ruefully that they did not know. He later told the leader of the American delegation that in twenty years of discussion with U.S. leaders he had never been asked such a question.

One obvious conclusion from the Communist adherence to the dialectic is that the Communist goal can never be perceived by observing the direction in which the Communists are moving. Failure to understand this lies at the root of the numerous delusions about Communism that still exist throughout academia and other prestigious U.S. circles.

IDEALISM AND MATERIALISM

Hegel was a philosophical idealist. He believed that thought was primary and matter was secondary—that matter could be known only through thought.

Marx was a philosophical materialist; he believed that matter was primary and thought was secondary—that the brain secreted thought as the liver secreted bile.

Through the ages, philosophers have been divided into two schools—the idealists and the realists. The idealist insisted that since matter can be known only by thought, thought must be the basic reality. The realists insisted that the universe with its innumerable elements existed independently of human thought.

Maybe we can leave judgment to the poets. A. E. Housman expressed the central ideas of both idealism and materialism in a brief poem:

Good people do you love your lives
and have you ears for sense?
Here is a knife like other knives,
that cost me eighteen pence.
I need but put it in my heart
and down will come the sky,
The earth's foundations will depart
And all you folk will die.

The first five lines express materialism, while the final three express idealism.

As a young intellectual, Marx was confronted with a dilemma. He was enthralled by Hegel's dialectic, but rejected his idealism. He agreed with the convictions and conclusions of Ludwig Feuerbach who taught that matter is the totality of being, that man is what he eats. The materialism espoused by Feuerbach was summarized by a later disciple of Marx—Mao Tse-tung—who wrote in his book *On Contradiction*, "There is nothing in the world except matter in motion."

Marx resolved his dilemma by combining the dialectic of Hegel with the materialism of Feuerbach, creating the philosophy known as dialectical materialism. This philosophy provided the prism through which he viewed human activities as he formulated his social diagnosis, prescribed his therapies, and predicted future developments.

The fingerprints of dialectical materialism are all over the ideas that Marx, along with his lifelong friend, colleague, and benefactor, Friedrich Engels, presented in their famous *Manifesto of the Communist Party* published in 1848. Millions were convinced and inspired by it, among them Lenin, Stalin, Mao, Pol Pot, Fidel Castro, and countless college professors and economists throughout the world.

This is an incomplete list of conclusions and practices that were guided by dialectical materialism.

HISTORICAL MATERIALISM

Marx formulated a doctrine of history known as "Historical Materialism," which is the basic foundation of *The Communist Manifesto*. In his preface to the 1888 English edition Engels states:

> *The Manifesto* being our joint production, I consider myself bound to state that the fundamental proposition, which forms its nucleus, belongs to Marx. That proposition is: that in every historical epoch, the prevailing mode of economic production and exchange, and the social organization necessarily following from it, form the basis upon which it is built up, and from which alone can be explained, the political and intellectual history of that epoch. (30 January 1888)

Thus to Marx and Engels, the mode of production was the creator of human character and ideas. Here is how he refutes the claim that eternal values exist independently of property relations:

> "Undoubtedly," it will be said, "religious, moral, philosophical and juridical ideas have been modified in the course of historical development. But religion, morality, philosophy, political science, and law, constantly survived this change.
> "There are, besides, eternal truths, such as Freedom, Justice, etc., that are common to all states of society. But Communism abolishes eternal truths, it abolishes all religion, and all morality, instead of constituting them on a new basis; it therefore acts in contradiction to all past historical experience."

What does this accusation reduce itself to? The history of all past society has consisted in the development of class antagonisms that assumed different epochs.

But whatever form they may have taken, one fact is common to all past ages, viz., the exploitation of one part of society by the other. No wonder, then, that the social consciousness of past ages, despite all the multiplicity and variety it displays, moves within certain common forms, or general ideas, which cannot completely vanish except with the total disappearance of class antagonisms.

The Communist revolution is the most radical rupture with traditional property relations; no wonder that its development involves the most radical rupture with traditional ideas.

A corollary of this Marxist doctrine is that control of the mode of production gives control of the formation of human character and ideas; that a selected mode of production can create a desirable character and philosophy of life. Future disciples of Marx applied this doctrine in practice with deadly consequences for millions of victims.

The conviction that all men and women consist solely of atoms, molecules, and other physical elements is another expression of materialism. Even mental and spiritual qualities are considered essentially material. Man is an animal with machinery somewhat more complex than other animals but with no transcendental qualities such as soul and spirit. There is no God and no life after death. Human beings can be changed and improved by methods that have been successful in changing other animals through animal husbandry.

All religions are superstitions. The idea of God was projected into human consciousness by the universal existence of class struggle. Religion is an enemy of progress since it diminishes revolutionary fervor. Therefore religion is the opiate of the masses.

Materialism means atheism. Lenin stressed this throughout his life. He insisted that atheism was natural and inseparable from

Marxism, a conviction still held by Communists throughout the world. This is illustrated by the answer Clark Bowers received from the representatives of the Chinese Communists during their discussion in Beijing in 1994 when he asked the question, "Must you be an atheist to be a Communist?"

> CLARK: Is the concept of religious practice part of your right of religious belief, and do members of the Communist Party also have the right to believe in God?
>
> MR. MO: First, you must realize that membership in the Communist Party is very demanding and is only for the disciplined few. If one chooses to join the party, they must understand and believe in the scientific laws of socialism. The first of these scientific laws is atheism. If a party member chooses to believe in religious superstition, he is free to leave the party.

The materialism that underlies Marxist doctrines seems to deny any scope for personal initiative and activity. Since we are all programmed by material forces, what possibility exists for individual choice? Surely this is expressed in the following limerick:

There was a young man who said "Damn!
It appears unto me that I am,
An engine that moves in predestinate grooves,
I'm not even a bus, I'm a tram."
[a tram is a streetcar on fixed rails]

Marx escaped from this dead end by turning to the dialectic, which enshrined "the unity and interpenetration of opposites." Thus objectivity was united with subjectivity and was also interpenetrated by it. Therefore a role remained for human initiative and choice. If this seems logically contradictory, it must be remembered that the dialectic conflict, often termed "contradiction," is a dynamic of human progress.

Conclusions influenced by the dialectic abound in *The Communist Manifesto*.

THE MANIFESTO—CLASS AND CLASS STRUGGLE

Chapter 1 opens with, "The history of all hitherto existing societies is the history of class struggles."

Class struggle is a manifestation of contradiction. Before class struggle can exist, classes must exist. What is a class?

A class is formed when "the mode of production" gives similar or identical experiences to many people and thereby creates similar ideas, emotions, ambitions, and institutions. The individuals of a class possess a similar "class consciousness." Therefore all men are not born equal. Classes are not equal; they are in conflict.

Marx analyzed the existing mode of production, Capitalism, and claimed that it had produced two major conflicting classes. One class consisted of those who owned the instruments of production, the other of those who were employed to use those instruments without ownership. They were wage slaves. He called the class of owners the "bourgeoisie," and the class of wage laborers the "proletariat." The struggle between these classes was the dynamic of progress.

Progress proceeded dialectically. The proletariat was the progressive class, and the bourgeoisie was the reactionary class. This dialectical conflict would inevitably reach a critical nodal point at which the proletariat would negate the bourgeoisie. Slow steady progress would be transformed into rapid explosive change, and a synthesis would emerge. This synthesis would be Socialism. Therefore the transformation from Capitalism to Socialism could not be consummated by an accumulation of incremental changes known as reforms. It must be revolutionary. All the material forces involved in the class struggle were in the process of producing a revolution. The class-consciousness of the proletariat must consequently be revolutionary. Reformism was reaction.

THE REVOLUTION

The purpose of the revolution was to produce a new mode of production with new relations of production. This new system was called Socialism. Would this revolution be peaceful or violent? The *Manifesto* climaxed with the clarion call—

> *The Communists disdain to conceal their views and aims.* They openly declare that their ends can be attained only by the forcible overthrow of all existing social conditions. Let the ruling classes tremble at the Communist revolution. The proletarians have nothing to lose but their chains. They have a world to win.
>
> The Communist Manifesto, 96

According to Marx, force would be necessary. He likened force to the midwife who would deliver the babe (Socialism) from the womb of an aging and decaying Capitalism.

When force is resisted it leads to violence, so the revolution would be violent. Engels wrote the following eulogy of violence:

> Have these gentlemen [the anti-authoritarians] ever seen a revolution? A revolution is certainly the most authoritarian thing there is; it is the act whereby one part of the population imposes its will on the other part by means of rifles, bayonets, and cannon—authoritarian means, if such there be at all; and if the victorious party does not want to have fought in vain, it must maintain this rule by means of the terror which its arms inspire in the reactionaries. Would the Paris Commune have lasted a single day if it had not made use of this authority of the armed people against the bourgeois? Should we not, on the contrary, reproach it for not having used it freely enough?
>
> Quoted by Lenin in The Proletarian Revolution and
the Renegade Kautsky

Violence must be an action—not a mere reaction.

One of the objectives of the revolution was the abolition of individualism, a bourgeois characteristic. Marx makes this clear in his *Manifesto:*

> . . . by "individual" you mean no other person than the bourgeois, than the middle-class owner of property.

This person must, indeed, be swept out of the way, and made impossible.

Future disciples of Marx took this instruction seriously. One relatively recent example is the conduct of Pol Pot and his Marxist cohorts in the Khmer Rouge during the revolutionary transformation of Cambodia, now Kampuchea. After seizing power they took pains to "make impossible" all bourgeois individuals. They defined as bourgeois any person who could read or write, all soldiers in the previous government, all civil servants, all members of professions such as doctors and lawyers, and all who had not engaged in physical labor in prerevolutionary years. The possession of horny hands was the badge of survival.

Academic apologists for Marxism claim that Marx did not mean killing by his statement, "this individual must be swept out of the way and made impossible," but many believed that he did. Thus ideas have consequences, and false ideas often have deadly consequences.

Lenin was an expert on the use of violence. He announced categorically that the revolution must be violent. He insisted, however, that violence should be used scientifically and be related to the revolutionary stage. He prescribed different types of violence for prerevolutionary, revolutionary, and postrevolutionary stages.

In the prerevolutionary stage, Communists should refrain from individual acts of violence, which he called "terrorism," because it limited their usefulness to the revolutionary cause and was therefore counterproductive. The primary function of each Communist was to lead the masses and to organize mass actions such as demonstrations, strikes, and riots. It was preferable to stimulate mass violence than to engage in such actions as assassinations and bombings that were likely to lead to imprisonment, and thereby destroy opportunities for more effective revolutionary activity. In the prerevolutionary season, killing should be confined to mass actions such as strikes and riots, whereas during a revolution it was open season for all violent acts, and after a successful revolution, the "liquidation of the bourgeois" would take place.

Well-wishers have often warned me that I should take precautions because Communists might decide to kill me to stop my anti-

Communist activities. I would serenely reply that I had a protector. Most assumed I was referring to God, but I was actually referring to a mortal, Vladimir Ilyich Lenin. Since I was active in what the Communists considered to be the prerevolutionary phase in the United States, and most other countries, Lenin had instructed that I not be killed.

In a revolutionary stage Leninists would act differently. For example, my foster son John Whitehall was engaged in anti-Communist activities in the Philippines during the Communist revolutionary war, and he was on the assassination list of the Communist New People's Army.

DIALECTICAL SEMANTICS

Marx, Engels, and Lenin readily acknowledged that the revolution would be violent, but their modern disciples have applied dialectics to semantics in order to claim the respectability that non-violence bestows.

During a discussion with the Chinese Communist theoreticians, the following interchange took place.

> CLARK BOWERS: Do you believe that it is possible for a revolutionary to be violent?
> MR. MO: No. It is the counter-revolutionary who commits acts of violence as he tries to work against peace and history's will.

Were the Chinese Communists lying? In light of their undisputed history of unlimited brutality, including the slaughter of millions, it seems obvious that they were. Nevertheless I do not doubt that they believed they were speaking the dialectical truth. They were applying "situational ethics."

Consider the action of taking a knife and plunging it into the abdomen of a living person. Is that a violent act? The answer depends on the purpose of the act. If an assassin is responsible it is certainly violent and murderous, but if a surgeon does it in order to remove an inflamed appendix it is nonviolent, life-saving.

In situation ethics, the morality of an act is not determined by its intrinsic nature but by the purpose for which it is performed.

In the linguistic universe of the Communists the revolution produces progress and is therefore good. Consequently, actions which serve the revolution are good.

The existing state is one of class warfare. The revolution will bring this class warfare to a progressive end and create peace. Therefore, revolutionary acts are peaceful.

Such revolutionary deeds as the "liquidation of the Kulaks as a class," which resulted in the deportation and death of over six million Kulaks in 1933–34, were therefore peaceful and nonviolent. As George Orwell wrote in his classic novel *1984*, war is peace.

If you are an actual or a suspected member of the bourgeois class, the Communists serenely take a nonviolent gun and use it to put a nonviolent bullet into your violent brain in order to produce peaceful progress. Deception has been dialectically sanctified.

THE DIALECTICAL CHIEF OF STAFF

In Hegelian theory, impersonal forces determine when the nodal point, at which the negation takes place, has been reached.

Marx taught that the forces generated by the mode and relations of production would necessarily produce the negation, or revolution. In order to survive, the Capitalists needed to employ workers. As Capitalism continued, due to the tendency of enterprises to merge, the number of capitalistic owners or bourgeoisie diminished, while the number of employed workers or proletarians increased. The conditions of labor became increasingly miserable for the proletarians as their hours grew and their wages shrank. This produced a revolutionary consciousness in the proletariat. The breaking point would ultimately be reached, and the workers would revolt and smash the mode and means of production and destroy Capitalism. As the *Manifesto* states:

> But not only has the bourgeoisie forged the weapons
> that bring death to itself; it has also called into existence
> the men who are to wield those weapons—the modern
> working class—the proletarians . . .

> What the bourgeoisie, therefore, produces, above all,
> is its own grave diggers. Its fall and the victory of the
> proletariat are equally inevitable.
>
> *The Communist Manifesto,* 51, 60

Unfortunately for Marx and the Marxists, history failed to follow Marx's scenario. But Lenin came to the rescue. He decided that the proletariat needed a brain and a mind that would decide when the nodal point of negation, or revolution, had been reached. This role was to be filled by the Communist Party, which Lenin first conceived, then organized, and finally led to power.

Clark Bowers asked the Chinese Communist leaders, "Who speaks for the people of China?" They replied, "The Communist Party acts on behalf of the workers. We are their mind."

Above the entrance to the headquarters of the Communist Party of the Soviet Union, this declaration was inscribed, "The Communist Party is the wisdom, the honor, and the conscience of our epoch."

Who speaks for the Communist Party? Lenin designed an internal party structure called "Democratic Centralism," which chose a spokesman who made the ultimate revolutionary decisions and exercised supreme power.

While ultimate authority was alleged to be the province of the people, or the masses, in practice it was transferred to the party, which transferred it to the central committee, which transferred it to the politburo, which transferred it to the general secretary, who ultimately became the dictator. This led to the emergence of such powerful figures as Stalin, Mao Tse-tung, Pol Pot, and, yes, Gorbachev.

During the years when Gorbachev, as secretary of the Communist Party of the Soviet Union, was promoting his programs of *perestroika, glasnost,* and democratization, Kremlinologists reported that a man called Ligachev led a conservative faction in opposition to Gorbachev. After the collapse of the Soviet Union, Ligachev announced that he could not remember any meeting of the politburo at which the vote for the policies of Gorbachev had not been unanimous.

This unanimity, and the power of one individual, was created by two submissions demanded of each party member. These were:

1. The voluntary submission by each party member of all his or her critical qualities of mind and will to the party. As Liu Shao-Chi, the former president of the Chinese Communist Party and China, wrote in his book, *How to Be a Good Communist:*

Whether or not a Communist Party member can absolutely and unconditionally subordinate his personal interests to the Party's interests under all circumstances is the criterion with which to test his loyalty to the Party, to the revolution and to the Communist cause . . .

To sacrifice one's personal interests and even one's life without the slightest hesitation and even with a feeling of happiness, for the cause of the Party, for class and national liberation and for emancipation of mankind is the highest manifestation of Communist ethics. This is a Party member's highest manifestation of principle. This is the manifestation of the purity of proletarian ideology of a Party member.

Liu Shao-Chi, *How to Be a Good Communist,*
(Foreign Languages Press, Peking, China, 1952, 51–52)

2. The requirement that once a vote is taken by a party committee, it is unanimously binding in thought and deed on all members of that committee and upon all members of the party below that committee.

Since the secretary controlled the agenda of the politburo and provided most of the information on which decisions were based, his ideas usually prevailed.

Thus the Communist Party secretary directed the dialectical progress of history. This created the possibility of human error.

The policies of the secretary, a fallible human, did not always produce the anticipated dialectical results. The negation was not invariably followed by the "negation of the negation."

Lenin's policy of surrendering land and people to the Germans by the Brest-Litovsk Treaty of 1918 was successful, as was his New Economic Policy of 1921, in which he reintroduced Capitalism in the Soviet Union. Stalin's policy in 1928, by which he negated Lenin's negation and abolished the New Economic Policy, was also successful since it achieved the objective of collective ownership. However, the policies of Gorbachev—*perestroika, glasnost,* and democratization—which were designed to purify and reinvigorate the Communist Party of the Soviet Union (CPSU), and to solve economic problems, failed miserably, and the Soviet Union is no more.

TOTAL FLEXIBILITY

When visiting universities I was frequently asked, "Do you speak on the economics of Communism?" My answer usually startled the questioner: "How can I? Communism has no economics. Economic programs are merely temporary tactics designed to enable the Communist Party to conquer and retain power."

But Communism has an economic objective. Marx expressed this clearly in the *Manifesto:* "the theory of the Communists can be summed up in a single sentence: Abolition of private property."

The Communist objective *is* the abolition of private property, but this objective must be reached by a long dialectical pathway. All economic programs along the pathway need not reduce private property.

The precise program at each stage of the journey to Communism must be designed to deal with each actual existing situation. Lenin, Stalin, Mao, and other Communist leaders constantly stressed this.

Communist economic policies have been numerous and "contradictory." The pathway to Communism passes through several stages. These include: the prerevolutionary stage, the revolution, Socialism, and Communism. Each stage has its own economic imperatives.

In the prerevolutionary stage, the Communist Party must be organized and the people enticed to support the Communist cause. The guiding principle at this stage is "Find out what the people want, promise it to them, work hard to get it for them so that they will submit to Communist leadership."

Lenin and the Bolsheviks followed this principle during their conquest of Russia. Marx's Communist theory taught them that land should be owned collectively. When Lenin returned to Russia from his exile in Switzerland in early 1917, he discerned that the majority of the Russian people wanted food, peace, and land. Therefore he came up with the slogan, "Bread, Peace, and Land" to describe the program of the Bolsheviks.

Since Marxism had previously taught the necessity of collective land ownership, various Marxist theoreticians castigated Lenin for deserting Marxism and said, "Farewell Lenin the Marxist; welcome Lenin the anarchist."

Thus the Communist Economic Program during the prerevolutionary stage was to create land owners, and thereby create capitalists.

During the Russian Revolution and the civil war that followed, all economic resources had to be devoted to attaining a Bolshevik victory. Personal sacrifice was the order of the day. At all costs, the Red Army must be fed and armed. Bread, peace, and land must be sacrificed. The economic aspirations of the people were put off.

After victory the Communist Party set out to build Socialism, which it called the "First Stage" of Communism. During this stage the people needed incentives to work hard and efficiently, such as wage scales that rewarded work. Wage equalization must be spurned; the Socialist Economic Program created significant differences in pay for different classes of workers, thereby fostering inequality.

During speeches to such groups as chambers of commerce, I would enjoy reading portions of a published speech that strongly condemned wage equalization. I would then ask the audience to guess who the speaker was. They were almost invariably astonished to learn that the author was none other than Joseph Stalin. Here is an extract from that speech:

> What is the cause of the heavy turnover of labor power? The cause is the wrong structure of wages, the wrong wage scales, the "Leftist" practice of wage equalization. In a number of our factories wage scales are drawn up in such a way as to practically wipe out the difference between skilled and unskilled labor, between heavy and light work. The consequence of wage equalization is that the unskilled worker lacks the incentive to become a skilled worker and is thus deprived of the prospect of advancement; as a result he feels himself a

"visitor" in the factory, working only temporarily so as to "earn a little" and then go off to "seek his fortune" elsewhere. The consequence of wage equalization is that the skilled worker is obliged to wander from factory to factory until he finds one where his skill is properly appreciated.

Hence, the "general" drift from factory to factory; hence, the heavy turnover of labor power.

In order to put an end to this evil we must abolish wage equalization and discard old wage scales. In order to put an end to this evil we must draw up wage scales that will take into account the difference between skilled and unskilled labor, between heavy and light work. We cannot tolerate a situation where a rolling-mill hand in a steel mill earns no more than a sweeper. We cannot tolerate a situation where a locomotive driver earns only as much as a copying clerk.

Joseph Stalin, *Problems of Leninism,*
(Foreign Languages Publishing House, Moscow,
1953, 463)

The economic program of the Communists during this Socialist stage was to increase inequality among the workers. Stalin proceeded to justify this promotion of inequality by claiming that he was following the teachings of Marx and Lenin. He continued:

Marx and Lenin said that the difference between skilled and unskilled labor would exist even under socialism, even after classes had been abolished; that only under Communism would this difference disappear and that, consequently, even under socialism "wages" must be paid according to work performed and not according to needs. But the equalitarians among our business executives and trade union officials do not agree with this and believe that under our Soviet system this difference has greatly disappeared. Who is right, Marx and Lenin, or the equalitarians? We must take it that it is Marx and Lenin who are right. But if that is so, it follows that whoever draws up wage scales on the "principle" of wage equalization, without taking into account the difference between skilled and unskilled labor, breaks with Marxism, breaks with Lenin.

More than fifty years later, Gorbachev repeated Stalin's condemnation of wage equalization when he wrote in his book *Perestroika:*

> Equalizing attitudes crop up from time to time even today. Some citizens understood the call for social justice as "equalizing everyone." But society persistently demands that the principle of socialism be firmly translated into life. In other words, what we value most is a citizen's contribution to the affairs of the country. We must encourage efficiency in production and the talent of a writer, scientist or any other upright and hard-working citizen. *On this point we want to be perfectly clear: socialism has nothing to do with equalizing.* Socialism cannot ensure conditions of life and consumption in accordance with the principle "From each according to his ability, to each according to his needs." This will be under communism. Socialism has a different criterion for distributing social benefits: "From each according to his ability, to each according to his work."
> [italics added]
> Mikhail Gorbachev, *Perestroika,*
> (Harper & Row, New York, 1987, 100)

To the Communists, Socialism was the stage during which productivity must be increased so as to attain an abundance of all things. In theory, this abundance would be accompanied by a change in the consciousness of the mass of the people so that selfish people would be transformed into unselfish people devoted to the general well-being.

Once abundance had been created and human nature regenerated, then, and only then, would it become possible to distribute goods produced on the basis of need. Then, Communism could and would come to pass. The slogan of Communism was, "From each according to his ability, to each according to his need."

Where a great skyscraper is to be built, the first stage is to create a large hole in the ground. The bigger the building, the deeper the hole. Socialism can be likened to the creation of the hole that will enable the magnificent edifice of Communism to rise.

No enlightened Communist claims that Communism exists anywhere. Many countries have been ruled by Communists but these rulers have concentrated on building Socialism. Thus the official name for the Soviet Union was the Union of Soviet Socialist Republics (USSR). The Chinese Communists claim they are building Socialism with Chinese characteristics.

Lenin once defined Socialism as "The Dictatorship of the Proletariat plus Electrification." This signified that the political monopoly of the Communist Party must be maintained while economic procedures to increase production were followed. If these procedures were capitalistic, so be it.

After victory in the civil war, Lenin was faced with a critical economic situation. He introduced Capitalism temporarily in order to increase production and utilized the energy and skill of Capitalists. He wrote:

> The political situation in the spring of 1921 was such that immediate, resolute and very urgent measures had to be taken to improve the conditions of the peasantry and to increase their productive forces . . .
>
> Our poverty and ruin are so great that we cannot *at one stroke* restore large-scale factory, state, Socialist production . . . Hence, it is necessary, to a certain extent, to help to restore *small* industry, which does not need machines, does not need either state reserves or large stocks of raw material, fuel and food, and which can immediately render some assistance to peasant farming and increase its productive forces.
>
> What will be the effect of this?
>
> The effect will be the revival of the petty bourgeoisie and of Capitalism on the basis of a certain amount of

free trade (if only local). This is beyond doubt. It would be ridiculous to shut our eyes to it.

Lenin then asks the question, "Can the Soviet state, the dictatorship of the proletariat, be combined, united with state Capitalism? Are they compatible?" His answer is categorical: "Of course they are."

> *Selected Works,* V. I. Lenin, Vol. II Part 2,
> Foreign Languages Publishing House,
> Moscow, 1952, 539, 542–544)

As long as the Communists controlled the machinery of the state, which included the army, the police, and the bureaucracy, they could reverse their "Capitalist" policy when the circumstances demanded. A negation would then take place. Meanwhile the state should continue to hold the reins that guided the Communist–Capitalist steed. Lenin wrote:

> The whole problem—both theoretical and practical— is to find the correct methods of directing the inevitable (to a certain degree and for a certain time) development of Capitalism into the channels of state Capitalism; to determine what conditions to hedge it round with, how to ensure the transformation of state Capitalism into Socialism in the not distant future.
>
> (Ibid., 544)

Some of the nondialectical Marxists were so outraged by the return to Capitalism in Lenin's New Economic Policy that they committed suicide in protest.

Many of the leaders in the governments, universities, and press of the Western nations rejoiced in what they considered to be the death of Communism in the Soviet Union.

In 1928 Stalin proved the validity of Lenin's contention that Capitalist economic policies could be introduced and then reversed when the time was ripe. He replaced individual farm production by collectivization. He sent Red Army units into the countryside to arrest all the farmers who had prospered during the New Economic Policy era and to deport them with their entire families to Siberia.

Those who resisted were executed. Many were deposited in the frigid snow in Siberia and left to scrounge for shelter and food on their own. Stalin called this dialectical negation the "liquidation of the Kulaks as a class."

The peasants were divided into three classes—Kulaks, middle peasants, and poor peasants. Those who employed labor were classified as Kulaks; those who managed to survive from what their land produced, without employing labor, were classified as middle peasants while those who had to supplement their income by working for wages part of the time were called poor peasants.

Thus Kulaks were peasant farmers who had farmed the land so successfully that they employed labor. They had not been landlords under the czar. Most landlords had been killed during the distribution of "land to the peasants."

Many of the Kulaks were extremely poor. Nevertheless every village was given a quota of those who must be arrested, deported, or executed. Pity for the impoverished was not permitted. Bolsheviks must not yield to bourgeois sentimentality. They must be "men of steel" as their leader was.

The land owned by the deported Kulaks became the base of a collective farm. Middle and poor peasants were persuaded or coerced to give their land and animals to the collective farm. Many resisted; they killed and ate their animals.

A great famine developed in Ukraine during the winter of 1931–32, during which six to eight million died, but collectivization prevailed. Agricultural production remained inadequate, and food shortages were chronic throughout the years of the Soviet Union. Naturally, these shortages were blamed on the weather. Notwithstanding the reality, Communists claimed that collectivization was a success, since it stopped the creation of a Capitalist consciousness among the peasants of Russia and consolidated the Communist dictatorship.

Over fifty years later, Mikhail Gorbachev eulogized the program and success of collectivization when he wrote in his book *Perestroika:*

> Collectivization was a great historic act, the most
> important social change since 1917. Yes, it proceeded

painfully, not without serious excesses and blunders in methods and pace. But further progress for our country would have been impossible without it. Collectivization provided a social basis for updating the agricultural sector of the economy and made it possible to introduce modern farming methods. It ensured productivity growth and an ultimate increase in output which we could not have obtained had the countryside been left untouched in its previous, virtually medieval, state.

Perestroika, 40

Since Communism has not been reached, Communist economic programs are decided and enforced by the Communist rulers with the primary purpose of maintaining the Communist monopoly of political power.

PSYCHOLOGICAL DIVIDENDS OF THE DIALECTIC

Self-Esteem

In his speech following the death of Lenin, Stalin assured the Communists that they were a special and chosen people. He said:

Comrades, we Communists are people of a special mold. We are made of special stuff. We are those who form the army of the great proletarian strategist, the army of Comrade Lenin. There is nothing higher than the title of member of the party whose founder and leader was Comrade Lenin . . .

Departing from us, Comrade Lenin adjured us to hold high and guard the purity of the great title of member of the party. We vow to you, Comrade Lenin, that we will fulfill your behest with credit.

Selected Works of V. I. Lenin, (Foreign Languages Publishing House, Moscow, 1952, 21)

The Communists consider themselves to be members of a special club. To them the mysteries of the dialectic have been revealed.

Whereas the great mass of mankind merely observes the consequences of the operation of the forces of nature, *they* discern the origin of the forces and the laws by which those forces operate. This enables them to influence the consequences and to predict the future accurately.

This understanding and ability make them members of a dialectical elite, and bestow upon them the right and the responsibility to lead and direct the untutored masses. These pilots can guide the ship of state throughout the reefs of capitalism until it reaches the dialectically promised land of Communism. This inflates their self-esteem. Thus the dialectic nurtures their pride.

Destiny

Most people like to be members of a winning team, and the Communists are sustained by this certainty. They are the progressives, and "progress is inherent in being." The ultimate triumph of Socialism is therefore as certain as the rising of tomorrow's sun. Both are guaranteed by the operation of objective laws—for example, the law of progress guarantees Communist victory, as the earth's rotation guarantees dawn.

This certainty of ultimate victory gives them great fortitude during difficult days. Setbacks are not defeats; they are dialectical retreats.

Thus Communism resembles the phoenix, a mythical bird of great beauty which, after being burned on a funeral pyre, rises from the ashes in the freshness of youth and lives through another cycle of years. The true Communist, though down, knows that Communism will rise again.

At the present time it is widely believed that Communism is dead, a conviction at best premature, and at worst delusional. The Communists await their day of deliverance, which they "know" is coming.

Righteousness in Hypocrisy

Hypocritical techniques are often effective but they penalize the practitioner who has a conscience. As Shakespeare wrote:

Thrice is he armed that hath his quarrel just,
And he but naked, though lock'd up in steel,
Whose conscience with injustice is corrupted.

(II Henry VI III, ii)

Tennyson teaches how a sense of righteousness and justice magnifies strength when he quotes Sir Galahad, the personification of selfless altruism:

My strength is as the strength of ten,
Because my heart is pure.

The dialectic enables Communists to experience and enjoy the strength and protection that purity of motive gives while they practice the techniques of hypocrisy and commit the most heinous crimes. It transforms hypocrisy into service, cruelty into kindness, and evil into good. Thus it delivers bountiful psychological dividends to its devotees.

Those who will not learn the lessons of history are condemned to repeat them, and those who will not learn the deviousness of the dialectic are condemned to be deceived by it.

7

....

Foreign Ventures

The world is small when your enemy is loose on the other side.
—JOHN BOYLE O'REILLY, 1844–1890

I HAVE NEVER KEPT A diary, so I must depend on my memory as I attempt to recapture and report times and details of events that happened more than forty years ago. But I shall strive for accuracy, and I promise honesty.

Upon returning to Australia from our visit to America, I resumed my medical practice, my evangelical activities, and my study of Communism.

Toward the end of 1951, I was invited to participate in a conference of the "International Council of Christian Churches," to be held in Manila. I accepted, and I agreed to speak on the subject, "Christianity and Communism."

My Australian accent again caused occasional confusion and merriment. At the airport, Carl McIntyre asked me to lead a group of Americans in a farewell prayer. I prayed that our Lord would be with me as I flew in the plane "today." Some of those present claimed that I had prayed for the divine presence as I flew in the plane "to die."

70

My accent notwithstanding, my message in Manila was understood and deemed relevant to the current situation in the Philippines. At that time, the Communists were leading a rebellion against the government. The rebels, known as the "Huks," followed the common Communist pattern. The leaders were university-trained intellectuals, and they were recruiting peasants by promising to abolish their poverty and oppression.

The goal of the Communists, however, is often contrary to that of the masses. Whereas the peasants want a fair share of the resources of the state, the Communists seek the destruction of the state. This was made lucidly clear by Lenin in his classical work, *The State and the Revolution,* which, at that time, was reportedly the world's most-translated book, even surpassing the Bible. My experience in the Philippines confirmed my conviction that my message on the undesirable and lethal consequences of the ideas of Communism was relevant and important for people of every class and nation.

JAPAN

While in the Philippines I was invited to Japan to speak to missionaries and interested Japanese people. So I sent the following cable to my lovable, long-suffering Lillian, "GOING ON TO JAPAN; DON'T KNOW WHEN I WILL BE HOME; ARRANGE FOR THE PRACTICE. LOVE, FRED."

Not then, nor on any other occasion, did Lillian offer one word of complaint concerning my absence.

In Japan I was guest of the Reverend Timothy Pietsch and his wife Helen. Timothy was the son of Dr. W. E. Pietsch, who later wrote the invitation letter that enabled me to enter the United States and establish the Christian Anti-Communism Crusade.

My schedule included lectures to missionaries, church congregations, and students. One experience with a Japanese student illustrated how difficult it is to communicate ideas across language barriers by either the written or spoken word. The student, a friendly, intelligent young man told me that he was attracted by the teachings of Marx. When I asked him if he had read *The Commu-*

nist Manifesto, he replied that he had tried but when the opening sentence referred to a ghost he gave up.

The Communist Manifesto begins, "There is a specter haunting Europe; the specter of Communism." Apparently the translator had used the word "ghost" for "specter." The student thought the *Manifesto* was a ghost story.

The art of communication is difficult. What the listener hears is filtered through past experiences and present interests, and sometimes the message received is quite different from what the speaker intended. To illustrate this I would often tell the following anecdote:

"While advocating the prohibition of alcoholic beverages, a Temperance orator thundered, 'There are over one hundred taverns in this county, and I am proud to say that I have never been in one of them.' An alcoholic voice interjected, 'And whish one was that?' "

I tried to overcome this communication problem by using illustrations taken from the daily experiences of my audience.

To convey abstract thoughts it is necessary to agree on the meaning of the terms used. "Define your terms," is a basic rule.

What is a definition? To me it is the description of the unfamiliar in terms of the familiar. We are all provided with familiar images through our senses, and from these images we construct our universe of language.

An effective speaker begins where the audience is. It is futile to use unfamiliar terms and images, but to discover and select suitable terms and images is often difficult.

On one occasion, in Alabama, I was invited to speak to students at the Perry County Christian School. I was able to communicate with the high school students, but was at a loss when I came to the grade school pupils.

I looked at the bright and smiling faces of eight-, nine-, and ten-year-old boys and girls, and I wondered, "What can I say to these children that will enlighten them about the nature of Communism?" First I established rapport by talking about koalas and kangaroos. I then asked, "Has anyone here heard of Joseph Stalin? If so please raise your hand." Not one hand was raised. It was obviously useless to talk about the crimes of Stalin.

I then asked, "Have any of you ever been in a group of children when one of you did something wrong and everyone in the group was punished?" Hands went up everywhere.

So I proceeded to tell them that Communism taught that you were good or bad, and should be rewarded or punished, because you belonged to a group, or class, whereas Christianity taught that each person is responsible for his or her own choices and actions and should be rewarded or punished accordingly. I believe that many young minds understood the message.

After an interesting, instructive, and fruitful visit to Manila and Tokyo, I returned to Sydney in time to celebrate Christmas and a twelfth wedding anniversary joyously with Lillian, John, Rosemary, and David.

8

....

The Communist Blueprint
for the Conquest of the U.S.A.

When the Cambrian measures were forming,
They promised perpetual peace,
They swore, if we gave them our weapons, that the wars
of the tribes would cease.
But when we disarmed
They sold us and delivered us bound to our foe,
And the Gods of the Copybook Headings said:
"Stick to the Devil you know."
—RUDYARD KIPLING, 1865–1936

"WHICH DO YOU CONSIDER TO be the greater danger, external or internal Communism?" I was frequently asked this question when I lectured on the nature and strategy of Communism.

I often responded by asking, "If you were on a ship that was sinking, such as the *Titanic,* which would be the greater danger, the water outside or the water inside?" I was illustrating that the external and internal forces were manifestations of the same danger. To use dialectical terminology, they constituted a unity of interpenetrating opposites.

To Marx, Lenin, and their disciples, the question was not "if" the Communists would conquer the world, it was "when." Lenin illustrated this on November 25, 1921, by his statement on the future use of gold:

> When we are victorious on a world scale I think we shall use gold for the purpose of building public lavatories in the streets of some of the largest cities in the world.
>
> *Selected Works*, vol. 2, part 2, 608

While Communist victory was certain because of the laws of history, the Communist Party was the instrument history had chosen to direct the victorious struggle. What strategy should it use?

The Communist Manifesto presented this clarion call: "Workers of the World, Unite. You have nothing to lose but your chains. You have a world to win."

The unity of the proletariat of the world was a necessary and important element in Communist strategy. It must be guided by proletarian internationalism. Marx taught that class struggle existed in every country in the world and that Capitalism was creating a bourgeoisie and proletariat everywhere. Consequently, the class struggle was international.

The proletariat, under the leadership of its mind, the Communist Party, had established its dictatorship in the Soviet Union, which had therefore become its strategic headquarters. As a result, every worker everywhere was a citizen of the Soviet Union. True patriotism meant giving support to all its policies.

This imposed great responsibilities upon the Communist leaders of the Soviet Union. Konstantin Chernenko, when he was dictator of the Soviet Union, claimed that Soviet policies complied with instructions from Lenin that international needs must take precedence over the national needs of Soviet citizens. This explained why the Soviet Union was spending in excess of $12 million a day to subsidize Communism in Cuba.

For the Communists, prediction guides prescription. They do not relax and complacently await a future being created by the "mode of production." They work like beavers to make the inevitable come to pass.

As the historically chosen vanguard of the proletariat, the Soviet Communist leaders designed and executed a basic strategy for world conquest. To them, the major enemy to defeat was world Imperialism, a conviction affirmed by Lenin in his influential book *Imperialism: the Highest Stage of Capitalism.*

The leader of world Imperialism was the United States of America; therefore, in Communist propaganda, "Imperialism" became a synonym for the United States. In thousands of speeches and articles in scores of languages, America was called the "Evil Empire." It was Communist leader Gus Hall's anti-American appellation. It is amusing to remember the condemnation that ingenuous liberals poured upon President Reagan when he called the Soviet Union the "Evil Empire"—once, in a single speech.

I don't remember when I finally perceived the basic strategy of the Soviet Communists to consummate the conquest of the world—by the surrender of the United States. But after years of study it emerged with clarity, and I chose the words for a formula that best described their strategy: "External encirclement, plus internal demoralization, plus thermonuclear blackmail lead to progressive surrender." The formula was not officially announced by Communist leaders, but the policies directed by this formula created the phenomenon called "Peaceful Coexistence."

This strategy was pursued by the Soviet Union until the Communist Party, under Mikhail Gorbachev, renounced it in 1985 when the leadership ruled that peaceful coexistence was no longer a form of class struggle. This acknowledged that their strategy for world conquest had failed. The Communists attributed this failure to the destructive power of nuclear weapons, which made avoiding nuclear war take precedence over the class struggle.

Gorbachev wrote:

> With the emergence of weapons of mass, that is, universal destruction, there appeared an objective limit for class confrontation in the international arena: the threat of universal destruction . . .
>
> Specifically, we deemed it no longer possible to retain in it the definition of peaceful coexistence of states with

different social systems as a "specific form of class
struggle."

Perestroika, 146–7

For nearly seventy years the Soviet Union followed this formula
and made considerable progress toward achieving its goal. The strategy included four primary elements: (1) Encirclement, (2) Demoralization, (3) Avoidance of nuclear war, and (4) Piecemeal surrender.

ENCIRCLEMENT

Numerous forces were cooperating in the effort to encircle the
United States. These could be classified as numerical, military, economic, and psychological.

Numerical Encirclement

At the peak of their power the Communists controlled one-third
of the world's population and exercised substantial influence over a
second third.

In 1903 Lenin created Bolshevism with about twenty-five supporters. In 1917, the Bolsheviks, now "the Communist Party of Russia," conquered Russia.

When Lenin returned to Russia from his exile in Switzerland and
announced that he had returned to lead the Communist Party to
conquer Russia, his party had about 50,000 members. After the conquest the Communists ruled about 160 million. The conquest of
Eastern Europe added another 100 million; the conquest of China in
1948 brought to total to over 1 billion, one-third of the world's population at that time. Numerous other countries fell to the Communists in subsequent years, including Korea, Vietnam, Cambodia,
Yemen, Somalia, Ethiopia, Angola, Mozambique, and Cuba. Revolutions led by Communists and supported by the Soviet Union
engulfed scores of other countries.

The figures support the claim that the Communists were making
remarkable progress toward world conquest.

Since progress is dialectical, the process of numerical encirclement
necessarily experienced reversals. These occurred when the mono-

lithic unity of the world Communist movement was shattered. The major reversal happened in 1959 when the Chinese Communists under Mao Tse-tung renounced and denounced the leadership and activities of the Soviet Communists under Khrushchev.

Despite divisions in the Communist ranks, all branches retained their devotion to the policies of Marx and Lenin and maintained their opposition to "Imperialism."

Military Encirclement

The Soviet Union set out to encircle the United States with such massive military might that any U.S. military action that could conceivably lead to war with the Soviet Union would be deterred. The proliferation of increasingly destructive nuclear weapons made such a war unthinkable.

To achieve military encirclement the Soviet Union created the largest army in the world and an overwhelming arsenal of nuclear weapons. The number and megatonnage of nuclear warheads and missiles to deliver them increased exponentially.

This military might enabled the Soviet leaders to:

(1) Deter any hostile military action by the United States and thereby maintain peaceful coexistence.

(2) Ensure that fraternal Communist Parties that had come to power could retain their power. If the people of any country rose up to overthrow their Communist rulers, the Red Army could and did rush to the defense of the Communists. Reflect on what happened in Hungary and Czechoslovakia, and what was attempted in Afghanistan. This policy was formalized in the "Brezhnev Doctrine."

(3) Provide arms and military advisors to Communist and national revolutions throughout the world. The objectives of such revolutions need not be Socialist, as long as they were anti-Imperialist or anti-colonialist. A successful rebellion would weaken world Capitalism; the Socialist revolution could come later.

(4) Provide the Soviet Union with bridgeheads and bases from which it could threaten the United States, illustrated by the placement of atomic missiles in Cuba that led to the 1962 missile crisis.

(5) Threaten neighboring countries. One Soviet objective was to take over West Germany, but this ambition was thwarted when the United States and its allies placed nuclear-tipped missiles in West Germany, which brought the European Russian heartland within range. These were installed by NATO forces under President Ronald Reagan's guidance and support. This deterred the Soviet Red Army forces, under the umbrella of the Warsaw Pact, from colonizing West Germany and Western Europe.

Economic Encirclement

The Soviet leader, Khrushchev, became notorious for his famous boast, "We will bury you." This was widely interpreted as a threat of military conquest but Khrushchev later claimed that he had intended only to convey that the workers of America would carry out the interment. He was convinced that the centralized economic system of the Soviet Union would soon outproduce the doomed "dog eat dog" capitalist system and that this would cause the American people to choose Socialism.

In the book *Khrushchev Remembers* he states:

> I allowed myself at one point to use the expression "We will bury the enemies of the Revolution." I was referring, of course, to America. Enemy propagandists picked up this phrase and blew it out of proportion: "Khrushchev says the Soviet people want to bury the people of the United States of America!" I said no such thing. Our enemies were purposely distorting a few words I'd just let drop.
>
> Later at press conferences I elaborated and clarified what I'd meant. We, the Soviet Union, weren't going to bury anyone; the proletariat of the United States would bury its enemy, the bourgeoisie of the United States.

Marx had taught the Communists that the Capitalist system was doomed because of the increasing "proletarianization" it inevitably caused. Lenin, however, perceived that Capitalism was being kept alive by "Imperialism," which enabled the United States and other countries to steal the resources of the undeveloped nations and use them to inflate the wages of the workers in the Imperial heartland, thereby delaying the development of their "revolutionary consciousness."

The basic imperialistic method for this theft was to export capital to underdeveloped countries. This capital produced agricultural and mineral products which were owned by the investors of the capital. Starvation wages were paid to the national workers to keep cost of production low.

These primary products were then transported to the investing Imperialist country where they were processed in Imperialist factories to produce finished products that were then sold on the world market. The buyers were often the countries from which the raw materials had been extracted.

The profits from this cycle were enormous, and this accounted for the poverty of the "Third World" and the relative prosperity and stability of the "First World."

Consequently, one way to hasten the collapse of Capitalism was to break the cycle of Imperialism. This could be done if Nationalist or Socialist leaders, who were anti-Imperialist, could grasp power in underdeveloped countries. Therefore all anti-Imperialist revolutions should be supported.

The Soviet Union also invested vast sums in assistance to underdeveloped countries in order to foster anti-Imperialist policies. This was done by direct gifts, indirect gifts through favorable trade relations, and low-interest loans. A country needed only to declare its opposition to U.S. Imperialism to receive Soviet beneficence. Thus the Aswan Dam was built on the Nile in Egypt and steel mills were built in India.

Cuba is one example of the Soviet endeavor to encircle the United States economically. As soon as Castro had conquered Cuba and announced his devotion to Communism, Cuba was given vital Soviet economic support. This went hand in hand with military support. It was conservatively estimated that Soviet support for Cuba exceeded $12 million per day.

During the Brezhnev era in Russia, Seymour Hersch, the famous journalist who reported the infamous "My Lai" massacre in Vietnam, was the featured speaker at an Accuracy in Media Conference in Washington, D.C. He claimed that the actions of the Soviet Union were primarily defensive and that the Cold War was due to the anti-Communist hysteria in the United States.

After his speech I asked him, "Why is the Soviet Union giving Cuba at least $12 million a day? Is it because they have so much money that it's a burden to them? Is it because they like the Cuban girls? Why?"

His reply was a typical non sequitur: "No one thinks much of Cuba." Apparently, the Soviet leaders did.

The poverty in Cuba stands in stark contrast to the prosperity in such former, underdeveloped countries as Taiwan, Singapore, South Korea, and Hong Kong.

The cause of poverty in Cuba is Socialism. It is Socialism, not Capitalism, that is producing its own grave diggers.

Psychological Encirclement

The Soviet Union conducted a massive campaign to encircle the United States with hatred. While the Soviet Union was depicted as an example of the glorious future which awaited all nations that embraced Socialism, the United States was described as a country that impoverished and oppressed its workers and threatened to destroy mankind with nuclear weapons. The USSR invested large sums in a worldwide propaganda campaign of hatred.

The central message portrayed the United States as an Imperialist predator. It was disseminated by literature and radio in an attractive style that appealed to the audience. This audience consisted of two major groups—the intellectuals and the mass of the people. The disinformation was divided into two categories: Propaganda and Agitation.

(1) Propaganda

The appeal of propaganda was primarily intellectual, while the appeal of agitation was basically emotional. Propaganda was defined as "that which conveys many ideas to a few people," whereas agitation was "that which conveys one idea to many people."

The organization that directed this campaign was known as the "Agitprop" department of the Soviet government.

Propaganda attempted to teach the basics of Marxism and Leninism to the elite few whom the Communists considered potential recruits for the party; these were mainly university-trained intellectuals, and the Soviets established schools in Russia to recruit and train them. Talented young people from underdeveloped countries were given scholarships to study at these schools with the hope that they would return to their own countries and organize guerrilla campaigns to seize political power.

Marxist and Leninist classics were also translated into numerous languages and distributed for a mere pittance.

The propaganda literature was comparable to the theological treatises which religious movements publish. No attempt was made to simplify the message and to dress up the presentation. The language was esoteric, polysyllabic, and difficult.

Through propaganda, the Communists hoped to create the enlightened individuals who would be worthy of membership in the party, which was the "mind" of the masses.

(2) Agitation

Agitation, "that which conveys one idea to many people," had the primary purpose to woo the masses by promises of future benefits, and to activate them to rectify present grievances, invariably in abundant supply.

Every modern technique was used. Magazines were printed on high-quality paper and adorned with colorful art. Special magazines were designed for different sections of the community—attractive magazines for children with stories and fables; magazines for women that featured beauty aids and the nurture of the family and children; and magazines for men on sport, engineering, health, and recreation.

On my lecture tours I carried a selection of Communist agitational literature. After examining it some people would often say in bewilderment, "What's wrong with this? I can't find any Communist message in it." I would then explain that the purpose of the magazine was to persuade the reader that conditions in the Soviet Union were almost heavenly; that the Communists, in a few short years, had transformed a backward country of poverty and oppression into a land of freedom, abundance, and happiness. Its message: "Go thou and do likewise."

No expense was spared to spread this "agitation" throughout the world. Huge semitrailers were purchased and outfitted as mobile libraries, which moved through the impoverished villages of India with the message that their future could be bountiful if they followed the path that had been pioneered by the people of the Soviet Union (see picture section).

While Russia was glamorized, America was demonized. It was the land of racism and crime in which a privileged and decadent few held all the power and kept the workers in check by distributing to them a small portion of wealth stolen from the poor of the earth through Imperialist practices.

Russia was the country promoting world peace, while the United States threatened mankind with nuclear destruction.

It should be noted that the Communist campaign to demonize America was aided and abetted by a significant non-Communist minority in the States who accepted many, if not all, of Lenin's doctrines of Imperialism. Their guiding principle was "America is to blame."

This campaign to demonize America was also aided by the small but influential Communist movement in America. Despite its small size the U.S. Communist Party received generous support from the Soviet Union. Evidence to this effect was confirmed after the demise of the Soviet Union.

Despite this effective Communist agitation, the United States still drew the poor of the earth to its shores. While Communist regimes had to create Iron Curtains and Berlin Walls to prevent their citizens from fleeing, the United States needed to erect border fences and maintain coastal patrols to prevent a flood from surrounding countries.

Nevertheless, the Communist strategy to encircle the United States numerically, militarily, economically, and psychologically attained significant success during many years.

DEMORALIZATION

The overthrow of the Capitalist system in the United States was to come about through the demoralization of the masses, not from their democratic choice of Socialism.

The demoralization would be primarily spontaneous but it could be aided and abetted by the activities of the Communists and their allies.

The Communists were convinced that Capitalism was in its dying stages. They believed the doctrine of Karl Marx, that the mode of production formed the base from which all the institutions of society were constructed. This base also engendered the emotions and ideas that formed the character of those employed within the institutions.

In Marxist jargon, the mode of production was the base while the institutions were the superstructure. The institutions of Capitalism included the family, the government, the schools, the military, the banks, the corporations, and the churches. All these were suffering from the decline of the moral fiber essential to the health of the institutions. A decline in the patriotism, honesty, and unselfishness needed to sustain a stable society would continue.

Family Breakdown

Marx believed that demoralization was already in progress when he wrote the *The Communist Manifesto*. This is illustrated by what he said about the family:

> Abolition of the family! Even the most radical flare up at this infamous proposal of the Communists.
>
> On what foundation is the present family, the bourgeois family, based? On capital, on private gain. In its completely developed form this family exists only among the bourgeoisie. But this state of things finds its complement in the practical absence of family among the proletarians, and in public prostitution.
>
> The bourgeois family will vanish as a matter of course when its complement vanishes, and both will vanish with the vanishing of capital. . . .
>
> The bourgeois clap-trap about the family and education, about the hallowed co-relation of parent and child, becomes all the more disgusting, the more by the action

of Modern Industry [by which] all family ties among the proletarians are torn asunder, and their children transformed into simple articles of commerce and instruments of labor.

Some of the predictions of Marx have proved to be correct, others not. Family disintegration has taken place in the United States with grievous social consequences. It has transformed many areas in central cities into moral and material wastelands. This has led to increased crime and drug addiction with associated gang wars and the impoverishment and endangerment of women and children. As has become clear, dysfunctional families can produce sociopaths, men without conscience, who become predators upon the community.

The Economy

Among the causes of demoralization Marx emphasized the Capitalist system. It has not come about, however, in the way that Karl Marx predicted. It is largely a result of the enrichment of the American workers, not their impoverishment.

Australia's greatest medical scientist, Sir Frank MacFarlane Burnet, winner of the Nobel Prize, saw three primary threats to the continued existence of mankind—thermonuclear weapons, the population explosion, and the availability of leisure time to people who are morally ill-equipped. The last is due to the success of Capitalism, not its failure.

Marx's analysis of Capitalism, though reductionist, was convincing. He selected certain ingredients in the Capitalist system and assumed that these provided the complete picture. He detected a process that led to the overproduction of goods and the underdistribution of the money which would enable these goods to be purchased by the workers who produced them. This led to economic stagnation characterized by surplus goods, unemployment, poverty, and social unrest. Each social crisis was temporarily eased by the start of a war which caused enough money to be circulated to enable the accumulated goods to be purchased. Therefore war was a necessary consequence of Capitalism.

To abolish war, Capitalism must be abolished. Socialism, of course, meant peace.

History has refuted this Marxist solution to war because wars have continued to be caused by noneconomic factors such as national liberation, religious intolerance, and paranoia—take, for example, the situation in Bosnia.

The Communist Role in Demoralization

What role should the Communists play as demoralization in America continued? As the instruments of historic purpose they must harness the forces that Capitalism was creating and use them dialectically to help achieve two immediate objectives—the weakening of the United States and the strengthening of the Soviet Union. This required recruitment, infiltration, and leadership.

(1) Recruitment

As economic and social conditions deteriorated, a number of educated idealists lost hope that long-range solutions to misery and injustice could be found as long as the Capitalist mode of production continued. Capitalism must therefore be destroyed. This could be hastened by membership in the Communist Party.

One example was the wealthy U.S. Communist, Frederick Vanderbilt Field. He could have enjoyed the fortunes of the family but he became convinced that much of the misery of the world was caused by Imperialism, and that Capitalism led inexorably to Imperialism. He decided to join the Communist Party and devote his life to destroying Capitalism.

Once recruited, Communists must be active participants. They must not gather with like-minded people and discuss abstract ideas while the battles of the class struggle raged. To do this was to commit one of the major Communist sins—sectarianism.

Great forces influenced millions, and these forces must be harnessed and led. They included: industrial strife, ethnic and racial discrimination, environmentalism, feminism, peace proponents, and religion. Their movements must be infiltrated, influenced, and, if possible, led.

To attain leadership was not easy. It required dedicated and constant service in local struggles.

This sometimes led to amusing situations as reality overwhelmed fantasy. A reformed Communist, Philip Abbot Luce, tells of one such incident when he was a member of the New York chapter of the Progressive Labor Party (PLP), which split from the U.S. Communist Party in the 1960s to support the Chinese Communists against the Russian Communists. The PLP New York chapter was made up of students, professionals, and even an oil millionaire from Texas. They were somewhat bewildered and embarrassed that this "mind of the proletariat" contained no proletarian members, and they set out to rectify this anomaly.

They prepared appropriate literature and took it to the waterfront to inform the workers that they would help deliver them from their intolerable oppression. The proletarians took the literature, tore it up, threw it into the ocean, and threatened to treat the Communists in the same way. The Communists retreated to the comforts of their New York apartments—cast down but not in despair.

It was a primary purpose of the Communists at that time to persuade the masses that the policies of the United States were responsible for the Cold War and that the USSR was a beacon of hope for the peace and prosperity of mankind.

To gain the confidence and support of the masses it was necessary to assist them in their day-to-day struggles. Thus the Communists became involved in every strike, every struggle to abolish racial discrimination, every effort to protect the environment, and every program to "liberate" women.

As dialecticians, the struggle was progressive, so Communists could be active on both sides in a particular struggle. The dialectic teaches that conflict, or "contradiction," is the dynamic of progress. Therefore the promotion of conflict is often desirable and "righteous."

(2) Infiltration

Attempts must be made to infiltrate and capture control of organizations based upon social forces. If these efforts were unsuccessful, a competing organization should be created. The Soviet Union would provide assistance and guidance.

Agents of the Soviet Union created and financed international organizations to harness the forces created by universal human desires. Such organizations included the World Peace Council (WPC) and the World Federation of Trade Unions (WFTU). National chapters of such organizations were formed and operated in as many countries as possible. While these organizations engaged in struggles for local needs, their major objective was to strengthen the Soviet Union and to weaken the United States.

The alleged dedication to "peace" enabled the Communists to infiltrate many churches. The late Herbert Philbrick, who was my friend and associate for many years, tells in his book *I Led Three Lives* how he was trapped by Communists who were wearing the garments of peace. As a young Christian in Cambridge, Massachusetts, he joined a Baptist church. He enrolled in a peace society that met in that church and was elected president, only to become outraged when he discovered that his organization was controlled by the U.S. Communist Party.

He reported this to the FBI, and the FBI asked him to stay put, join the party, and report its activities.

He joined the Communist Party and rose to become a leader. He came out of the Communist closet to give evidence of Communist subversive activities in the Smith Act trials of 1951.

Interestingly, the WPC ceased to exist when the Soviet Union disintegrated and its financial subsidy ceased.

(3) Leadership: Spies and Spying

Communist membership provided a pool from which "espionage agents" and "agents of influence" could be chosen. Such agents could operate with a clear conscience because they were convinced that they were serving their country's real interests. Throughout the world a great "class war" was raging and proletarian victory was not only inevitable, it would also be beneficial to the people of every country. Bourgeois governments must be destroyed by the proletariat who were led by the Soviet Union. Thus to reveal official secrets to the Soviets was proletarian patriotism.

One of Lenin's first tasks after the Bolshevik conquest of Russia was to create a security apparatus to search for internal and external enemies so that they could be neutralized. This organization was led by Felix Dzerzhinsky, who was known as the "Conscience of the Party" because of his selfless dedication.

The original name of this espionage agency was the CHEKA. The entire Communist Party was urged to hunt for spies and enemies and to report them to the CHEKA. "Every Comrade a Chekist" was the reigning slogan.

In accordance with the principle that "a party grows strong through purging itself," leadership of this security apparatus was constantly purged. One after another of its leaders was arrested and executed. With each change of leadership came a change of name. The acronyms by which it has been known include NKVD, MGB, and KGB.

A parallel military intelligence agency, known as the GRU, was created, and it conducted independent espionage activity both internally and externally.

The CHEKA in its many incarnations set out to recruit foreign agents who would serve as spies in their own countries for the Soviet Union. These agents would obtain classified and secret information, and their Soviet controller would transmit it to Soviet headquarters.

Espionage Agents

One of the tasks of the CHEKA (NKVD, MGB, or KGB) operative in a foreign country was to select and control people who would serve as spies for the Soviet Union. A spy network was established in the United States.

After the atomic bomb was built, the Soviet search for information about nuclear weapons became increasingly urgent.

One dedicated Communist who became a spy was Whittaker Chambers. After giving faithful service to the Soviet Union for several years he renounced Communism and reported his espionage activities to the FBI. In his classical book *Witness* he revealed the steps he took on his journey to spydom, and away from it. He gave evidence in court about the espionage activities of the influential Alger Hiss, president of the Carnegie Endowment and confidant of President Franklin Roosevelt, which led to Hiss's arrest, trial, conviction, and imprisonment. The ensuing national controversy still rages, but recent evidence from the archives of the former Soviet Union confirm the accuracy of the testimony of Chambers.

Agents of Influence

Many devoted Communists and committed fellow travelers did not become spies, but served as "agents of influence." They obtained positions in the government or other institutions which influenced public opinion, including the news media, universities, the film industry, and churches. Unpaid agents of the Soviet agitprop campaign, they used their powerful positions to aid the Communist cause by exalting the Soviet Union and slandering the United States.

The success of Soviet espionage within the United States has been well documented. Many books have been written about the activities of such people as the Rosenbergs, who were executed for obtaining secret information about building the atom bomb and transmitting it to the USSR.

Did They or Did They Not?

As this is being written a controversy is raging around the possible role played by some of the leading United States and allied atomic scientists in providing valuable information on the construction of both the atomic and hydrogen bombs to the Soviets. Scientists who have been accused include Robert Oppenheimer, Leo Szilard, Enrico Fermi, and Niels Bohr.

The 1994 book *Special Tasks*, by Soviet spymaster Pavel Sudoplatov, who headed the atomic spy rings in America, reveals that a "Special Department S" was established in the Soviet Union in February 1944 to supervise atomic energy espionage. He states, "I was appointed head of the "Special Second Bureau" of the newly set up State Committee for "Problem Number One, whose aim was the realization of an atomic bomb through uranium fuel." He reports how their spies operated.

In 1941 Elizabeth Zarubina was a captain in the NKVD. After her husband's posting to Washington, she

traveled to California frequently to cultivate the Oppenheimer family through social contacts arranged by
Kheifetz. Kheifetz provided Elizabeth Zarubina with a
rundown on all the members of Robert Oppenheimer's
family, known for its left-wing sympathies, to enable her
to approach them. He then introduced Elizabeth to
Oppenheimer's wife, Katherine, who was sympathetic to
the Soviet Union and Communist ideals, and the two
worked out a system for future meetings. Katherine
Oppenheimer was not mentioned by name in the
reports, but we worked through a woman close to
Oppenheimer, and it was my understanding then and is
now that the woman was his wife.

Through Katherine, Elizabeth Zarubina and Kheifetz
convinced Oppenheimer to refrain from statements sympathetic to Communist or left-wing groups in order not to
call the attention of the FBI to himself. Zarubina and
Kheifetz persuaded Oppenheimer to share information
with "antifascists of German origin," which provided a
rationale for taking Klaus Fuchs to Los Alamos. Oppenheimer agreed to hire and promote these people, provided
he received confirmation of their opposition to Nazism
before they came to the project. Oppenheimer, together
with Fermi and Szilard, helped us place moles in Tennessee, Los Alamos, and Chicago as assistants in those
three labs. In total there were four important sources of
information who transmitted documents from the labs to
the New York and Washington rezidenturas and to our
illegal station, which was a drugstore in Sante Fe . . .

Special Tasks, 184

(Kheifetz was the resident Russian spy in the United States, and
Oppenheimer was the head of the Manhattan Project which pro-
duced the atomic bomb.)
Sudaplatov writes on:

When Morris was drafted into the U.S. Army in July
1942, their controller in New York, Anatoli Yatskov,

a/k/a Yakovlev, used Lona as a courier to Los Alamos to pick up information. Lona's trips to New Mexico were explained as visits to a sanatorium for a tuberculosis cure. Yatskov, code name Johnny, recounted in 1992 his work with Lona Cohen, a "pretty young woman." On one of her trips, August 1945, she traveled to Albuquerque shortly after the first atomic bomb was dropped on Hiroshima. She anxiously awaited a contact, who gave her a "thick wad" of tightly written pages that were "priceless" to Moscow Center.

As she left the security-infested town, she demonstrated her tradecraft. Carrying a suitcase, a purse, and a box of tissues, she arrived at the railroad station just as the train was supposed to leave. She dropped her suitcase and started rummaging nervously through her purse, searching for her ticket. She handed the tissue box to the conductor to hold while she looked for and found her ticket. Delighted, Lona boarded the train, leaving the box of tissues with the conductor. "I felt it in my skin, that the conductor would return the box of tissues, and indeed later he handed it to me." When Yatskov met her in New York City, Lona told him, "You know, Johnny, everything was all right except for one thing. The police held these materials in their hands." The tissue box contained a detailed description and drawing of the world's first atomic bomb.

On such a small axis the world turns.

Sudoplatov reports that the leading atomic scientists, Robert Oppenheimer, Leo Szilard, Enrico Fermi, and Niels Bohr, supplied vital atomic information to Soviet agents. They were not official Soviet spies, but they were opponents of the Nazis. Since the Soviet Union was an ally in the fight against the Nazis it was thought justifiable to provide its agents with atomic information. Only Oppenheimer could be considered pro-Communist. Moreover, as scientists, they believed that scientific knowledge should be shared internationally.

Sudoplatov states that Oppenheimer and Fermi were assigned the code names "Star" and "Editor," as information sources.

A Dialectical Contradiction

The Communist attitude to U.S. demoralization was based upon two conflicting ideas: (1) The degenerate character of Americans was caused by the existing economic system—the Capitalist mode of production, and (2) The Capitalist system had created U.S. citizens of such sterling character and intellectual excellence that they were worthy to become members of the Communist Party and assist the Soviet Union to conquer the United States and thereby liberate all mankind.

Their conviction that capitalism causes national degeneration is clearly expressed in an article in the September 10, 1994, U.S. Communist newspaper *People's Daily World*. Here are some extracts:

> To a great extent, most people agree on what the problems are and that they are of crisis proportions. Poverty, unemployment, homelessness, segregation, crime and violence, social decay, and crisis in education and health.
>
> Communists blame the system, the capitalist system. We proclaim it as far and as wide as we are able. The system that puts private corporate profit before people is to blame for our lousy state of affairs. Of course, the individuals who control and benefit from the system are to blame—but they are as much the products of it as its creators . . .
>
> Solutions to the problems we face under capitalism, to be most effective, should have this basic truth as their starting point. They should be firmly oriented on the working-class side of the class dividing line that is at the core of capitalism. And they should have on their horizon the aim of replacing this rotten system with the more just, progressive and truly democratic system of socialism.

The article also reveals the growing respectability of the U.S. Communist Party.

> Blame the "outside agitator." For years this meant blame the Communists, and anyone who could be labeled a Communist. It's holding much less sway now, as witnessed by the markedly friendly reception the Communists are finding among people—a fact that bodes badly for capitalism.
>
> Tom Hopkins, *World* op-ed editor

Who says, "Communism is dead"?

Thermonuclear Blackmail

For fifty years, atomic destruction has been suspended like the sword of Damocles over the head of mankind, threatening total destruction. This created a problem for the Soviet leaders as they formulated their plans.

How could they fulfill their historic duty to conquer the world without precipitating a nuclear conflict?

One way was to build enough atomic weapons to ensure that atomic war between the Soviet Union and the United States would defeat both sides and would therefore be deterred.

The Soviet Union embarked upon an ambitious program to build an arsenal of atomic weapons and the means to deliver them. The leaders were aware that numerous crises would occur as their program to encircle the United States progressed and that these might bring war between the Soviet Union and the United States. They also believed that the mutual realization that any such war would cause total destruction of both sides would deter it. Thus the policy of Mutual Assured Destruction (MAD) guided the conduct of both the Soviet Union and the United States.

This policy proved effective, and nuclear war has been avoided for over fifty years. Many crises have come and gone. Any list of them would include the Soviet invasion of Hungary in 1956, the Cuban Missile Crisis of 1962, the Berlin Blockade of 1949, and the installation of Pershing and cruise missiles in West Germany beginning in 1983.

The policy of MAD required the construction of increasingly sophisticated and costly nuclear weapons but forbade their use. From the Soviet standpoint these weapons were important. Their very existence protected the USSR from the use of NATO forces, however great the provocation.

In his book *Perestroika,* published in 1988, Gorbachev described the nuclear stalemate that existed:

> It is crystal clear that in the world we live in, the world of nuclear weapons, any attempt to use them to solve Soviet-American problems would spell suicide. This is a fact. I do not think that U.S. politicians are unaware of it. Moreover, a truly paradoxical situation has now developed. Even if one country engages in a steady arms build up while the other does nothing, the side that arms itself will all the same gain nothing. The weak side may simply explode all its nuclear charges, even on its own territory, and that would mean suicide for it and a slow death for the enemy. This is why any striving for military superiority means chasing one's own tail. It can't be used in real politics.

Madmen who were prepared to promote nuclear war did exist. Many were military leaders. One such was Mao Tse-tung, China's dictator.

Khrushchev reports how, during his visit to China in 1953, Mao endeavored to persuade him to provoke a war between the United States and the Communist empire:

> I remember once in Peking, Mao and I were lying next to the swimming pool in our bathing trunks, discussing the problems of war and peace. Mao Tse-tung said to me, "Comrade Khrushchev, what do you think? If we compare the military might of the capitalist world with that of the Socialist world, you'll see that we obvi-

ously have the advantage over our enemies. Think how many divisions China, the USSR, and the other Socialist countries could raise."

I said, "Comrade Mao Tse-tung, nowadays that sort of thinking is out of date. You can no longer calculate the alignment of forces on the basis of who has the most men. Back in the days when a dispute was settled with fists or bayonets, it made a difference who had the most men and the most bayonets on each side. Then when the machine gun appeared, the side with more troops no longer necessarily had the advantage. And now with the atomic bomb, the number of troops on each side makes practically no difference to the alignment of real power and the outcome of a war. The more troops a side has, the more bomb fodder."

Mao replied by trying to assure me that the atomic bomb itself was a paper tiger! "Listen, Comrade Khrushchev," he said, "All you have to do is provoke the Americans to military action, and I'll give you as many divisions as you need to crush them—a hundred, two hundred, one thousand divisions." I tried to explain to him that one or two missiles could turn all the divisions in China to dust. But he wouldn't even listen to my arguments and obviously regarded me as a coward.

Khrushchev Remembers, 469, 470

That these two men actually had the power to initiate a war that could have destroyed humanity is a terrifying thought.

Despite the nuclear stalemate, Gorbachev insisted that the Soviet Union must continue to build bigger and better bombs. He claimed that this was forced upon him by the United States.

It would seem logical, in the face of strategic stalemate, to halt the arms race and get down to disarmament. But the reality is different. Armories already overflowing continue to be filled with sophisticated new types of weapons, and new areas of military technology are being developed. The U.S. sets the tone in this dangerous, if not fatal, pursuit.

I shall not disclose any secret if I tell you that the Soviet Union is doing all that is necessary to maintain up-to-date and reliable defenses. This is our duty to our people and our allies.

Perestroika, 218

PROGRESSIVE SURRENDER

The Communist program to conquer the United States of America continued on its successful way. Statistics indicated that triumph was not far distant. But internal forces were operating within the Soviet Union that finally led to its disintegration.

I had long before discerned these forces, and in our May 2, 1968, Crusade newsletter I wrote this prediction:

> Today Communism is powerful and aggressive. It is stronger numerically, militarily, economically, propagandistically, and subversively than any comparable movement in human history. It has delivered shattering blows against the free world during the past 50 years. An objective analysis of the historic record would indicate that it is winning the battle for world conquest. However, today Communism is suffering from an internal hemorrhage that will progressively weaken it so that, if the free world can survive the next few years, the future is radiant with hope.

Since the program to conquer the United States appears to have suffered final defeat, some announce that the danger was exaggerated. Some even claim it did not exist: If it doesn't exist now, it never did. This is akin to claiming that Nazism was never a danger to Europe because Hitler was defeated. It is also like claiming that cancer never threatened a person's life because it was cured by appropriate therapy.

The conviction that Communism is the inevitable future for all mankind is still held by Marxists, but as world conditions have changed, their ideas on how this is to come to pass have also changed. Marx and Engels believed that a military conflict between the forces of a united proletariat and the bourgeoisie would probably occur during their lifetime. Engels studied military science to equip himself for a leading role in the conflict.

In pre-Leninist days, Socialists throughout the world anticipated such a conflict. Australia's "People's Poet," Henry Lawson, raised by a mother who was a devout Socialist, wrote the poem "Faces in the Street" when he was twenty-one years old. It described the coming solution to the problem of human poverty in 1888.

Once I cried: "O God Almighty! if Thy might doth still
 endure,
Now show me in a vision for the wrongs of Earth a cure."
And, lo, with shops all shuttered I beheld a city's street,
And in the warning distance heard the tramp of many feet,
 Coming near, coming near,
 To a drum's dull distant beat—
'Twas Despair's conscripted army that was marching down
 the street!

Then, like a swollen river that has broken bank and wall,
The human flood came pouring with the red flags over all,
And kindled eyes all blazing bright with revolution's heat,
And flashing swords reflecting rigid faces in the street—
 Pouring on, pouring on,
 To a drum's loud threatening beat,
And the war-hymns and the cheering of the people in the
 street.

And so it must be while the world goes rolling round its
 course,
The warning pen shall write in vain, the warning voice
 grow hoarse,
For not until a city feels Red Revolution's feet
Shall its sad people miss awhile the terrors of the street—
 The dreadful, everlasting strife

For scarcely clothes and meat
In that pent track of living death—the city's cruel street.
Poetical Works of Henry Lawson,
(Angus and Robertson, Sydney, 1970)

Many socialists believed that the formation, growth, and activity of trade unions would lead to the revolution. The accepted scenario included the following steps:

(1) Form a trade union

(2) Organize an industrial strike, one that seeks higher wages and improved conditions

(3) Transform the industrial strike into a political strike, with the objective of destroying the capitalist system itself

(4) Perform acts of violence in order to transform the political strike into a revolutionary strike

(5) Revolution. (The 1905 revolution in Russia followed this pattern.)

The Bolshevik conquest of Russia and the formation of the Soviet Union introduced a new element into the revolutionary process. Marxism became Marxism-Leninism, and the Communist Party of the Soviet Union became the higher command of the Communist armies wherever they operated. It also supplied all anti-Imperialist armies with weapons and funds.

The development of atomic weapons, however, demanded a new world strategy. World conquest could not now be achieved by a major war. It must be accomplished by incremental steps below the threshold at which nuclear war might erupt.

One way was to organize and support anti-Imperialist local wars. Many, but not all, of these would be led by Communists. Most of them would be wars of national liberation. Every successful war of national liberation would accomplish the following:

(1) Increase the number of people under Communist control or influence and thereby increase the numerical encirclement of the United States.

(2) Deprive U.S. Imperialism of a source of raw materials and markets for its manufactured goods. This would reduce the amount of money available to bribe U.S. workers. It would lead to unemployment and create a revolutionary consciousness among the workers.

Khrushchev confidently predicted that it would finally cause the workers to rise up and destroy the Capitalist system. Clarifying the meaning of his well-known statement, "We will bury the enemies of the revolution," he explained in *Khrushchev Remembers* that "the proletariat of the United States would bury its enemy, the bourgeoisie of the United States."

(3) And finally, increase U.S. reluctance to become involved in a war with the USSR and increase its willingness to compromise and make concessions.

As all this proceeded, the balance of power would tip in favor of the USSR, for as each local crisis developed it would become increasingly logical for the United States to make a concession rather than risk war. Thus concession would follow concession till no reasonable alternative to surrender remained.

This surrender would not be sudden, nor would it be called surrender. It would be similar to "Finlandization," in which the Soviet's superior military strength and economy would be acknowledged. The die would have been cast, and any future "Stalin" could commit his atrocities unhindered. To paraphrase T. S. Elliot, it might be said, "This is the way the class war ends, not with a bang but with a whimper."

Fortunately, this outcome never happened; its failure was caused to a considerable degree by the decay of the Soviet Communist Party. Instead of becoming increasingly unselfish and talented, as their false doctrines of human nature predicted, the Communists became increasingly selfish, greedy, incompetent, and criminal.

It is enlightening to contrast the reports on conditions in the USSR which Khrushchev made in 1969 and those Gorbachev made in 1987.

Khrushchev had held the position of first secretary of the Communist Party of the USSR from 1953 to 1964, while Gorbachev became first secretary in 1985. Khrushchev was still secretary of the CPSU when he made this statement:

> We Communists believe that capitalism is a hell in which laboring people are condemned to slavery. We are building Socialism. We have already been successful in many respects, and we will be even more successful in the future. Our way of life is undoubtedly the most progressive in the world at the present stage of humanity's development. To use the language of the Bible again, our way of life is paradise for mankind. . . .
>
> We have accomplished many things, and we have created the conditions for still greater successes.
>
> *Khrushchev Remembers*, 521–522

Gorbachev wrote:

> Decay began in public morals; the great feeling of solidarity with each other that was forged during the heroic times of the Revolution, the first five-year plans, the Great Patriotic War, and postwar rehabilitation was weakening; alcoholism, drug addiction and crime were growing . . .
>
> Many Party organizations in the regions were unable to uphold principles or to attack with determination bad tendencies, slack attitudes, the practice of covering up for one another and lax discipline. More often than not, the principles of equality among Party members were violated. Many Party members in leading posts stood beyond control and criticism, which led to failures in work and serious malpractices.
>
> At some administrative levels there emerged a disrespect for the law and encouragement of eyewash and bribery, servility and glorification. Working people were justly indignant at the behavior of people who, enjoying

trust and responsibility, abused power, suppressed criticism, made fortunes and, in some cases, even became accomplices in—if not organizers of—criminal acts.

(*Perestroika,* 22–23)

Gorbachev attempted to regenerate the character of Russian Communism and Communists by his programs of *perestroika, glasnost,* and democratization, but he failed, and the USSR is no more.

The sinfulness of human nature triumphed, and dreams of Communist beauty and hope became the reality of deception, deprivation, destruction, and despair.

9

....

The Vulnerability of Australia

And she came. She was beautiful as morning,
With the bloom of the roses on her mouth,
Like a young queen lavishly adorning
Her charms with the splendors of the South.
And the fierce old nations, looking on her,
Said, "Nay, surely she were quickly overthrown;
Hath she strength for the burden laid upon her,
Hath she power to protect and guard her own?"
—A. B. PATERSON (SONG OF FEDERATION)

IN THE 1950s and 1960s, my conviction grew stronger that Australia's safety depended upon the strength of the United States and its understanding of the character of the Communist menace. I remembered how American forces were needed to protect Australia from Japan during the Second World War.

When addressing audiences I would often draw attention to Australia's vulnerability by asking this hypothetical question: "If you were prime minister of Australia, and Soviet submarines with nuclear weapons were stationed in the ocean waters near Brisbane, Sydney, Melbourne, Adelaide, Perth, and Hobart, and the Soviet commander phoned you and demanded surrender, what would you do?"

I would explain that over half of the country's population live in those coastal cities, that Australia had no equipment to locate those submarines and no weapons to destroy them. I would suggest that the obvious response would be to call the president of the United States and plead for protection since it alone had the weapons that could deter a Communist attack. If the United States were either unable or unwilling to help, there would be no alternative to surrender.

When asked how the Communists could conquer Australia, I would answer, "By telephone."

I decided I could best contribute to my country's security by bettering American understanding of the true nature and objectives of the Communists.

THE BIRTH OF THE CHRISTIAN ANTI-COMMUNISM CRUSADE

During my 1952 visit to America, Dr. Billy Graham and Dr. W. E. Pietsch, among others, urged me to form an organization that would educate people about the Communist menace, and at the same time be in harmony with Christian evangelism. Since atheism was a basic doctrine of Communism, Communism was the enemy of the Christian message: "God so loved the world, that He gave his only begotten Son that whosoever believeth in Him should not perish but have everlasting life." (John 3:16) I decided that an appropriate name for the proposed organization would be "The Christian Anti-Communism Crusade." Lillian and I decided to go ahead.

Leaving my medical practice in the care of a locum, I returned to America in 1953. Lillian and the children hoped to join me later if the venture proved successful.

My one speaking engagement scheduled before my arrival was to address the annual banquet of Life Bible College of Angeles Temple, Los Angeles, which is the training ground for potential preachers and pastors of the Four Square Gospel Church. Their $50 honorarium financed the birth of the Christian Anti-Communism Crusade.

After the banquet, Carl Williams, a successful businessman and a foreign missions enthusiast of the Four Square Gospel Church, invited me to spend the night in his Long Beach home so that I could give my message and testimony at a breakfast meeting of the Christian Businessmen's Association the following morning. This was an important stepping-stone on the path that led to the Crusade's locating its offices in Long Beach.

After my message, Carl Williams phoned the Reverend James D. Colbert, the executive director of the Long Beach chapter of the national organization, Youth for Christ, to recommend me as a suitable speaker at one of his Saturday night Youth for Christ rallies. Jim was delighted. He had seen and heard me on a television program and was wondering how to reach me. This interesting contingency would have far-reaching significance.

After addressing the youth rally and learning that Jim was about to leave for speaking engagements in Phoenix, I asked him to try to arrange meetings there for me. He succeeded beyond my expectations.

My Phoenix meetings were held in churches. In my addresses I combined an exposure of Communism's doctrines and practices with Christian evangelism. I stressed the role that atheism played in the formation of Communist doctrines, and the logical consequences. I challenged Christians to be as dedicated to Christian regeneration as the Communists were to creating a godless utopia. Anti-Communism *aided* evangelism.

Some who were members of secular organizations in the audiences invited me to speak to their groups. A chain reaction started, where one lecture led to another and then another.

Dr. Pietsch, my official American host, called a small group of Christians together, and we formed the Board of the Christian Anti-Communism Crusade and registered it in Waterloo, Iowa, in May 1953. He became president, and I became executive director.

Jim Colbert became director of Missions of the Christian Anti-Communism Crusade when it was founded, and conducted anti-Communist seminars in Africa, Asia, and Latin America. He was also chairman of the Crusade Board until his recent death in 1996.

I chose the name. It was in harmony with my motivation and objective, and was an honest acknowledgment of the basic premises of the Crusade. We believed that God existed; that Christian doctrines were true while Communist doctrines were delusional; and that the Communist danger was real.

Some people charge that we are biased. I plead guilty. We are biased in favor of truth, freedom, and life; we are against deceit, slavery, and unnecessary death. We believe that Communism leads to classicide through the liquidation of the bourgeoisie, that it leads to the justification and practice of mass murder.

The choice of the word "Christian" was not meant to imply that non-Christians were pro-Communist or were excluded from the battle against Communism. It was an acknowledgment of our positive purposes, and was in keeping with common practice since many American organizations are called Christian. Look in the phone book.

I was genuinely astonished when the word "Christian" in our name became controversial. When Martin Luther King, Jr., formed the Southern Christian Leadership Conference, I never heard that the name offended Northerners because they were excluded, or that it offended Jews.

Names are significant, but the important things to consider when judging any organization are its doctrines, purposes, and programs. As Shakespeare's Juliet said, "What's in a name? That thing we call a rose by any other name would smell as sweet."

When challenged, as I frequently have been, by the question, "We know what you are against; what are you for?" I reply, "We are for the presentation of the Christian gospel; we are for truth, freedom, and continuing life; we are for feeding the hungry and healing the sick; and we endeavor to practice Christian love."

FINANCIAL SUPPORT

Every organism needs nourishment, and every organization needs financial support. How was the Crusade financed?

The primary means of support came from offerings taken after speaking to church groups. We gave those who believed in us the opportunity to contribute. While most gifts were small, they enabled the Crusade to survive and grow.

Dr. Pietsch insisted that we follow a policy of "Pay as you go," and I approved wholeheartedly. The life of the Crusade has been free of debt.

When asked how to finance a young organization, I enjoy telling the following story:

In the Washington, D.C., area, I spoke to four different gatherings in a single day. In the morning I gave evidence on "Communism in Hawaii" to the Territorial Committee of the House of Representatives of the U.S. Congress; in the afternoon I spoke to the National War College; during the supper hour I spoke to the Washington Bible College; and in the evening I spoke to the Pentecostal Church of God in Arlington, Virginia.

Who paid the expenses? The Pentecostal Church of God took up an offering after I had spoken.

The Crusade began with no financial angels. We have never employed fund-raisers, and we have followed a strict policy of using the entire amount of any designated gift for the designated purpose. The *message* has been our fund-raiser.

In harmony with our policy of keeping administration expenses to a minimum, I personally presented our request for tax-deductible status to an official of the Treasury Department; in due course, it was granted.

On later occasions, when the Internal Revenue Service examined our ministry, they invariably confirmed our tax-deductible status. When Walter Reuther of the United Automobile Workers Union sent the infamous Reuther Memorandum to the U.S. Attorney General asking him to have our tax-deductible status removed, his hopes were dashed.

THE AUDIENCES

Churches

Most of the churches where I was welcomed were evangelical and small. Occasionally, I would speak in a church of one of the more liberal "mainline" denominations. I welcomed any opportunity to preach—morning and evening services, special church groups such as adult Sunday school classes, and gatherings of women, men, or youth. Most of these churches were eager to expand their ministry, and the possibility that a message on Communism would attract non–church-goers appealed to many ministers.

Civic Clubs

Civic clubs are a feature of American life. A host of them hold weekly meetings, and finding speakers is not always easy. Consequently, program chairmen often welcome the offer of an unusual speaker.

Jim would go to a chosen city and exchange a five-dollar bill for nickels, the contemporary cost of a phone call, and sit in a hotel lobby with a phone book, tracking down the program chairmen of listed clubs. Though most clubs had a policy of not paying their speakers, he was sometimes able to negotiate a $25 honorarium. Honorarium or not, we gladly accepted.

An outstanding day was the one on which I visited New Hampshire in 1959. The Lions Club of Manchester, New Hampshire, and the *Manchester Union,* published by William Loeb, nationally known courageous fighter for freedom, sponsored my appearance to address the New Hampshire legislature at Concord and to speak to an evening mass rally in Manchester. Both meetings overflowed with people and enthusiasm. The Lions Club published the following cartoon.

Schools

I was often invited to speak to a school assembly, an experience I always enjoyed. Invariably, the students were interested and responsive. Question-and-answer periods were fascinating. Questions from junior high school students were direct and straightforward, but those from high school students were somewhat more sophisticated. College questions sometimes contained a trap.

The questions asked in adult audiences were often disguised opportunities for imparting, not receiving, information. Partisans would deliver a minor lecture or pose a question in a way that they hoped would entice me to respond by conveying the information the questioner wanted the audience to hear.

While I never hesitated to say "I don't know" when appropriate, I cannot remember being asked a question that surprised or embarrassed me.

Whenever possible I collected the names and addresses of those interested in further information. These received my newsletters. I also invited them to become members of the Crusade. The annual membership fee was ten dollars, a hundred dollars for lifetime membership. The membership did not grant voting rights. The Crusade survived and grew.

As the Crusade developed, in 1953 Lillian and I decided that the time had come to bring the family to America. We rented a cottage in Long Beach so that John, who was eleven, and Rosemary, nine, could attend school. David was five.

But the family move was not as successful as we had hoped. I was traveling and speaking constantly, so I was seldom home. Due to seasonal differences, the American and Australian school schedules do not dovetail, so John was enrolled in a class that was half a year behind, and he was unhappy. Lillian finally said, "I would sooner educate the children in Australia, and I see very little of you now. We would see each other about as much if I took them home, and you came home and stayed with us twice a year." The expression "quality time" was not then in common use, but it was what she had in mind.

I agreed reluctantly, and Lillian took the children home, where she cared for them while also serving as secretary of the Australian

Christian Anti-Communism Crusade. I remained in the States, and returned to Australia for six weeks twice a year.

We corresponded daily and lovingly. Lillian is the center of all the family activity. She fulfills the biblical promise, "Her family shall rise up and call her blessed." (Proverbs 31:28)

10

....

The Pathologist

It has been said that the anatomist never made a good surgeon,
that it was the pathologist who made the surgeon.
—William J. Mayo

I HAVE OFTEN BEEN ASKED, "How do you see your role in the
fight against Communism?"

I have seen myself as a medical doctor who is battling a deadly
disease—Communism; I have regarded myself as a pathologist who
researches and reports the nature of that disease.

One of the first pamphlets I wrote was entitled, "Communism, a
Disease." Here is an extract from it:

> Communism has already killed many millions of peo-
> ple and proposes to kill many millions more. Therefore,
> by definition, it is a disease.
>
> It is a threefold disease. It is a disease of the body,
> because it kills; a disease of the mind, because it is asso-
> ciated with systematized delusions not susceptible to
> rational argument; and a disease of the spirit, because it
> denies God, materializes man, robs him of spirit and

111

soul, and, in the last analysis, even of the mind itself, and reduces him to the level of a beast of the field.

The disease of Communism is making fast epidemic progress and we are confronted, not merely with the possibility, but with the probability that at present rates of expansion, within a generation it will have consumed the entire earth.

The most essential feature in the treatment of any disease is accurate diagnosis. We have a saying in the medical profession: "It is better to have the right operation done poorly than the wrong operation done very well."

When a patient consults a doctor, he or she will often hear, "We must run some tests." The physician then sends the patient to the pathologist so that necessary tests can be carried out before treatment is prescribed.

The pathologist does not prescribe treatment. But without the pathologist, even the best physicians and surgeons are handicapped, if not helpless. To quote William J. Mayo, founder of the Mayo Clinic, "It has been said that the anatomist never made a good surgeon, that it was the pathologist who made the surgeon."

The popular image of a surgeon as a nimble-fingered artist is fallacious. Knowledge is the basic requirement of a surgeon; manual dexterity is secondary.

During my medical student years this was stressed by our teachers who gave this advice, "If you're in a foreign country and you need surgery, and want to find the best surgeon, ask which one makes the biggest incision and go to him." A larger incision leads to greater knowledge.

I was often challenged by the accusation, "You alarm us but don't tell us what to do." The accusation had some justification but I viewed myself as the pathologist, not the physician. I considered the American people to be the physicians and urged them to study and study hard so they could decide on and apply the therapy that would preserve the liberty they took for granted. I urged Christians to apply the principles that Jesus taught in their daily lives, such as "Do unto others as you would that they should do unto you." (Matthew 7:12)

And I frequently quoted the biblical proverb, "Righteousness exalts a nation: but sin is a reproach to any people." (Proverbs 14:34)

When preaching Sunday morning sermons I would often base the message on the warning of the prophet Joel:

> Blow ye the trumpet in Zion, and sound an alarm in my holy mountain: let all inhabitants of the land tremble: for the day of the Lord cometh, for it is nigh at hand. (Joel 2:1)

While the danger was physical, the response which the prophet urged was spiritual:

> Therefore also now, saith the Lord, turn ye even to me with all your heart, and with fasting, and with weeping, and with mourning: And rend your heart, and not your garments, and turn unto the Lord your God: for He is gracious and merciful, slow to anger, and of great kindness, and repenteth him of the evil. (Joel 2:12–13)

As far as possible I avoided entanglement in local disputes, and I shunned partisan politics. My passion was to discover and proclaim the truth.

During later years I was astonished and bewildered when I was widely accused of being a right-wing extremist; an anti-Semite; a protofascist; or a leader of a "nativist" movement of "know-nothings," of which I had never heard. (More on this later.)

POSITIVE VERSUS NEGATIVE

Was I too negative? How often I heard this charge! I believe in both the positive *and* the negative. I reject the absurdity in "You should always be positive; you should never be negative." I believe in a police force that is against crime, not one that merely conducts clubs for boys. I don't think a fire engine, while rushing to extinguish a fire, needs to broadcast as it goes, "We are also in favor of city beautification."

It is sometimes difficult to distinguish the positive from the negative. I once asked an advocate of the positive imperative this simple question, "If my house catches on fire and I call the fire brigade, is that a positive or a negative act?" He replied, "If you put the fire out yourself, it is positive; if you call the fire brigade, it is negative." I remained unimpressed.

The name of the Crusade indicates our belief in *both* the positive and the negative. True Christianity is a positive force, and "Christian" is the first word in our name. Our record has proved that the Crusade practices religion as it is described by the apostle James:

> Religion that God our Father accepts as pure and
> faultless is this: to look after widows and orphans in
> their distress and to keep oneself from being polluted by
> the world. (James 1:27)

During its existence the Crusade has given lifetime support to thousands of orphans through the work of the Indian Christian Crusade, and to many Christian messengers throughout the world.

We are positive in our stand for truth and love. We are unashamedly "anti" in our opposition to Communism.

PROGNOSIS

One of the duties of the pathologist is to provide a prognosis so that appropriate therapy may begin. He must think about the future as well as the present. He must be ruthlessly honest and report the truth even if it upsets the patient, family, and physician.

Some diseases cause intense pain that is merely temporary and self-terminating. Others cause little or no pain till they become difficult or impossible to treat. Early and accurate diagnosis is the pathway to life.

Pain may be a warning signal but its message is not always trustworthy. Consider a child who is awakened by a severe abdominal pain. Her mother rushes her to the nearest emergency room, and if the child is diagnosed as having overeaten, the prognosis is good.

On the other hand, the doctor may diagnose an attack of acute appendicitis and advise immediate surgery. His report may distress mother and child but it is not callous and cruel. A truthful diagnosis and prognosis is the pathway to life.

After reading *The Communist Manifesto* more than fifty years ago, I made the accurate prognosis that the doctrines of Karl Marx would lead to classicide through the "sweeping away" of "the bourgeois, the middle-class owner of property." History has recorded the accuracy of this prognosis.

Many disagreed with this diagnosis and prognosis and nurtured the delusion that Marxism was essentially benign. But after many years in the service of Karl Marx they discovered that the mass murders committed by Communists were due to their devotion to Marxist doctrines and not to deviation from them.

Examples abound. Professor Eugene Genovese, who supported and taught Marxism for many years, now raises what he calls "the question" that almost never gets asked:

> "What did we know, and when did we know it?" In other words, when did members of the American left learn that the idealistic cause so many of them supported—the international communist movement— "broke all records for mass slaughter, piling up tens of millions of corpses in less than three-quarters of a century"?
>
> Genovese gives his own answer: "We knew everything essential and knew it from the beginning"—and therefore the left was guilty of abetting unspeakable crimes.
>
> Quoted from *Time* magazine, 22 August 1994.
>
> Source: "Dissent," summer edition

Eric Aarons, a leader and member of the Australian Communist Party for forty years, writes in his recent book *What's Left?*:

> We often used to speak of the "general crisis of capitalism," and today the capitalist world is indeed suffering from growing economic and social problems. But this only intensifies our chagrin at the fact that a general crisis in all fields, economic, political, social, and ideological, developed first in the socialist countries. The

effects of the long political monopoly of the ruling communist parties were even worse than anticipated, and their political bankruptcy far greater. The revelation of the details of crimes and repressions were sickening, though not unexpected. But the intensity of the economic crisis, the extent of environmental degradation, the depth of the corruption, and the degree of political backwardness of the populations were less expected. The "leading role of the Party" had led to—this!

Another, probably longer-lasting and more widespread response in the Left has been to acknowledge, even if reluctantly, the magnitude of the crimes committed in the name of socialism, and the many distortions that have occurred. Having done so, they then assert that socialism itself remains untarnished. After all, they argue, the torture practiced by the Christian Church during the Inquisition, the mass slaughter of people in various religious "civilizing missions," and the declaration that "God is on our side" in a host of dirty wars does not necessarily mean that religion itself should be condemned.

Such a stance has cogency, and I certainly would not want for a moment to identify Stalinism, the Tiananmen massacre, and a host of other distortions and crimes with socialism as we had envisaged it, or the values that we held dear. But saying "that wasn't socialism" won't overcome the underlying problems, or surmount public scepticism or serve to establish what *real* socialism would actually look like.

More than a dozen socialist countries, with diverse traditions and histories, and in many cases able and independently minded leaders, have all gone through a somewhat similar development. They have all, at a certain stage, run up against basically similar problems. All have seen their highly dedicated, self-sacrificing and popularly supported parties transform themselves into ruling groups exercising a monopoly of economic, political, and ideological power to, eventually, little or no positive purpose. Corruption and privilege have at least tainted, if not thoroughly permeated, them all.

Clearly these problems cannot just be attributed to the effect of hostile capitalist forces, to peculiar circumstances in the countries themselves or to the personal characteristics of those who rose to the top. It seems far more likely that underlying economic and social structures are more important factors, as indeed Marxism itself would indicate.

Eric Aarons, *What's Left?*
(Penguin Books Australia Ltd., 231–234)

Another disillusioned Communist who now faces the facts is the American ex-Communist Dorothy Healey, who held many high positions in the U.S. Communist Party. In her book, *Dorothy Healey Remembers,* published in 1990, she describes her reaction after attending a meeting at which Khrushchev's speech on the crimes of Stalin had been reported and discussed.

Nothing had prepared me for the magnitude of what we were hearing. We had marched for so many years with the purity of the Soviet Union as our banner. We had believed it completely.

It was around eleven o'clock in the evening when the reading of the report finally ended. I had been crying for several hours. I made a dash for the door because I didn't want to talk to anyone. Ben Davis came over, and I will always remember his kindness. He didn't say a word but put his arm around me as we walked downstairs and got me into a taxi. I went back to the hotel where I was staying. About half past twelve the phone rang and it was Bill Schneiderman, who wanted to talk to me. Word had gotten around about how upset I was. I just said, "No, I don't want to talk to you. I don't want to talk to anybody. I just want to think. Just leave me alone."

The next day there was another session. The thing I remember most about it was a comment by Jim Jackson, an up-and-coming black leader. He said, "I don't understand what all this emotional reaction is to that speech, all this great political to-do. Why, comrades, everybody knows you can't make an omelet without breaking eggs." I felt chilled by the repetition of that all-too-familiar cliche. Yes, we had always understood that in a revolutionary situation unfortunate things were bound to happen, people might be killed or be imprisoned unjustly. In the heat of battle many decisions might be made that in retrospect would not always seem defensible. But what Khrushchev's speech had described was not the convulsions that followed in the immediate wake of the revolution but rather a deliberate policy of torture and murder that lasted for decades. I had been very impressed with Jackson until then, but I never regained my respect for him afterward. In contrast, Ben Davis was very shaken by the report and said that thinking back over the history of our own Party, it seemed to him that had we come to power we might have committed the very same crimes. I was reminded of my vote to expel Roy Hudson in the early 1950s when I knew full well that the charges against him had been nonsense. Would I have voted the same way if we had been in power and it had been a question of life or death? The very fact that I was unsure as to the answer left me with a queasy feeling.

Dorothy Healey Remembers
(Oxford University Press, 1990, 153–155)

"I AM AGAINST COMMUNISM"

"You have no need to talk to me; I am against Communism." I wish I had a dollar for every time I have heard this said.

To be effective, opposition should be complemented by understanding. One of the most feared diseases of my young years was poliomyelitis, or infantile paralysis. The very word made parents tremble.

Today this disease is rare, but the triumph over polio was not due to the emotional opposition of parents. It was due to the dedicated research of scientific pathologists such as Jonas Edward Salk and Albert Bruce Sabin, who studied and researched the disease, discovered the virus that caused it, and designed vaccines to prevent its transmission.

When asked, "What can I do to defeat Communism?" I gave my standard answer: "Study the disease." The Crusade encouraged the formation of study groups, and I urged people to read Communist literature, which was abundant, so that they could know their enemy. But many wanted action, not knowledge. Though I stressed that action based upon ignorance often aided the enemy, my warning sometimes fell upon deaf ears.

During one of the Anti-Subversive Seminars held in Washington, D.C., in later years, a group of attending students reported with pride that they had picketed the Russian Embassy. Instead of applauding I stressed that our purpose was study, not action. Knowledge should precede activity, and adequate knowledge required continuing study. I again urged them to obtain and study Communist literature and even to attend Communist rallies.

Was this advice dangerous? To some degree it was. Communist literature was often seductive, and they might succumb. It was like the danger pathologists face in researching infectious diseases. Knowledge was necessary in order to protect the researcher. I tried to provide such knowledge.

Some voices urged me to form a disciplined action organization that would mobilize the rebellious energy of youth and direct it into practical projects. But I spurned such advice. In many situations I had no idea what should be done and felt incompetent to advise and direct others. Also, I realized that this kind of organization required mechanisms for controlling what the members said and did, and I had neither the desire nor the ability to control. I urged the formation of many independent organizations motivated by their own distinctive aims in the common battle. These organizations could cooperate and compete. Strength would be found in diversity, not in unified control. Freedom flourishes where choice is possible.

To many this policy was a prescription for futility. The quest for truth, however, is never futile. The truth engenders healthy offspring even though the gestation period may tax human patience. As Jesus taught, "You shall know the truth and the truth shall make you free."

From the perspective of many years it is clear that a bountiful harvest for freedom has been reaped from discovering and proclaiming the truth about Communism. Testimonials, which come constantly from one end of the world to the other, certify this. Many who were informed and inspired have entered spheres where they have applied the lessons they learned—leaders in government, education, communication, religion, business, and labor. Their number is legion.

As I traversed the United States and overseas I provided to an ever-increasing audience documented information on the pathological ideas, and the resulting deeds, of Communism. During the years 1953 through 1961 the response was overwhelmingly positive. I routinely received standing ovations after speaking to audiences. But after the Southern California School of Anti-Communism in Los Angeles in 1961, this honeymoon period came to an abrupt end when we were targeted by a malicious campaign of bigotry and slander.

11

....

The Pen, the Tongue, the Sword

Caesar had perished from the world of men had not his sword
been rescued by his pen.
—HENRY VAUGHAN (SIR THOMAS BODLEY'S LIBRARY)

IT HAS BEEN CLAIMED THAT "The pen is mightier than the
sword," but is it mightier than the tongue? That depends upon the
time, place, and circumstances.

In the development of the Crusade, speaking preceded writing,
but it soon became evident that the spoken message must be confirmed and complemented by the printed page. I learned this lesson
in 1952.

Dr. Pietsch had invited me to speak every night for a week on his
11:30 P.M. radio program over Station KXEL in Waterloo, Iowa. I
gave a series of brief messages on the laws on which Communism
was based and their historic consequences. Dr. Pietsch told his radio
audience that he would send a printed summary of my messages to
all who requested it. In order to fulfill this promise I wrote *The
Heart, Mind and Soul of Communism,* our first published booklet.
It described the homicidal essence of Marxist–Leninist doctrines and
conduct, which proved to be both accurate and relevant.

Though written in 1952, it is my answer to "the question" which Professor Genovese asked in 1994 about the homicidal essence of Marxist–Leninist doctrines and conduct, "What did we know, and when did we know it?" Here is an extract from my booklet.

> The mass-murder program of Communism is a logical and inescapable consequence of their basic beliefs. It is science in action. So many have been deceived on this point. They attribute the bestiality and excesses of Communism to the national characteristics of certain races— to Russian imperialism, to Asiatic cruelty, to a Jewish conspiracy of revenge; to anything and everything except the real culprit—that system of ideas and beliefs known as Communism. The murder of millions in Russia was not the excess due to a barbaric past; the liquidation of millions proceeding apace in China is not an example of Oriental cruelty. It is scientific Communism in action. Anglo-Saxon Communism will be just as scientifically ruthless, just as dehumanized as the Russian and Chinese varieties; it believes the same things, and it is as true today as ever, "As a man thinketh in his heart, so he is."
>
> *The Heart, Mind and Soul of Communism*, 20

Among my many other booklets are *Communism: a Disease*, *The Christian Answer to Communism*, *What is Communism?*, *Why I am against Communism*, *Why Communism Kills*, and W. P. Strube's, *Communism: a Religion*.

Soon after the Crusade was established in 1953, I began to publish a newsletter. Until 1958, issues appeared sporadically. Then it appeared twice monthly for nearly forty years until 1994, when it became a monthly. Any critic who is honestly interested in the Crusade's message and history can peruse these letters.

As editor and primary author of newsletter commentary, I tried to adhere conscientiously to certain principles. These included:

(1) The main source of information was the literature published by the Communists themselves. I preferred to discover what the Communists were thinking, saying, and doing from their own liter-

ature, and not from the writings of their opponents. The Crusade subscribed to a host of Communist periodicals.

(2) Controversial affirmations and conclusions must be supported by incontrovertible evidence. The source must be provided. Readers were not required to believe an affirmation merely because "Schwarz says so." I have never had any "secret" information.

Because this required constant documentation, I was occasionally accused of being a vehicle for Communist propaganda. Given that it was sometimes unclear where the Communist statements ended and my commentary began, we used a different typeface for Communist quotations.

(3) We attempted to classify specific Communist statements as propaganda or agitation—as did the Communists. Propaganda was designed to inform the mind, while agitation stimulated the emotions.

Propaganda was written for the Communists and fellow-travelers, and also for the educated elite who were considered potential Communist recruits. The primary audience for agitation were those who were angered by some real or perceived injustice and who could be stimulated to engage in some activity such as a strike or demonstration.

(4) We strove for accuracy, not sensationalism; tried to place each statement in its proper context; and spurned half-truths and falsehoods.

(5) We appealed to readers who were intelligent and self-critical, and we appealed to reason and compassion more than to emotion and selfishness.

I was sometimes challenged by the question, "You say that the Communists define as truth any statement that will advance their cause. How, then, can you believe a word they say?"

I would give an analogy. Consider an organization of confidence men. If their activities are to be coordinated they must have some method of internal communication in order to keep their agents informed about what tactics to use during specific campaigns. The more people involved in the organization, the greater the need for such channels of communication.

The World Communist Movement was, and is, a massive organization containing millions of agents. To be effective, it required a constant flow of consultation, criticism, contention, and command, and this was printed in their widely circulated newspapers and magazines. It was available to anyone who might be interested. I was interested. I read what they were writing to one another, and I endeavored to interpret and report it.

I had no access to the secret channels of communication in the Communist organization, and I am no expert on secret Communist espionage. My purpose was not to identify secret Communist members and spies. The only persons I identified as Communists were those who publicly acknowledged it. I have stated what Communists believe and the consequences of those beliefs. I have described their techniques of deception. I have sought to describe the Communist organization with its chain of command and its attempts to harness social forces for hidden purposes. I have indicated the various categories of Communist supporters, including collaborators and dupes. But I have accused no one falsely of being a Communist. After a lifetime in the forefront of opposition to Communism, I have never been sued.

A prominent Methodist minister in Los Angeles once accused me of having been a complete failure because I had not discovered and revealed a single secret Communist. I wear that accusation as a badge of honor.

These policies have had their rewards. I feel a glow of inner satisfaction when I am assured by readers of the newsletter that they can quote any of its information with total assurance.

I felt a similar glow when I was attacked by Professor Urban Whitaker of San Francisco State University and accused of being "The most dangerous demagogue in the United States." My pride was not due to the accusation but to the reason he gave for it. He said, "He can neutralize all the liberals." I assumed that the "liberals" to whom he referred were educated and intelligent men and women. To have been able to dispel their delusions about the benign nature of Marxism–Leninism was a justifiable cause for rejoicing.

SEEING IS NOT NECESSARILY BELIEVING

Statements and observations are usually interpreted by the hearer or observer after passing through the prism of his or her past experiences. This often leads to erroneous or even absurd interpretations.

One possible historic example of this was French Queen Marie Antoinette's "Let them eat cake," on having been told that the angry mob were protesting their lack of bread. Maybe this was not callousness, because in her experience cake had always been available.

Accurate observation divorced from understanding of motives and purposes may lead to bizarre and absurd conclusions. I would frequently entertain audiences by describing how I interpreted the behavior of the players when I attended my first American football match. Since childhood, I had been a fan of Australian "rugby" football, so this obviously influenced my interpretation of what my eyes saw.

Here is the description of my reactions following my first viewing of an American football match, taken from my book *You Can Trust the Communists (to be Communists)*, published in 1960.

Seeing is not necessarily believing. If seeing is believing, you cannot tell me anything about American football because I have seen it with my own eyes. . . .

The University of Southern California was playing the University of California in a homecoming match. It was a magnificent spectacle. A hundred thousand people were gathered together. . . . They must be entertained . . . so with typical American genius the organizers hit upon a remarkable scheme. They dressed all the football players up like clowns. They put them in the most ridiculous and grotesque garments I have ever seen. They were padded and patted in every direction like an Eskimo bride at a winter wedding breakfast. They had baggy pants. They protruded at the rear and at the knees. They wore enormous helmets with protruding jaws. It was the funniest looking sight I had ever seen.

About fifty of these clowns ran on to the playing field and a strange thing happened. Instead of bursting out laughing as would have been quite natural everybody began clapping and cheering. I admit bewilderment at this incomprehensible manifestation of American psychology. After these clowns had run around throwing the ball to one another for ten or fifteen minutes, most of them became weary or bored and went to sit down on some benches at the side of the field. Eleven clowns remained on each side of the line running across the middle of the playing field, and seven of them knelt down opposite one another and started to pray. When they had said their prayers, one of them flicked the ball back to a guy standing behind. He apparently took a liking to it, and thought he would take it home, so he cut across that field like a streak of lightning. The others saw what he was doing and rushed after him. He swerved and he weaved. He approached the sideline. It looked as though he was going to get away. But suddenly, hurtling through the air came a massive body which crashed into him and knocked him right over. This was rather cruel, but maybe it was fair enough since he was trying to steal the ball like that.

At this point nobody seemed to know quite what to do. A clown in a costume all of his own with up and down stripes which made him look like a convict blew a whistle and the game stopped. One side called a committee meeting. What took place at this committee meeting, I do not know exactly. One thing they did was to interchange a few of the clowns who had apparently grown tired in the struggle.

They resumed with another session of prayer. I feel that this recurrent prayer in American football is one of the hopeful signs of the day. When the center man flicked the ball back to the one standing behind him, he played them a dirty trick. In all my living days, I have never seen a dirtier deed. How he had the gall to do it before two hundred thousand staring eyes, I will never know. He changed his side right in the middle of the game, he turned and ran round backwards. When he had gone back about ten yards, however, someone caught him and knocked him over. Wasn't that a dirty trick to change his side in the middle of the game like that? I know he did. I saw him with my own eyes.

You say to me, "Oh, you're crazy! That man hadn't changed his side at all. He'd gone back to get in a good position to make a forward pass and they trapped him." You know this because you know the rules of the game. You know its purposes and you know its motives. You are in tune with its spirit. But if you knew none of these things; if you came, as I do, from another land where the rules for football are quite different, where the game has no forward pass, and if you took the rules which were familiar to you and interpreted what you saw in terms of them you would be apt to make conclusions very similar to those I reached.

When we observe what the Communists do without knowing the rules of the game, without knowing Communist doctrine, morality, objectives, and methods, when we project on them our own basic Christian standards, our conclusions are as ridiculous as my interpretation of an American football match. They are far more dangerous. There must be assiduous study of the doctrines of Communism if the necessary understanding of their psychology, morality, and program is to be achieved. There is no substitute for knowledge. Ignorance is evil and paralytic.

The greatest ally Communism has is the existing ignorance concerning its true nature. War must be declared on this ignorance.

Well-meaning but ill-prepared tourists have often served as unconscious vehicles of Communist deception.

Malcolm Muggeridge was one visitor to Russia who did not put his intelligence and integrity in cold storage before he went. He went to Russia as a journalist for the British newspaper *The Manchester Guardian*. Reared by socialist parents, he was sympathetic to the "Soviet Experiment." He was accompanied by his wife, who was a member of the British aristocracy but who, determined to identify with the Russian proletariat, discarded all her expensive wardrobe before leaving for the "Workers' Homeland."

What they saw horrified them. They were unprepared for the cruelty, the brutality, the terror of Communist rule, but they observed and reported it.

They were also horrified by the willful blindness and intellectual dishonesty of many of the world-famous visitors who saw but ignored the evidence before their eyes. Muggeridge describes this in his book, *Chronicles of Wasted Time:*

> Wise old Shaw, high-minded old Barbusse, the venerable Webbs, Gide the pure in heart and Picasso the impure, down to poor little teachers, crazed clergymen and millionaires, drivelling dons and very special correspondents like Duranty, all resolved, come what might, to believe anything, however preposterous, to overlook anything, however villainous, to approve anything, however obscurantist and brutally authoritarian, in order to be able to preserve intact the confident expectation that one of the most thorough-going, ruthless and bloody tyrannies ever to exist on earth could be relied on to champion human freedom, the brotherhood of man, and all the other good liberal causes to which they had dedicated their lives. All resolved, in other words, to abolish themselves and their world, the rest of us with it.
>
> William Morrow & Company Inc.:
> New York, 1973, 275–276

Another journalist who also retained his senses during his sojourn in Russia was Eugene Lyons, who later became a lecturer at our Anti-Communism Schools.

He, too, went to Russia as a sympathizer, only to be disillusioned and horrified by what he saw, and expounded on it in his book *Assignment in Utopia.* And he was pilloried by much of the literary establishment for daring to tell the truth and disturb their delusions. He dedicated the remainder of his life to educating the American people and wrote *The Red Decade.*

Consequently, I felt no great desire to make a tour of Russia; I did not believe it would significantly increase my knowledge of Marxist–Leninist doctrines. In the minds of some, the fact that I had "been there" might add credibility to my messages, but there was no shortage of living testimonials to the realities of Communist rule. Millions of refugees with authentic experiences of Communist terror were eager and willing to tell their stories to anyone who would listen.

I have never believed that it is necessary to suffer from a disease in order to understand it. If this were true every medical pathologist would need to suffer from a multitude of diseases.

Understanding requires study. A proverb states, "A fool learns by his own experience; a wise man learns by the experience of others." I considered that it was much more important to learn, interpret, and report the authentic experience of refugees from Communism than to enhance my reputation by a brief and privileged visit.

12

....

Indian Safari

I look upon the world as my parish.
—JOHN WESLEY (JOURNAL, JUNE 11, 1739)

THE YEAR 1956 WAS AN important one. Events of great significance took place: The valiant Hungarian people attempted to break
their Communist chains and establish "Socialism with a human
face," but they were defeated by the tanks and guns of the Soviet
Union's invading Red Army. Egypt's president, Gamal Nasser,
decided to nationalize the Suez Canal, and the two countries who
controlled the canal, Britain and France, failed to retain control by
military action, due in large measure to opposition from the United
Nations and the United States.

While these events were taking place, I made my first visit to India.
Almost forty years have passed since then, and I do not remember
how my correspondence began with a young Indian Christian.
Ch Devananda Rao was a young evangelical Christian and an Indian
schoolteacher who lived in a small village called Vijayawada near
Hyderabad in Andhra State. He had received copies of Crusade
newsletters and had urged me to visit India, pledging to help combat
the spread of Communism in that populous nation.

Earlier in these pages I mentioned Communism's "proletarian internationalism." Lenin embraced this international vision with fervor. Even during the darkest days of Bolshevik power, he stressed that the needs of the international revolution must take precedence over the needs of the Soviet Union itself. To promote and direct the world revolution, he organized the Comintern, commonly known as the "Third Communist International." He and his disciples were confident that India would play an important role in future revolutionary triumphs.

One example of the importance that Soviet Communist leaders assigned to India was their use of semitrailers as mobile libraries to carry the Communist message to the poor of India's villages.

When I made my first visit to India in 1956, the Communist conquest of India did not appear to be an impossible dream, or a nightmare.

ANDHRA STATE

My plane landed in Bombay, a large city on India's west coast. Devananda Rao met me and we traveled by train across the Indian subcontinent to Hyderabad, then to Secunderabad. Finally, we reached the Rao home in Vijayawada village.

Devananda was a handsome young man in his early or mid-twenties. He spoke good English, had been recently married, and his young bride Suvarna greeted me shyly but charmingly.

Their marriage had been arranged by their parents. In those days teenage dating was practically nonexistent. The girls were taught to be modest and to refrain from flirting. Their objective was to impress the parents of prospective husbands, not the young men themselves.

When a young man reached marrying age the parents looked for a suitable bride, negotiated with her parents, and then made arrangements for the dowry and the wedding.

So it was with Devananda and Suvarna. But theirs has been a happy union. They have loved and respected each other, and raised a family of five fine children.

The conditions in which the Raos lived would have been classified as extreme poverty in America, England, or Australia. I quote from a letter that I wrote to Dr. Pietsch during my flight to Australia:

I visited the village and home of brother Rao's parents. It was an illuminating experience. That such a splendid Christian family could be raised in such unbelievably primitive conditions is a miracle of Grace. Their home is a one-roomed hut with mud floor, straw roof, and mat walls with practically no furniture and certainly not even the most primitive facilities. Yet here a consecrated family of six children [among them Devananda] had been raised and educated. It is impossible to believe without having been actually seen.

This incontrovertible fact should place another nail in the coffin of the widely held delusion that poverty is the primary cause of the epidemic of crime and illegitimacy which currently rages in the United States.

Christians are a small minority among the Indian people, and the Rao family was part of that minority. Devananda and Suvarna were both fervent disciples of Jesus, and they gathered a group of Christians for a worship service at which I preached. They even took up an offering. It was truly a collection of widow's mites. As Jesus taught, the value of the gift is measured not by what is given but by what is retained.

The prophet Joel affirms that young men shall see visions. Devananda told me about his vision. He wished to establish an Indian Christian Crusade that would enlist and enable Indians to preach the Christian Gospel of redeeming love, and expose the false doctrines and deceptive practices of the Communist enemies of God and freedom. Also, he hoped to establish orphanages where children could be provided with a home, good food, education, and Christian teaching by devoted Christian care-givers.

His vision inspired me, and I pledged help in whatever way I could. I stressed that the organization should be created and controlled by Indians and not by a subsidiary of a foreign institution; to be considered a subsidiary of "American Imperialism" could destroy its effectiveness.

Rao proceeded to form The Indian Christian Crusade and Indian Christian Orphanages, which have ministered to many Indians for nearly forty years. Thousands have been won to Christ, thousands have become fine Christian adults, and thousands have learned the true nature of Communism.

On my return to America I presented the needs of the Indian Crusade and Orphanages, and the opportunity to demonstrate Christian love. Anyone could become an orphan's foster parent by contributing ten dollars a month. This would house, feed, educate, and train a child to become a good Christian citizen. Above all, the children would know they were loved.

We also support Christian Anti-Communism evangelists for twenty-five dollars per month, which often provides for an entire family. These evangelists travel on bicycle from village to village with their message.

The orphans and workers have been supported by voluntary contributors. Not one cent has ever been received from government sources. The Crusade sends the full amount of the gifts to the Indian Christian Crusade, retaining nothing for administrative expenses.

As this is being written, 300 orphans and 350 evangelists are being supported. These are two of the many projects that justify the word "Christian" in the name of the Crusade.

KERALA

Following an address I gave in Seattle, Washington, a young man introduced himself as George Thomas, from the state of Kerala in India. He had recently been awarded his Ph.D. degree, and he was about to return to his homeland.

Kerala, situated on the southern tip of India, had recently elected the Communists to power in the state assembly. This gave the Communists considerable, though not complete, power, because of the constitutional restraints of a non-Communist central government. Consequently, certain basic liberties such as freedom of speech made it possible to oppose Communism openly.

Kerala was simultaneously the most Christian and the most Communist state, or pradesh, in India. Tradition teaches that the Apostle Thomas—"doubting Thomas"—visited India after the resurrection of Jesus and established the Christian Church, which has endured and grown. A substantial number of Kerala's citizens are professing Christians.

George and his family were members of a small group of Christians known as the Plymouth Brethren, who are devoted students of the Bible.

George was eager to obtain a printing press and publish a daily newspaper that could cover world, national, and local news, spread the Christian gospel, and expose Communism. I presented the opportunity to the Crusade's growing constituency. Their response enabled him to buy a printing press, publish a newspaper, and later, a magazine. We continued our subsidy for many years. George and his father also established and directed the Indian Gospel Mission.

As the publisher of a daily newspaper with an anti-Communism policy that featured editorials exposing the atheism, deceitful tactics, and deadly objectives of the Communists, George became known and respected. He ran for office and was elected to the state legislature, where he was a strong voice against Communism.

In Kerala, conditions under the Communists deteriorated so seriously that Prime Minister Nehru, amidst violence and terror, used his government's constitutional powers to expel the Communist state government and order a new election.

The newspaper, *Keraladhwani* (The Voice of Kerala), informed Moslems and Hindus as well as Christians that Communism opposed all religions. The Communists were defeated in the election. George Thomas wrote: "It is with a sense of pride that I write you this letter. This morning a new democratic cabinet assumed charge of the government of Kerala. Our paper went out into all of Kerala with a full page heading, 'Democratic government reestablished in Kerala.' I have the satisfaction that we have played our reasonable share in the victory of democratic parties. . . ."

The idea that a small organization such as the Christian Anti-Communism Crusade could influence the destiny of such a nation as India may appear to be a delusion of grandeur but I retain great faith in the power of truth to keep men free.

13

....

Debating the Communists

Come now and let us reason together.
—ISAIAH 1:18

"I AM WILLING AND EAGER to debate any Communist on any aspect of Communist doctrine, organization, objectives, and history, on any platform at any time." I have issued and reissued this challenge many times, and it has led to numerous debates with Communists.

My first debate, in 1940, with the Australian Communist leader, Max Julius, taught me several valuable lessons which I have endeavored to apply in subsequent debates. These include: (1) *Take the offensive*. Keep the spotlight on Communism. Do not permit the Communist spokesman to control the agenda. He will probably attempt to spotlight the defects of Capitalism, such as unemployment, poverty, depression, Imperialism, and war, and make the unproven and unprovable assumption that Communism will cure them all. If the debate is permitted to proceed on these lines a Communist win is assured, since Capitalism is a human system operated by imperfect people and therefore has weaknesses and imperfections. If it is contrasted with some hypo-

135

thetical system of perfection its weaknesses tend to obscure its virtues.

Communism has real doctrines, real organizations, and a real record of delusion, dictatorship, tyranny, impoverishment, and mass murder. Attention must be focused upon these.

(2) *Debate the audience, not your opponent.* Your purpose is to expose the delusions, deceitful tactics, and deadly deeds of the Communists and to make as many people as possible aware of them. If the spokesman for Communism begins to discuss theoretical details which are interesting to the debaters but not the listeners, the purpose of the debate is defeated.

While an opponent may be converted during a debate, this is unlikely since debates don't usually create an emotional climate favorable to conversion. The saying "convince a man against his will; he's of the same opinion still" is in harmony with human nature. The probable attitudes of the debaters are described by the cynical observation, "My mind's made up; don't confuse me with the facts." The hope and objective must be to persuade the audience.

(3) *Attempt to recruit an audience that contains as many uninformed, uncommitted, and skeptical people as possible, and then present the truth in words and examples that will appeal to them.* It is exciting and exhilarating to speak to an audience of supporters and fellow-believers who applaud and cheer, but the stroking of personal pride is not the purpose of the debate. Emotion is temporary, but a truthful idea endures and develops in the mind once it is implanted.

Many of my debates took place before university audiences. These included Harvard, Massachusetts, Columbia, New York, the University of California at Berkeley, and the University of Texas at Austin.

One debate that did not take place in the mid-1950s was at the University of Maryland. Though scheduled and announced, the governor of the state vetoed it. I sent him a letter of protest but it was disregarded.

As some debates took place many years ago and the speeches were not recorded, I must depend upon my memory, which is not infallible, to report what was said.

HARVARD

The debate at Harvard University took place on October 12, 1959.

My opponent was the chairman of the Communist Party of Massachusetts, Otis Archer Hood. I regard him as the most intellectually agile Communist I have ever debated. He refused to be drawn into a discussion of the Communist record of delusion and death.

I addressed him as follows:

Mr. Hood, since you are a Communist, I assume that you place great credence in the statements and doctrines of Marx and Lenin.

As you undoubtedly know, Karl Marx taught that in the final analysis character and ideas are created by the prevailing mode of production, and the private ownership of the means of production has created greedy and selfish characters. He called the class made up of such owners, the bourgeoisie.

Marx attributed the degenerate and greedy characteristics of the bourgeoisie to their class of social origin and affirmed that once the abolition of the private ownership of the means of production had taken place, superior characters with superior ideas would be created. This conviction forms the foundation for the Communist program to create an improved and superior "New Man."

The great disciple of Marx, Lenin organized and led the Communist conquest of Russia and the establishment of the Union of Soviet Socialist Republics (USSR), in which socialism replaced Capitalism. Lenin declared that this success was due to the superb characters of the members of the Central Committee of the Bolsheviks, as the Communists were called at that time. Most of them were persons of outstanding intelligence and erudition who had forsaken comfort and security and had dedicated themselves to the service of the poor of their country. During many years they had willingly suffered privation, danger, imprisonment, torture, and even risked death for the cause. They had proved themselves to be incorruptible. Lenin classified them as the greatest individuals to have ever been gathered into one organization.

It is noteworthy that these magnificent characters had been formed under Capitalism. When their day of triumph arrived and the socialist environment replaced Capitalism, what wonderful characters they must have become.

Let the Communists tell us what happened to them. Under Socialism, the large majority of that wonderful committee degenerated into such traitors, fiends, and scum that they were unfit to live and it was necessary to put them to death. Stalin alone retained his intellectual integrity and devotion to the workers.

Now, Mr. Hood, let us be honest. When you learned what had happened to these heroes of your youth and young manhood once they lived in the environment of Socialism, didn't a tiny trace of doubt about the inevitable perfection of human character by the environment of Socialism enter your mind?

Hood executed an intellectual sidestep brilliantly. He replied:

Those were the days of the Great Depression here in the United States. A lot of people lacked food and were hungry; a lot of people lacked fuel and were freezing. I was so busy trying to get a little more food for the hungry and fuel for the freezing that I did not have time to think about these things.

What an intellectual acrobat! Anyone with the slightest acquaintance of Communists knows that they paid immense attention at that time to what was happening in Russia, the land of their hopes and dreams.

I remember being hissed at at one point in the debate but I cannot remember what I said that triggered the hissing. For many years I reported that I was "hissed at at Harvard." I did not dream that the day would come when a post-doctoral fellowship at Harvard would be named after Lillian and me.

Harry Bridges

Many of the debates with Communists were spirited but, for sheer rancor and venom, none can compare with my debate with Harry Bridges. It took place in front of the prestigious Commonwealth Club of San Francisco on October 22, 1962.

WHO WAS HARRY BRIDGES?

The *World Book Encyclopedia* gives this summary:

> Harry Bridges served as president of the International Longshoremen's and Warehousemen's Union (ILWU) from 1938 to 1977. He came to the United States in 1920 as a seaman and joined the International Longshoremen's Association (ILA). In 1934, he led a West Coast maritime strike which became a general strike. In 1937, he brought his ILA group into the Committee for Industrial Organization, a forerunner of the Congress of Industrial Organizations (CIO). Later, the CIO expelled the ILWU on grounds of Communist domination. Bridges never denied his sympathy for Communist and related causes, but he denied that he was a member of the Communist Party. The government tried unsuccessfully several times to revoke his citizenship and deport him. He was born Alfred Renton Bridges in Melbourne, Australia.

The slander war against the Crusade, and against me personally, that began in late 1961 was raging in 1962, and Bridges joined the ranks of the slanderers with enthusiasm. He launched a war of words against me. In a speech at San Francisco State College, he told the audience that he was the one man with whom I would never get on the platform because he knew all about me, and I would be unmasked as a fraud and a charlatan.

I was in Honolulu when I heard about this. I cabled Bridges immediately and invited him to come to Honolulu at our expense so that I *could* get on the platform with him. He declined, yet continued to charge that I would never dare to debate him.

In due course a debate before the Commonwealth Club of San Francisco was arranged. Bridges continued his nerve war. A friendly labor official told me that he was renowned in labor circles for this kind of tactic.

Contending that I would find some excuse to default on the debate, he demanded that each of us deposit $5,000, which would become the property of the other, if either failed to appear for the debate.

A friend loaned me the money, and it was duly deposited, but a discomforting thought struck me. Did I now have a bounty on my head? Previously, I had never been troubled about my personal security, because Lenin had instructed the Communists not to assassinate an opponent in a nonrevolutionary time. But this was different. If I was unable to participate in the debate, Bridges would receive $5,000. Uncharacteristically, I took a few precautions. I kept my travel arrangements private, and I asked my friend Jim Colbert to go with me. And I stipulated that the $5,000 was to be given to charity if I were unable to attend.

The auditorium was crowded. Representatives of all the major news media were present. Someone remarked that the excitement was greater than on any day since the great San Francisco fire.

The debate title was, "The Schwarz Schools of Anti-Communism are Good for the Students of this Community." I spoke first. I told the audience, "I've been looking forward to this debate for a long time. . . . Harry Bridges said he was the one man with whom I would not get on the platform because he knew all about me, both in the United States and in Australia, and I would be revealed as a fraud and a charlatan. So here I am. I'm waiting with interest to see what charges the International Communist Conspiracy can dredge up from its sewers of accumulated moral filth."

I then addressed the announced subject and expounded on the *magnitude,* the *method,* the *morality,* the *monopoly,* and the *malignancy* of Communism, and concluded: "The alternative to the monopoly of Communist tyranny is incarnate in the traditions and institutions of American society. Among these cherished freedoms is freedom of speech, leading to freedom of persuasion. This is the freedom utilized by the Schools of Anti-Communism. These schools are obviously in the interests of the students in this area, and they merit the support of student and businessman, housewife and worker, as they contribute to the defeat of tyranny and the retention and extension of freedom for all mankind."

When Bridges went to the podium he delivered a vicious, personal attack of infinite dishonesty. I lost count of the false statements he made. As a climax he charged, "In the hospital, Dr. Schwarz was in charge of some young student nurses fifteen, fourteen, sixteen years old. He was run out of that medical district for using his doctor's authority to make them submit."

He then sprang his trap. "I just want to say one thing. What I have just said is libelous. Let Dr. Schwarz sue me."

I replied, "As I said, I was interested to know what the International Communist Conspiracy could dredge from its sewers of accumulated moral filth. Now we know. I offer anyone the money for a long-distance call to the Medical Board of New South Wales, and the British Medical Association, to enquire of my status as a medical practitioner. Callers will find that my medical status in Sydney, Australia, is unimpaired."

When the chairman announced, "Mr. Bridges has one minute to put a question to Dr. Schwarz," Harry Bridges said, "That will take me half a minute, and if Schwarz wants to take half an hour to answer that's all right with me. Number one. Are the statements I made about you true, and number two, will you sue me?"

I answered, "Question number one: The statements are false, utterly false, completely false, totally false. Number two: You don't sue a skunk for stinking!"

When Bridges was asked about phoning the Medical Board in Australia, he turned from the obscene to the absurd. He said, "It's no use calling them. They haven't heard of this yet. They're waiting on the outcome of this debate."

Skunkology

Reports of the debate were many and varied. *Newsweek* magazine, under the caption "Skunkology," reported:

The setting, a gilded ballroom in the Fairmont Hotel on San Francisco's Nob Hill, couldn't have been more elegant, nor the audience, 1,250 Commonwealth Club members, more respectable. And as it turned out, the main speakers—Dr. Fred C. Schwarz and Harry Bridges—couldn't have sounded more out of place.

Invited last week to debate the value of the Schwarz anti-Communist schools, the professional anti-Red crusader and the hard-nosed, pro-leftist longshoremen's union boss—both of them Australians—wound up instead in a venomous exchange which left the civic-minded Commonwealth Clubbers, if not enlightened, then entertained. They whooped the "debaters" on.

While Schwarz, a fleshy 49, suggested that Bridges was getting his material from Communist conspiracy's "sewers of . . . moral filth," the 61-year-old labor leader, with equal warmth, said Schwarz's anti-Red schools were organized for union busting, race hating, and to make money for Schwarz.

Highlight of the "debate"? Unprintable. It took the form of a purely personal charge by Bridges, who, admitting it was libelous, dared Schwarz to sue. Dr. Schwarz rejoined: "You don't sue a skunk for stinking."

Somewhat more objectively, the *Oakland Tribune,* published a report by Dave Hope, entitled, "Bridges-Schwarz Meeting a Brawl."

Harry Bridges, president of the International Longshoremen's and Warehousemen's Union, turned a Commonwealth Club debate with Dr. Fred Schwarz, president of the Christian Anti-Communism Crusade, into a Pier 6 brawl yesterday.

In a vicious personal attack on Schwarz, Bridges charged the Crusade head is a union buster and race hater, and accused Schwarz of misconduct while he was a doctor in Australia.

"The statement I have just made is libelous unless I can prove it," Bridges yelled as the usually decorous club

luncheon erupted in a storm of boos. He challenged
Schwarz to sue him for libel.

"That is false, utterly false, totally false," Schwarz
countered. "Sue? Well, you don't sue a skunk for
stinking."

Schwarz coupled his denial with an offer to pay telephone charges for any responsible agency that will call
authorities in Sydney to check the charge.

During his opening statement, Schwarz said he was
waiting to hear from Bridges "to see what charges Communism can dredge up from its sewer of accumulated
filth."

After Bridges spoke, Schwarz declared: "Now we
know."

The announced topic of the debate, lost in the tur-
moil when Bridges exploded was: "Are the Dr. Schwarz
Anti-Communism Schools Good for Students of this
Community?"

Schwarz insisted they are, claiming: "Since they
present the truth and help to preserve freedom, they are
in the best interests of the students."

Schwarz said his schools teach the magnitude of the
Communist danger, the method of its conquest, the
morality and monopoly of Communism and its malignancy. . . .

Bridges called Schwarz a fake and declared he conducts schools to make money for himself. He specifically
charged that Schwarz attempted to break a longshore
strike in Hawaii, and fought the Mine, Mill and Smelter
Workers Union in Idaho.

"I'll stand with the AFL-CIO leaders who have
declared both the longshoremen and the mine workers
are Communist dominated," Schwarz countered.

"I did speak in Idaho because I felt the union there
had betrayed the working people in the interests of the
Communist Conspiracy.

"But the longshore strike in Hawaii was over six
months before I got there," Schwarz declared, "And I

was in Hawaii only one day on my way to the United
States mainland." ...

The debate, an on-and-off affair for nearly a year,
attracted a near record attendance of more than 1,250.
Bridges got some applause, but he was also jeered and
booed, while Schwarz was given an ovation as he
stepped up to rebut Bridges' charges.

What led Bridges to launch his campaign of character assassination? I have always hesitated to ascribe motives to others since I am not always sure of my own. I am well aware of the biblical admonition, "Judge not, that you be not judged. For with what judgment you judge, you shall be judged." (Matthew 7:1–2)

I have never believed that the majority of my critics and opponents was motivated by a sympathy for Communism, but I do make an exception in the case of Bridges. He set out to destroy the Crusade's campaign to expose the pathology of Communism, by attempting to channel my time and energy into legal conflict instead of education about Communism.

In the debate he had been careful to stress that he was speaking as an individual and not as a representative of the International Longshoremen's and Warehousemen's Union, so that the union could not be charged.

The charges of Bridges were not reported in the ILWU newspaper, *The Dispatcher*. As far as I am aware, the only newspaper that reported his specific charges was the Communist paper, *People's World*. The Crusade newsletter also published them, with rebuttal.

From the day of the debate till the day of his death in 1990 I did not hear one word from Harry Bridges.

THE FREEDOM TO STARVE

My debate with Ben Dobbs, the executive director of the Communist Party of California, lingers in my memory. It took place in a studio of Los Angeles television station KTTV/Channel 11.

Ben Dobbs was accompanied by Dorothy Healey who, at that time, was chairman of the Communist Party of Southern California. She was friendly, and we chatted while waiting for the debate to begin. She asked, "How can you support the dreadful monopolies in America?"

I looked at her in pretended astonishment and said, "Did I hear you correctly? A Communist talking against monopoly! It's a wonder the word doesn't shrivel in your throat. That's like Al Capone talking against crime; like Hitler talking against bigotry. Communism is the distilled essence of monopoly. No monopoly in America is comparable. Compared to the monopoly of the Communist Party in Russia, General Motors is a corner service station."

Communism exercises a political monopoly. The Communist Party is the only party; no competing political party is permitted. The Communist Party controls the entire economy; it is an economic monopoly. Since it controls the legislative, executive, and judicial branches of government, it is also a governmental monopoly. It has a military and police monopoly; a labor monopoly; an educational monopoly; a communications monopoly. Communist power is monopoly power.

This monopoly power can stop any person's food supply, and can starve anyone. One of my definitions of Communism in power is, "Control by Potential Starvation."

The awesome power conferred by the Communist monopoly soon became the focus of the debate with Ben Dobbs. He spoke first and said, "But what's wrong with Communism? We Communists believe in full employment. What's wrong with that? We believe in medical care for the sick and elderly. What's wrong with that? We believe in the end of war for all time. What's wrong with that? We believe in universal peace and human brotherhood. What's wrong with that?" Turning to me he asked, "Don't you believe in these things, Dr. Schwarz?"

Taking the offensive, I replied, "That reminds me of the mackerel swimming by and observing an enticing piece of fish. It says to itself, 'High protein content, what's wrong with that? Delicious aroma, what's wrong with that? Highly nutritious, it will build splendid fish tissue, what's wrong with that? Just the right size. I can take it in one delectable mouthful. What's wrong with that? What's wrong with it is the hook in it! And what's wrong with what you just said, Mr. Dobbs, is the hook of Communist dictatorship through monopoly and its imposition of universal tyranny."

I then asked Ben Dobbs, "Can you answer a question that has perplexed me for some time? Did the Soviet author, Boris Pasternak, who was awarded the Nobel Prize for writing the book *Dr. Zhivago,* and who died recently, starve to death?"

Ben Dobbs countered, "He had plenty of money. He was paid well for his translations of Shakespeare."

I said, "Let us review Pasternak's plight. He had been a prominent Russian author and poet and was a distinguished member of the union of Soviet Writers, which is controlled by the Communist Party.

"He dared to write the novel *Dr. Zhivago,* which was critical of the Communist Party. As a consequence he was rewarded by receiving the Nobel Prize for Literature and punished by expulsion from the Union of Soviet Writers.

"This expulsion had dire consequences. He became unemployable, and his income ceased.

"Presumably he had saved some money and had deposited it in the bank. What bank? A bank that was controlled and directed by the Communist Party that issued the instruction, 'This man's funds are frozen. Don't give him any money.'

"He is indignant, and maybe he thinks, 'This is my money; I will appeal to the court.' What court? A court that is controlled by the Communist Party that has written the laws, appoints and controls the judges and lawyers, and has the power to choose the verdict the court gives. His appeal to the court is futile.

"He considers selling some of the furniture in his house in order to buy food. How would he do this? Could he place an advertisement in the newspaper? What newspaper? The existing newspapers were *Pravda,* published by the Communist Party of the Soviet Union (CPSU) and *Izvestia,* published by the Soviet government. They do not accept advertisements, and both are controlled by the Communist Party.

"What about his friends? Would they help? To do so would place them in danger as they would be helping 'an enemy of the people.'

"Pasternak was confronted by the greatest monopoly that has ever existed. If it decided to starve any individual it had the power to do so."

At the time of the debate, the suggestion that Pasternak may have starved seemed extreme. Later, evidence surfaced that Pasternak himself was worried by the possibility of starvation.

The evidence appears in the book *Moscow Under the Skin,* by the Italian author Vero Roberti. He was a journalist who served in Moscow for the Italian newspaper *Corriere della Sera.*

Roberti was in Moscow when the award of the Nobel Prize to Boris Pasternak was announced on October 23, 1958. He managed to interview Pasternak on that day, and several times thereafter, until the poet's death. He wrote:

> On the evening of October 23, 1958, I telephoned to my newspaper a short interview I had with Boris Pasternak. Fear of the Censor had made my colleagues, Nicolas Chatelain, and Michel Tatu, and myself describe our meeting with the poet in a matter-of-fact way. It was easy to guess that the award to Pasternak of the Nobel Prize for Literature would anger the Soviet leaders and the guardians of the so-called Soviet "realism." It was the first time that a major literary award had been given to a Russian author resident in the Soviet Union.

Nicolas, Michel, and I were the only ones who managed to reach Pasternak's "dacha" at Peredelkino. . . .

Here is the dispatch I sent to my newspaper. The words in italics and parenthesis are those that did not pass the Censor. I still have the original copies with the Censor's stamp on them.

> Pasternak shakes our hands and invites us to sit down. He had kept us waiting because he wanted to change. He apologizes and says he has been for his daily walk. "There is something wrong with my right knee, and the doctor has advised me to walk for at least an hour every day." . . . "I haven't received the official con-

firmation yet," he replied to a question of mine (*and I shall defer my decisions until the Soviet authorities let me know their intentions*). I cannot tell you therefore whether I shall go to Stockholm.

Roberti again visited Pasternak on October 30. His report to his newspaper was totally censored by the Soviet authorities. However, he kept a copy and reports Pasternak as saying:

> *"The Union of Soviet Writers has expelled me," he said, "and today they have sent three doctors to check my health. They are waiting over there. Why? I just do not understand!" Then after a pause he added: "Why did they cover me with mud from head to toe? It isn't true that I'm a superfluous person, a poisonous creature, an emigrant in my own country, a petty Philistine and a traitor. My goodness, such insults and lies. Now today they have sent three doctors to see me, but everyone knows I suffer from a mild form of sinovitis. Why? I must go and see them now: please wait here for me."*
>
> *A horrible thought came to me, and I asked Boris Leonidovich whether he wanted me to be present at the examination. But he replied: "Thank you, but I think it would be better if you waited here." I tried to insist, and suddenly the poet realized what was in my mind. He turned pale and with a deep sigh, put a hand on my shoulder and said gently, "Thank you, thank you! I understand your concern but what can I do now? I am already dead!"*
>
> *After about twenty minutes he returned and exclaimed: "They found nothing wrong with my health!"*

Roberti's report of his final meeting is as follows:

> On March 15, 1960, I met Boris Pasternak for the last time. A common friend had told me that he would

be pleased to see me. I went to Peredelkino on the electric train. I was again very cold. The countryside was covered with snow. Pasternak was a ghost of his former self. He was much thinner. There was no expression in the eyes of his pale emaciated face. He talked about his sadness and his anguish: "I have no strength left to work, and I sit for hours without any thoughts in my poor head. Perhaps I am paralyzed and don't realize it yet. I cannot even reply to the letters from friends which are piled up on my table . . . *I have been expelled from the Union of Soviet Writers so I shall starve. No one publishes my poetry or my translations anymore, which was my daily bread. The first payments from my editor have been confiscated by order of the authorities . . .*

Suddenly his eyes lit up and in a harsh voice he exclaimed: "They have taken away this money in the hope that I will go down on my knees and disown my novel and my poetry. But nothing will ever make me yield . . . I yield only to death!"

Two days later the same friend, whose name I cannot reveal, came to see me at the Central Telegraph Office and told me that Boris Pasternak was "gol kak soko" (hungry as a hawk), extremely poor, and had to borrow money to exist. "All his works have been ostracized. Boris Leonidovich is unaware that his brother Alexander helps him and seeks help for him from his friends. If he knew this he would rather starve to death. He is very ill."

The Communist system of government is based on the power to starve. This power to starve may be imposed purposefully or it may operate spontaneously.

A United Press International communiqué from Moscow, published in the Long Beach *Press Telegram* on February 2, 1966, gives a report by the Communist youth newspaper *Komsomol Pravda*, the organ of the Young Communist League, of how a young girl was driven to suicide by starvation. The paper told how Galina Ozornina had worked at a textile factory in the Tadzhikistan capital of Dushanbe when the factory, finding its plan unfulfilled, ordered her and other girls to work at nights.

"Teenagers are not allowed to work nights," the paper said. "That factory administration knew about this law but its plan was failing."

When the girls failed to show up, the shop foreman, Mrs. E. Chetverikova, went to the girls' dormitory, scolded them, and fired Galina. Galina became caught in a vicious circle of red tape that ended in her death.

The factory demanded that she be cleared by the factory library, personnel department, and dormitory before she could collect her pay. But she could not pay her dormitory rent until she got her pay. And her internal passport—which she needed to get a new job—had been taken from her until she paid her rent.

Galina wandered around Dushanbe for two months and occasionally crept into the dormitory to sleep. Eventually she killed herself, and the factory (suddenly magnanimous) gave her back pay to her family.

As the Bible teaches, the devil may appear as an angel of light, and so may Communism. The Communists may appear to be bearers of desirable gifts, but the ancient warning "Beware of Greeks bearing gifts" should be heeded.

The alleged economic and moral benefits of Communism are simply the bait adorning the hidden dictatorial hook. Every proud boast of Communist achievement can be matched by conditions in a well-kept penitentiary. Most people would be unconvinced by the argument that imprisonment is desirable because the following statements are true:

(1) Alcoholics become sober
(2) Economic security is universal
(3) Shelter is adequate for protection against tornadoes and hurricanes
(4) Medical and dental care are freely available
(5) Educational opportunities exist
(6) An environment of law and order prevails.

The universal passion for liberty would spurn these benefits and prefer the insecure environment where a person can choose. Without freedom to choose, there is no freedom and no morality.

Years later both Dorothy Healey and Ben Dobbs became disillusioned with Communism and resigned from the American Communist Party.

TROTSKY LIVES

The city was Chicago. The hour was midnight. The time was in the 1960s. Three of us were gathered in the studio of a powerful radio station. We were: the moderator of a popular radio program that featured discussion and debates between persons with conflicting viewpoints; a representative of the Young Socialist Alliance; and I.

The moderator was handsome and articulate. He told me that he had attended an Anti-Communism School conducted by the Crusade in Columbus, Ohio, and had not been favorably impressed.

My opponent was a young university student who represented the Young Socialist Alliance, which was having considerable success in recruiting students and creating crises on the campuses of colleges and universities. Peter X was a well-groomed and likable young man, and the atmosphere was respectful, if not exactly friendly.

The moderator introduced the contestants and said to Peter, "I understand that you advocate Socialism, not Communism."

I could not let that pass unchallenged, so I interrupted and said, "May I ask Peter a few questions?"

> SCHWARZ: What is the relationship of the Young Socialist Alliance to the Socialist Workers Party?
> PETER: The Young Socialist Alliance is an independent youth organization which has a close association with the Socialist Workers Party.
> SCHWARZ: Would it be fair to state that the Young Socialist Alliance is the youth group of the Socialist Workers Party?
> PETER: That would be fair.
> SCHWARZ: What is the relationship of the Socialist Workers Party to Leon Trotsky?

PETER: The Socialist Workers Party is a working class organization which agrees in large measure with the viewpoints and teachings of Leon Trotsky. For legal reasons it is not an actual member of the "Fourth International" [which Trotsky founded after his expulsion from Russia] but it cooperates closely with it.

SCHWARZ: Would it be correct and fair to state that the Socialist Workers Party is Trotskyist?

PETER: That would be accurate.

SCHWARZ: Does the Socialist Workers Party also support and apply the teachings of Lenin and Marx?

PETER: We certainly do.

SCHWARZ: Then you are Marx–Leninist–Trotskyist. Doesn't that mean that the Socialist Workers Party and the Young Socialist Alliance are Communist?

PETER: Of course we are. We are the only genuine Communists.

I was glad to have made that clear, since considerable confusion continues to exist concerning the relationship of Socialism to Communism. Socialism is a generic term with many subordinate species. It does not mean much until the species of Socialism is indicated.

The word Socialism is akin to the word Christian in this regard. To say that someone is "Christian" does not say much until the specifics of the "Christian" relationship are given. There are evangelical Christians and liberal Christians; violent Christians and pacifist Christians; Catholic Christians and Protestant Christians. The Southern Christian Leadership Conference, founded by Martin Luther King, Jr., and the Ku Klux Klan both claim to be Christian. It is little wonder that the onlooker is confused. As the saying goes, "The devil is in the details."

So it is with the term "Socialism." Its meaning often depends on who uses the term. If a Communist uses the word Socialism, its meaning is clear. It is a synonym for the system of doctrines, organization, objectives, and activities known as Marxism–Leninism. The Communists define Socialism as "the First Stage of Communism." To use a biological analogy, Socialism is the caterpillar; Communism is the butterfly.

Our discussion continued. The moderator asked Peter, "What is your attitude to profit?

> PETER: We are against it. It is theft of one man's labor by another.
>
> MODERATOR: Are you against it always and in all circumstances?
>
> PETER: Yes.
>
> SCHWARZ: Will you admit that in some circumstances the quest for profit by certain individuals has conferred great benefits upon many others?
>
> PETER: I will not.
>
> SCHWARZ: Will you admit that health is better than sickness?
>
> PETER: Certainly.
>
> SCHWARZ: Will you acknowledge that those who discovered the life-saving drugs such as penicillin and other antibiotics that have defeated most of the infectious diseases such as lobar pneumonia, and infectious meningitis, which formerly killed millions of young people, benefited mankind?
>
> PETER: I will.
>
> SCHWARZ: Since the mid-1930s, over one hundred life-preserving drugs have been discovered in the capitalist world; not one in the socialist world. Most of them have been discovered by pharmaceutical companies in their quest for profit.

At that stage the moderator introduced a red herring: "The pharmaceutical companies have also created a lot of drug addicts."

I have not heard of Peter since. He was young, attractive, friendly, and honest. I wish him well.

14

....

The Progressive Reality

Capitalist production begets, with the inexorability of a law of
nature, its own negation.
—KARL MARX (*MANIFESTO OF THE COMMUNIST PARTY*)

IN 1953 I ATTENDED A Billy Graham evangelistic campaign in
Detroit, Michigan. An Australian friend, Max Bushby, who later
served for many years as speaker of Parliament in the Australian
state of Tasmania, introduced me to the man known and loved as
the prince of Christian evangelists.

Billy welcomed me as a Christian brother. He told me that he had
heard my interview on a Christian radio program and had listened
with interest to the statements I made about Communism. We discussed the Communists' program for human regeneration by the
creation of a suitable environment after they attain power by violent
revolution, and I contrasted this with the Christian program for personal regeneration by the indwelling power of God. I also outlined
some of the principles of the Communist philosophy—dialectical
materialism—and showed how these principles were applied in
practice.

Greatly interested, he incorporated some of the information into
one of his messages. Billy had friends in Congress, and he wanted me

154

to take my message to Washington. He arranged for me to address a luncheon meeting for congressmen, senators, and cabinet staff officers in the Congressional Dining Room in Washington, D.C.

Following my address, the Honorable Frank Boykin sent an "official day letter" to Billy Graham.

FRANK W. BOYKIN
1ST DISTRICT, ALABAMA

HOME ADDRESS:
MOBILE, ALABAMA

ALPHONSE LUCAS
SECRETARY

COMMITTEE:
MERCHANT MARINE
AND FISHERIES

Congress of the United States
House of Representatives
Washington, D. C.

FEBRUARY 26, 1953

DR. BILLY GRAHAM
MONTREAT, NORTH CAROLINA

THANKS TO YOU AGAIN FOR BRINGING US ANOTHER GREAT MESSAGE THROUGH YOUR FRIEND, DR. FRED SCHWARZ. IT WAS TERRIFIC. HE KNOCKED THEM COLD. WE HAD PRACTICALLY ALL THE LEADERS IN THE REPUBLICAN AND DEMOCRATIC PARTIES. I HAD THE MESSAGE RECORDED AND EXPECT TO PLAY IT FOR PRESIDENT EISENHOWER. ALSO PLAY IT IN MOBILE AND OTHER PLACES. I AM ALSO GOING TO GET THE MESSAGE FROM THE TAPE AND PUT THE ENTIRE STORY IN THE CONGRESSIONAL RECORD AND MAKE MANY THOUSANDS OF COPIES. YOU WERE MENTIONED MANY TIMES BY DR. SCHWARZ AND ME. LOOKING FORWARD TO SEEING YOU IN JACKSONVILLE ABOUT THE TENTH. LOVE TO YOU AND YOURS.

FRANK W. BOYKIN, M.C.

OFFICIAL DAY LETTER

Billy Graham wrote to me:

Dear Fred:
I have already heard excellent reports of your ministry
in Washington and the contact in New York. They were
greatly pleased and challenged by your conversation and
address. I am certain the Lord has opened a wonderful
door there, and that much good will come of it. You are
a faithful servant of the Lord, and I believe He is using
you to advance His Kingdom in this particular message
He has given you. It is certainly needed at this hour.
We shall be upholding you to the Throne of Grace. . . .

Some time later I again addressed a group of congressmen in
Washington, D.C. This time it was a breakfast meeting of the 83rd
Congress Republican Club. After the meeting, Congressman John R.
Pillion sent me the following letter:

June 4, 1957

Dear Doctor Schwarz:
Your address to the 83rd Congress Republican Club
was one of the outstanding events of our experience.
Since actions speak louder than words, you will know
our appreciation from the steps we immediately took to
refer you to the House Un-American Activities Commit-
tee and to arrange a personal interview between you and
an Assistant to the President of the United States.
We are accustomed to a Cabinet Member or to an
Administrative Leader being the Speaker at our Club
Breakfast. This makes us a critical audience. I can hon-
estly say that your understanding of the Communist
mind, your unusual ability to present their mental
images with clarity and vividness, your eloquence and
obvious devotion to the cause of freedom equipped us to
serve better the people of America whom we represent in
Congress.

The father of Dr. Fred Schwarz in 1908, while a missionary at Peel Island Leper Colony near Brisbane, Australia, directs a funeral. (He is the one with a tie.)

The wedding of Fred and Lillian, July 26, 1939.

The harvest—recent family picture.

The family doctors (left to right)—John Whitehall, Pediatrician; John Schwarz, Family Medicine; Murray Esler, University Professor, Medical Research and Clinical Therapist; Rosemary Schwarz Esler, Psychiatrist; Fred Schwarz, M.D. (Two grandchildren are also doctors now and two more are in medical school.)

Happy grandchildren.

Dr. Schwarz and Lillian with their great-grandson Maxwell and his mother Katherine.

The audience at the Southern California School of Anti-Communism, held in the Los Angeles Sports Arena, Aug. 28–Sept. 1, 1961. The program was televised live for 2 1/2 hours each evening. (Photo: John Hartley).

On the platform (left to right) are Ed Ettinger, Pat Boone, Ronald Reagan, Nancy Reagan, Geradine Frawley, Lillian Schwarz, Fred Schwarz, and Roy Rogers (Photo: John Hartley).

John Wayne at the podium.

Bring your own tape recorder (Photo: John Hartley).

Mobile library distributing Communist literature in villages of India.

Inside the Communist mobile library.

Literature published and distributed worldwide by the Crusade.

Rev. Colbert with children of Indian Christian Orphanage (supported by the Crusade since 1956).

Rev. Colbert serves the food.

Rev. Colbert with Indian Christian anti-Communism evangelists.

Using a printing press in India, which the Crusade provided to combat Communist propaganda.

*I hope the people of America may continue to hear
your message.*

Yours very sincerely,
Signed: John R. Pillion

The congressman wasted no time. Shortly after I returned to my hotel room, the phone rang. Richard Arens, director of the House Committee on Un-American Activities, invited me to give evidence on "The Communist Mind" to the committee. I asked, "When?" I was somewhat surprised when he answered "Now," but I said "Certainly."

I went to the Capitol, where Mr. Arens questioned me in an executive session of the committee. No congressmen were present. His questions and my answers were recorded, and I left the Capitol not expecting much from the interview.

The committee published the interview and distributed it to its mailing list. One recipient was a freedom-loving American Jew from New York, Alfred Kohlberg, founder of the Jewish Anti-Communist League. He in turn sent the interview to those on his mailing list. Later, Alfred and I became friends and collaborators.

A journalist who was writing the story of one of America's leading electrical companies, the Allen-Bradley Company of Milwaukee, Wisconsin, received a copy. After reading it, he gave the copy to Fred Loock, president of the Allen-Bradley Company. He read it on a flight from New York to Milwaukee and told me later that it was the first time he had ever read anything that presented the seductive appeal of Communism so clearly and understandably. He could now understand how they had been able to recruit educated and intelligent students.

In Milwaukee, Fred Loock gave a copy of the interview to Harry Bradley, the company chairman. Harry read it and said, "We should do something about this."

The company decided to publish the entire interview in many of the nation's major newspapers, including *The New York Times, The Washington Post,* the *Wall Street Journal,* and *The Los Angeles Times.* It appeared as a double page advertisement under the caption, "WILL YOU BE FREE TO CELEBRATE CHRISTMAS IN THE FUTURE?"

The initiative of the Allen-Bradley Company did not stop there. They offered to supply copies of the interview to anyone. Unlimited numbers of copies would be sent to schools and churches, and twenty-five copies were sent to individuals. The demand was overwhelming, and I learned that the testimony has had the largest circulation of any congressional document of modern times.

During this exciting time, I had been in Australia. On my return to the States I got in touch with the company. Harry Bradley and Fred Loock invited me to go to Milwaukee to meet them; they treated me royally, and we became personal friends. The company supported the Crusade generously as long as Harry Bradley and Fred Loock lived.

The concluding paragraphs of my testimony before the House of Representatives Committee on Un-American Activities stimulated criticism and controversy:

MR. WEIL: If the present rate of Communist advances continues, how long do you think it will be, in your analysis of world events, before the Communists take complete control of the world?

DR. SCHWARZ: I think the Communists have more or less tentatively set the deadline for about the year 1973. Mao Tse-tung and Stalin in their last conference thought it would take four more five-year plans, approximately 10 years for the conquest and consolidation of Asia, with the immediate threat to Africa and Europe, while the weakening, softening, and degeneration of America continues, and avoiding an atomic-hydrogen war, their conquest is contemplated about that time.

MR. WEIL: You mean 10 years from now for the consolidation of Asia, and this program does not envision a hydrogen bomb war?

DR. SCHWARZ: The basic Communist strategy in 1952 renounced the inevitability of World War III. World conquest without war, which is called peaceful co-existence, became their basic strategy. I would not be surprised that they would like some disarmament, as all they look to from military might is a stalemate. If they can reduce the armament burden and retain this stalemate, they will have more funds available for propaganda, and political and economic warfare.

Evidence to support the accuracy of this statement is given in the 1994 book *The Private Life of Chairman Mao*. The author of this book is Dr. Li Zhisui, who was the personal physician of chairman Mao Tse-tung from 1954 till the chairman's death in 1976. He accompanied Mao to Moscow in November 1957 to attend the fortieth anniversary celebrations of the founding of the Soviet Union. At this celebration Mao made a speech which Dr. Li describes thus:

> Mao was optimistic about the future, exhilarated by the prediction he had made in his own speech. Within fifteen years, Mao said to the assembled delegates, the Soviet Union will overtake the United States in the production of steel and other major industrial products and China will overtake Great Britain. Within fifteen years, he asserted, the material conditions in the communist world will be transformed, their economies surpassing those of the capitalist West. With the transformation of the material base, the whole world would be ripe for the communist revolution.
>
> Dr. Li Zhisui, *The Private Life of Chairman Mao,*
> (New York, Random House, 1994)

This speech was made by Mao in November 1957. Add fifteen years, and the anticipated date of the world revolution becomes late 1972. At that time world conquest by Communism seemed less unlikely than did the Communist conquest of China when Mao led the retreat, known as the Long March, in 1934–35.

The harvest from the publication of *The Communist Mind* has been incalculable and bountiful. Many who later became national leaders, such as Dr. James Kennedy and Dr. James Dobson, have told me that they were profoundly influenced by it. It presented an idea whose time had come.

Once again I discovered that truth begets healthy progeny even if the length of the gestation is a trial of patience.

15

Anti-Communism Schools

A little learning is a dangerous thing;
Drink deep, or taste not the Pierian spring:
There shallow draughts intoxicate the brain,
And drinking largely sobers us again.
—ALEXANDER POPE

I BELIEVED THIS WARNING WAS appropriate for many anti-Communists: their knowledge of Communism was too superficial. To illustrate, I frequently used the analogy of what was needed to combat an epidemic of a deadly disease—that effective treatment depended upon research and study so that the vulnerabilities of the disease could be discovered and appropriate measures taken.

I had long entertained the vision of intelligent and responsible anti-Communist gatherings to study in depth the doctrines, organizational principles, methods, and objectives of Communism. This could dispel some of the widespread delusions about Communism.

Some of these delusions are as follows:

Delusion No. 1: *The policies and programs of the Communists are revealed by their choice of the name "Communism."* The name implies that they are devoted to common ownership or sharing.

160

It was often said that the early Christians were actually Communists because they shared "all things in common."

I explained that the word "Communism" was simply a name that had been given to a complex of doctrines, organizational principles, and objectives that could not be understood by looking up the meaning of the name in a dictionary. The same word often has several meanings. I pointed out that it would be foolish to judge the engineering of a Dodge automobile from the dictionary meaning of the word "dodge" and that, in practice, the world Communist movement had little, if anything, to do with common ownership and sharing.

Delusion No. 2: *Communism stands for human equality.* The fact is that the doctrines of Communism are based upon inequality. They affirm that mankind is divided into unequal and conflicting classes.

Delusion No. 3: *Communism is primarily an economic system.* Economics is a tool that is used to serve an organized movement with pseudo-religious objectives. Communism has a set of doctrines that are accepted by faith; it is an elite organization like a church that works to spread and apply its doctrines. In this sense, then, the "church" is the Communist Party, and the doctrines include the beliefs in inevitable human progress, the material essence of reality, and the positive power of conflict. These beliefs are formalized in such categories as dialectical materialism, historical materialism, democratic centralism, and proletarian internationalism.

Delusion No. 4: *The part equates the whole.* Those familiar with one aspect of Communist conduct may think they understand the whole.

This tendency is illustrated by the old fable about the six blind men who inspected an elephant. The first bumped into the elephant, felt along its side, and said, "An elephant is like a house." The second bumped into the elephant's leg, felt up and down, and said, "An elephant is like a tree." The third touched the trunk, felt it move, and said, "An elephant is like a snake." The fourth touched the tail of the elephant and said, "The elephant is like a rope." The fifth touched the ear and said, "The elephant is like a fan." The sixth felt the point of the tusk and said, "The elephant is like a spear."

Our objective must be to see the whole elephant.

In 1958 I decided that the time had come to transform my vision into reality, by conducting week-long Anti-Communism Schools.

St. Louis, Missouri, was chosen as the host city for our first "School of Anti-Communism." The reasons were practical—mainly, because the Tower Grove Baptist Church had offered us use of their educational building, free of charge.

The Crusade, moreover, had friends in the St. Louis area. I had spoken to a number of churches there and had addressed the St. Louis Medical Society, after which I received the following letter from attorney Fred Schlafly, the husband of the beautiful and talented lady who later became "The Sweetheart of the Moral Major-

VERLIE, EASTMAN, SCHLAFLY & GODFREY

LAW OFFICES

FIRST NATIONAL BANK BUILDING

ALTON, ILLINOIS

EMIL J. VERLIE (1891-1940)
C. DANA EASTMAN
J. F. SCHLAFLY, JR.
CHARLES B. GODFREY
HARRY H. MARSHALL
R. EMMETT FITZGERALD

TELEPHONE 3-8808

May 18, 1957

Dr. Fred C. Schwarz
Lennox Hotel
825 Washington
St. Louis, Missouri

Dear Dr. Schwarz:

I wish to compliment you on the splendid address you gave at the St. Louis Medical Society on May 14. I have heard most of the great American anti-Communists speak, namely Congressman Martin Dies and his most able successor as Chairman of the House Un-American Activities Committee, Francis E. Walter, Senator Patrick McCarran, Senator Joseph R. McCarthy and Louis Budenz. Able and informed as these men have been on the subject of Communism, I believe that your knowledge of the subject is greater and your ability to impart that knowledge to your audience is even more effective.

I hope that you will keep in touch with me as you continue to diagnose and treat the disease of Communism.

Sincerely,

J F Schlafly

JFS:ag

MR. J. F. SCHLAFLY IS A MEMBER OF THE SPECIAL COMMITTEE OF THE AMERICAN BAR ASSOCIATION ON COMMUNIST TACTICS, STRATEGY, AND OBJECTIVES.

ity" and the real "First Lady" of the United States. He was a member of the special committee of the American Bar Association on Communist Tactics, Strategy, and Objectives.

The agent whom we sent to promote and organize the school found the task impossible. He phoned me and urged me to cancel the project. But I knew that if we canceled this one, we would meet up with the same problems the next time and cancel it. So I said, let's go ahead with this one, and if no one comes, so be it. The project took off, and a movement was born.

Under the caption, "St. Louis School a Success," the following report was published in the May 1958 edition of the Crusade newsletter.

> The school for anti-Communists was an outstanding success. One hundred and thirty people attended. They came from as far away as Canada and Florida, with one, of course, from Australia. They represented many professions. There were preachers from many denominations, including Catholic priests. Businessmen mingled with men of manual labor. Attorneys jostled with housewives. Some had given many years to the struggle against Communism, while to others it was an entrance into a new world. Many of the latter were shaken to the very foundation of their lives. As they gained an insight into the appalling world of Communist intrigue, advance, and terror that surrounds us, living a life of complacent self-indulgence felt almost criminal. One young businessman, a Lutheran layman leader, expressed this to the friend who had invited him to the school, when he said to him, "Why did you bring me here? I will never sleep soundly again."

The following letter is typical of many. It came from Mr. William J. Henderson, who represented the Associated Industries of Missouri.

> Just a note of appreciation for the inspiring and well-organized school which you and your staff conducted in

St. Louis. Without exception, this was one of the great experiences in my life. Others have told me the same thing. A good number of us were utterly exhausted from the emotion stirred by a number of the speakers, the excitement of working together as an organization, and watching you perform daily with such vigor and enthusiasm. It was indeed a wonderful week well-spent.

A group of us are meeting today to continue the good work. Our long-range goal is a clinic of this type next year with twenty times the number of people attending and one hundred times more work involved. I sincerely believe that the approach to this problem is a POSITIVE one. Our short-range goals are convincing others of the seriousness of the problem, aligning others to the cause by getting their active participation, meeting and discussing common core subjects with other speakers, and if need be, developing a few fronts of our own. . . .

A significant movement had been born. I believed that the course on the doctrines, organization, deeds, and objectives of Communism should have a skeletal structure, and I agreed to provide it by giving a series of lectures on the doctrines of Marx and Lenin, the organization and role of the Communist Party, and the dialectical methods which the Communists were using in pursuit of their objectives. The other issues such as muscles, glands, and skin should be added by selected speakers with expertise gained from experience. These convictions guided the selection of the syllabus and faculty of the first and future schools.

THE CARDINAL MINDSZENTY FOUNDATION

Those who attended included a group of Catholic friends, among them a Catholic priest, Father C. Stephen Dunker, who had served as a missionary in China. He had been imprisoned by the Chinese Communists and had endured great suffering. He was accompanied by Fred Schlafly, Fred's wife Phyllis, and Fred's sister Eleanor.

They suggested that we form a united Protestant–Catholic organization to combat Communism. Somewhat to their surprise I made an alternative suggestion. I proposed that we should develop independent Protestant and Catholic organizations which could both cooperate and compete.

I pointed out that unity does not always provide strength; that it may foster weakness; that it may inhibit and paralyze powerful motivations; and that monopoly excludes the dynamic which competition often provides.

Protestant–Catholic unity could also present some practical problems. Support from Evangelical Protestant Christians had contributed substantially to my ministry and the Christian Anti-Communism Crusade; if I associated with Catholics in that way, I would be suspect in certain circles. I also suggested that their Catholic connections might be weakened if they operated under a Protestant leader.

In short, I urged them to form a Catholic organization so they could express, without restraint, the dynamic motivations of their Catholic convictions.

They agreed and proceeded to form the Cardinal Mindszenty Foundation, which has given magnificent service to Catholics and others for more than thirty-five years.

I have a profound conviction that unity in diversity is preferable to uniformity. I believe that diversity facilitates choice and thereby freedom. Too often we confront the predicament of the purchaser of the automobile who was told, "You may choose any color you like as long as it's black." I believe competition is preferable to monopoly. I do not think that competition necessarily generates hostility. I believe in a plurality of organizations, whether parties, teams, denominations, foundations, or crusades.

I remember attending a meeting in Australia of Baptist ministers who were welcoming an American Baptist pastor who had come to pastor a church in Australia. After thanking the Australian pastors for their welcome, he warned, with a smile, "Look after your members because I'll be after them." Was he promoting hostility and inefficiency or helping the Christian cause?

I have never thought of the Christian Anti-Communism Crusade as the sole answer to Communism, or thought that everyone who wishes to oppose Communism should join it. Above all I have never seen myself as "The Leader," the "Man on a White Horse" whom others must obey. Often I do not know what should be done; I lack the competence to direct or even advise others. I am well aware of the truth of Lord Acton's maxim—"Power tends to corrupt; Absolute power corrupts absolutely." The hideous deeds of Stalin and Mao Tse-tung bear eloquent testimony to this truth.

The activities of the Christian Anti-Communism Crusade have been in harmony with the spirit of democracy, never fascism; to state otherwise is to participate in slander.

The St. Louis School of Anti-Communism was followed by scores of others in many cities, including Los Angeles, Long Beach, New York, Chicago, Houston, Dallas, Miami, St. Petersburg, San Francisco, San Diego, Seattle, and Portland.

A school was organized as follows:

(1) A person or group wanting a School of Anti-Communism in their city invited the Crusade to cooperate.

(2) They were advised to form a local committee to sponsor the Crusade.

(3) This committee issued a formal invitation to the Crusade to conduct the school.

(4) The Crusade agreed to provide the school program on behalf of the committee.

(5) The committee accepted the responsibility of providing the logistics of the school, such as the location and financial support.

(6) Donations to finance the school would be given to the Christian Anti-Communism Crusade so that they would be tax-deductible. These donations were then given to the committee to be dispensed by the appropriate officers, such as the committee treasurer.

(7) The Crusade provided the school's faculty and program. I agreed to select and arrange the faculty. Each faculty member was granted "academic freedom," and the ideas he or she expressed did not necessarily express the opinions of either the local committee or the Crusade.

(8) If a financial surplus remained after all the expenses of the school had been paid, it would be given to the Crusade.

(9) When the school had been held and all the bills paid, the committee disbanded.

THE FACULTY

We had many faculty members. Some served frequently and others only occasionally. Some were nationally known, while others were relatively unknown. All were opposed to Communism.

Since the selection of the faculty was my responsibility I was always on the lookout for persons with specific knowledge of some aspect of Communism, or those with experiences that revealed Communist strategy or tactics. No examination into affiliations, associations, or private lives of the prospective faculty members was conducted. The Crusade had no access to official government secrets, and it had no espionage agency of its own.

Some who have served as faculty members:

(1) *Herbert Philbrick*. He was well known as the author of the book *I Led Three Lives,* and writer of the television program with the same name.

(2) *Dr. Walter Judd*. He had extensive experience with the Communists as a medical missionary in China. He had also served many terms as a Republican congressman from Minnesota and was an orator of great eloquence and persuasiveness.

(3) *Senator Thomas Dodd* of Connecticut. He was a U.S. Democratic senator who was well informed about Communism and very active in the struggle against it.

(4) *Cleon Skousen*. He was a lifetime student of Communism and had written the book *The Naked Communist*. He had also been the chief of police of Salt Lake City and was an active member of the Mormon Church.

(5) *Juanita Castro*. She was a sister of the Cuban Communist dictator, Fidel Castro, and had played a role in Castro's conquest of Cuba and during the early days of his rule. She became disillusioned and defected to the United States.

(6) *Dr. Fred Schwarz.*

Scores of others made a significant contribution.

We were not always successful, however, in our attempts to recruit faculty members. On one occasion Jim Colbert and I met with the officials of the International Longshoremen's Association (ILA), based in New York City. Their union was fervently anti-Communist, and we arranged for one of their leaders to speak at a school, but the arrangement fell through.

I was privileged to sit beside Senator Hubert Humphrey on a plane during the days when the Christian Anti-Communism Crusade had become highly controversial, but he was very cordial. We discussed the Anti-Communism Schools, and I invited him to speak at one. He expressed interest, but the proposed event never took place.

My own role on the faculty was important. I was both moderator and major teacher. I usually gave the daily opening and closing lectures, and I tried to arrange the lectures so that each one would lead naturally to the next. Usually, the audience grew as the series proceeded. I never used notes, and I always enjoyed the question sessions.

The subjects I covered usually included: (1) Marxism, (2) Leninism, (3) The Dictatorship of the Proletariat, (4) Communist Techniques for Conquest, (5) The Structure and Creation of Communist Fronts, (6) Communist Philosophy: The Difficult, Devious, and Dangerous Dialectic, (7) The Communist Program to Conquer the United States, (8) Allies of Communism, and (9) The Christian Answer to Communism.

All lectures were tape recorded, and the recordings were made available to all who requested them. No lectures were "off the record." We had no secret or hidden agenda.

Dr. George Westcott of Ypsilanti, Michigan, recorded the lectures. After serving as a Christian missionary in Africa, he returned to the United States and established a medical practice in Michigan. His dedication knew no bounds. Whenever we held a school he would close his medical practice and come with his recording equipment. Sometimes he was assisted by his son, Dr. Robert (Bob) Westcott, who followed in his father's footsteps and became a Christian missionary.

NO SMOKING

Circumstances compelled a policy on smoking. When the Tower Grove Baptist Church of St. Louis generously offered their premises, we had to comply with their no smoking rule.

Somewhat hesitantly, I announced the no smoking rule. The applause surprised me and led to our repeating the policy for all future schools.

At each school commencement I announced:

> We cherish freedom and wish to grant maximum personal freedom to each person present. One freedom that most of us desire is the freedom to breathe air which is uncontaminated by cancer-causing toxins. While I know that some of you wish to inhale tainted tobacco fumes you have no right to compel your neighbors to inhale them also. Therefore, in order to maximize freedom, we must forbid you to smoke inside this building.

The policy proved to be popular with a majority.

16

....

A Book Is Born

My desire is that mine adversary had written a book.
—Job 31:35

MY COMMUNIST ADVERSARIES, INCLUDING MARX, Engels, Lenin, Stalin, and Mao, had written many books. I thought that the time had come for me to write one also.

I enjoyed speaking, but I was not as keen on writing. Speaking was a joy, not a chore. The response of an audience inspired me, so I preferred the self-indulgence of speaking to the self-discipline of writing.

During the early years of the Crusade I had written a few booklets as well as many articles for the Crusade newsletter. But I knew the power of the pen, and I agreed with those who urged that a more substantial book should be written. My problem was finding the time and the self-discipline.

I decided on a shortcut. I would combine speaking and writing. I would deliver a series of lectures on Communism which would be tape recorded, transcribed, edited, and then published in book form..

I hired a hall in San Francisco, and, without notes, I delivered a series of lectures on successive evenings on the subjects: (1) Trust the Communists?, (2) The Recruiting of a Communist, (3) The Molding of a Communist (The Communist Party: Origin and Organization), (4) The Communist at Work (Communist Fronts and Captive Organizations), (5) Techniques for Seizing Power (Philosophy of Violence), (6) Successful Techniques for Seizing Power, (7) Consolidation of Power: (The Dictatorship of the Proletariat), (8) Allies of Communism, (9) Brainwashing, (10) The Difficult, Devious, and Dangerous Dialectic, and (11) Program for Survival.

The lectures were duly transcribed, and Dr. Marion Crowhurst, now a professor of English on the Education faculty of the University of British Columbia, served as a most competent editor. The book was published in 1960 by the well-known national publisher Prentice-Hall Inc.

I called the book *You Can Trust the Communists (to do exactly what they say)*, and later changed it to *You Can Trust the Communists (to be Communists)*. I have never regretted the choice despite occasional protests that it suggests approval of Communism.

That year, 1960, was a time when the message of the Crusade was almost universally respected and applauded. The only articulate opponents were the Communists and their left-wing supporters.

In 1961, after the remarkable Southern California School of Anti-Communism in Los Angeles, the honeymoon period ended and a politically motivated storm of slander engulfed the Crusade; the book's publisher was caught in the storm. False accusations of right-wing extremism, neo-fascism, anti-Semitism, nativism, and fanaticism began to take their toll, and all aspects of the work of the Crusade became controversial. Prentice-Hall's salesmen began to meet with strong opposition in selling their textbooks to educational institutions.

In the end, Prentice-Hall decided to stop promoting *You Can Trust the Communists (to be Communists)*. The book was withdrawn from bookstores, and Prentice-Hall gave the copyright to the Crusade.

Despite this disappointment, the book has been an immense success. It has served as a powerful rebuttal to the slanderous accusation that the Crusade had been primarily concerned with demonizing all progressive forces in the United States by associating them with Communism, and that we were "looking for a Communist under every bed."

The truth was greatly different. We constantly emphasized the international dimensions of the Communist movement and focused on the Communist formula for the conquest of the United States:

External encirclement plus internal demoralization plus thermonuclear blackmail lead to progressive surrender.

Many more words were devoted to describing the encircling Communist forces than to the internal activities of the numerically small U.S. Communist Party. I would also reason that the possibility of the U.S. Communists being elected to power by vote of the American people was infinitesimal and that the danger was surrender, not conversion.

I said frequently that if every Communist in the United States were to miraculously disappear, external encirclement, internal demoralization, and the threat of thermonuclear destruction would still remain, and consequently, so would the potential for success of the Communist program.

I did not belittle the significance and power of the American Communists. They saw themselves as social scientists who were skilled at harnessing and exploiting social forces. This skill enabled them to exercise greater influence than their numerical numbers would suggest.

I also stressed that the Communists did not always, or even usually, create the forces that they harnessed and used. I did not accuse the Communists of causing the demoralization of the United States. This demoralization was proceeding owing to many forces, among them the beliefs, attitudes, and policies which are typical of what is often called secular humanism. This led some dishonest or superficial critics to charge that I was accusing the secular humanists of being Communists.

INTERNATIONAL PUBLICATION

Most countries of the world were experiencing Communist infiltration and subversion. Consequently, the message of the book was well received abroad, its appeal enhanced by its clear message. The reader did not need to be a scholar in order to understand it.

The book's message was the primary force behind its wide distribution and translation into many languages, including Spanish, Portuguese, French, German, Italian, Korean, Japanese, Chinese, Vietnamese, Africaans, Swahili, Telegu, and Malayalam.

Louis La Coss, an editorial writer for the *Globe Democrat* of St. Louis, Missouri, summarized the substance of the book in a review published in the August 28, 1960, issue.

> This detailed expose of Communist machinations toward its long objective of world conquest should be read by every American, especially by the millions who are unaware of the insidious and subversive tactics employed by our enemy in its determination to win the class war which it believes will destroy Capitalism, which means the United States. It is a terrifying account of intrigue, deception, fake promises, illegal acts, "brainwashing," seduction of the intellectuals and shrewd manipulation of dupes, many of whom believe they are anti-Communists but actually are tools of the Kremlin. And the hour is late to meet this challenge.
>
> The title, *You Can Trust the Communists,* is deceptive in that you can trust the Communists only to do precisely what they have said they will do. Their intentions, beliefs, and methods have been stated many, many times, and there has been no deviation from the course they plotted under Lenin, carried on by Stalin and Khrushchev. They have proclaimed a fight to the finish with Capitalism, and the war is prosecuted relentlessly on schedule. The author is Dr. Fred Schwarz, an Australian who has traveled around the world to attack the Communists and to warn all of us of impending danger. He has spoken in St. Louis.
>
> For those who have the will to be informed—hence, able to meet the Red challenge—this is an invaluable handbook.
>
> He describes how cells and fronts are formed. He reveals the studied technique of "brainwashing." He tells about discipline and sacrifices demanded from every party

member as well as the fellow travelers and sympathizers, even to the point of confessions of guilt which actually does not exist but which causes men and women to stand in the dock and admit they are "traitors and unfit to live" because they have betrayed the working class, which they have not.

It is not easy to become a party member. The Communists have never aimed at the conversion of great masses of people. "Their whole concept," writes Dr. Schwarz, "is that of a small party, compact, mobile, disciplined, and dedicated, consisting largely of an intellectual elite. It is the task of this small group to utilize scientifically the social forces that move and direct the masses of the people, so that the Communist party may come to power over them, and impose forcibly the Communist program.

"The program of Communism is to recruit into the services of the party great numbers of individuals most of whom are unconscious that they are serving the Communist purpose. . . .

"The answer to the problem of combating the Communists lies in the area of education—education of the masses to the menace that is engulfing them while they are not aware of it. The Communists have stated their plans, and they are right on schedule."

Every American should read this book. . . . Education concerning Communism should promote greater love of the Christian heritage of freedom and a dedication to the defeat of the Communist enemy. . . . It is suited for classroom study and would make a fine textbook for high school and college.

Initially, the book was accepted and promoted by such bodies as the United States Information Agency (USIA), individual states, unions, schools, and churches. A special edition, with the alternative title *Communism, the Deceitful Tyranny,* was printed for the state of Louisiana, and 50,000 copies were purchased for distribution to schools and libraries.

When a labor union in Latin America appealed to U.S. labor unions for assistance in combating Communist infiltration, the book chosen was *You Can Trust the Communists (to be Communists)*.

Those who were perplexed by the question, "What can I do to combat Communism?" found that the distribution of the book was an effective answer, as this letter illustrates:

EVANS LUMBER COMPANY

POST OFFICE BOX 1056
SANTA ROSA, CALIFORNIA

February 4, 1964

Dr. Fred Schwarz, President
Christian Anti-Communism Crusade
P.O. Box 890
Long Beach, California 90801

Dear Sir:

Perhaps you know that our family sent out a paperback edition of "You Can Trust The Communists (to be Communists)" with each outgoing Christmas Card. It might be a source of inspiration to you to know that the response has been nothing short of phenominal. Many of these people are fine, well-educated Americans that have never previously read an anti-communist book.

From one of our retired school teacher friends, we received the message "I have read the book with considerable alarm. Due to my interest, I was able to induce my children, my grandchildren, and friends to read the book. We made attempts to purchase additional copies in bookstores, drug stores, and other places. Not a copy was to be found in any of these places."

One family of four read the book and then contributed their copy to the school library. One party started reading the book in the evening upon going to bed. He started thinking about what could happen to his family under Communism, and promptly got out of bed and continued reading until the book was finished. Next morning he called me long distance to state that because of me he didn't sleep all night, and that the whole gruesome, Communist prospect came to him almost at once. He wanted more copies of the book so that his friends could be awakened to the dangerous situation as he had been.

The responses have been too many to repeat in this letter. If every one of your supporters would take their Christmas Card list, even today, and mail out the paperback book, millions could be awakened almost by magic. This experience has enriched my life greatly and led me to believe that with the utilization of our resources and the distribution of your book, as well as other materials, we can yet save this great nation and the world.

Trusting that God, in the year 1964, will help us to bring about a miracle in the minds of the people in the world, and may His Blessings be with you.

Sincerely,

Lee Evans

LE:bh

In some countries, those who opposed Communism placed their lives on the line. This was certainly true in the Philippines and Italy.

THE PHILIPPINES

A friend of the Crusade sent a copy of a report published in the March 1986 edition of the magazine, *Asiaweek,* known as the *"Time magazine of Asia."* It described the critical hours prior to the resignation of the president of the Philippines, Ferdinand Marcos, during which the nation trembled on the brink of major civil war. The chief of staff of the Philippine army, Fidel Ramos, had just forsaken the Marcos camp to join the forces of Cory Aquino. He was entrenched in Camp Crame in Manila, which was surrounded by nuns and citizens, as they awaited the threatened artillery bombardment from troops loyal to Marcos. The report states:

> At midnight Gen. Ramos took a jog around the perimeter with two guards but no sidearm. Back at headquarters at 2.03 A.M., he lit a cigar and reported that a Huey helicopter had been flown by defecting air force pilots. *On his mahogany table were a book by Dr. Fred Schwarz entitled "You Can Trust the Communists (to be Communists),"* a Bible open at Psalm 91, and a back issue of *Asiaweek* with himself on the cover.
>
> [italics added]

At that time General Ramos was leading the Philippine army against the guerrillas, the Communist New Peoples Army. At this writing he is president of the Republic of the Philippines.

Fidel Ramos was vitally interested in the struggle against Communism, no mere academic interest. Many areas of the country were already controlled by the Communists, who maintained their authority by acts of terror.

General Ramos was aware of the work of the Christian Anti-Communism Crusade led by Dr. John Whitehall, who reported one example of Communist conduct—the massacre of Christians in Digos—thus:

When the shattering noise of gunfire stopped and the stillness of death descended over the small church deep in the jungle of the Philippines, only the crying of a child could be heard by survivors of an atrocity in which 11 children under the age of thirteen, including two one-year-olds, fourteen teenagers, eight women (some of whom were pregnant), and seven men were massacred by a unit of the Communist New People's Army.

The massacre occurred on Sunday morning June 25, 1989, in the home of the pastor of a church affiliated with the United Church of Christ of the Philippines in a tiny village called Rano in the district of Digos in Southern Mindanao.

The reason for the massacre appears to be the participation of the Rano village in widespread refusal to continue paying "revolutionary taxation" to the Communists. This taxation has been going on for years and has been a cruel burden to the poor in the mountains who sometimes have nothing to eat but roots. The 5 to 20 pesos which have been demanded from each family each month could be construed as nothing when converted into U.S. dollars where one dollar is worth 22 pesos, but in reality it is a pitiful commentary on the poverty of the Philippines and the cruelty of the party with its monthly extortion of 25 cents of flesh from the fleshless.

The casualty list confirms that the Communists massacred an unsuspecting Sunday School. The children and teachers ran into the pastor's house which was about 5 meters away from the church. They thought there would be more protection in that building if only because the thatched and split bamboo walls reached from floor to ceiling, unlike the church whose walls only went halfway. Inside the house, they began to sing hymns and pray.

The pastor and his brother who lead the men's and youth work of the church remained outside to face the

Communists. They were beheaded. The Communists surrounded the bamboo house and began to jeer at the children and women inside, demanding to know "Where is your God . . . your God will not protect you now." Then, they opened fire, without warning or mercy. Survivors say the firing went on for an hour. All that is sure is that over 900 spent cartridges were counted around the house and 39 corpses inside.

When the firing was over . . . the Communists went inside the church, someone took up a guitar, and they began to sing victory songs, including the Filipino version of the Communist Internationale.

The Rano massacre was Leninism in practice. With a morality of its own, the party would both punish and warn all those threatening its vital system of supply. In doing so, it would squander 900 cartridges on the massacre of a Sunday School . . . 23 bullets per dead infant . . . is a boast of ruthlessness and invincibility.

Dr. John Whitehall openly opposed the Communists in the Philippines with literature and seminars, informing preachers of the true nature and objectives of the Communists. Because of this, the Communists listed him among those they planned to kill. Fortunately, their plans were not successful.

ITALY

In 1978 the Red Brigades of Italy were conducting their campaign—kidnapping and assassinating their opponents and national leaders. Those who opposed Communism faced great danger. Despite this, our Italian colleagues published and distributed the Italian translation of *You Can Trust the Communists (to be Communists)*. In February the Italian distributor wrote,

We have been working hard in the midst of a thousand difficulties, including strikes of printing houses, paper mills, fabricators, etc. Our Italy is really a poor country.

However, thanks be to God, the book has been published. The text has been made fluent and easily comprehensible for every kind of person. . . . We wanted a high quality production, considering the high quality of the contents of the book.

Concerning the circulation:

1. We have sent copies to all religious book shops, both Evangelical and Catholic in Italy.

2. We are now sending 3,000 copies to newspaper reporters. We are also sending copies to all mayors of cities and towns and to all teachers and professors.

Naturally this has provoked reactions. Threats to blow up our headquarters have been received both by anonymous phone calls and by posters. We have informed the police and are trusting in the Lord but can't help being somewhat worried because guerrilla warfare is common and the newspapers report wounded and dead every day. We appreciate your standing by us and your prayers. . . . [italics added]

TURKEY

We received this letter in November 1975.

I served as a senator for 12 years (1961–1973) in the Turkish Senate. During this time, in the Inter-Parties Anti-Communist Commission which I established in the parliament, and also in the activities of the numerous organizations which we established in Turkey to combat Communism, I repeatedly made use of your book on a vast scale. In addition, during the years 1962–63 in a 12-session seminar which I arranged in the Ankara Turkocagi (a Turkish Youth Organization), using your book as a basis, I had taught your writings to the young people.

I, too, am a medical doctor, pediatrics is my field, but I have also dedicated myself to fighting against Communism since 1932.

STRANGE BEDFELLOWS

In America, some who did not agree with our Christian philosophy nevertheless supported our campaign to expose the pathology of Communism, as the following letter attests.

> Although our political and social beliefs are almost diametrically opposed (I am an atheist and an anarchist), I feel that there are grounds for dialogue. In this decade of the 20th century, Communism represents the greatest threat to human freedom. This may not always be true. Perhaps in the future, Communism will take the libertarian road, however, this is doubtful. . . .
>
> What is tragic about Communism is that it has not and, most likely, will not live up to its message of freedom. It has replaced tyranny of the old social order with its own brutal bureaucracy. Because of this, I find myself supporting some of your goals. Politics has indeed made strange bedfellows. Enclosed is a small contribution.

When challenged as to why I accepted help from such sources, I would reply, "If my house was burning down I would accept help in extinguishing the fire from the arsonist himself."

EDUCATION AND INDOCTRINATION

I have constantly urged that a course on Communism should be based upon the conviction and teaching that individual freedom is preferable to tyranny. Because of this, I was accused of advocating "indoctrination," not "education."

I do not believe that indoctrination and education are always antithetic. Indoctrination has its place in education. I believe that children should be indoctrinated with the addition, multiplication, and division tables in mathematics, and with the correct spelling of words and the proper use of English grammar. Once when I was a guest on a radio talk show in Boston, Massachusetts, I said something to this effect, and a listener called to protest that this might inhibit the genius of an Einstein. I replied that I thought such a potential genius should learn the basic mathematical tables first and demonstrate his genius later, and that such indoctrination might even water the flowering of genius.

It is difficult to teach elementary geometry without axioms, and it is difficult, if not impossible, to teach ethics and good citizenship without moral guidelines.

GUILT BY ASSOCIATION

The following article appeared in the August 27, 1962, edition of *The New York Post* under the heading, "USIA: We Bought Book by Schwarz."

At the time, *The New York Post* was viewed as left-wing and the paper was actively participating in the campaign to classify the Crusade as a "right-wing extremist" organization with a hidden partisan political agenda.

The U.S. Information Agency today confirmed that it has subsidized the Korean printing of a book by right-wing anti-Communist Dr. Fred C. Schwarz.

The USIA also distributed copies of *You Can Trust the Communists* to USIA libraries and "leading citizens" in Korea, an agency told *The Post* today.

The book by Dr. Schwarz, who has the endorsement of Robert Welch, leader of the John Birch Society, is regarded by the USIA as an "extremely clear exposition of the Communist threat," according to Asst. Director Herb McGushin.

"You could call it a subsidization," McGushin said, "but it only cost $380.31. We spent $100 for publication rights and $280.31 for publication support—that means for an initial order of 210 copies to insure the publisher against loss. Of course, that wouldn't insure an American publisher, but foreign printing is extremely cheap.

"We used the 210 copies for presentation to leading citizens to put in our libraries as part of a program of stimulating foreign publication of American books. We give publishers an initial order to try to induce them to take the risk."

Dr. Schwarz is an Australian-born physician and lay preacher who heads the Christian Anti-Communism Crusade. He has conducted "schools of anti-Communism" in a score of cities, in which speakers have ranged through all shades of the radical right.

Their more extreme statements have occasionally been deplored by Dr. Schwarz, who has claimed he permits his speakers "academic freedom."

His book, however, is regarded by the USIA as a "clear explanation of the Communist threat," McGushin said, "although I haven't read it myself."

The Korean publisher printed 5,500 copies of the book, McGushin said, and the printing, with the exception of the 210 USIA copies, was privately distributed.

The USIA sponsorship of his book was revealed by Schwarz yesterday on a "Meet the Press" TV program.

The author of the article was faced with a dilemma. The facts he was about to disclose were favorable to the Crusade. He discovered that:

(1) The United States Information Agency judged the message of *You Can Trust the Communists (to be Communists)* to be "An extremely clear exposition of the Communist threat."

(2) It had spontaneously arranged for the translation of the book into Korean.

(3) It had invested USIA funds to distribute the book to Korean leaders.

How could he lessen the impact of these positive facts? He inserted the irrelevant information that I had "won the endorsement of Robert Welch," the "leader of the John Birch Society," and that the speakers at the Schools of Anti-Communism "have ranged through all shades of the radical right."

He employed the well-known but discreditable tactic of "guilt by association," a practice roundly condemned when used against so-called "liberals," who have advocated Communist-supported programs.

The ownership of *The New York Post* has changed since 1962 and its editorial policy with it. But the mindset that equates a critical evaluation of the pathological doctrines and programs of Communism with right-wing political extremism still lingers in many academic and media circles.

17

....

Making Friends

The friends thou hast, and their adoption tried,
Grapple them to thy soul with hoops of steel.
—SHAKESPEARE (*HAMLET*)

"I HOPE I CAN MAKE many friends tonight." With these words I
would often begin an appeal for financial support for the Crusade at
one of our evening rallies.

I explained that doing things for people did not always lead to
friendship, and that persuading people to invest in a common cause
is a surer method of sealing friendship. I often quoted Jesus, "Where
your treasure is, there will your heart be also." (Luke 12:34) I illustrated this by showing how the sacrifices a mother makes for her
baby strengthen the bonds of love that unite them.

I tried to establish bonds of friendship by persuading the audience to donate a sacrificial gift to support the Crusade work. I sincerely believed, and continue to believe, that those who did give
were enriched, and I felt no embarrassment in making such an
appeal. The bulk of the support came from individuals, not institutions—thousands of small gifts from people of low and moderate
means.

One person who established a close bond of friendship by her constant support is a charming woman named Jan Conner. During the past twenty-eight years she has contributed more than $40,000 to the Crusade.

How did a housewife manage to do this? Jan tells her story.

In 1964 I was elected as a Goldwater delegate to the Indiana Republican State Convention. I soon became involved in selling items to raise money for the campaign from our home.

Among the 300 volunteers involved in the Goldwater campaign was Ruth Burroughs. She and her husband Floyd . . . invited my husband Dick and me to attend a public meeting in Clowes Hall to hear Dr. Fred Schwarz speak. We went and heard the message and were also introduced to Dr. Schwarz. I became eager to learn more about Communism but hardly knew where to begin.

Floyd Burroughs suggested that we commence a study group. . . . The studies were based upon *You Can Trust the Communists (to be Communists)* and patriotic books. On reading Dr. Schwarz's book, I was shocked to learn that the Communists believe that men and women are "sinful" due to the corrupting influence of the capitalist system and that a new quality of human-kind could be created scientifically by providing a socialist environment.

Dr. Schwarz explained that the Communists were right about the sinful nature of mankind but their diagnosis of the cause of this was wrong. I accepted the Bible teaching that the answer to human depravity comes from faith in Jesus Christ and the experience of being born again. I was thrilled to learn these truths, and I acknowledged that I was a sinner and placed my faith in the finished work of Christ on the Cross and became "born again."

Believing that "Faith without works is dead," I set out to work to raise money to help the Crusade. The Federation of Women's Clubs was selling beautiful jeweled flag pins, and I decided that I would sell them also and give the profit to the Crusade. Soon I was buying and selling jeweled earrings to match the pins. . . .

It was not long before our home was filled with items for sale. . . . At present my inventory includes boxed greetings cards, napkins, jewelry, gadgets, and flashing buttons, mirrored lipstick cases, an entertainment book, hand-decorated T-shirts, sweat shirts, collars, and sweaters. Over the years the inventory has varied enormously and has sometimes included candies. . . .

I have always been a character, and I arranged my wardrobe so that I can be easily identified. I always wear red, white, and blue, and usually add inventory accessories. I also carry items in a tote bag or in the car for sales to impulse buyers.

Above all I am always prepared to share my personal testimony of how I began by trying to save my country and learned of my lost condition and became a Christian.

The Lord has richly blessed my hobby of raising money for the CACC, and my family and friends have enabled me to give $40,000 to the Crusade from my "nickel and dime" business. They have helped by carting, buying, wearing, and selling my wares.

I will be eternally grateful to Dr. Schwarz, and I trust that my efforts have been of value to him and our cause.

Floyd and Ruth Burroughs were significant in the work of the Crusade. Not only did they direct an office of the Christian Anti-Communism Crusade in Indianapolis with efficiency and devotion for many years, they were also board members, and they became special friends. It was always a delight for me to visit with them and enjoy their friendship and hospitality.

Although fund-raising has been essential, fund-raising expenses have been minimal. External auditors have estimated that they did not exceed 3 percent to 4 percent of the Crusade income. This low cost was maintained by adhering to the following principles:

(1) No individual or institution was employed to raise funds.

(2) No commissions were paid to individuals for soliciting donations. This applied to me personally and to all members of the Crusade staff.

(3) No financial or material inducements were promised or given to prospective donors.

(4) No debt was accumulated. Our policy was "pay as you go." I am not immune to accident or illness, and I had no wish to leave a burden of unfunded debt as my heritage.

(5) All lecture fees, and all royalties paid on books published by the Crusade, became the property of the Crusade. For example, I have never taken one cent of the royalties paid for the book *You Can Trust the Communists (to be Communists),* though these have been substantial. When the state of Louisiana purchased 50,000 copies of *Communism: the Deceitful Tyranny,* the royalty of $20,000 became Crusade income.

Pardon a personal anecdote. When I was thinking about writing *You Can Trust the Communists (to be Communists)* I told Lillian that any royalties would be given to her. I later realized that this could provide grist for the mill of those who accused me of being in the fight against Communism "for the money," so I decided that all royalties must go directly to the Crusade.

One accusation used to discredit the Crusade and me is that personal gain has been my primary motivation. The evidence clearly shows that the accusation is absurd. As a practicing medical doctor, my income in Australia was well above the average income. Our major financial asset is our family home.

The accusation of my greed reveals far more about the accuser than about me. As the Bible teaches, "Unto the pure all things are pure, but unto them who are defiled and unbelieving is nothing pure." (Titus 1:15)

Many people judge others by themselves. Those who charge greed are confessing that greed would be their motive if they were engaging in a similar activity.

The Crusade publishes an annual financial statement prepared by independent external auditors, which is available to all Crusade supporters. On several occasions the Crusade has been audited by the Internal Revenue Service and the State of California. One of their duties is to examine my personal income tax return. Most have commended the Crusade's work, and me personally.

THE MAJOR FUND-RAISER

The message, delivered by word of mouth and by printed page, has been our major fund-raiser. During the early days most of the Crusade's income came from my lectures; it now comes from the newsletter. The primary purpose of the newsletters and books is of course to tell the message. Occasionally, small to moderate fees came from civic clubs, colleges, or business associations, but we employed no lecture agency.

For many years our newsletter was published twice monthly. It is now published monthly. There is no subscription charge. It is sent freely to all who ask for it, and to the members of selected groups such as the United States Congress.

People who receive the newsletter fall into two groups: those who support the Crusade and its message, and those we hope to inform and recruit as supporters. A more personal cover letter, with news of our current programs and our financial needs, accompanies the newsletter to our supporters.

Since our ruling passion is to present the truth, no restriction is placed on those who wish to spread the message. Permission is granted to anyone to reprint any portion with or without giving credit. I am aware that this policy carries dangers, such as taking statements out of context, but this is a risk we are prepared to take. We are guided by the experience of St. Paul, who wrote from prison:

> Some indeed preach Christ even of envy and strife;
> and some also of good will: The one preach Christ of
> contention, not sincerely, supposing to add affliction to

my bonds: But the other of love, knowing that I am set
for the defense of the Gospel. What then? notwithstanding every way, whether in pretense, or in truth, Christ is
preached; and I therein do rejoice, yea, and will rejoice.

(Philippians 1:15–18)

SUPPORT FROM BUSINESSMEN

Communist theory teaches that Communists and businessmen are
natural enemies, but practice does not always confirm that. They
sometimes walk hand in hand.

The infant Crusade grew for two to three years supported by people of very modest means, and then, gradually, the message attracted
various prosperous individuals.

The word "individual" must be stressed. Support did not come
from big corporations or business associations but from individual
businessmen who were drawn to the work of the Crusade after hearing a lecture or reading a newsletter or booklet.

The following letter explains the motivation of one businessman.

Sunmark Capital Corporation

Dear Dr. Schwarz:

*As we review the assets of our business it is quite
obvious that one of the most valuable assets we have is
our stake in the free enterprise system. We can buy
insurance covering all the other assets of our business
but the only way we know how to insure this one is to
help further educational efforts such as yours in the
effort to enlighten the American public as to the future
of our free enterprise system if the forces of collectivism
throughout the world are successful in achieving their
goals.*

*Accordingly, we are enclosing an "insurance pre-
mium" to help further your work. . . .*

Sincerely,
Menlo Smith
President

Occasionally, friends of the Crusade have tried to enlist the support of large public corporations but they have always failed. Most large corporations are controlled by business bureaucrats, not owners, and they avoid controversial associations or activities. They dread potential stockholder suits or governmental displeasure.

But one by one, some courageous and far-seeing businessmen began to support the Crusade. Here are some examples:

Walter Knott

I remember my excitement when a check for $500 arrived from Walter Knott, the founder and president of Knott's Berry Farm in Los Angeles, California. When I called to thank him I found him to be a warm-hearted and generous lover of liberty. We became personal friends, and he supported the Crusade until his death.

The Chicken House at Knotts Berry Farm became the favorite location for Crusade rallies. Walter, who usually attended, was unpretentious and utterly genuine in his love for America. These words of Shakespeare describe him well:

His life was gentle, and the elements
So mixed in him that nature might stand up
And say to all the world,
"This was a man!"

(*Julius Caesar* V.v.)

Charles Stewart Mott

I was guest speaker at a dinner meeting of engineers in Flint, Michigan. The chairman was a dignified gentleman named Charles Stewart Mott. I later discovered that he was a member of the board of General Motors.

At the conclusion of my address he pulled a checkbook from his pocket and wrote a check for $1,000 to the Crusade.

On several occasions I enjoyed lunch with him in the cafeteria at the top of the Mott Building. When asked, "What does a billionaire eat for lunch?" I answered, "Poached eggs on toast."

During our personal meetings he often gave me a lecture on how to make money. His method was infallible provided two basic assumptions were true: (1) You already had ample funds, and (2) You did not need to spend any that you made. He never explained why, under such circumstances, it was necessary to make money. Unfortunately, neither of these assumptions has ever applied to the Crusade.

The financial support of C. S. Mott was personal and moderate. The Crusade never received money from the corporations with which he was associated or from the foundation that he had endowed, a foundation with present assets of over one billion dollars.

J. Howard Pew

Dr. Howard Kershner, director of the Christian Freedom Foundation, invited me to address one of its meetings. This Foundation published the magazine *Christian Economics*.

After the meeting, Dr. Kershner said to me, "J. Howard Pew had to leave but he asked me to to ask you to call on him."

I knew who J. Howard Pew was, and I responded promptly. The patriarch of the Pew family, he had served as president of Sun Oil Company for many years. He and other members of the Pew family were well-known philanthropists.

I called on Mr. Pew in his office in the Sun Oil Company building in Philadelphia. He received me graciously and warmly. Our mutual devotion to the Christian faith soon developed into a close friendship, and he became a major supporter of the Crusade. He introduced me to his brother J. N. Pew and his sister Mrs. Mabel Pew Myrin.

J. Howard Pew arranged an appointment for me to address the Philadelphia Rotary Club. After delivering my speech, I needed to leave promptly to catch a plane to another city where I was booked to speak. He carried my bags and helped put them in a taxi. I have often said that this was the most prestigious bellboy service I have ever received.

The Pew family had established a number of philanthropic foundations. These were administered by the Glenmede Trust Company, whose director was a Christian gentleman named Allyn Bell. Later, when we conducted an Anti-Communism School in Philadelphia, Allyn served as chairman. He became, and remains, a close friend.

The Pew family and their foundations became major Crusade supporters. Each year the Crusade received over $50,000 from the foundations, and Mrs. Mabel Pew Myrin donated shares of Sun Oil stock worth $10,000. This support ended soon after the death of brother and sister. Soon after J. Howard's death, Allyn retired and all support for the Crusade stopped. It is worth noting that the Pew Charitable Trusts now contain over $3 billion.

On each and every occasion our message has been our fund-raiser.

Rarely, if ever, did I ask anyone for a donation during personal visits. I have a psychological block that makes such personal pleas difficult for me, but the block dissipates when I am speaking in public.

Patrick J. Frawley, Jr.

One morning in 1960 the mail brought a check for $10,500. It came from Mr. Patrick J. Frawley, Jr., and I immediately called to thank him. He invited me to visit him in his home in Bel Air, California.

Patrick and his charming, gracious wife Geradine were the personification of Irish hospitality. With nine children, their home was a hive of constant activity. They were active in their Catholic church, and their children attended Catholic schools. They became aware of the danger that Communism presented to their Christian faith and home, but it was Geradine who first became aware of the menace. "But warning him about it," she said, "was like talking to a wall," and then Castro shook Patrick awake with a takeover of his Schick business in Cuba. Schick also had a blade manufacturing plant in Venezuela and another in Sweden. Technicolor, for which he was both chairman and CEO, had factories in England and Italy.

He phoned me in alarm and arranged for me to meet his corporate executives. Though a dedicated Catholic, Patrick was not sectarian. Edward Ettinger, his right-hand man, was Jewish, and Curtis Kent was a Baptist.

Illustrating how blind he had been to the Communist danger, he told me that earlier when he owned PaperMate and had a factory in Puerto Rico he would travel there three or four times a year, spend time in the home of Dick Godfrey, head of the FBI for the Caribbean, and listen to Communist speeches and tapes of Communist plots, but the magnitude of the menace didn't strike him as significant.

His love of reading, instilled in him by his parents from an early age, had much to do with his success and wealth: Shakepeare, George Bernard Shaw, and the Bible. But upon venturing into business, the book *Giant of the West,* the story of A. P. Giannini, founder of the Bank of America, captivated him.

By age twenty-one Patrick had virtually memorized Dale Carnegie's *How to Win Friends and Influence People.* He later had his executives take the Carnegie course. He tells that when five hundred successful American businessmen were asked what books had the most impression on them, some said the Bible was first, others said Shakespeare, but all said that the Carnegie book was a solid second.

Trying to understand why it took him so long to perceive the Communist danger, he wondered if he may have taken too far the book's stress on businessmen not getting involved in discussions about religion and politics.

While it is natural for an intelligent man to wonder, "Why didn't I wake up sooner?" many never do awaken. Not only did Patrick become lucidly aware, he became an ally valiant in fight, and also a personal friend.

Patrick arranged a small gathering of his friends, and I discussed with them the nature of Communism and the work that the Crusade was doing to expose and diminish the Communist threat. They were eager to become involved with the Crusade. I explained that we thought it more efficient to have a number of independent organizations combating Communism than one united organization. In this way, specific motivating forces could be retained. In a united organization, specific aims are sometimes paralyzed through fear they might offend others in the organization. I explained that freedom flourishes best in an environment where choice exists and that uniformity can dampen initiative.

I told Patrick about the Cardinal Mindszenty Foundation and urged him to join it since he was a Catholic. He became an active member and supporter, but he also did the same for the Christian Anti-Communism Crusade.

He introduced me to an unfamiliar world—the world of business. He was a strategic thinker and overflowed with ideas. And he was willing to pay to transform them into reality. His generosity knew few bounds.

With Patrick's permission, I report a personal problem of his. He was a victim of alcoholism. He entered Shadel Hospital in Seattle, Washington, voluntarily and underwent "Aversion Therapy," which controlled his disease. Ever since, he has dedicated his life to the diagnosis and treatment of this deadly disease, and established a chain of treatment centers for victims of alcohol and drug addiction that have a record of outstanding success.

18

As Others See Us

Oh wad some power the giftie gie us
To see oursels as others see us!
It wad frae monie a blunder free us,
An' foolish notion.
—ROBERT BURNS, 1759–1796 (*TO A LOUSE*)

THE YEARS 1953 TO 1961 were ones of growth and development
for the Crusade. I traveled extensively, gave thousands of lectures,
debated Communists, appeared on talk shows, and wrote hundreds
of articles for our newsletters and a number of booklets. Major
accomplishments included the book *You Can Trust the Communists
(to be Communists)* and the inauguration of our Schools of Anti-
Communism.

We tape-recorded the lectures delivered at our schools and at
many rallies, and distributed them widely. Consequently, I left a tape
and paper trail that was and is accessible to anyone interested in my
message.

My audiences were diverse. Though I adapted my lectures to
accommodate different interests, my basic message remained unchanged—that the Communists are Communists with a basic philosophy, predetermined goals, and predictable activity.

195

One lecture led to another. I made it known that I would address any audience on condition that I was free to choose what I said. This offer did not exclude meetings of the Communist Party and its fronts.

I delivered lectures at all of the following, and to other audiences too numerous to mention:

Committees of the U.S. Congress; state legislatures; the CIA; universities, colleges, and high schools; military schools and the armed forces; theological seminaries; churches and church organizations; civic clubs; patriotic organizations; political clubs; public rallies; radio and television; and, of course, our own Schools of Anti-Communism.

Responses were almost invariably positive. The letters at the end of this chapter, all unsolicited, are selected from many.

Any unbiased investigator of my talks and writings will search in vain for partisan political statements. What he will find are two constant themes: the pathological nature of Communist doctrines and practices, and the Christian gospel of redemptive love.

Toward the end of the 1950s our week-long Schools of Anti-Communism increased in frequency and enrollment. I continued to deliver most of the lessons, to select faculties, and to serve as master of ceremonies. I was busy.

We ended each school with a banquet. Typical was the banquet held in the Disneyland Hotel, March 6–10, 1961. The atmosphere was festive though no alcohol was ever served. We had an open microphone for students to share their experiences of the week. I remember my good friend Dr. George Westcott, after sitting at a tape recorder from early morn till late at night each day, telling one of his funny stories.

> The temperance lecturer presented an object lesson to teach children the dangers of alcohol. He stood a glass of clear water and a glass of whisky side-by-side on a table. He then dropped an angle worm into the clear water where it writhed and wriggled. He then removed the worm and dropped it into the whisky, where it stiffened and died.
>
> Turning to the class, he selected a ten-year-old boy and asked, "Now, Billy, what does this illustration teach you?"

After humming and hawing Billy blurted out, "I would say this teaches me, 'If you've got worms, drink whisky.' "

By July 1961 the Crusade had reached its zenith. Its message was being used by agencies of the U.S. government, major institutions of the United States, and throughout much of the world. Audiences were large and enthusiastic. Opposition was inarticulate and minimal. I had no presentiment of the storm of bigotry and slander that was about to engulf us, and that the test for manhood described by Rudyard Kipling in his poem "If" lay ahead.

If you can bear to hear the things you've spoken,
Twisted by knaves to make a trap for fools.

But first, the crowning event that surpassed our most extravagant fantasy: the Southern California School of Anti-Communism in the Los Angeles Sports Arena.

Speaker
WADE VAN VALKENBURG

HOME ADDRESS
1118 Cherry Street
Kalamazoo 39, Michigan

HOUSE OF REPRESENTATIVES

Lansing 1, Michigan

March 20, 1956

Dr. Fred C. Schwarz
Box 508
Waterloo, Iowa

Dear Dr. Schwarz:

This letter is to express to you the thanks and appreciation of
the members who were able to listen to your most excellent address
given to an informal joint convention of the Legislature on
Thursday, March 15.

The message which you delivered should be heard by every American
citizen as certainly it is important that public opinion be formed
in such a way as to stem the continued growth of communism if we
are to maintain the liberties which we all enjoy.

The illustrations which you gave pointed up the importance of the
understanding referred to above as nothing else could do. No person
would need to be a college graduate to understand the current
danger confronting this country.

In addition, every citizen in the United States is indebted to you
for the giving of your time in bringing this very vital message to
the people.

Again, I wish to express not only the thanks of the members but
mine personally for the time which you gave in bringing to us this
most impressive message.

Also, I wish to extend greetings to Mrs. Schwarz as I know that the
wives of the members particularly were very happy in meeting her.

Sincerely yours

Wade Van Valkenburg

g

THE NATIONAL WAR COLLEGE
OFFICE OF THE COMMANDANT
WASHINGTON 25, D. C.

11 June 1956

Dear Dr. Schwarz:

To present the last official lecture of the academic
year at The National War College is an honor, but because of
the long list of distinguished speakers who preceded you, lec-
turing at the end of the year could also have been a handicap.
However, your humor, experience and unusual ability to clarify
and simplify the ideology and unchanging objectives of the Communists far outweighed any disadvantage that might have been
involved in following so many outstanding predecessors.

Your excellent lecture was interesting and valuable.
On behalf of all members of the College may I thank you for your
outstanding contribution to the work of The National War College.

Sincerely yours,

E. T. WOOLDRIDGE
Vice Admiral, U. S. Navy
Commandant

Dr. Fred C. Schwarz
c/o Mr. J. Colbert
3356 East First Street
Long Beach, California

HEADQUARTERS
CONTINENTAL AIR DEFENSE COMMAND
ENT AIR FORCE BASE
COLORADO SPRINGS, COLORADO

OFFICE OF THE DIRECTOR
CIVIL AIR DEFENSE

8 August 1956

Dr. Fred Schwarz
Box 890
Long Beach 1, California

Dear Dr. Schwarz:

I would again like to tell you how much I got out of your presentation here at ENT Air Force Base last week. Since then I have heard a number of officers indicate how good they thought your presentation was and how great is the need for similar presentations to be made to people throughout this country. One officer summed it up with these words: "That is the first time that I have heard a lecture where I was told the dangers of communism in terms that I clearly understood." We, at this headquarters, do appreciate your taking the time to come and give us such a worthwhile presentation.

I have reviewed the booklets that you left with me on communism, namely: "The Heart, Mind and Soul of Communism" "The Communistic Interpretation of Peace" and "The Christian Answer to Communism". With your written permission, we would like very much to reproduce the pamphlet "The Heart, Mind and Soul of Communism" in a quantity of approximately 10,000 copies for distribution to the officers assigned to the Air Defense Command and to the leaders in the Ground Observer Corps program. We would like to reproduce it as is, giving you full credit and indicating we had your permission to do so. I realize that to buy the pamphlet would be a more practical approach. However, we do not have the money available for buying it at this time, but we do have the materials for reproduction.

If you have no objection to our doing this, and will give us your written permission to reproduce this pamphlet, we will be very grateful to you and will give it as wide circulation as possible, at the same time giving you full credit.

Sincerely,

BROUN H. MAYALL
Colonel, USAF
Director

FEDERAL CIVIL DEFENSE ADMINISTRATION
~~WASHINGTON 25, D.C.~~
Battle Creek, Michigan

OCT 2 2 1955

Dr. Fred C. Schwarz
3356 East First Street
Long Beach 3, California

Dear Dr. Schwarz:

You will be happy to know how enthusiastic the reaction of the
employees of the Federal Civil Defense Administration was to your
address yesterday, October 20, 1955, here in Battle Creek.

It doesn't happen often that a speaker can hold the rapt attention of his audience for better than an hour, as you did yesterday.
After the address the reaction was that they would have been glad
to listen to you still longer. Many of the top officials expressed
their personal appreciation to me for having brought you in.

Your thorough acquaintance with the Communist philosophy and history was impressive to all of us. We feel that you are rendering
an invaluable service to the western world and, indirectly, to
the mission of Civil Defense. Your presentation gave our work a
significant rationale and encouraged our employees in their various responsibilities in connection with Civil Defense.

I would be pleased if we could arrange a return engagement.

Thank you for coming and thank you for your clear and inspired
message.

Sincerely yours,

Fred W. Kern, Th.D.
Director
Religious Affairs Office

PHONE GRAND 121   SINCE 1909

Lernor Iron & Metal Co., Inc.
"LIGHT SCRAP FOR BALING OUR SPECIALTY"
OFFICE AND RAILROAD SIDING
540 COLBY STREET
BELOIT, WISCONSIN

NON-FERROUS
——
COPPER - BRASS
ALUMINUM - BATTERIES
RAGS - PAPER

FERROUS
——
IRON AND
STEEL SCRAP

OCTOBER 26, 1953

DR. FRED SCHWARZ
392 XIMINO AVENUE
LONG BEACH, CALIFORNIA

DEAR DR. SCHWARZ:

I AM RATHER PROUD OF THE FACT THAT I WAS INSTRUMENTAL
IN BRINGING YOU TO BELOIT. FOR THE LAST FEW DAYS, I HAVE
HEARD NOTHING BUT RAVE COMMENTS ABOUT YOUR SPEECH.

I HAVE BEEN STOPPED BY FRIENDS ON THE STREETS, CALLED BY
BUSINESS PEOPLE OF OUR COMMUNITY AND PRAISED BY THOSE WHO
KNOW ME, FOR THE TERRIFIC JOB YOU DID IN YOUR SPEECH TO
OUR ASSOCIATION OF COMMERCE MEMBERSHIP FORUM.

IN THE HUNDREDS OF SPEECHES I HAVE HEARD FROM SUPPOSED
AUTHORITIES TO THOSE OF LESSER REPUTATION-NEVER HAVE WE
HAD THE TERRORS OF COMMUNISM SO APTLY AND SO CLEARLY
PLACED BEFORE OUR GROUP OR ANY OTHER GROUP TO MY KNOWLEDGE.

I CAN SAY, WITHOUT RESERVATION, THAT UNTIL A GROUP HAS
HEARD YOUR TALK ON COMMUNISM THEY KNOW ABSOLUTELY NOTHING
OR HAVE THE LEAST SUSPICION OF WHAT IS PLANNED FOR THE WORLD.

I CONSIDER MY SELF RATHER FORTUNATE TO HAVE HAD THE OPPOR-
TUNITY TO SPEND THE ADDITIONAL TIME WITH YOU IN TRANSIT
FROM THE AIRPORT.

KINDEST REGARDS AND GOOD FORTUNE IN YOUR PROJECT OF EXPLAINING
THE TRUTH TO AMERICA.

SINCERELY,

TOM CHEKOURAS
PAST STATE PRESIDENT
WISCONSIN JUNIOR CHAMBER OF COMMERCE

TC:N

301 PRESS-TELEGRAM BUILDING • LONG BEACH 12, CALIFORNIA
TELEPHONE 6-1920

September 16, 1953

Dr. Fred Schwarz
c/o Mr. Alan Shearman
Box 508
Waterloo, Iowa

Dear Dr. Schwarz:

I wish to express the appreciation of our Rotary Club for your fine address on "The Heart, Mind and Soul of Communism." We have had many speakers on similar subjects but your approach is unique. You are the first one who ever gave us an insight into the inner thought life of Communism so that we can correctly interpret their actions.

The rapt attention to every word was indicated by every member remaining to the end even though it was considerably past our closing time. Your technique of presentation proved itself the equal of the superior quality of your subject matter.

We unhesitatingly recommend that you be heard by every Rotary Club in this and every country.

Sincerely,

J. H. DAVIES
President

JHD/db

FIRST
CONGREGATIONAL CHURCH
of
LOS ANGELES

535 SOUTH HOOVER STREET

LOS ANGELES

Telephone —
DUNKIRK 9-3125

October 30th, 1952.

Dr. Fred Schwarz,
354 South Ardmore,
Los Angeles, Calif.

Dear Dr. Schwarz:

Enclosed please find check for $100.00 as our contribution to the splendid work you are doing.

Your address before the Freedom Club of the First Congregational Church last Tuesday was one of the most informative and convincing discussions of Communism any of the more than 1500 who attended ever heard.

The standing ovation given you by the audience was the only one of its kind ever accorded any speaker before the Club. That tells you better than any words of mine could how we all felt.

May God bless you and keep you and further your efforts for the preservation of Freedom under God in this distracted world.

Continued kindest personal regards.

Sincerely,

Jacob D. Allen,
Director, Freedom Club.

JDA:a

FAR EAST BROADCASTING CO., Inc.

"Christianity to the World by Radio"

BOX 1 WHITTIER, CALIF.   TELEPHONE: OXFORD 6-7711   CABLE ADDRESS: FEBCOM

September 2, 1953

Dr. Fred C. Schwarz,
Lafayette Hotel,
Long Beach, California.

Dear Dr. Schwarz:

Your series of thirteen transcribed radio broadcasts on Communism have been
forwarded to Manila. They have been broadcast over the seven transmitters of
the Far East Broadcasting Company, both Philippine service and overseas service.

We have recently received the following report from our stations in Manila concerning these programs: "You will be interested to know that the Psychological
Warfare Division of the Philippines Government is very much interested in these
lectures. We have loaned them several of the tapes and they called their whole
staff together to hear them. General Duque, Chief of Staff, says he has never
heard anything like them before. They now want permission to translate them
into the various Philippine dialects and send their own people out 'preaching'
Dr. Schwarz' lectures on Communism!"

We are at present engaged in having these lectures translated and transcribed
on a tape by a Russian member of our staff. He is also going to take the
material which I recorded from your series of eight lectures at Trinity
Methodist Church, in Los Angeles, and make additional programs in Russian from
them. We feel that the material which is contained in these programs, and
your basic approach to the problem of Communism, is the most effective weapon
we have yet found to aid in the battle against the evil forces of Communism.

We are most anxious to secure an additional series of fifteen-minute broadcasts
from you. As soon as any more are available, we would appreciate it greatly if
you could make them available to us at the earliest possible moment.

May God's richest blessing be upon you in the great work you are doing throughout the United States and the world to awaken people to the terrible dangers
which are confronting them at this time.

Sincerely yours in Him,

Robert A. Reynolds

ROBERT A. REYNOLDS,
Assistant to the President.

RAR/ht

TRANSMITTERS	AT MANILA	BROADCASTING:
DZAS—680 KC.	DZH-9—11.855 MC.	20 HRS. DAILY
DZH-6—6.030 MC.	DZI-6—17.805 MC.	IN
DZH-7—9.730 MC.	DZB-2—5.885 MC.	34 LANGUAGES
DZH-8—15.300 MC.		AND DIALECTS

MICHIGAN STATE UNIVERSITY

OF AGRICULTURE AND APPLIED SCIENCE · EAST LANSING

CONTINUING EDUCATION SERVICE

November 14, 1955

Mr. Fred C. Schwarz, M. D.,
Box 508,
Waterloo, Iowa.

Dear Dr. Schwarz:

We want to express our sincere appreciation for the splendid contribution you made at our recent Management Conference which was attended by more than seven hundred people.

At the close of the day's activities we asked each participant to anonymously evaluate each phase of the program. It should be gratifying for you to know that your outstanding luncheon address received a higher rating than any of the thirteen workshops and was even better received than the keynote address. Unquestionably you awakened the members of the audience to the dangers of communism in American industry.

66% rated your address excellent; 24% evaluated it as very good; 9% thought it was good. It is significant that of the seven hundred people present only 6 thought your speech was fair or poor.

You are doing an important job and doing it very well indeed. You have our best wishes.

Sincerely yours,

Paul L. Moore, Assistant to the
Director of Continuing Education Service

HAWAII RESIDENTS' ASSOCIATION
INCORPORATED

CABLE ADDRESS
"IMUA"
TELEPHONES
54-0005 AND 50-1109

HEADQUARTERS
ROOMS 2-A, 2-B AND 3-A
PIER 7
HONOLULU 13, HAWAII

October 11, 1955

Fred C. Schwarz, M.D.
Box 508
Waterloo, Iowa

Dear Dr. Schwarz:

After six years of operation for the Hawaii Residents' Association, I am prepared to say that the week of October 2 - 8, while you were here as our guest speaker, was the high spot of our existence.

During these seven memorable days, you gave 24 lectures in the public schools, at our University and over the Island-wide radio. The message was heard by thousands.

In my opinion, you have done more to make our people aware of the dangers of Communism than any person who has spoken on the subject in Hawaii.

This is true because of your complete grasp of the subject and because of your delightful personality and charming sense of humor.

We are indebted to you and trust we may have the privilege and the opportunity of having you with us again in the not too distant future.

May God speed you and your message as you leave us to spread the word in other parts of the world.

Cordially yours,

Lawrence M. Judd, President
HAWAII RESIDENTS' ASSOCIATION, INC.

PROGRAM

1. COMBAT COMMUNISM AND ALL UN-AMERICAN SUBVERSIVE ACTIVITIES
2. LIVE AND WORK TOGETHER IN RACIAL HARMONY
3. DEMONSTRATE AND MAINTAIN THE AMERICAN WAY OF LIFE

19

....

The Southern California School of Anti-Communism

Whither is fled the visionary gleam?
Where is it now, the glory and the dream?
WILLIAM WORDSWORTH, 1770–1850
(*INTIMATIONS OF IMMORTALITY*)

ON SUNDAY, AUGUST 27, 1961, THE *INDEPENDENT PRESS-TELEGRAM*, Long Beach, California, carried this editorial:

TOP SPEAKERS FEATURED
Anti-Red School to open Monday

The biggest anti-Communist meetings in history are predicted by the organizers of the Southern-California School of Anti-Communism, which opens at 8.30 a.m. Monday in the 16,000-seat Los Angeles Sports Arena.

The five-day school features several well-known speakers, Hollywood stars and anti-Communist films. Among its highlights will be Youth Dedication Night, starting at 7 p.m. Wednesday, for which there will be no admission charge.

MONDAY'S program: 8:30 a.m. registration; 9 a.m.
"Philosophy of Communism," Dr. Fred Schwarz, head
of Christian Anti-Communism Crusade. . . .

Weeks before, I had gazed at the vast array of seats in the Los
Angeles Sports Arena with something approaching awe, and had
difficulty imagining them filled. At that time it was the largest covered auditorium in the United States, and it had never been filled.

I went at the urging of Dr. William (Bill) Brashears, an Orange
County dentist, chairman of the Orange County School of Anti-
Communism that had been held in the Disneyland Hotel, Anaheim,
from March 6 to March 10, 1961. That school had attracted the
largest attendance of any to that date and Bill had decided to hold a
sequel in the massive sports arena.

Though I liked the idea I was not convinced of its practicality.
Somewhat halfheartedly, I promised to cooperate by providing the
faculty and program of the school if he could provide the students. I
had little hope that his vision would become reality, for up until that
time a school attendance of 1,000 had been considered large.

PREPARATIONS FOR THE SCHOOL

Bill proceeded to organize a committee to issue an official invitation to the Crusade to conduct the Southern California School of
Anti-Communism.

Patrick Frawley cooperated wholeheartedly and generously and
accepted the chairmanship of the committee and the proposed school.
He recruited the support of prominent citizens from his business associates, Hollywood personalities, and personal friends. He hired professional help and paid many of the bills from his own pocket. And he
arranged for the actor, George Murphy, who later became a U.S. senator, to serve as master of ceremonies during the school.

Subcommittees to promote the school were also organized. These
recruited students from churches, schools, veterans' organizations,
women's clubs, and businessmen and patriotic associations.

On opening day, August 28, 1961, a *Los Angeles Times* editorial
announced the event.

SIX LECTURES SET TODAY
AS ANTI-RED TALKS OPEN

Six lectures are scheduled today for the opening session of the five-day Southern California School of Anti-Communism at the Memorial Sports Arena.

Dr. Fred C. Schwarz, president of the sponsoring Christian Anti-Communist Crusade will lead off the proceedings with a talk on the philosophy of Communism after registration, scheduled for 8:30 a.m.

Rear Adm. Chester Ward, USN, ret., former navy judge advocate general, also will appear during the morning session with a 10:30 a.m. talk entitled "National Suicide by International Agreement."

The *Los Angeles Examiner* called the school an Anti-Red Meet.

ANTI-RED MEET

PROCLAIMED by more than 30 Southland cities, backed by civic leaders in all walks of life and jointly sponsored by a citizens committee and the Christian Anti-Communism Crusade, the Southern California School of Anti-Communism is now in session at the Los Angeles Sports Arena. . . .

We hope no Southlander misses this authoritative clinical analysis of the enemy's mind and plans.

At that time the Crusade was not controversial. We were not commonly regarded as right-wing extremists, and wide sections of the community cooperated with us.

PREPARATORY BUSINESSMEN'S LUNCHEON

Patrick Frawley secured the help of the Los Angeles Chamber of Commerce in arranging a luncheon of businessmen to promote the school. The chamber provided its mailing list for our invitations. I can still remember Jim Colbert helping me carry large boxes of envelopes to the chamber office as we worked on the mailing.

The luncheon was a great success; 641 businessmen attended. I spoke on the nature and potential consequences of the threat that Communism presented to the free enterprise system, and many promised their support for the school.

COMMITTEE MEETINGS

Regular and well-attended committee meetings were held. Jim Colbert attended all of them. The message was my responsibility and passion, and I rarely attended a committee meeting at which I did not deliver an exhortation.

One committee in which I was active was the Literature Committee. Enthusiastic supporters of a variety of causes who had attended our previous schools were eager to distribute their own literature. But we insisted that permission should be obtained for any display. We were eager to avoid the apparent sponsorship of "hate literature," which placed the blame for Communism on some specific race or religion, in particular, any anti-Semitic literature. But though we tried to be vigilant we were not always successful.

THE PROGRAM

The program of the Southern California School of Anti-Communism was similar in content to our schools that had been held elsewhere. A copy of the published schedule is on page 212.

THE FACULTY

The faculty was selected from people who represented a wide spectrum of institutions. I followed my usual criterion for choice: their ability to shed light on some aspect of Communist doctrine or activity. Some were nationally known, most were not. A copy of the published faculty list is shown on page 213.

TELEVISION

As an advertising expert, Patrick Frawley was well aware of the power of television. In order to publicize the coming school, he purchased three half-hour sessions during prime-time on Los Angeles

The Southern California School of Anti-Communism

New Schedule — The Faculty and Class Sessions — New Schedule

SESSIONS	MON., AUG. 28	TUES., AUG. 29	WED., AUG. 30	THURS., AUG. 31	FRI., SEPT. 1
A.M. 8:30-9:00	Registration	American Adventure Series Film	American Adventure Series Film	American Adventure Series Film	American Adventure Series Film
9:00-10:15	PHILOSOPHY OF COMMUNISM Schwarz	PHILOSOPHY OF COMMUNISM Part II Schwarz	COMMUNIST PARTY Schwarz	COMMUNIST FRONTS AND CAPTIVE ORGANIZATIONS Schwarz	HOW TO DEBATE WITH COMMUNISTS AND FELLOW TRAVELERS Schwarz
10:15-10:30	Coffee Break	Coffee Break	Coffee Break	Coffee Break	Coffee Break
10:30-12:00	NATIONAL SUICIDE BY INTERNATIONAL AGREEMENT Ward	THE COMMUNIST CRISES IN ASIA & INDIA Colbert	COMMUNISM PSYCHIATRY AND CRIME Skousen	I LED THREE LIVES Philbrick	PARIS VIA PEKING Judd
12:00-1:30	Lunch Hour	Lunch Hour	Lunch Hour	Lunch Hour	Lunch Hour
1:30-2:00	Film	Film	Film	Film	Film
2:00-3:15	PROLETARIAN STOCKHOLDER John G. Powers	THE COMMUNIST CHALLENGE TO U. S. EDUCATION Trillingham	FIDEL CASTRO 15 YEARS A RUSSIAN AGENT Del Junco	THE COMMUNIST CRISES IN LATIN AMERICA Sluis	PROGRAM OF
3:15-3:30	Coffee Break	Coffee Break	Coffee Break	Coffee Break	
3:30-5:00	MORAL FOUNDATION OF MILITARY POWER Barnes	TOTAL MOBILIZATION FOR TOTAL CONFLICT - Ward	EDUCATION'S PART IN RESOLVING COMMUNISM - Drakeford	CYBERNETIC WARFARE Philbrick	ACTION W. P. Strube, Jr.
5:00-7:00	Dinner Hour	Dinner Hour	Dinner Hour	Dinner Hour	Recess
7:00-8:15	AMERICA'S INTERNAL SECURITY Dodd	THE NAKED COMMUNIST Skousen	COMMUNISM AND YOUTH Philbrick	"A" BOMB TESTING de Seversky	BANQUET 7 P.M. Address "DESIGN FOR VICTORY" Schwarz & Team
8:30-9:45	COMMUNIST APPEAL TO THE INTELLECTUAL Schwarz	CAUSE & COURSE OF COMMUNISM Schwarz	TREATMENT OF COMMUNISM Schwarz	AN EFFECTIVE FOREIGN POLICY Judd	

YOUTH DEDICATION DAY — WEDNESDAY, AUGUST 30, 7:00 P.M.

IN PERSON — Pat Boone, Dale Evans, Ronald Reagan, Roy Rogers

Herb (I Led Three Lives) Philbrick, Paul Mickelson, Lee Childs, Dr. Fred Schwarz

Everyone Invited — No Admission Charge

★★★★★★FACULTY ★★★★★★★

E. RICHARD BARNES, Captain, U.S.N. (Ret.), San Diego, California. Former District Chaplain, Eighth Naval District.

JAMES D. COLBERT, Long Beach, California. Vice-President of Christian Anti-Communism Crusade.

TIRZO DEL JUNCO, M.D., General Surgeon, Pasadena, California. Cuban by birth. School mate with Fidel Castro at University of Havana, Cuba, where Castro was studying law and Dr. Del Junco was studying medicine.

MAJOR ALEXANDER P. de SEVERSKY is famous for his definitive, "Victory through Air Power". General Douglas MacArthur says of Major de Seversky: "All of his statements, all of his predictions have been proved eternally right". He is the author of the best selling book, "America: Too Young to Die".

THOMAS J. DODD, U.S. Senator, member of Senate Internal Security Committee and Vice Chairman of the Committee on the Judiciary.

DR. JOHN DRAKEFORD, Fort Worth, Texas. Professor at Southwestern Baptist Theological Seminary.

WALTER H. JUDD, M.D., U.S. Congressman. An expert on foreign affairs in the United States Congress.

HERBERT PHILBRICK, Author and Lecturer, Rye Beach, New Hampshire. Former counterspy for the F.B.I., author of "I Led Three Lives" which has been dramatized on television.

JOHN G. POWERS, President Prentice Hall Inc., Inglewood, Cliffs, New Jersey.

FRED C. SCHWARZ, M.D., Sydney, Australia. President of the Christian Anti-Communism Crusade, student and diagnostician of Marxian theory and philosophy.

W. CLEON SKOUSEN, author, Salt Lake City, Utah. Formerly with the F.B.I., author of "The Naked Communist".

JOOST SLUIS, M.D., orthopedic surgeon, San Francisco, California. Medical missionary and a Director of Christian Anti-Communism Crusade.

W. P. STRUBE, JR., President of Mid-American Life Insurance Company, Houston, Texas. Secretary and a Director of Christian Anti-Communism Crusade.

DR. C. C. TRILLINGHAM, Superintendent of Schools, Los Angeles, County.

CHESTER WARD, Rear Admiral, U.S.N. (Ret.). Former Judge Advocate General of Navy. Former Asst. Professor of Law, George Washington Law School. Recipient of Legion of Merit from Secretary of Navy.

★ ★ ★

"Eternal Vigilance is the price of Liberty"

TV Station KTTV/Channel 11 in the preceding week, and gave me my assignment—"Speak!"

I did not enjoy television. I much preferred the inspiration of a live and visible audience where people could react by nodding or shaking their heads, smiling or frowning, clapping or booing. I disliked the insensitive television spotlight that never even flickers at the most hilarious joke. But I heard the call of duty and obeyed, sitting in a chair in the studio, talking to the blazing light as conversationally as I could.

I presented the basic ideas and motivations of the Communists and described their consequences. I warned that similar programs would be enacted in America if the Communists were successful in achieving monopoly power here.

To my surprise Geri Frawley considered my television talks the best she had heard me give. The president of Channel 11 was also impressed. He suggested that the four evening sessions of the school should be televised. He even offered to secure a sponsor. We accepted gladly, of course. The Richfield Oil Company became the sponsor, and each evening program of the school was televised for two-and-a-half hours. Happily, it proved to be highly profitable for the sponsor.

I never met any representative of the company and they never attempted to influence the content of the message in any way.

On the editorial page, *The Los Angeles Times*, August 28, 1961:

ANTI-COMMUNISM SCHOOL ON KTTV

Television station KTTV (11) will broadcast live coverage of all four evening sessions of the Southern California School of Anti-Communism tonight through Thursday.

The series, which will pre-empt normal "prime time" evening programs, will be sponsored by Richfield Oil Corp. as a public service.

Evening telecasts will begin at 7:30 p.m. and end at about 10 p.m. Sessions of the school will be held at the Memorial Sports Arena.

The program was simple. It consisted of a recital of the Pledge of Allegiance to the Flag, an invocation, a few announcements, and two lectures. I delivered the second lecture.

My memory of that opening evening is vivid. Senator Thomas Dodd spoke first, using written notes, for about forty-five minutes. Announcements and introductions took a little time, and then I was faced with the task of speaking for one-and-a-half hours.

I had often been warned that audiences have a short attention span, lasting no more than half an hour. How could I hold their interest for an hour-and-a-half?

I spoke to my audience in my usual way and tried to ignore the television cameras. I told my jokes, used my illustrations and anecdotes, and developed the chain of reasoning in my customary forthright and forceful style. The audience responded in the usual fashion with claps and cheers.

Frankly, the response of the live audience did not surprise me. It was the reaction of the television audience that amazed me. It proved that those who accused Americans of having a short attention span were deluded. The attendance at the Sports Arena increased and the television ratings were high.

I'm sure that this sounds somewhat egotistical, but as that great American philosopher Yogi Berra said: "If it's true, it ain't braggin'."

The *Los Angeles Examiner,* Friday, September 1, 1961, reported:

RED EXPOSE

Capacity crowds which attend the Los Angeles sessions of the Southern California School of Anti-Communism eloquently attest to the thoughtful determination of patriotic citizens to realize the nature and intentions of a universal enemy.

The event has surpassed all expectations of success.

It has presented a group of distinguished authorities who exposed the Marxian conspiracy as calmly and minutely as scientists dissecting a deep-sea monster.

They refuted with scholarly precision the superficial appeals with which the oldest form of tyranny baits a trap for the ignorant and the unwary.

One after the other, political experts, social philosophers, criminal investigators, and military strategists drew on their experience and knowledge to confirm with logic the natural repugnance of a free nation to the modern version of total slavery.

It is a tribute to the quality of the Los Angeles audiences that their attention and response were immediate.

Altogether the sessions supplied the facts and aroused the resolution to meet them, an attitude that has always sustained Americans in every crisis.

The tremendous Los Angeles success of the School of Anti-Communism now gives promise of its extension to other metropolitan centers. We hope this is done, for this invaluable service should be available to all Americans.

On youth night the attendance was so great that the chairman, Patrick Frawley, and the speaker, Herbert Philbrick, had difficulty getting through the overflow crowd outside.

The whole community was aroused. Morrie Ryskind, in *The Los Angeles Times,* wrote, "The evening sessions, featuring nationally known speakers, were televised, and those who should know tell me that some three million people listened in nightly. At any rate, I can honestly say that in my 25 years in Los Angeles I have never known a local event that so completely captured the enthusiasm of the city."

OVERFLOW CROWD AT SPORTS ARENA

Anti-Red Youth Program Draws 17,000
An overflow crowd of 17,000 persons jammed the Sports Arena in Los Angeles for Youth Dedication Night in the five-day anti-Communism school in progress there.

There was no admission charge for this event, and all 15,700 seats were filled. The others heard the proceedings and music from loud-speakers outside.

The program's all-star cast included Pat Boone, Ronald Reagan, Roy Rogers, Dale Evans, John Wayne and Lee Childs. . . .

Editorial, *Press-Telegram,* August 31, 1961

The *Los Angeles Examiner* gave a large headline to an article by Vincent X. Flaherty.

ANTI-RED SCHOOL IMPRESSIVE

AS FAR AS I'M CONCERNED, the most refreshing movement to be launched here in many a day is the Southern California School of Anti-Communism. As you know, it drew thousands to the Sports Arena to hear qualified speakers. The most impressive part of it all was the large turnout of young people.

It is to the everlasting credit of Richfield Oil that it sponsored these meetings for the benefit of large television audiences, thereby enabling many thousands more to hear and see what was going on.

The Anti-Communism School founded here very well may be a powerful nationwide antidote to shake the country out of its 11th hour complacency. It is almost certain to sweep into other large population areas, increasing the momentum it developed here.

The *Los Angeles Herald-Express* devoted pictures and a long report on the banquet, the school's concluding event.

ANTI-RED CRUSADE HERE ENDS

Capacity Crowd at Banquet

Los Angeles' largest "crusade" against Communism came to a successful end last night in Shrine Exposition Hall with a fervent call to "continue the fight against this insidious ideology."

A capacity crowd of 3,500 persons attended the banquet ending the five-day session of the Southern California School of Anti-Communism, and heard most of the same speakers urge continued vigilance against Communism. More than 2,000 were turned away because of Fire Department regulations.

Dr. Fred C. Schwarz, eloquent adversary of Communism, gave a short history of the School and then asked the audience to spread the doctrine of anti-Communism to their friends and neighbors.

Need Thinkers

"We need to create thinkers," he said, "to inform intelligent and dedicated people of the dangers that are prevalent to the survival of this wonderful country.

"We spend billions of dollars in Iraq, Laos, Cuba, Bolivia and other places. What happened to all that money? Nothing, money is useless if the people aren't informed and dedicated.

"In strategic areas throughout the world, there is a crying need for information. It is our duty to fulfill this need if we expect to stop the torrent of Communistic imperialism and tyranny that is going on today."

Dr. Schwarz spoke of future plans that included the spreading of literature, newspapers and even comic books throughout the world that would push the American idea over to all.

Will to Win

"Through earnest efforts and a will to win," he said, "we will defeat Communist propaganda with our own truthful statements. Bit by bit, a little at a time, if we persist, we will win and send the Communists back to Russia.

"We need to plant the seeds of truth and nurture the growth into a sturdy plant of freedom."

Dr. Schwarz ended his talk with the hope that the five-day seminar brought a realistic approach to the dangers of Communism saying:

"In analyzing the Communist program, some people can only see within, while others can only see without. I hope we will be able to see both sides and bring it into the open."

Among the speakers introduced were Dr. George Westcott, Capt. E. Richard Barnes, USN (Ret.), Dr. James Colbert, Dr. John Drakeford, Patrick Frawley, and many others.

Dinner music was provided by the El Toro Marine Base band, and Lee Childs sang several numbers. Actress Dale Evans offered the invocation.

George Murphy

Actor George Murphy was master of ceremonies and led the delegation of filmdom personalities which included cowboy Roy Rogers and Don Defore.

Following the speeches, which were again televised, donations that ran into thousands of dollars were submitted through checks and pledges by the audience.

SEPARATE AND IDENTIFY LETTERS

Letters to newspapers flowed across editors' desks. One editor, rebuked because letters about the school had taken up most of the space, said, "What can I do? These are the only letters we're getting." These few excerpts illustrate the tone of most of the letters.

A recent letter-writer referred to dedicated people, working to save our freedom as "hate mongers." He says not to let the anti-Communists "sell us their wares of anti-this or anti-that."

These people are selling us self-preservation, not hate. If you are not against anything as aggressive as Communism, you must be for it. Actually, no neutral position is possible.

Let me point out that "anti" is justified when opposing policies such as those of Hitler, which were based on greed and cruelty. An anti-Communist policy for the United States is based on our desire and our right to live the way we want to.

I am 17 and have never written a letter before. Now I feel I must speak out for what I believe in.

Re: the letter "What are Americans For?"
May I suggest that what Americans are "FOR" is the privilege of being "anti" anything we wish.

I would like to thank you for giving so much coverage to the Southern California School of Anti-Communism. In a day when there are so many pressures to expose the Communistic philosophy and tactics, your newspaper is doing a great deal to keep the public informed.

Many of your readers, I'm sure, viewed the telecast last week of the anti-Communist school held here in Los Angeles. I'm certain most all agreed these schools are a tremendous step in the fight for our freedom. . . .

After the first session of the Anti-Communist School at the Sports Arena we find ourselves delighted with the call for unity between liberals and conservatives of Sen. Dodd presented as it was with feeling and intelligence. The stirring eloquence of Dr. Schwarz was rewarding because of his intimate knowledge of the Communist dogma and ploy. Both of these gentlemen made a real contribution to the understanding of the insidious nature of international Communism.

Occasionally in recent weeks, letters have been appearing on this page written by people who apparently think that if there were no poverty, unemployment, etc., in the world Communism would be no threat. Their theme seems to be that no one should lift a finger (or even speak out) against Communism as long as such adverse economic conditions exist anywhere.
If the U.S. should spend itself to the point of pauperism, and if as a result all people on earth should retire

some night in warm clean beds and with full bellies—
would the Communists inside our country and out be
any less dedicated to our destruction on the morrow?

Ha! Ask one, and he'll ask you if you've heard a
shrimp whistle.

How can I recapture the public mood of that time?! The televised
programs had gained a high rating, and I was constantly recognized
and greeted by strangers. On several occasions people clapped when
I entered a restaurant.

ATTACKS

Though the public response was overwhelmingly favorable, a few
critical voices were raised. The following article was published in the
September 1 edition of *Life* magazine, the companion publication of
Time magazine, and was deeply resented by those familiar with the
message of the Crusade and the school.

FAR-RIGHT REVIVALISTS

A new kind of "revival meeting" serving the nonreli-
gious ends of an outfit called the "Christian Anti-
Communism Crusade" is being held with full hullabaloo
and political portent in Los Angeles this week. Like nine
other crusades in U.S. cities during the last year, it is
presided over by Frederick C. Schwarz, 48, an Australian evangelist gone secular. Schwarz preaches doomsday by Communism in 1973 unless every American
starts distrusting his neighbor as a possible Communist
or "comsymp" (Communist sympathizer).

Schwarz tries to appear less extreme than the John
Birch Society, and he publicly disavows Birchism. However, his local steering committees have often included
known Birchers. Schwarz himself landed in this country
with $10 in his pocket in 1953, but he has built the
"crusade" into a $500,000 business. Having persuaded

41 California mayors to proclaim this week as an official "anti-Communism week," he now plans to take the road show on to New Orleans and Columbus, then, tentatively, to Chicago, Washington, and New York.

Some months later, Patrick Frawley arranged an interview between Henry Luce, the founder and chairman of the publishing empire that included *Time, Life,* and *Fortune* magazines, and me. It took place in Los Angeles. We spent a friendly hour talking and Henry Luce told me that he regarded the extreme liberalism that had engulfed such institutions as the Methodist Church, the Unitarians, and the World Council of Churches as a threat to the future liberty and well-being of America comparable to the threat from Communism.

At the time of our interview the politically motivated propaganda war against the Crusade and me was raging. He acknowledged that his publications had played a role in this war and suggested that an objective article in *Time* magazine would be preferable to a public apology.

In the February 9, 1962, edition of *Time* magazine, the following article was published.

CRUSADER SCHWARZ

In the steadily heating controversy over mass-meeting anti-Communism, Frederick Charles Schwarz, 49, founder and director of the Christian Anti-Communism Crusade, is rapidly becoming the hottest thing around. Last week the keen, spellbinding Dr. Schwarz sallied out from Southern California, heartland of his movement, into another terrain, the San Francisco Bay area. There, in Oakland, he put on a five-day anti-Communist "school"; later this year he expects to carry his message to the Middle West and to New York.

Schwarz means to stir people up, and he does. He arouses an automatic-reflex hostility in the liberal-to-left camp, and an equally instinctive support on the far right. But for those Americans who are themselves less easily classified, Schwarz is a hard man to classify. For his crusade poses a question that is deeper than it looks: What is the role of the individual U.S. citizen in anti-Communism?

Rising Furor. "We're not angels," Schwarz says. "We haven't right wings, left wings, any wings." For those critics viscerally disposed to dislike his "Crusade," but not disposed to study it, Schwarz does not make things easy. He has not uttered any simple, memorable piece of nonsense, like Robert Welch's statement that Eisenhower was a Communist dupe. The Schwarz Crusade proceeds right out in the open without any of the conspiratorial folderol of Welch's Birchites.

Schwarz had an interest deeper than doctoring. In 1949 he fell into an argument with an Australian Communist. After this debate, he determined to find out all he could about Communism. He steeped himself in the works of Marx, Engels, Lenin, and Stalin, to the point that friends recall his wife, Lillian May, saying: "I'm never alone with Fred. He always has Karl Marx along."

He recalls one triumphant debate in his younger days with a Communist leader in a Sydney park: "I mentioned Dialectical Materialism, whereupon the Communist leader challenged me. 'What is Dialectical Materialism?' he asked. I replied, 'Dialectical Materialism is the philosophy of Karl Marx that he formulated by taking the dialectic of Hegel, marrying it to the materialism of Feuerbach, abstracting from it the concept of progress in terms of the conflict of contradictory, interacting forces called the Thesis and the Antithesis, culminating at a critical nodal point where one overthrows the other, giving rise to the Synthesis, applying it to the history of social development, and deriving therefrom an essentially revolutionary concept of social change.' The questioner looked at me with wide-open eyes. I added: 'Don't blame me. It is your philosophy, not mine.' "

In 1953 Schwarz returned to this country again, developed his idea of a mass-effort Christian Anti-Communism Crusade, and eventually sold his medical practice in Sydney. Why did he do it? Explains Lillian May Schwarz who remains in Australia with their three children and serves as secretary of the Christian Anti-Communism Crusade organization in her native country: "We feel that if Fred worked every hour of every day in Australia, he could not achieve nearly as much as he is achieving in America. If he awakens the U.S. to the full danger of Communism, he is automatically getting that great country on the side of Australia."

Schwarz starts with the laudable premise that Americans should be informed about Communism; if they understand it, they will be better able to combat it. "In the battle against Communism, there is no substitute for accurate, specific knowledge. Ignorance is evil and paralytic." Schwarz therefore sets out to inform—and in some ways he succeeds admirably. In his book, his treatment of such a difficult subject as dialectical materialism is a model of instructive popularization.

But it is on the susceptibility of modern society, especially American society, to exploitation for Communist ends that Schwarz really bears down. He notes that the number of actual, hard-core U.S. Communists has never been great. But they are surrounded by fellow travelers, sympathizers, and "pseudo liberals." Most of these liberals "are to be found in the ivory cloisters of colleges and universities"; they are, in effect, the "protectors and runners of interference for the Communist conspirators."

After Knowledge, What? Presumably, a citizenry well informed about the evils, strengths, and tactics of Communism would be equipped to make itself felt in the voting booth, in letters to Congressmen, and other normal methods of political expression, on the specific issues of cold war policy—defense spending, foreign trade policy,

foreign aid, atomic testing, fallout shelters, the role of
the U.N., etc.

Crusader Fred Schwarz does indeed leave his readers
and listeners eager to do something about Communism.
The question is: What specifically does he give them to
do that can be translated into national policy and
action?

I had only one criticism, which I made reluctantly. Apparently the talented journalists of *Time* magazine did not fully understand the limited role of the pathologist in the treatment of disease.

Returning to the days of the Southern California School, I am so glad that Lillian was there to enjoy the exhilaration and sense of achievement. We had no premonition of the propaganda war that was about to burst upon us. While the days were far from quiet, they preceded a raging storm.

20

······················

Hollywood's Answer to Communism

There was a time when meadow, grove, and stream,
The earth, and every common sight, To me did seem
Apparelled in celestial light,
The glory and the freshness of a dream.
—WILLIAM WORDSWORTH, 1770–1850
(*INTIMATIONS OF IMMORTALITY*)

FOLLOWING THE UNPRECEDENTED SUCCESS OF the Southern California School of Anti-Communism, Patrick Frawley conceived a great idea. Since Hollywood, with its dominant role in the formation of public opinion, had been a prime target of Communist infiltration, it would be enlightening to conduct a big televised rally at which luminaries of the film industry would demonstrate their devotion to freedom and their opposition to Communist tyranny.

His idea was translated into reality when the rally, "Hollywood's Answer to Communism," drew over 15,000 to the world-famous Hollywood Bowl on the evening of October 16, 1961.

Announcing the event, journalist Terry Vernon wrote the following article, published in the *Long Beach Press-Telegram* under the caption, "3-Hour Anti-Communist Crusade on Tonight":

226

The summer season's most highly rated new television personality returns with his crew tonight to compete with Fall fare.

He's Dr. Fred C. Schwarz, president of the Christian Anti-Communism Crusade.

From 8 to 11 p.m., Dr. Schwarz will present "Hollywood's Answer to Communism" on KTTV/Channel 11.

Assisting him in the speaking department will be Sen. Thomas Dodd, D-Conn., Rep. Walter Judd, R-Minn., and Cleon Skousen, author of *The Naked Communist.*

Actor George Murphy will serve as master-of-ceremonies, and numerous other Hollywood celebrities will participate.

Last Aug. 28–31, the prime-time telecasting of Dr. Schwarz' "Anti-Communism School" at the Sports Arena clobbered all video opposition.

From the standpoint of viewers' response, it was the most successful series of telecasts in KTTV's history. The station received 8,000 letters and more than 1,800 telephone calls about the program.

Richfield Oil, which sponsored the TV presentations, reported receiving "hundreds and hundreds" of applications for credit cards, according to Richard A. Moore, KTTV president.

Tonight's show, which basically is a recap of what was presented last summer, will be aired by 32 other West Coast stations.

Most of the 32 are affiliates of ABC, CBS, or NBC, which means that these three networks will pre-empt major shows for the special three-hour program.

In our area, only KTTV is carrying it.

In the 32 other areas, the program will be sponsored by Richfield Oil, which also wanted to back the Southland presentation.

However, Pat Frawley, who is prominent in the Anti-Communist Crusade, is also a high executive for Schick Razors. The Southland presentation will be sponsored by Schick Razors because Frawley put in the first sponsorship request.

Individuals desiring to attend tonight's session may do so at the Hollywood Bowl. There is no admission charge.

The rally fulfilled or even surpassed all expectations. A large delegation of nationally known film stars graced the platform. *The Los Angeles Times* reported in its October 17 edition that the master-of-ceremonies, "Actor George Murphy,"

> introduced a dozen or more stars whom he identified as "some of the crowd in Hollywood that for years have been opposing Communism."
>
> They included John Wayne, Cesar Romero, Pat O'Brien, Lloyd Nolan, Jimmy Stewart, Linda Darnell, Robert Stack, Roy Rogers and Dale Evans, Andy Devine, Edgar Bergen, Wendell Corey, and Walter Brennan.
>
> An hour-long entertainment program, headed by singer Connie Haines, preceded the talks. Two hundred American Legionnaires served as ushers, and 350 Boy Scouts formed a massive color guard in the opening ceremonies.

The *Los Angeles Examiner* included Jane Russell, Ronald and Nancy Reagan, Gene Raymond, and Tex Ritter in the list of film stars supporting the event.

The scheduled speakers were Senator Thomas Dodd, Congressman Walter Judd, W. Cleon Skousen, and me. I was to deliver the final address, and I waited nervously as the program began to run late. When I finally spoke, only ten minutes remained, so I delivered an uncharacteristically brief message. It was sufficiently forceful to earn me a comparison to Adolph Hitler in the student newspaper of Stanford University.

A special feature of the program was an apology by *Life* magazine publisher for a calumnious article that had appeared in its September 1 issue, entitled "Far-Right Revivalists." *The Los Angeles Times* reported:

C. D. Jackson, vice president of *Time,* Inc., and publisher of *Life* magazine, apologized for articles in *Life* critical of the recent Southern California School of Anti-Communism at the Sports Arena and the Christian Anti-Communism Crusade headed by Dr. Fred C. Schwarz. The crowd cheered.

"Dr. Schwarz will be subject to oversimplified misinformation," Jackson said. "Regretfully, my own magazine recently published an oversimplified misinterpretation. I believe we were wrong, and I am profoundly sorry."

The *Life* publisher made a special trip from New York for the Bowl appearance.

"It's a great privilege to be here tonight to align *Life* magazine with Sen. Dodd, Rep. Judd, Dr. Schwarz, and the rest of these implacable fighters," Jackson declared.

The *Los Angeles Herald-Express,* October 17, 1961, reported:

Producer Jack Warner was the first speaker. He told how Communists invaded the motion picture industry and how a few succumbed to their propaganda, saying:

"Twenty-five years ago the Communists made Hollywood a prime target. Through domination of this vast media, they knew they could control a good percentage of our thinking. It was regrettable that some of our people believed in their deceitful propaganda.

Fought in Open

"It is with pride that a majority of these people—some who are no longer with us—had the guts to fight them in the open and bring about an eradication of Communist infiltration in Hollywood. To these people a great debt of gratitude is owed."

In addition to being televised live on thirty-two television stations in the West, the entire program was televised for future showing in wide areas of the rest of the nation. The patriotic industrialist Roger Millikin sponsored a twelve-station hookup through North Carolina, South Carolina, and Georgia on December 11, 1961.

Mr. Millikin wrote:

> The response was absolutely unbelievable. All of the stations involved have advised us that never in their history have they had such a tremendous and overwhelming support for any program they have ever run.
>
> Several of the stations that turned down the program have since admitted that they made a great mistake and have said that if they had to do it over again they would certainly have rushed to accept. You will be interested to know that after we had selected one station in Charleston, South Carolina, to run this program, the other station there called us up and told us that they would have to be included because they could not be the only station in Charleston which did not run a program which dealt with anti-Communism. We therefore decided to include them. Subsequently, they were told by their ABC network that they had to put on the Bing Crosby Christmas Show at 9 o'clock which conflicted with the last hour of our program. Thereupon they asked us if we would not let them have the program for the first two hours following which they would tell their listeners to turn to their competitor's channel to watch the completion of the show. They did this, and I am advised by our agency that this is probably the first time in the history of television that any one station has told its listeners to turn to its competitor.
>
> My office has been deluged with letters and telegrams, the general tenor of them being that they never thought they could sit through a three-hour program but that it turned out to be the shortest three hours they had ever seen. Secondly, they were enthusiastic about the marvelous presentation of the subject by all the main speakers and have written in and asked us to

have copies made of speeches and also asked us if we
could make a film so they could take it to small groups
and have it shown over again. Almost without exception
they have regretted that it was not possible that everybody knew that this program was going to be run and
have asked whether it would not be possible to run it
over again.

Who would have dreamed that a few months later, television stations in New York and Washington would be afraid to sell us time
to present our programs?

Did they fear the possible loss of their license due to the hostility
of the administration?

21

. . . .

Early Opposition

There is nothing more dreadful to an author than neglect,
compared with which reproach, hatred and opposition are
names of happiness.
—SAMUEL JOHNSON (*THE RAMBLER*)

FROM 1953 TO 1961 THE Crusade grew in stature and influence.
Opposition was an irritation more than a handicap. My reaction to
the irritation was tinged with amusement and pride.

During this period the opposition came from expected sources.
After 1961 it increased exponentially, from a trickle to a torrent, and
included many who should have been supporters.

Initially, the motivation of the opposition came from two categories: the ideological and the personal.

IDEOLOGICAL OPPOSITION

Opposition based upon ideology came from the pro-Communists.
This statement does not claim that the majority of those who
opposed were Communists; rather, that they had a benign attitude
toward Communism.

232

In *You Can Trust the Communists (to be Communists)* I stated, "The program of Communism is to recruit into the service of the Party great numbers of individuals, most of whom are unaware that they are serving the Communist purpose." I listed those who served in Communist fronts as: (1) Communists, (2) Fellow travelers, (3) Sympathizers, (4) Pseudo-liberals, or (5) Dupes. Certain members of each of these categories considered me guilty of sins of both commission and omission.

THE GOOD IN COMMUNISM

One common criticism was based upon my failure to point out the good in Communism as well as the bad. In rebuttal I explained that a pathologist is a specialist in the characteristics of disease, not health, and that a mixture of good and evil is often more deadly than an undiluted evil.

Examples abound. I based one of my favorites on the hook and the bait used in fishing. The hook is pure evil. Its sole purpose is to trap the fish. The bait is often pure good, both appetizing and nutritious. Judging by the consequences for the fish, when the good bait is added to the evil hook does it dilute or increase the evil?

Many of the elements in snake venom are benign. It is the toxin that is deadly. When warning of the danger from snake bite, is it necessary to specify the benign and nutritive elements of the venom?

Communism often presents the dilemma, "How shall we respond to those doing good that evil may come"? The Bible warns that Satan may be transformed into an angel of light. (2 Corinthians 11:14)

Most of the "enlightened" opponents during this early period believed they were "progressive." They accepted the Marxist concept that "progress is inherent in being" and that people were divided into two conflicting camps, "the progressive and the reactionary." The pro-Communists believed that the Communists were in the progressive camp even if sometimes mistaken and extreme. The motto of many progressives was, "No enemies on the Left."

Opposition also came from the Soviet Union. I felt a sense of pride, regarding it as a tribute to the effectiveness of the Crusade and me.

GUT-LEVEL OPPOSITION

The second group in opposition consisted of people who resented or disliked me personally or who thought that I was poaching their preserves. That was their privilege. I am not exactly a social charmer.

I am also contra-suggestive by nature and have a tendency to look for fallacies in statements and to point them out. And I am not a good listener, often lacking sensitivity in appreciating the problems of others. It is difficult for me to sympathize with those suffering from self-inflicted wounds.

I am not a social snob, as I lack the heritage, the sophistication, and the desire to be one of the social elite, but I do tend to be an intellectual snob. My argumentative temperament makes me argue forcibly. Lillian tells me that I am so forceful that I sound angry. I don't blame anyone for disliking me.

Yet, despite these less than charming characteristics, I have been able to make and keep lifelong friends.

On the positive side I believe that I have a great devotion to truth and to the one who is truth incarnate, Jesus Christ.

SHOOT THE MESSENGER

The initial reaction to unpleasant truth is often anger. I spoke one rainy evening in the City Hall auditorium of Berkeley, California, which seats three thousand. About two hundred to three hundred were present so that the hall appeared almost empty. The program consisted of an invocation and the pledge of allegiance, followed by a lecture lasting one-and-a-half hours, which I delivered sitting on a stool behind a podium. Any experienced speaker would understand how difficult it is to convey emotion in these circumstances.

When the rally ended a number of people came to the platform. Among them was a tall, handsome young man. When I extended my hand, he rejected it angrily, saying, "I won't shake hands with you, you've upset me too much! Your logic is magnificent but you're too emotional! You're like Billy Graham."

The truth was that my facts and logic had upset his emotions. When the message is unpalatable it is traditional to blame the messenger.

Those who were emotionally unwilling to accept my message found justification by attacking my motives and character. Most commonly, I was accused of exploiting the Crusade for personal financial enrichment. This charge was an indirect confession of their own character.

LOUIS LOMAX

One person who displayed both ideological and personal hostility was the television host Louis Lomax. This confrontation took place in 1967, but it illustrates attitudes that were prevalent earlier.

Lomax was an African American intellectual, renowned as an author, orator, and television personality. He classified himself as a convinced liberal, and rarely missed an opportunity to ridicule conservatives. He conducted a syndicated television interview program each Thursday and Sunday evening over KTTV/Channel 11, in Los Angeles.

He invited me to be a guest on his program in February 1967. I arrived at the appointed time and waited while he interviewed others, and announced periodically that I was to be a guest. Finally, some five minutes before the end of his program he said he believed that people conducting anti-Communism programs were racketeers, and then added that he was about to interview one of the leaders of an anti-Communism program.

At that point a commercial announcement came on, after which almost immediately the time ran out, so I was unable to respond. What an example of "freedom of speech"!

Fortunately, my protest secured me the right of reply. The spot came on Sunday evening, February 19, 1967.

Here are some excerpts.

> LOMAX: Lomax here. I happen to believe that the nongovernmental groups fighting Communism border on nothing short of a racket. My first guest is one of the leaders of such a group, the Christian Anti-Communism Crusade, his name is Dr. Fred Schwarz, and . . . he and I are going to tangle.

Lomax: How do you earn your living?

Schwarz: I receive a salary from the Christian Anti-Communism Crusade, and I was interested in your comment that it's a racket. I haven't the slightest expectation of convincing you otherwise tonight because every man must judge in terms of his own character, and a person who is dominated by commercial interests will be quite unable to understand anybody else who sacrifices his financial interests and does it on principle.

Lomax: Well, because of what you suggest, I don't think you are so much dominated by principle and by any particular concern for Communism. After all, you admit you make a living from the foundation.

Schwarz: But long before, I made a living and a better one from my medical practice.

Lomax: I make a living from working on television and writing books and . . .

Schwarz: Of course! But I haven't accused you of being in a racket.

Lomax: I haven't accused you of being in one *yet.*

Schwarz: You came mighty close to it.

Lomax: Did I? When I said it, I didn't mean you personally. But I do happen to feel very strongly that these guys wandering around with their anti-Communism crusades, and all these anti-Communist organizations *are* really making a racket out of it, and I will develop that later on; but first of all, more about your organization. What do you do? And what do you believe?

Schwarz: Our organization believes that Communism comes to power by deception and remains in power by force. Therefore, if you are to be effective against the phase of deception you must educate, and provide knowledge of the nature, the philosophy, and the program of Communism. For example, we're interested in Thailand at present. I have prepared a series of lectures entitled, "What is Communism?" that over one hundred universities in the U.S. have requested. We are translating this series into the Thai language for distribution in Thailand where they can be used on radio and possibly television. We also plan to translate my book, *You Can Trust the Communists (to be Communists),* for distribution there. We believe that no more than a tiny percentage of people will be attracted to Communism if they know what it is; so while they still have a choice, we try and tell them.

LOMAX: As you probably know I've just come back from a month tour of Thailand. In fact I'm doing a book right now on the Communist insurgency in Thailand. I'm not completely ignorant on the question so let's move from that. What do you propose to do in Thailand?

SCHWARZ: We propose to provide the information, so that people may learn what Communism is.

LOMAX: Don't they know?

SCHWARZ: No, the foreign minister says that they are so preoccupied with the very important, present program of subversion and guerrilla warfare that they haven't given sufficient attention to the theoretical underpinnings of Communism.

We teach the philosophy of Communism, its history and organization, and its techniques of deception, for it doesn't matter how anti-Communist you are, and how dedicated to freedom you are, if an individual appeals to you in terms of a program tuned to your self-interest and you don't know the true nature and objectives of Communism, you may be deceived.

LOMAX: So you're going over to alert the people in Thailand?

SCHWARZ: Just as we did in British Guiana. We put on an educational program on the nature of Communism while the people still had a choice to do something about it.

LOMAX: I submit that Communism, and I oppose it as much as you do, that Communism is like a vulture; it thrives only in death, or when something is dying. I sub-

mit, Sir, that if you really wanted to convince the Thais
that you are concerned for them, you would do a much
better job saving them from Communism if you went to
work in your own country to change its immigration
practices. I know, because I talked with Thais for an
entire month. You can't walk up to a Thai and say,
"Look man, I want to save you from Communism but
you're not good enough to be my neighbor. You're not
good enough to be my citizen. And I submit that your
Crusade would do a good deal better if it really worked
on Australia itself, if you concerned yourself with Australia rather than trying to go to Thailand to sell them
your books and your lectures.

SCHWARZ: Just a minute. Firstly, we're not selling anything. We're giving it. Get that point straight. And secondly, if you were a medical man, do you know what
we'd call you? A quack!

LOMAX: Really?

SCHWARZ: Because your whole approach is the
approach of the quack.

LOMAX: Really?

SCHWARZ: Yes! Consider for example the disease of
tuberculosis. When a person is in a run-down condition,
he's more susceptible to contracting it. But any physician
who merely concentrated on environmental measures to
cure tuberculosis and ignored the pathological organism
which took advantage of the environment, would be a
quack. In terms of Communism, there are two causative
elements—one is the environment, which, as you say,
includes poverty and social discrimination. Another is
the Communist party, which takes advantage of the
environment. Any legitimate medical practice must
give attention to the pathological agency as well as the
environment.

We're trying to give attention to that pathological
agency. We're just not big enough and qualified enough
to change the environment of the whole world.

LOMAX: If you are really concerned about the Thai people, where were you when the Thai people were put under military government? Where were you when their constitution was suspended? Where were you when they were denied the right to vote? Where were you when it became martial law in Thailand? Where were you when they made a law in the country that no more than five people can gather together at any one time to discuss political issues? Why didn't you go and save them then?

Break for commercial.

SCHWARZ: You're like the man who says, "This man was drunk and he brought the accident on himself therefore I won't treat his wounds." I'm no quack. You expect me to solve all the problems of everyone everywhere. Every country in the world has serious problems, but I believe that Communism is the biggest monopolistic tyranny in the world, and therefore I'm concentrating on it. In the medical world would I refuse to treat people who had appendicitis because they also have rheumatism, ingrown toenails, and a number of other things which I cannot treat adequately? I'd be as stupid as you apparently think I am.

LOMAX: All I'm saying is that you seem to come running like a fire truck once Communism rears its head, but you don't seem to go running when other problems which create the climate for Communism rear their head.

SCHWARZ: Of course, because I can't run in all directions everywhere at the same time. In the medical profession a specialist consultant is skilled in *one* field, not in every field. If you go to an orthopedic surgeon you wouldn't level an attack on him because he wasn't a psychiatrist. Let's get down to some intelligent questions if possible.

LOMAX: But I think these are quite intelligent.

SCHWARZ: I don't. I think they're stupid.

LOMAX: You may think they're stupid, but you see, I happen to know, I've just come from there. The people you are out to save are asking the questions I am asking you.

SCHWARZ: The question that most people ask is: "Even though our lot is bad, is this going to make it worse?" If they're convinced that the alleged solution will make it worse, they'd sooner keep what they have. For example, in British Guiana their lot was not good, but when they realized that Communism was a totally monopolistic totalitarian tyranny they thought it was better to put up with what they had.

LOMAX: Are you saying then that you saved the day in British Guiana?

SCHWARZ: I'm saying that we made such a contribution that Cheddi Jagan, at that time president, who is an acknowledged Communist, declared us prohibited immigrants. Since the present Burnham government has been installed the prohibition has been lifted.

We believe that folks don't only value economic well-being, though that's very important. They also value freedom, and if they think they're going to lose it they resist.

LOMAX: So you have no feeling that you should go back home and clean up Australia?

SCHWARZ: Certainly not, because I don't think I'm competent to clean up Australia, and I'm certainly not competent to clean up Los Angeles.

LOMAX: But you are competent to stop Communism here, apparently!

SCHWARZ: I'm not competent to stop Communism here. I hope to add information and knowledge to aid the opposition to Communism, and I do the best I can in that regard.

LOMAX: What are you doing, Sir, in the United States that our government itself is not doing?

SCHWARZ: The government is not an educational organization.

LOMAX: It isn't?

SCHWARZ: No, in the philosophy of the United States, education is the privilege of the people. There is a glorious free market for educational ideas. We are educating—printing books, leaflets, newsletters; delivering lectures; conducting anti-Communism schools. I have recorded fourteen short messages on the nature of Communism, and offered them free to university radio stations. Over a hundred of these have requested them for broadcast. We are simply trying to educate. May I use a medical analogy?

LOMAX: Go ahead.

SCHWARZ: Pathology is a field where they don't treat any disease. Would you abolish every pathologist in the United States because not one of them is treating the condition he or she helps diagnose? They simply investigate the disease and give information about the disease to the physicians. The physicians then combine that information with knowledge of the age of the patient, past medical history, other prevailing social and economic conditions, consider the pharmaceutical weapons available, and treat.

We're pathologists in the field of Communism. We try to explain its philosophy, morality, and prognosis and to describe the deceitful techniques by which it operates. In no sense are we a universalist organization thinking we're stopping Communism here or anywhere else.

LOMAX: And in the process of giving out this information, you're making speeches at universities, and admitting in your newsletters you're asking people to give you money. In fact to one man you said, "Give me a thousand dollars."

SCHWARZ: I had spoken at the University of Louisiana when this man jumped to his feet and said, "That's a very challenging message, but I want to do something. What can I do?" And at that stage we needed the money to support this program and so I said, "Give me a thou-

sand dollars to fight Communism in British Guiana."
The Crusade was supporting two teams there.

LOMAX: How much money are you going to spend in
Thailand?

SCHWARZ: That will depend on what the opportunity
is, and what resources we have. If we are able to have
the book translated, and they ask us for a hundred thousand copies, we'll make every effort to give that number.
We'll try to do whatever we can do effectively, hoping
that it will prevent the necessity for military action.

LOMAX: Dr. Schwarz, when did your organization discover Thailand?

SCHWARZ: We became active there during the last two
or three years. We began in the United States and Australia, and when a crisis develops in another country, we
give attention to the best of our ability.

LOMAX: The question I raised with you earlier
which you think is stupid—you didn't know there was
anything wrong in Thailand until the Communists
popped up.

SCHWARZ: Of course I knew there was something
wrong. I know there's something wrong in the United
States, and I know that if every Communist in the world
died tomorrow there'd be lots of things wrong everywhere. What I think is stupid is your thinking that I am
not entitled to teach the philosophy of Communism anywhere because I haven't cured everything everywhere.

LOMAX: No, no, no. You misread my position. I think
you're entitled as an American; you can do anything you
wish; and I'm letting you on my program to say it—

SCHWARZ: I'm entitled to attempt to persuade people
to contribute to education about Communism. What I'm
not entitled to do is use their money for my own personal advantage, and so the Crusade books are audited.
I always like the investigations by the federal and state
auditors because we always make new friends and usually get some new contributions when they come.

LOMAX: OK. When you first hit the United States and made the big splash, I think it was 1961, wasn't it?

SCHWARZ: That's when the big splash came.

LOMAX: I was in New York at the time. As I remember, you had a big meeting here and a number of celebrities were involved. How much money did you net then?

SCHWARZ: We published the audit in the newspaper. It was out of this world, we had never experienced anything like it. The gross income for the week was, I think, about $313,000, and the net on that was close to $200,000. That was the outstanding week in our history. We held a banquet at the end of it, and some $85,000 was contributed. To tell you the spirit of those days, the Los Angeles Rotary Club was meeting; we'd been on television for two-and-a-half hours every evening and somebody stood up at the Rotary Club and said, "Have you been following these programs on TV? We ought to do something about it," and they spontaneously took up an offering and sent in $5,000. That was the spirit of that week.

LOMAX: Where did all that money go?

SCHWARZ: It went into the fight against Communism. For example, we support a daily newspaper in Kerala, India; we have an orphanage with eighty-five underprivileged boys we're supporting in Andhra State; we're operating in twenty-one countries around the world. We are very active worldwide in the battle to preserve freedom. The money is spent in these areas.

Our income for the year is no secret; you may examine our books. Our annual income is a little under three-quarters of a million dollars.

LOMAX: I want to go on to some of the things you talk about. I've been reading your newsletters the last couple of days. You seem to believe that Russia and China are good friends, that there's really no hostility between them.

Schwarz: What?! You have been reading my material, and you say that! The quarrel between them is of a bitterness and an intensity that is indescribable, like the quarrel between Stalin and Trotsky. It is vicious, bitter, and dialectical. Each believes the other is a heretic, and heretics are usually hated more than the heathen. The quarrel is intensely bitter.

Lomax: So what does this say about the worldwide Communist conspiracy? Is it cracking up?

Schwarz: It says that instead of being monolithic it's now multicentral. Instead of just one focus of Communist activity, there are a number competing with each other. In some ways this weakens it. In other ways it strengthens it. We have a doctrine in capitalist countries that competition improves efficiency. However, I'm much more optimistic about the final outcome now than I was ten years ago.

Lomax: What do you think of the possibility that the United States and Russia may one day combine in a war against China?

Schwarz: I think that possibility is exceedingly remote. I don't expect any open warfare between Russia and China. What I expect to happen over there is that Russia will support the so-called revisionists in China and try to have Mao Tse-tung and his group overthrown, while China will try to promote people's warfare everywhere. I can't foresee any open conflict between them.

The proudest boast of the Communists is that they are scientists who use social forces as levers. Archimedes was a scientist who said, "Give me a lever and somewhere to stand, and I will move the world."

A sailor is a scientist who can take the wind and make it drive a ship against itself. He doesn't create the wind; he understands and harnesses it.

The Communists study the existing social forces and attempt to harness them for world conquest. There are always some forces the Communists can exploit. Where there's human nature you'll have problems. If people are being paid, they aren't being paid enough. Racial intolerance is almost universal, and anywhere in the world where you have different nationalities living in proximity in quantity there seems to be potential for trouble.

LOMAX: I'm amazed at you, a doctor, because it seems to me that if I know that a cold germ, if indeed cold comes from a germ, is flying around in the air waiting for my child to stand in a draft, that the way to stop the cold is to keep my child away from the draft. Close the window.

SCHWARZ: But I also know that if there's no opportunity to keep children away from a draft—that they have to go to school, where they're going to get into drafts, where other students are going to breathe on them—I must have some specific treatment for the cold if they get it.

I'm not arguing with you for one moment that these social forces don't need attention; they do. I'm delighted if you are giving attention to the force of racial discrimination. I'm also delighted if you're giving attention to the force of poverty. I'm delighted for everyone who is giving attention to these things because millions of people need to become involved; but just as one person can often only do one thing, I'm trying to give attention to the pathological ideology of Communism.

LOMAX: I'm trying to have you understand that here you are now, wanting to save a man in Thailand, from Communism. Fine, but the man in Thailand right now, under his own government, cannot even vote. He does not even have a constitution. He cannot sit as you and I are, arguing, and talk publicly on television. The newspapers are censored by the government. In other words, what are you going to do to save him?

SCHWARZ: If the threat of Communism diminishes, his opportunities will increase. There is not an equality of

evil. Some systems are bad, other systems are worse.
You know for example that there are things wrong in
the United States.

I contend that the ultimate and most dangerous per-
manent form of totalitarianism tyranny is Communism,
and unless we deal with this we won't have the opportunity to deal with the others.

LOMAX: If the current government in Thailand will
not let its citizens vote, it is just as dangerous as Communism is, because there's nothing Communism can do
to them that hasn't already been done.

SCHWARZ: Oh, there are lots of things Communism
can do to them.

LOMAX: What can they do?

SCHWARZ: Communists can arrest them and put them
in concentration camps. They can take their children
away from them. They can exterminate them because
they belong to the wrong social class. Tyranny is not
always equal; there are degrees of tyranny. Did *you* get
into Thailand? Communism could set up a state where
you couldn't get into Thailand, and think how dreadful
that would be.

LOMAX: They could even do like Australia; even if I
got there I couldn't become a citizen. I'd like you to tell
us what you can do in Thailand and these other countries that the Peace Corps isn't already doing. I happen
to know from first-hand information that we are doing a
tremendous job. We have turned the entire Peace Corps
of the United States aid service in Thailand into an infor-
mational, educational machine to educate the people in
the northeast section of Thailand about the danger of
Communism.

SCHWARZ: I'm delighted to hear it. I know that the
American government is getting involved in certain educational matters and it has made use of the educational
material of the Crusade for this purpose. But tradition-
ally, education has been a local responsibility. I know for

example that by congressional law, the United States Information Agency cannot educate within the United States. It only educates outside the borders of the U.S.

I'm happy for whatever education the government is giving. We are hoping we'll be able to do more, a little more effectively.

The foreign minister of Thailand told us that he thought they were not giving enough attention to the theoretical underpinnings of Communism. We are helping in that area.

The Peace Corps can do a thousand things we can't do, and do them very well. They give attention to some of the problems you raise so fluently and so rightly. But we can, I believe, add specific and valuable information on the philosophy of Communism and its implications.

LOMAX: Are you then, in the process of your education, prepared to tell the prime minister of Thailand, "For God's sake, let the people in your country vote"?

SCHWARZ: No. We are not. I don't believe I'm qualified to tell governments everywhere everything they should do in their own backyard. I'm conscious of my limitations and I'll stick to my tools. I'll stick to my specialty, which is the philosophy, the morality, the nature, and the techniques of Communism. And I hope that *you* told that to the prime minister of Thailand while you were over there.

LOMAX: Yes, indeed. You know that one of the techniques of Communism then is to come in where there is discontent?

SCHWARZ: Always.

LOMAX: And yet you're not going to do anything to address yourself to the discontent itself.

SCHWARZ: No, because there is discontent everywhere in the world. For example, I know that alcohol is one of the causes of road accidents but I'm not going to devote all my energies to a fight against alcohol. I'll treat the victims of the road accidents that happen as best I can. I would like to spend more time in the fight against alcohol, as it murders millions, but I can't do everything. Frankly, as a medical man, I find the argument that you must not do something, because you can't do everything, absurd. That is the domain of the quack. The very progress of medical science depends on specificity, not universality.

LOMAX: Dr. Schwarz, I want to thank you for being a guest on the program; we like to hear all sides of every possible issue. I will conclude this interview by making an editorial comment, purely my own, and that is this: We are not going to cure the evil sickness of Communism until we deal with the situation in which it grows.

I, too, made an editorial comment, albeit a delayed one. Obviously I did not convince Louis Lomax. He retained his personal hostility and his ideological delusion that poverty is the primary cause of Communism, as the dialogue with Mr. M. E. Thompson on his March 2, 1967, program shows:

THOMPSON: Well, I just wish to comment on that savior of our country that you had on last Sunday, that Fred Schwarz. Do you think that men like that are doing our country any good?

LOMAX: I do not, and I hope it came over very clear on the screen what I think.

THOMPSON: And, do you think we should allow to come, to leave their own country where they have professions and a lot of discriminations, to come over here in our behalf and try to save the country?

LOMAX: Well, I don't know how we can stop them. . . .

THOMPSON: . . . Oh, yes we can. We should just put up a protest, a mass protest, and have the Immigration catch them by the seat of the pants and throw them off the end of the pier.

LOMAX: Hey, you know what, you know what? You have raised an interesting question. I know any number of very worthy people who are foreigners who are now in the process of being deported from this country because their visas have expired. It may be interesting to find out one day how long Fred Schwarz has been in this country, what kind of visa he is here under, and why he is not being subjected to the same kind of harassment some other people that we know have.

THOMPSON: But it isn't only that, Mr. Lomax. It is the thing that he is violating. He is violating a right of Americans over here who were born and raised and living peacefully, without his injecting a lot of fear and hatred. That's all he is doing, and he only does it for one reason. It's because he and "Skousen," that man that quit the FBI for the purpose, he must be making pretty good money, too. They both are making more money than they could make in their professions by holding their hand out, and then on top of that they insult us by going to foreign countries and give the money away to help them where they are discriminating. For instance, in, ah . . .

LOMAX: Thailand and British Guiana.

THOMPSON: Thailand and those places.

LOMAX: Okay, thank you very much for coming into the dock and expressing your views.

THOMPSON: I am going to write to immigration myself, and I hope that everyone here who feels as I, do the same thing.

LOMAX: Okay, when you get your answer from them, let me know.

Mr. Thompson was a little confused. If he had wanted to protest about his and Mr. Lomax's money being sent overseas, he should have directed his criticism to the government. The only money we have ever sent overseas is money given by voluntary contributors for specific purposes.

22

....

The Rage of Leviathan and the Fulbright Memorandum

Heaven has no rage like love to hatred turned,
Nor hell a fury like a woman scorned.
—WILLIAM CONGREVE, 1670–1729 (*THE MOURNING BRIDE*)

DURING THE 1950S THE INFLUENCE of the Crusade increased as its message was heard and accepted by millions of people in major institutions of society. Doors were open everywhere, and the response to the message was overwhelmingly favorable.

Unsurprisingly, there were attacks upon the message and me from Communists and pro-Communists but these were usually tangential and ineffective.

Suddenly, this changed. The Crusade and its message were attacked in force by people who could not be considered pro-Communist by any stretch of the imagination. Many of them claimed to be opponents of Communism, and I believe that in some instances this was true.

With the advantages of hindsight, I now submit my considered answers to questions concerning the campaign of misinformation, falsehood, innuendo, and slander, a campaign that engulfed much of the nation and deceived many. I will endeavor to answer the ques-

250

tions, "What? Who? and Why?" concerning the authorship, content, and objectives of this campaign.

WHAT?

Suddenly, in 1961 and 1962, we were confronted by these dramatic changes:

(1) Doors which had previously been open into military institutions were suddenly slammed shut.

(2) The policies of the United States Information Service (USIS) and the United States Information Agency (USIA) toward the book *You Can Trust the Communists (to be Communists)*, and to the Christian Anti-Communism Crusade, were reversed.

(3) The Internal Revenue Service (IRS) was instructed to investigate the financial policies and practices of the Crusade in order to remove its tax-deductible status.

(4) Crusade-friendly television stations were intimidated and refused to sell television time for future broadcasts.

WHO?

Who has the power to direct military policy; to control the USIS and USIA; to order the IRS; and to intimidate the television stations?

Communist and pro-Communist forces lacked that power. Their influence was indirect rather than direct.

The only possible source was the highest echelon of the U.S. government. It alone had the power. The government in 1962 was the Kennedy administration, and it would be absurd to accuse President John Kennedy or Attorney General Robert Kennedy of being pro-Communist. The motive for the attack on the Crusade must have been otherwise.

WHY?

The assignment of motivation is always difficult, and I am reluctant to speculate. Motives are usually complex, not simple. They involve various factors which are both objective and subjective.

With reluctance, therefore, I submit the following hypothesis, acknowledging beforehand that it may be incomplete or even wrong. I believe the motive was primarily political. The administration was Democrat, and it had concluded that the ministry of the Crusade was helping the Republicans.

It has been said that "Hell hath no fury like a woman scorned." A competing fury is a politician threatened. As contemporary political campaigns testify, such virtues as honesty and courtesy are often suspended during political campaigns and any half-truth or insinuation which can denigrate the opponent is permissible. Loyalty to the team becomes the dominant virtue, and honorable people behave dishonorably.

In some aspects the game of politics can be compared to baseball. Anyone who has attended major league baseball games is familiar with the following scene:

The pitcher throws a ball that hits the batter. Thinking that the attack was deliberate, the batter rushes toward the pitcher, sometimes waving his bat. Immediately and spontaneously every member of the fielding team rushes to support the pitcher, and all members of the batting team rush to support the batter leaving the dugout empty.

Team loyalty determines opinion and conduct. Truth and falsehood, guilt and innocence, right and wrong become irrelevant. A wild melee takes place on the field in which the only unbiased participants are the umpires who seek to restore order and who may finally express their judgment of guilt or innocence by ejecting from the game the one they consider guilty of the original offense.

I believe that this anecdote illustrates the actions and attitudes of those involved in the campaign of misrepresentation and slander against the Crusade that raged during the 1960s.

While many critics believed that the Crusade activities were helping the John Birch Society, powerful Democrats believed its activities were worse—that we were helping the Republican Party. Both conclusions were based upon what was perceived as the outcome. To them, correlation indicated causation.

I was bewildered when professing liberals allowed their party loyalty to take precedence over their loyalty to freedom of speech, freedom of association, and opposition to censorship. They claimed to abhor "guilt by association" but they condemned me because of some alleged tenuous association with members of the John Birch Society. Only later did I understand their motivation.

At the time I was politically naive and believed that the campaign was the result of misinformation and misunderstanding and that the attackers would change when they learned the truth. In some instances this was the case but in many instances prejudice and bias, intermingled with political loyalty, prevailed.

The first major shot in the politically inspired war was fired by Senator William Fulbright, the chairman of the U.S. Foreign Affairs Committee, when, endorsed by President John Kennedy, he compiled and submitted the "Fulbright Memorandum" to the secretary of defense.

This memorandum succeeded in its objective—to close the doors of all military institutions to the Crusade and to several other moderate and intelligent organizations that drew attention to the pathological consequences of Communist doctrines, organizations, and programs.

FULBRIGHT MEMORANDUM

In 1961 Senator William Fulbright produced a "Memorandum submitted to Department of Defense on propaganda activities of military personnel." It was published in the *Congressional Record* on August 2, 1961.

Senator Fulbright was chairman of the Foreign Relations Committee, as indicated, but the memorandum was not authorized by the committee. Fulbright stressed this when he reluctantly consented to its publication in the *Congressional Record*. He hoped to keep the memorandum secret but he submitted to the demands of senators who were aware of it. He stated:

> Madam President, I have been surprised in the past
> few days by a display of intense interest in a memoran-
> dum on propaganda activities of military personnel
> which I have submitted to the Secretary of Defense . . .

The memorandum was based on my strong belief in the principle of military subordination to civilian control. . . . Military officers are not elected by the people, and they have no responsibility for the formulation of policies other than military policies.

I was unaware that it was the custom, the practice, or the right of senators to demand access to the private correspondence of their colleagues. Although I should not have thought it my duty to open my private files, I would have been quite willing to show the memorandum in question to any senator who courteously requested to see it. I was not willing, however, to comply with an ultimatum such as I received from the junior senator from South Carolina [Strom Thurmond] on July 21 demanding that he be provided with a copy of the memorandum "within the next hour."

I have now been apprised of the misapprehensions under which I was laboring. . . . I therefore ask unanimous consent that it be printed in the *Record* at this point.

Although Fulbright claimed that the memorandum was personal, it produced powerful public consequences. The author and philosopher James Burnham stated in an article in the August 26, 1961, edition of the *National Review*:

Is this memo important? It was important enough to make the Pentagon start dancing, immediately, to its tune. It was important enough to get from the President, in his press conference of August 10, an unconditional endorsement.

Fulbright acknowledged that the activities of the military forces to which he objected were authorized by official U.S. policy. The memorandum stated:

Under a National Security Council directive in 1958, it remains the policy of the U.S. government to make use of military personnel and facilities to arouse the public to the menace of the Cold War.

Fulbright gave two reasons for advising that this policy be changed:

(1) The application of this policy had endangered the principle of military subordination to civilian control. (The memorandum presented no evidence to justify this fear.)

(2) The programs in which military personnel and properties were involved were contrary to the president's program. They made use of radical right-wing speakers and they fostered suspicion of the motives of people in authority. The memorandum stated:

In at least eleven instances of what apparently are implementations of the National Security Council policy, the actual programs, closely identified with military personnel, made use of extremely radical right-wing speakers and/or materials with the probable net result of condemning foreign and domestic policies of the administration in the public mind.

As a generalization, the instances described in the attached list involve the participation of military personnel in programs on the nature of the Communist menace and proper methods of combating it. Under such names as "alerts," "seminars," "freedom forums," "strategy for survival conferences," and perhaps others, military personnel of various services and rank have participated to such a degree as to identify themselves with the fact of the program and, at least to some extent, its content.

The content has no doubt varied from program to program, but running through all of them is a central theme that the primary, if not exclusive, danger to this country is internal Communist infiltration. Past and current international difficulties are often attributed to this, or ascribed to "softness," "sellouts," "appeasements," etc. Radical right-wing speakers dominate the programs.

The thesis of the nature of the Communist threat often is developed by equating social legislation with Socialism, and the latter to Communism. Much of the administration's domestic legislative program, including continuation of the graduated income tax, expansion of Social Security (particularly medical care under Social Security), federal aid to education, etc., under this philosophy, would be characterized as steps toward Communism.

The memorandum revealed antidemocratic convictions. It assumed that once American citizens were in the military forces they lost their basic rights and became automatons who should applaud and obey all the orders they received from higher authorities.

Fulbright referred, apparently favorably, to a memorandum from Secretary of Defense Robert McNamara that stated:

After the President has taken a position, has established a policy, or after appropriate officials in the Defense Department have established a policy, I expect that no member of the department, either civilian or military, will discuss that policy other than in a way to support it before the public.

It is difficult to imagine a better prescription for censorship.

The verdicts in the Nuremberg trials that followed the Second World War rejected the defendants' pleas that their actions were justified because they were obeying orders.

The Crusade and Dr. Fred Schwarz received dishonorable mention in the memorandum, but we were not the primary focus of the attack. Fulbright apparently harbored the prevalent delusion that the Crusade and its officers personified "radical right-wing extremism" and assumed that most enlightened people thought the same. Consequently, it was merely necessary to mention our participation in an anti-Communism program in order to condemn it. He stated, "For a description of Dr. Schwarz's viewpoint and purposes, see *The New York Times,* May 21, 1961, p. 54."

I was unaware of this article until I read the statement in the memorandum which classified it as a description of my "viewpoint and purposes." I secured a copy of the article and read it carefully.

It is long—approximately eighty column-inches—and the author is Cabell Phillips. The caption is "ANTI-RED DISPUTE GRIPS ILLINOISANS," and the subheading is "Intensive Right-Wing Efforts Arouse Controversy."

The article featured a description of an allegedly typical anti-Communism School. It stated:

> On August 29, 1960, Dr. Schwarz opened a five-day school on anti-Communism at the Glenview Naval Air Station. Sessions were held three times a day in an auditorium on the base, with an attendance of several hundred at each session. The audience consisted of base personnel, naval reservists, and civilians from surrounding communities.

Cabell Phillips called this event "Dr. Schwarz's School" but ignored entirely the subject matter of my lectures. Those seeking information on my "viewpoint and purposes" would search the article in vain, and justifiably conclude that my role was ceremonial and ornamental. However, I am not handsome enough to serve as an attractive pot plant.

Phillips was a gifted writer. He could create the impression that he was objectively describing an event while ignoring the living essence of it and selecting only items that sustained his own bias. I suspect he could have described a trek by dogsled to the South Pole without mentioning ice, and have it considered comprehensive.

The truth is that my lectures were the core and essence of the school.

I delivered two major lectures each day, and I also served as "master of ceremonies." Phillips made no mention of the titles or substance of these lectures, no mention of such words as Marxism, Marxism–Leninism, democratic centralism, the dictatorship of the proletariat, proletarian internationalism, surplus labor, class struggle, and dialectical materialism. In their place I found such perfidious statements as the following:

The common denominator in the thinking of these groups, as observed in several weeks of travel, is that "the American way of life" is being attacked by fifth columnists frequently operating under such "socialistic" guises as "liberalism," "the welfare state," and "one worldism."

These ideological convictions are often accompanied by an opposition to existing tax, foreign aid, and civil rights policies of the Federal Government, and by a belief that the religious and moral fiber of the nation is deteriorating because of Communist machinations.

Two organizations that have been most active in fostering this drive at the community level are the John Birch Society, headed by Robert H. W. Welch, Jr., of Belmont, Mass., and the Christian Anti-Communism Crusade, of which Dr. Fred C. Schwarz of Long Beach, Calif., is president.

Their tactics differ somewhat, but their aims are almost identical. The Birch Society advocates not only "education," but also the adoption, on occasion, of Communist methods to combat Communist subversion. Its belligerency goes so far, for example, as to demand the impeachment of Chief Justice Earl Warren for furthering Communist aims.

Schwarz Doctrine

The Schwarz doctrine advocates much the same sort of "education" about the Communist menace but stops short of urging particular acts of reprisal.

Unedited tape recordings of all the messages which I delivered at the Schools of Anti-Communism exist, and no intelligent and unbiased researcher could find in them any direct or indirect evidence to substantiate this categorization.

The Christian Anti-Communism Crusade and the John Birch Society were and are two independent and separate organizations. It is true that from time to time individual members of the John Birch Society supported programs of the Christian Anti-Communism Crusade, but so did members of the American Civil Liberties Union, the Democratic Party, and the AFL-CIO.

I can speak only for the Crusade, as I have never been a member of the John Birch Society and I never met Robert Welch, its founder and leader.

The Crusade had no means of investigating the convictions and associations of those who attended and supported our schools. As far as I am aware, no member of the John Birch Society was ever a member of a school faculty; this may occasionally have been the case since I had no means of knowing, nor any desire to know, the private lives of faculty members.

It was patently misleading and unfair to judge my "viewpoints and purposes" by the statements and alleged activities of Robert Welch and the John Birch Society. To do this was a betrayal of the liberal principles to which many of our most articulate critics professed allegiance.

Many national leaders have testified spontaneously that they found my lectures on the pathological nature of Communism illuminating and valuable. One example is former Congressman Jack Kemp. When I met him many years later in the U.S. Capitol he said, "So you're Dr. Schwarz! You have an unusual ability to present Marxist ideas so that ordinary people can understand. When I was quarterback for the San Diego Chargers I often listened to recordings of your lectures."

I have heard many similar statements from both friends and intelligent opponents. I remember one critical student at the University of California at Berkeley saying, "You can expound the ideas of Karl Marx better than any Marxist I have ever heard."

It was this ability, combined with my devotion to personal liberty and the teaching of Jesus, that contributed substantially to the appeal of my messages at the Schools of Anti-Communism.

Cabell Phillips's bias toward the Crusade and me was shown by an article he wrote later in *The New York Times*, April 30, 1961, for which I received an official letter of apology from *The Times*, dated August 22, 1961 (see chapter 1).

The primary purpose of the Fulbright Memorandum was to denigrate two fine moderate organizations, the Foreign Policy Research Institute and the Institute for American Strategy, both of which had high intellectual and academic stature. Their crime was that they studied the official literature of the Communists and understood Communist motivations, tactics, and strategy. The memorandum stated:

> The chief force behind these meetings of businessmen, teachers, servicemen, and church leaders has been an organization called the Institute for American Strategy.
>
> The varied activities of the Institute for American Strategy to date have included the National Military-Industrial Conference held annually since 1955 in Chicago, and two strategy seminars for Reserve officers held at the National War College in the summers of 1959 and 1960. The annual conference is a cooperative effort undertaken by prominent business and military leaders, while the War College seminars have been held under the official auspices of the Joint Chiefs of Staff and the Secretary of Defense. Most recently, the institute has sponsored the publication of a book called *American Strategy for the Nuclear Age,* prepared by the Foreign Policy Research Institute of the University of Pennsylvania, and edited by two members of that group, Walter F. Hahn and John C. Neff. The book is described as a master curriculum for strategy seminars, and advertised as consisting largely of the lectures given at the first National War College seminar. It was used, in page proof, as a text for the 1960 course at the War College, and plans are being made for the widest distribution. Ten thousand copies have already been furnished by the institute to the National University Extension Association for distribution to public school libraries and debate groups throughout the country.

I had no association with these organizations but I was acquainted with some of the leaders, and I held them and their message in high regard.

One objective of Senator Fulbright was attained by the mere compilation of his memorandum. The doors to military institutions were suddenly slammed shut.

Senator Fulbright became one of the leading opponents of U.S. involvement in Vietnam. The *Sydney Morning Herald* is one of Australia's most respected newspapers. On December 30, 1969, it published the following article by Denis Warner, one of Australia's most respected journalists:

> Beginning in June, 1962, when Canberra sent a team of 30 advisors [to Vietnam] under Colonel F. P. Serong, it was paying the premium on what was considered to be Australia's most vital insurance policy: the American alliance.
>
> From the fall of Dien Bien Phu, in 1954, the always implied, if never explicitly hinted, Australian policy was to ensure the maintenance of an American presence in South-East Asia. With the benefit of hindsight, and the barbed comments of Senator Fulbright, who told me 18 months ago that he did not care if all countries in South-East Asia became Communist, it is easy to look back and question many aspects of the policy.

I did not doubt Denis Warner's statement, and I considered his revelation that Senator Fulbright "did not care if all the nations of South-East Asia became Communist" was worth publishing and analyzing. Consequently, I wrote the following report, which was published in the cover letter of the Crusade's newsletter on March 15, 1970.

> "Senator Fulbright, who told me eighteen months ago that he did not care if all the countries in South-East Asia became Communist . . ."
>
> These words appeared in an article in the *Sydney Morning Herald,* Australia, on Tuesday, December 30, 1969. The article is written by Denis Warner, one of Australia's most prestigious journalists and a leading expert on Vietnam.

This incredible statement is a symptom of the malaise that afflicts so many educated and otherwise intelligent people. This intellectual affliction is a blindness to the true nature of Communism. The victims of this disease find it impossible to believe that the Communists are sincere in their devotion to their doctrines and that their activities are designed to achieve the objectives demanded by these doctrines. This makes them unaware of the international significance of every national Communist advance. To the Communists, the conquest of Southeast Asia is a stepping-stone to the conquest of the United States. A logical extension of the statement of Senator Fulbright would be "he did not care if all states in the U.S.A. became Communist." I am not accusing Senator Fulbright of being logical and do not suggest that this later statement expresses his sentiments in any way. I do state that indifference to Communist advance anywhere contributes to Communist danger everywhere. The Communist conquest of Cuba threatens all Latin America, and the Communist conquest of Southeast Asia would threaten India, Japan, and Australia.

This intellectual blindness is primarily an affliction of the highly educated, many of whom are teachers, who pass it on to their students. A generation which sees no evil in the materialism, dictatorship, and classicide of Communism is emerging. The transition from benign neutrality toward Communism to positive support for Communism is an easy one for the young to make. This transition was made by the leadership of SDS with lightning speed. SDS was formed as an anti-Communist organization in 1962. It rapidly evolved to an organization that accepted Communists and finally to an organization dominated by fanatical, self-confessed Communists.

A hard-hitting, aggressive program to reveal the doctrines, morals, methods, and objectives of communism to high school and college students is imperative. Our New Year's resolution is to carry out such a program with energy and skill.

May I suggest that you consider making a resolution
to give regular monthly support to the Crusade if you
are not already doing so. A letter from you informing
me of your resolve to do this will be a great encouragement for this New Year.

This led to the following angry letter from Senator Fulbright to
the editor of the *Sydney Morning Herald* in which the senator categorically denied that he had made the statement attributed to him by
Denis Warner. The letter also contained a malicious, vicious, and
slanderous personal attack upon me and my motives.

> SIR.—The reason for this letter is that in the "Her-
> ald" of December 30, 1969, an article entitled "The
> Australian in Vietnam," by Denis Warner, contains a
> serious misstatement of fact concerning me.
>   Mr. Warner states: "With the benefit of hindsight, and
> the barbed comments of Senator Fulbright, who told me
> 18 months ago that he did not care if all countries in
> South-East Asia became Communist, it is easy to look
> back and question many aspects of the policy."
>   I wish to state unequivocally, with no reservations
> whatever, that this statement is false. I have never at any
> time to anyone stated that I did not care if all or any
> countries in South-East Asia became Communist.
>   I think it most unfortunate for any country to fall
> under the sway of any Communist regime, because I
> believe that Communism is not a system designed to
> serve the best interests of civilized human beings. I am
> opposed to authoritarian systems, and especially those
> which have a doctrine so inconsistent with the best inter-
> ests of normal human beings, as have the Communists.
>   It is inconceivable to me why a reporter should make
> such a statement, unless he is desperate to draw atten-
> tion to his otherwise dull and uninteresting article by an
> outrageous misrepresentation of a public official's views.
>   It would not have been too serious if this falsehood
> had been confined to your paper, but a notorious

exploiter of the gullible and uninformed in the country, Mr. Fred Schwarz, has picked up this statement and given it very wide distribution in this country as a part of his money-raising campaign which has been going on continuously for years.

I think it is unfortunate that a reputable paper such as yours has become the vehicle contributing to the despicable programs sponsored by Mr. Schwarz. For this reason I write you this letter in the hopes that you will correct the statement carried in your newspaper.

J. W. FULBRIGHT
Chairman,
Committee on Foreign Relations,
United States Senate.
Washington.

Denis Warner replied to the letter of Senator Fulbright and gave details of the time, place, and content of the interview which the senator claimed had never taken place. This reply was printed in the *Sydney Morning Herald* on February 24, 1970.

DENIS WARNER'S REPLY

I share Senator Fulbright's misgivings about the campaigns conducted in the United States by Dr. Fred Schwarz.

There is, however, no question that Senator Fulbright made the statement that he now denies. His memory seems short, for, in an earlier protest to the Australian Embassy in Washington about the article, the senator not only denied that he had made the statement but that he had ever talked to me.

I saw him by appointment in his office in the U.S. Senate in March 1967. The appointment was made by the Washington bureau of the "Reporter" magazine. Though the magazine has since closed down, former members of the staff are still in Washington and could no doubt confirm that the appointment was made.

Perhaps the senator failed to identify me as an Australian and was unaware that, in addition to my work for the "Reporter," I also wrote for "The Sydney Morning Herald."

Certainly, in a long career of reporting international affairs I have never talked to a senior public official in any country who was so ready to denounce his own country's policies and the views of senior officials to a foreign newspaperman.

The United States had to get out of Vietnam, he said, because it was inevitably leading to a major war. His country had always been militarily irresponsible, and he suggested that I should talk to a senior serving military officer, who also came from Arkansas, if I doubted him. He was not concerned whether all of South-East Asia became Communist, or countries became Communist, and he cited U.S. relations with Yugoslavia as an example of what the United States might have achieved with North Vietnam if it had pursued more sensible policies.

In a dispatch sent from Washington after the interview and published in Melbourne on March 21, 1967, I contrasted what Senator Fulbright had to say with the deep sensitivity of Senator Mike Mansfield, who also gave me an interview on the same day. In this article, I described Senator Fulbright's remarks as "blunt, direct, and, I can find no other word for it, irresponsible." I have not changed my opinion since.

—Denis Warner

Warner did not report Senator Fulbright's statement in order to support me, since he agreed with the attack on my character and motives made by Fulbright.

Some of my friends and supporters rallied to my defense, as the following two letters indicate:

The *Sydney Morning Herald*

Saturday, February 28, 1970

SIR.—It is unfortunate that, in publishing Senator Fulbright's letter ("Herald," February 24), you should have given hospitality to this unsubstantiated attack on the character of Dr. Fred Schwarz, an attack which, it is plain from Denis Warner's reply, is irrelevant to the veracity or otherwise of the senator's statement on Communism and South-East Asia.

Dr. Schwarz is an Australian of unusual ability and was formerly a medical practitioner in this city. He gave his first public address on the nature of Communism in 1946 to a meeting in Sydney at my invitation, and I have a reasonable knowledge of his attempt to awaken the general public to an awareness of the professed policies of Communism.

He certainly takes a more serious attitude than does Senator Fulbright to the implications for the United States of Communist advances in South-East Asia, but to insinuate, as Senator Fulbright does, that he has mercenary motives in conducting his Christian Anti-Communism Crusade is ludicrous. Nor is it part of Dr. Schwarz's method to engage in the kind of personal denigration that Senator Fulbright has been betrayed into by his evident resentment over Mr. Warner's quoting of him. It is regrettable that the senator should use his responsible position as a platform from which to abuse someone from whose approach he differs.

(The Reverend Canon) D. W. B. ROBINSON, Sydney.

Canon Donald Robinson has been a lifelong friend of Lillian and me. Soon after writing this letter he became Anglican archbishop of Sydney, and served with honor and distinction for many years until his recent retirement.

Another supporter, with whom I have no memory of being personally acquainted, but to whom I am grateful, wrote the following letter to Denis Warner:

April 3, 1970

Mr. Denis Warner
Sydney Morning Herald
Sydney, Australia

Dear Mr. Warner:

I have just received the current newsletter and a form letter from Dr. Fred Schwarz. Both are dated March 15, 1970, and are enclosed. You, the *Sydney Morning Herald,* and the U.S. Senator J. W. Fulbright are subjects of comment in these papers. Dr. Schwarz defends himself very well against Senator Fulbright's slanderous remarks, and I would let it go at that but for a comment of yours in your reply to the senator. You say in the *Herald,* "I share Senator Fulbright's misgivings about the campaigns conducted in the United States by Dr. Schwarz." In other words, you say you approve of the "irresponsible" language used by the Senator in commenting on Dr. Schwarz and his activities. I can not let this pass without reply. I am a longtime small contributor to the Crusade. I have followed its activities closely because I do not wish to be associated with irresponsible persons or activities, and so many charges have been leveled at Dr. Schwarz from the left. All of them false. All, I repeat, All. He has had to weather vicious smears over and over and has done so every time to his credit. You can't possibly talk to Dr. Schwarz and read his newsletters without being impressed by his sincerity, knowledge of Communism, gentle manners, and good common sense and dedication to his cause, a most worthy cause to my mind. There are, of course, liberal-left ideologues, like Senator Fulbright, who get very angry at him for exposing their points of view to the light of reality. They never seem to learn that you can't trust, appease, or negotiate with Communists except from positions of strength, that we must have the will to win over the Communists or we are lost.

Dr. Schwarz speaks highly of you and the *Herald*. He calls you eminent and respected and the *Herald* one of Australia's leading and most responsible newspapers. Did you know that the Christian Anti-Communism Crusade has a branch in Australia (in Sydney) led by his wife, Lillian? Your remark must have been extremely harmful to her anti-Communism activities in Australia, and her sacrifices to stay in Australia separated from her husband in order to bring up her children as loyal Australian citizens. I looked back in my files and enclose a copy of a newsletter dated November 14, 1966, from Dr. Schwarz which contains a photo of his family and tells why he came to the U.S. and why he remains an Australian. It is most revealing in answer to criticisms. Also enclosed is a copy of his book *You Can Trust the Communists (to be Communists)* and a booklet *What Is The Christian Anti-Communism Crusade?*

The magazine, *The Reporter*, impressed me as a radical, liberal-left publication. I would expect them to disapprove of Dr. Schwarz. If you approved of this magazine then we are on totally different wavelengths and unable to communicate meaningfully. You should be reading the *National Review* to balance the conservative view against the liberal. I hope that you and your paper can find it in your heart to withdraw your derogatory remarks about Dr. Schwarz and give him a small boost instead.

Sincerely yours,
Robert R. Hammond

I must depend upon my memory as I report the following anecdote. While this controversy was raging a man approached me following one of the rallies at which I had spoken. He told me that a close relative of his was on Senator Fulbright's staff and that this relative had told him that the senator had sent an emissary to Australia to investigate me. The emissary had returned with the report, "It's no use; he's as clean as a whistle."

The attack upon my character left me emotionally undisturbed. I like to think that this was due to the clarity of my conscience as expressed by William Shakespeare:

Thrice is he armed who hath his quarrel just
And he but naked though locked in steel
Whose conscience with injustice is corrupted

Senator Fulbright played the role of the Pied Piper as described in the poem by Robert Browning, "The Pied Piper of Hamelin." The following stanza describes the result of his "piping."

And ere three shrill notes the piper uttered
You heard as if an army muttered;
And the grumbling grew to a mighty rumbling;
And out of the houses the rats came tumbling.
Great rats, small rats, lean rats, brawny rats,
Brown rats, black rats, gray rats, tawny rats,
Grave old plodders, gay young friskers,
Fathers, mothers, uncles, cousins,
Families by tens and dozens
Brothers, sisters, husbands, wives—
Followed the piper for their lives.

Please pardon my use, or misuse, of poetry. I do not wish to allege or insinuate that all those who responded favorably to the piping of Senator Fulbright were rats, but only that the response was similar.

The statements and activities of some who responded to Fulbright's "piping" follow.

PRESIDENT JOHN F. KENNEDY

When President John F. Kennedy visited Los Angeles on Sunday, November 18, 1961, he made a speech in which he attacked "extremism" and the far Right groups. This speech received great publicity. Here are extracts as reported in *The New York Times,* November 19, 1961:

In the most critical periods of our nation's history, there have always been those on the fringes of our society who have sought to escape their own responsibility by finding a simple solution, an appealing slogan, or a convenient scapegoat.

Good Sense Prevailed

But in time the basic good sense and stability of the great American consensus has always prevailed.

Now we are face to face once again with a period of heightened peril. The risks are great, the burdens heavy, the problems incapable of swift or lasting solution. And under the strains and frustrations imposed by constant tension and harassment, the discordant voices of extremism are heard once again in the land. Men who are unwilling to face up to the danger from without are convinced that the real danger comes from within.

They look suspiciously at their neighbors and their leaders. They call for "a man on horseback" because they do not trust the people. They find treason in our finest churches, in our highest court, and even in the treatment of our water. They equate the Democratic Party with the welfare state, the welfare state with Socialism, and Socialism with Communism. They object quite rightly to politics intruding on the military—but they are anxious for the military to engage in politics.

But you and I and most Americans take a different view of our peril. We know that it comes from without, not within. It must be met by quiet preparedness, not provocative speeches. . . .

Let us not heed these counsels of fear and suspicion.

The distinguished journalist, Tom Wicker, commented:

Mr. Kennedy chose a region in which the John Birch Society had some of its strongest support to make his third and sharpest attack on what he tonight called "the discordant voices of extremism."

The statements of President Kennedy seemed to endorse the delusions of Senator Fulbright, and the campaign of misinformation and slander against the Crusade gained momentum.

The Bible warns us that "Evil communications corrupt good manners" (1 Corinthians 15:33), so the consequences of this storm of misinformation and slander were not surprising.

Those who were uninformed tended to accept the false charges as truth, particularly since the scurrilous charges emanated from persons in responsible governmental positions. No person's judgment is better than the information on which it is based, so many became hostile to the Crusade and to me. The trickle of falsehood grew into a stream, and then a torrent. Many believed the big lie that I was a radical right-wing extremist who was engaged in a nefarious program of character assassination and self-enrichment.

This big lie infected important members of the national news media, the upper echelons of educational institutions, various church dignitaries, and large segments of the liberal intelligentsia. It created a fog of misunderstanding and a climate of hostility that destroyed the consensus that had previously welcomed my exposition of the pathological nature of Communism's doctrines. Henceforth, wherever I went, I faced opposition based upon delusions.

IDEAS HAVE CONSEQUENCES

Some of those who knew the truth were immobilized by the campaign of falsehood. The Crusade and I became "controversial." And since many businessmen had been taught to avoid controversy wherever possible, this neutralized some of our former allies.

One experience drove this lesson home. Prior to the Southern California School of Anti-Communism, when we were planning to hold a promotional dinner for businessmen, we asked the Los Angeles Chamber of Commerce for their mailing list to send out invitations. They agreed without hesitation.

When the school was over and the storm of slander was raging, we decided to invite businessmen to another dinner meeting. We hoped to get support to distribute a Portuguese copy of *You Can Trust the Communists (to be Communists)* to every university student in Brazil.

When Jim Colbert and I visited the chamber we were welcomed with open arms. The chamber officers congratulated us on the school's success and told us that the quality of our education on Communism was far superior to that of the chamber itself. But when we asked for the use of the chamber's mailing list, their hesitation was apparent. One said, "We'll need official permission to do that."

Permission was not granted.

I cannot recall one supporter who became an opponent because of the slander campaign, but some, because of social or financial pressures, were transformed from active into passive supporters.

On the positive side, many who had attended our schools or rallies, or who had heard our message via literature or tape recordings remained courageous friends and supporters. Despite the deluge of falsehood, the stream of truth flowed on. Their number is legion.

Recently while reading the December 2, 1994, edition of the conservative publication *Human Events,* the name "Schwarz" in a caption caught my eye. Naturally, I wondered if it referred to me. This is what I read:

> If all the conservative leaders in the country were polled, probably over 90% would say that they had gotten their start, or at least a huge push, by the influence of Dr. Fred Schwarz and his classic book, *You Can Trust the Communists,* published by Prentice-Hall. That book, along with one or two others, basically kicked off the conservative, anti-Communist revolution started in the late 1950s.

I then noticed that this paragraph was part of a letter written by James C. Bowers. His son Clark is one of my closest friends. Clark became the "Fred and Lillian Schwarz Distinguished Visiting Fellow" at Harvard University. Clark had told me that he was nurtured on the message of *You Can Trust the Communists (to be Communists)*.

As noted previously, the truth produces healthy offspring but the gestation period is sometimes so extended that it tries human patience severely.

MOTIVE FOR SLANDER

Since the stream of misinformation seemed to be coming from the political and information headquarters in New York and Washington, D.C., I decided to visit these cities and expose the Crusade and its message to those who generated public opinion. In my naïveté, I believed that factual evidence would convince rational opponents. It took me some considerable time to discover that the hostility was not based upon the message but upon what the misinformers perceived to be the outcome of the message. With customary optimism I set out for New York.

23

....

The Slanders of Attorney General Mosk

I will be hang'd, if some eternal villain,
Some busy and insinuating rogue,
Some cogging cozening slave, to get some office,
Have not devis'd this slander.
—SHAKESPEARE (*OTHELLO*)

AFTER THE FIRST SAN FRANCISCO Bay Regional School of Anti-Communism, January 29 to February 2, 1962, ended, the attorney general of California, Stanley Mosk, launched an unprovoked attack on the Christian Anti-Communism Crusade's school. On February 5 he appeared on television station KTVU/Channel 2, in Oakland, California, and made the following statement:

I said the Crusade was not a school but a promotion, and was challenged to prove my point or to apologize. I will prove the point.

The sessions have not been organized as a school under the laws of any city or county and none of the alleged instructors have teaching credentials issued by the state of California. Thus, legally, this could not qualify as a school.

274

[AUTHOR'S NOTE: What about the presence on the faculty of Dr. C. C. Trillingham, who was Los Angeles superintendent of schools?]

That this is a promotion is indicated by the fantastic economic nature of the movement. Just listen to these verified figures. For the first 90 days following June 30, 1961, the so-called Crusade took gross receipts in Los Angeles alone in the sum of $311,253. It expended $96,496 in rent, pay to its speakers, advertising, printing, and so forth, leaving a net profit of $214,757. This is indeed big business; nearly a quarter of a million dollars net in 90 days. At that rate, there would be a million dollars a year in just one city.

No one is told, except in generalities, what is happening to the Oakland profits or to the $100,000 taken out of Philadelphia; the $40,000 taken out of Phoenix; and so on, city after city.

No wonder this whole movement has been called "Patriotism for Profit." Those who attended the meetings received a Schwarz price list. If an individual bought one of each available tape and one of each booklet, it would cost him $689.10. There is a presumption in the eyes of these promoters that anyone who fails to buy all this material is uninformed and perhaps unpatriotic. The theme of these entrepreneurs of indignation is that the American policy with respect to Communism is all wrong and that in many instances the policies are implemented by men whose loyalty is suspect.

They tell us we are losing the Cold War. Orators of the radical-right dwell longingly upon such topics as Cuba and Red China, and they say, "Isn't it awful!" But have you ever heard these men describe the tremendous bastion of freedom which we have helped to construct in the common-market countries of Western Europe? Have they told the stories of intense and sustained effort made by the domestic Communist Party to win over minority-group Americans, and how these Americans have com-

pletely spurned the siren call of Communism to remain
steadfastly loyal to America? Do they tell of the steady
diminution of the strength and influence of the Communist Party in the United States?

And when they talk about Berlin, do they point out
that the flow of refugees is from Communism to freedom, and not vice versa; that it is freedom, not Communism, which has "laid ahold" on the hearts and minds of
these people; and that it is freedom for which they risk
their very lives?

Let's discuss patriotism. The orators of the radical-
right have tried to preempt the term "patriotism." It
reminds me of the time that we almost let the Communists preempt the word "peace."

Is it patriotic to demand that the Chief Justice of the
United States be impeached? Is it patriotic to sow dissension by insisting that some of the very highest leaders of
the United States are disloyal? Is it patriotic to debase
free and open debate by heckling and shouting and hooting? Is it patriotic to deride democracy by calling it a
perennial fraud? Does it help America or hurt America?

Many good people have written to me and asked,
"How can I fight Communism? Are there any alternatives to these promotions?" Of course there are. There
are just as many alternatives as there are free men. Each
individual must be more than anti-Communist. He must
find for himself through our legitimate institutions how
he can constructively serve America and liberty and
democracy.

Let us turn aside from these shrill-voiced apostles of
despair. The leading anti-Communist is not to be found
among them. He is to be found in the White House. He
is the president of the United States. Every president of
the United States.

In these difficult times, let us rally to his support and
to the support of our government, our churches, our
schools, our universities, where these defeatists sow dis-

sension. Let them reap a reaffirmation of faith in our free institutions. The radical-rightist suggests defeatism in his slogan, "I'd rather be dead than Red." The thoughtful American responds, "I intend to be alive and free."

If this statement had been made by a person of lesser stature than the attorney general of California, it would have been laughable to scorn. It was puerile. He seems to have been unaware that the word "school" has many meanings. Nothing, to his mind, can be rightly called a school unless it has been *legally* classified as such and unless the teachers have been issued credentials by the state.

The *Random House Dictionary* includes in its definition of a school, "Any place, situation, etc., tending to teach anything," and "Any group of persons having common attitudes and beliefs." Mosk attacked the school, its sponsors, and its faculty. He implied dishonest motives by dubbing our efforts "Patriotism for Profit," but failed to name anyone receiving the profit, and thereby he cast suspicion on all associated with the school.

I presented the following rebuttal:

> This brief speech contains *sixteen* distortions of the truth, either by direct misstatement or obvious inference. This statement discusses two themes:
> 1. The finances of the Schools of Anti-Communism.
> 2. The message of the schools.
> In each case he gives an inaccurate and biased account.

Finances

> Where his figures are taken from the published audits of the Southern California School of Anti-Communism, they are accurate. His other figures are false.
>
> The Christian Anti-Communism Crusade did not take $100,000 out of Philadelphia. I challenge Mr. Mosk to give the source of these figures. Many of his other alleged financial facts are equally incorrect.

The books of the Christian Anti-Communism Crusade have recently been audited by both the federal
government and the state of California. This is in addition to a regular annual audit by a CPA, which has been
published.

The Message of the School

With reference to the message of the school, Mr.
Mosk criticizes things that were never said or done at
any School of Anti-Communism we have conducted and
implies that these were features of the school. Every
message given at San Francisco Bay Region School of
Anti-Communism was recorded, and the following can
be easily proved.

1. It was never suggested that the Chief Justice of the
United States be impeached.
2. It was never suggested that some of the very highest leaders of the United States are disloyal.
3. There was no heckling, shouting, and hooting to
debase free and open debate.
4. Democracy was exalted and was not called a
perennial fraud.

Attorney General Stanley Mosk created a straw man
without substance to demolish.

As Mosk continued his campaign of slander, we considered suing
him for libel. In those days the Supreme Court had not delivered the
Sullivan Decision, which made public figures immune from conviction for libel unless malice could be proved.

An attorney, Herbert Sturdy, contacted Mosk, who sent him
the documents on which he was basing his charges. Not one docu-
ment referred to any statement or activity of the Christian Anti-
Communism Crusade or any of its Schools of Anti-Communism.
They all dealt with other alleged "right-wing extremist" movements.
Mosk said he would consider making a retraction.

While the negotiations were proceeding, the statute of limitations for legal action expired, whereupon Mosk terminated all discussion.

Stanley Mosk later became a justice of the Supreme Court of California.

I venture to add this anecdote. Sometime later, Mosk was under consideration for a responsible federal appointment. I was visited by an agent of the FBI who asked me if I had any information to confirm a charge that Mosk had been "pro-Communist." I replied that I had no knowledge of any pro-Communist attitudes or activities of his, but that I did know one thing from personal experience. He was a liar.

Mosk did not receive the appointment.

24

....

The Reuther Memorandum

The dictum that truth always triumphs over persecution,
is one of those pleasant falsehoods which men repeat
one after another till they pass into commonplaces,
but which all experience refutes.
—JOHN STUART MILL, 1806–1873 (ON LIBERTY)

I WAS NOT A POLITICAL partisan, and I was not fully cognizant
of the power of political passions. But I soon discovered that these
passions can overwhelm honesty, reason, and truth, and transform
cultured and sophisticated individuals into rabid primitives. Political
passions transformed professed opponents of "McCarthyism" into
ardent practitioners of "reverse McCarthyism," those who practiced
guilt by association, semantic sabotage, impugnment of motives,
condemnation before trial, and flagrant falsehood.

As previously mentioned, I discovered the political motivation of
the anti-Schwarz campaign by hindsight. I did not find it overnight.
The conclusion that a deliberate political campaign was taking place
was reached after an accumulation of convincing circumstantial
evidence. The alternative possibility—that informed, intelligent,
patriotic, and successful national leaders actually believed that the

ineffable nonsense that Robert Welch and the John Birch Society presented was as great a danger to the security of America as the nuclear bombs of the Communists—did not, and does not, seem credible.

In a newsletter dated November 1963, I wrote:

> During the past eighteen months a ferocious campaign has been waged relentlessly to discredit and destroy the Christian Anti-Communism Crusade. There has been no limit to the dishonesty practiced by participants in this slanderous attack. It has been very difficult to discern the motives of some of those who have taken part. It is easy to understand the hostility of the Communists, but many of those who have joined in the attack on the Crusade have records of hostility to Communism rather than sympathy toward it. Their attitude has been puzzling in the extreme. Light has now been shed on this perplexing problem through the publication of a memorandum prepared by Walter and Victor Reuther of the United Workers Union and submitted to the Justice Department on December 19, 1961.

The memorandum was first revealed in the book *The Far Right*, by Donald Janson and Bernard Eismann. They wrote:

> In the fall of 1961, Walter Reuther, President of the United Auto Workers' Union, and a Vice President of the AFL-CIO, discussed the matter [the alleged danger from right-wing extremists] with Attorney General Robert Kennedy and promised to write a memorandum for him.

Thus the Reuther Memorandum was born. Judging from the events of the previous eighteen months, it appears that this memorandum was instrumental in forming the official policy of the administration toward the Christian Anti-Communism Crusade.

LACK OF DEFINITION OF RADICAL RIGHT

No attempt is made to define the radical right. The Christian Anti-Communism Crusade is simply classified, without a breath of evidence, as an extremist radical right organization. The authors moreover reveal great ignorance of the history, philosophy, and general activity of the Crusade. No hint is given in the document that they are even aware of our worldwide, anti-Communist, educational work.

The memorandum states: "All of these radical right organizations have the same general line. The danger to America is domestic Communism. While their particular traitor will vary from Harry Hopkins to George Marshall; from President Truman to President Eisenhower; from Senator Fulbright to some labor leader; there is no question that anybody even slightly to the left of Senator Goldwater is suspect. They traffic in fear. Treason in high places is their slogan, and slander is their weapon."

By placing the Christian Anti-Communism Crusade in this category, the Reuthers proved that they themselves were skilled in the techniques of slander. The Christian Anti-Communism Crusade had an intelligent, effective anti-Communist program in twenty-one countries extending from Japan to Mexico. The Crusade had long since enabled George Thomas, an American-educated Indian and a Christian freedom-loving patriot, to establish a daily newspaper in Kerala, India, and to cooperate with other groups in the democratization of a Communist state government. It had been active in the sugar and rice plantations of British Guiana, teaching workers what they might expect from a Communist takeover. These activities gave rise to repeated attacks on the Crusade in the Communist press of the entire world. About all this the Reuther brothers were silent, and I suspect their silence was due to their ignorance.

The memorandum proposed practical measures to destroy the financial support of the Crusade. One was that the IRS investigate "right-wing organizations" in order to rescind their tax-deductible status. "Schwarz's Christian Anti-Communism Crusade" was specifically mentioned.

Benson's National Education Program, Schwarz'
Christian Anti-Communist Crusade, Hargis' Christian

Crusade and William Volker Fund, Inc., are among the radical right groups which are reported to have federal tax exemptions. It would appear highly doubtful, to say the least, that any or all of these groups properly qualify for a federal tax exemption. Prompt revocation in a few cases might scare off a substantial part of the big money now flowing into these tax exempt organizations.

The proposal of Reuther was followed by an IRS audit of the Crusade. We welcomed it.

In the summer of 1962, auditors representing the federal government and the state of California thoroughly investigated the financial records of the Crusade. They soon discovered that big business was not the primary source of support for the Crusade, but small gifts from thousands of devoted donors. They also discovered that a substantial portion of the Crusade income was sent abroad to teach the true nature of Communism in numerous countries.

The auditors also investigated whether the Crusade was engaged in political activity. They found no evidence of political activity or financial misconduct by the Crusade. The attempt to use the IRS to destroy the Crusade failed miserably.

25

....

The Victims of the Lie

One of the most striking differences between a cat and a lie
is that a cat has only nine lives.
—MARK TWAIN, 1835–1910 (*PUDD'NHEAD WILSON*)

Matilda told such Dreadful Lies,
It made one Gasp and Stretch one's Eyes;
Her Aunt, who, from her Earliest Youth,
Had kept a Strict Regard for Truth,
Attempted to Believe Matilda;
The effort very nearly killed her.
—HILLAIRE BELLOC, 1870–1953 (*MATILDA*)

ONCE THE ELEPHANTS HAVE CRASHED through a protective
fence, lesser animals have no difficulty in following. After the barriers of truth and intellectual integrity were breached by the attacks
that emanated from the administration, a herd of smaller animals
followed. Some of these were predators but many were just going
along with the stampede. The participants in the stampede included
members of the U.S. Congress as indicated by the following statement of Ohio's Senator Stephen M. Young, made under parliamen-
tary privilege, on August 7, 1962:

MR. YOUNG of Ohio: Mr. President, the increased
activity in the last few years of what is commonly
referred to as the radical right, or the right-wing lunatic
fringe, and the publicity given it has proven to be a vir-
tual gold mine for a few opportunistic rabble rousers.
These circuit riders of the new anti-Communist evangelism have discovered that spreading their messages of
prejudice and hate can be a very profitable occupation.

One of the foremost among them is Fred Charles
Schwarz, a part-time doctor from Australia, who in the
United States has become a plain medicine man. The
cure-alls of this witch doctor are fear, suspicion, hate,
and hysteria. He is a flamboyant faker.

Schwarz recently announced that he is bringing his
show known now as the Christian Anti-Communism
Crusade to my home city of Cleveland, Ohio, where he
will stage a 5-day anti-Communist school. These so-
called schools are in reality exercises in revivalist emotion and hysteria rather than exercises in logic and
understanding. His teachers are for the most part
extremists of the radical right who see Communists
under every bed. Also associated with this witch doctor
may be a few retired high-ranking military officers who
want our Nation to wage preventive war tomorrow, if
not today-plus some plain old-fashioned rabble
rousers. . . .

Unfortunately, Dr. Schwarz and his instructors have
very little to say against the threat of aggression from
the Soviet Union and Red China. They retreat from
emphasis on opposition to the grave Communist aggres-
sions from the Soviet Union and Red China. Instead,
they prefer to denounce Communists at home, where
they are weakest and well under control. They try to create the suspicion that many of our neighbors are Communists or Communist sympathizers.

In an ominous voice, this unscrupulous demagogue,
Fred Charles Schwarz, opened his recent address in

Cleveland stating that he was repeating the words of
Nikita Khrushchev, "Tomorrow the Red Flag will fly
over the United States." Of course, he is reporting the
big lie. He could not prove where and when Khrushchev
made that boast, if he ever did. In his meetings, he
spends most of his time denouncing Communists he
claims are boring from within. Of course, no one in the
audience asked the speaker regarding the recent report
of the Federal Bureau of Investigation on the decline of
the Communist Party in the United States.

(*Congressional Record*—Senate, August 7, 1962)

This tirade of falsehood bore the imprimatur of the U.S. Senate.

The stampede included major elements of the news media such as
Newsweek magazine and CBS television, faculty members of various educational institutions, leaders of liberal churches, and sundry
authors.

The central delusion of the slanderers was that the Crusade and I
were leading an extremist right-wing political crusade and that the
Christian Anti-Communism Crusade was the ideological twin of the
John Birch Society.

Examples abound. Here are a few of them.

THE CBS PROGRAM "THUNDER ON THE RIGHT"

A team from CBS television, led by Bill Leonard, who later
became president of CBS News, attended the Anti-Communism
School held in St. Petersburg, Florida, November 27 to December 1,
1961. This team recorded the entire school program on 35mm film.
The subsequent telecast pieced together selected fragments of the
proceedings.

The team was courteous and friendly, and Bill Leonard was
charming. He assured me that he was unbiased and said that he
would be pleased to sit down with me so that we could watch the
program together when it was telecast.

Impressed with his sincerity, I shrugged off warnings from friends
that the program would misrepresent the Crusade and its message.

My friend and colleague Bill Strube was in Hawaii when he saw the telecast. He immediately called me to say that the program was an attack on the school, but I was unconvinced.

But then I saw the program. Bill Strube was right. The CBS team had recorded thirty hours of lectures delivered at the school, and the televised program included about ten minutes of carefully selected material to confirm the pre-reached conclusion that the Crusade was a right-wing extremist organization.

The CBS program was not in fact devoted to the Crusade's Anti-Communism School at all. It featured the policies and activities of a number of "right-wing" organizations including the school. Once the school had been classified as "right-wing extremist," the damage was done.

I later told Bill Leonard that the central mistake of his program had been to classify the Crusade as "right-wing extremist," and I illustrated this as follows:

Let us assume that CBS television had produced a program called "Criminal Organizations of America," had included the Salvation Army in that category and then showed members of the Salvation Army engaged in fund-raising. Even though the scene was genuine, would this be a fair presentation of the nature and ministry of the Salvation Army? The inclusion of the Army in such a program condemned it in advance. Similarly, the inclusion of the Crusade in the program "Thunder on the Right" was condemnation in advance.

I immediately dispatched the following letter to Bill Leonard.

Mr. Bill Leonard
C.B.S.
485 Madison Avenue
New York City, New York

Dear Bill:

My confidence in my judgment of character is severely shaken. I have seen the CBS Reports television program "Thunder on the Right" and it did what so many of my friends warned me it would do. Whenever they warned me to be careful, I replied that I had met and talked with you and that, if the presentation was not objective and fair, I was the world's worst judge of character. I consider the program the most effective forgery by film I have ever seen.

When you first contacted me, I told you that I would cooperate fully if the desire was to be objective and factual but that I had no interest if conclusions had already been reached and selective material was required to illustrate these conclusions. You assured me this was not the case. Apparently the decision had already been made that we were an extremist right-wing organization and should be thus reported. When the decision was made to concentrate on me as a pitchman I do not know.

I am happy to see that you were not the major commentator. I would like to think that your responsibility was limited. As far as I am concerned, the only honest portion of the entire film as it relates to me was the part where you questioned me concerning the accusation that our anti-Communism schools gave indoctrination, not education.

I was presented in the film in various scenes. As I recall them, they were:

1. Selling books.

2. Bragging about the results of the Los Angeles school.

3. Talking about taking an offering. No hint of the purpose of the offering was given anywhere. Apparently this may have destroyed the image it was desired to create.

4. Teaching how to spell "dialectical."

5. Speaking via television to the students of the high schools in the area. It is my impression that the message I was heard giving was not the message I gave on this occasion. Could you let me know if this is correct, as I do not wish to misjudge?

6. Answering your question concerning education or indoctrination.

Nowhere was there any intelligent presentation of the message which consumes the great majority of the time at the schools. This I consider basic dishonesty.

In spite of this, I am glad that the program was presented. I am hopeful that I will be able to secure a copy of the film and utilize it as an example of the use of the fine techniques for dishonest purposes.

If I have been harsh in my judgments, I hope you will enlighten me concerning any facts of which I am unaware.

Yours very sincerely,
Fred Schwarz
President
Christian Anti-Communism Crusade

I also sent this letter to the president of CBS television.

The President
CBS Television
485 Madison Avenue
New York City, New York

Sir:

I viewed your program "Thunder on the Right" with astonishment tinged with reluctant admiration. I consider it the most effective "forgery by film" I have seen. By the process of selection and elimination, an entirely false picture of the Christian Anti-Communism Crusade and my message was presented.

The Christian Anti-Communism Crusade was classified as an extremist right-wing organization. No evidence was submitted for this classification. The message of the Crusade was completely ignored. The practical worldwide projects of the Crusade for which the offerings are received was not even mentioned.

I apply for equal time on your television stations to dispel the false image you created.

Could the Christian Anti-Communism Crusade purchase a 16 MM film presentation of the program? I
would like to use it at our anti-Communism schools to
illustrate great technical proficiency in the service of
dishonesty.

Yours very sincerely,
Fred Schwarz
President
Christian Anti-Communism Crusade
FCS/ed

P.S. I have enclosed a copy of this letter to the Federal
Communications Commission, Washington, D.C.

After receiving his letter Bill told me, "You sure can write one hell
of a letter." CBS refused to sell a copy of the program to me.

As a commentator on the CBS Radio Network, Bill Leonard, on
December 9, 1961, delivered this much more informative and favorable report of my activities. It included:

This is Bill Leonard with an analysis of the news for
the CBS Radio Network.

This week in Nashville, Tenn., 2,300 persons struggled through a driving rainstorm to reach the War
Memorial Auditorium, where for some three hours they
listened to an anti-Communist rally dominated by Dr.
Fred Schwarz, an Australian preacher, one-time doctor,
and currently the president of the Anti-Communism
Crusade.

Schwarz would have been surprised at anything less
than a packed house, and by anything less than a series
of interruptions for cheers and applause during the
course of his 90-minute sermon on the Communist Blue-
print for World Conquest. For he is currently enjoying
such a vogue that he is leaving the nation's other professional and semi-professional anti-Communists far in his
wake. At a time when the so-called right-wing political
revival, coupled with a growing national anxiety over

the Communist threat, has provided a fertile ground for all sorts of political pitchmen to plow, Schwarz has been making his competitors—if that's the word—look like rank amateurs at the game. . . .

Schwarz came to national attention some weeks earlier when his Crusade packed Hollywood Bowl attended by and supported by a large number of film and industrial luminaries. It was in Hollywood that C.D. Jackson, of *Life* magazine, apologized profusely and publicly for a *Life* article about Dr. Schwarz—and the story of that apology has become a juicy highlight of Dr. Schwarz's fascinating routine.

The success of Dr. Schwarz—and there is no reason to think he has yet reached his peak of renown—may be explained by two things. First, in an area in which persuasive oratory has been noticeably absent, Dr. Schwarz is a spellbinder. He's a stocky bundle of energy with a classic Australian twang, well trained in the evangelical techniques. He makes exceedingly good listening. But perhaps more important, is the content—some would say the lack of content—of Dr. Schwarz's remarks. Although he has been placed by much of the press in the category of those who maximize the role of Communist recruitment and subversion within America, he vigorously denies that this is where he belongs. And, in fact, he would be the first to stress his "program" is not only not a right-wing program, but not really a program at all. In his own words it "stresses the magnitude of the external Communist danger, the necessity for personal integrity, courage, study of Communism and devotion to freedom, at the same time acknowledging allegiance to Christian doctrine."

At the popular level the apparently non-political tone of his exhortation have made it possible for him to enlist enthusiastic supporters on a much broader base than the so-called "lunatic fringe" of the professional anti-Communists.

Despite our friendliness, Bill Leonard never acknowledged specifically that classifying the Crusade as "right-wing extremist" in the program "Thunder on the Right" had been a mistake.

SANITY RETAINED

In the midst of the campaign of slander some critics retained their intellectual integrity and based their criticism upon observation and research. One such was the journalist and author Fletcher Knebel, whose article, "Rightist Revival," was published in *Look* on March 13, 1962.

Before writing his critique, Knebel took the unusual step of interviewing me as well as actually attending Crusade rallies.

In his report he frankly acknowledged that his criticism was not based upon what I said but upon the outcome of what I said. And he refrained from ad hominem attacks. He wrote:

> Dr. Schwarz, 49-year-old Australian physician and lay Baptist preacher, is a witty, knowledgeable, and articulate speaker who stokes his Crusade with evangelical fervor. After firing the West and parts of the South, he will invade New York City in June. He also plans to found an anti-Communist university in this country.
>
> The Crusade is no personal moneymaking venture for Dr. Schwarz. He says he takes only $5,000 in salary. The Crusade also pays all his expenses, including hotels, food, clothes, and travel. His wife in Australia receives $5,400 annually as a secretary in the Crusade office. The bulk of the CACC contributions defrays costs of the anti-Communism schools, staff salaries, upkeep of a big new headquarters in Long Beach, Calif., and such projects as sponsoring an anti-Communist newspaper in India and a mission headquarters in Japan.
>
> Dr. Schwarz considers it unfair and, in some contexts, libelous, to bracket his message with that of the right-wing. His message capsuled: Communism will seize the United States by 1973, unless we alter policy radically.

Great military budgets and massive foreign aid have
failed to do the job. Communism marches on, in Cuba,
Laos, the Congo. We need a fresh approach.

It is true that very little of what Dr. Schwarz utters
could be classified as right-wing. Why then is he mentioned in this article (which is titled "The Rightist
Revival")? Because this writer is convinced, after more
than 100 interviews on the ramparts of the right, that
the Christian Anti-Communism Crusade is by far the
most important single factor in the rightist revival. In the
wake of Dr. Schwarz's immense rallies and "anticommu-
nism schools" sprout militant "study groups" that
expand, subdivide, and multiply like human cells. The
Rev. James D. Colbert, vice-president of the CACC, says
the Crusade itself has founded 5,000 study groups.
Starting with basically sound Schwarz material, many
"students" go on to find Communists in the White
House, the income tax sapping America for a Communist coup, and Red plots behind such proposals as coun-
tywide governments for municipalities.

Dr. Schwarz says his mission is to "educate," and
declares he has no answers. It is for others, he says, to
find methods to halt the Communist menace. Thus, in
the wake of his emotional rallies, he leaves a vacuum
into which missionaries of the far right promptly pour.
Dr. Schwarz says this isn't his fault. He urges that
churches should guide the study groups to keep extremists from gaining control. . . .

In sum, Dr. Schwarz is like the man who warns that a
forest fire is raging toward town from all points of the
compass, but shrugs his shoulders when asked how to
put it out. "I don't believe in giving the government
advice."

Knebel argues that because I sounded the alarm and then failed to
give instructions to those whom I alarmed, I was favoring the activities of real "right wingers."

Knebel likens me to a "man who warns that a forest fire is raging toward town from all points of the compass, but shrugs his shoulders when asked how to put it out." I plead guilty and point out that such a man is performing a valuable service even if he merely warns. He does not need to be an experienced fire fighter himself. His information could help guide the fire fighters of the community.

I am reminded of the well-known poem, "Horatius at the Bridge," by Lord Thomas Babington MacAuley. He describes the scene in Rome as the invading army of Tuscans, under the leadership of Lars Porsena, drew near.

> Just then a scout came flying,
> All wild with haste and fear:
> "To Arms! to Arms! Sir Consul
> Lars Porsena is here."
> On the low hills to westward
> The consul fixed his eye,
> And saw the swarthy storm of dust
> Rise fast along the sky.

Apart from the general advice "To Arms," the scout did not advise further. The designing of the plan to combat the forces of Lars Porsena was left to the Consul and Horatius, the keeper of the bridge.

I again make reference to my self-identification as a pathologist reporting the results of his investigation of a deadly disease, Communism.

My criticism of the article by Knebel is that he seemed to have little understanding of the role of a pathologist, which is to study the organisms and conditions that are causing the disease and so inform the physician. The pathologist is not expected to treat the disease or even advise the physician about treatment. The truth may be unpleasant, but should this cause the pathologist to make the report less alarming?

To extend the medical analogy a little further: Society is comparable to a living organism such as the human body. The body is made up of minute individual cells with a common origin, but they develop special characteristics and functions. One important function of certain cells is to serve the body's immune system.

The immune system of society consists of such institutions as the military, the police, and the courts. Who and what should direct the activities of these bodies? In a democratic society the ultimate source of authority is the people.

Some elements of the news media subordinated truth to prejudice and bias. This puzzled me initially.

As already confessed, I was politically naive and I believed that most of the attacks on the Crusade and me were due to misinformation and that a presentation of true information would lead to more honest and less biased reporting.

This was partly true: several major segments of the news media did change their attitude toward the Crusade, such as the magazines *Life* and *Time* and the newspaper *The New York Times.* Some did not. *Newsweek,* for one, demonstrated persistent bias and contempt for the truth. For example: An election in the Dominican Republic took place in October 7, 1963. Juan Bosch was elected president and subsequently ousted by a lightning-fast bloodless military coup.

NEWSWEEK

In its edition dated October 7, 1963, *Newsweek* wrote:

> In his short reign, Bosch really accomplished little,
> but he talked a lot, and his talk sounded radical to both
> the army and the rich. Even before his election, he was
> denounced as a "Marxist–Leninist," and afterward,
> rightist agitators, including members of the California-
> based Christian Anti-Communist Crusade, tried to stir
> up trouble. Their charges were picked up by some U.S.
> newsmen.

This report was egregiously false. At that time, the Crusade had never had a representative or speaker in the Dominican Republic, and I have no knowledge of any Crusade literature having been distributed there. I knew nothing of the political philosophy and policies of Juan Bosch. I hardly knew his name. I sent the following letter to *Newsweek:*

> Your edition of October 7 adds another false statement to the many your magazine has already published concerning the Christian Anti-Communism Crusade. No rightist agitators are spokesmen for the Christian Anti-Communism Crusade, and this organization has never tried to stir up trouble for President Juan D. Bosch of the Dominican Republic, nor have we denounced him as a Marxist–Leninist.
>
> Yours very sincerely,
Fred Schwarz
President
Christian Anti-Communism Crusade

I received no reply, and no correction was published in the magazine. Subsequent protests were also ignored.

I was so incensed by the magazine's censorship and falsehood I refused to accept interviews from its reporters. I remember an occasion when a *Newsweek* reporter phoned me while I was in San Francisco. I told him that his magazine owed me an apology. He said, "That will have to come from New York." I said, "Until it does I have nothing to say to you." I am still waiting.

The silence of the *Newsweek* editors contrasts with the policy of *The New York Times* which is to reply to every responsible communication.

LIFE AND *TIME*

Though the first reports of the magazines *Life* and *Time* about the Crusade's lectures and schools were biased and derogatory, they were later retracted and replaced by fair comment.

In its September 1, 1961, edition, *Life* magazine published this statement:

> A new kind of "revival meeting" serving the nonreligious ends of an outfit called the "Christian Anti-

Communism Crusade" is being held with full hullabaloo
and political portent in Los Angeles this week. Like nine
other "crusades" in U.S. cities during the last year, it is
presided over by Frederick C. Schwarz, 48, an Australian evangelist gone secular.

Schwarz preaches doomsday by Communism in 1973
unless every American starts distrusting his neighbor
as a possible Communist or "comsymp" [Communist
sympathizer].

I did not contact *Life* magazine personally but many others did,
among them Patrick Frawley. The publisher of the magazine, C. D.
Jackson, acknowledged the article's misrepresentation and volun-
teered to make a public retraction. He flew from New York to Los
Angeles and appeared on the program "Hollywood's Answer to
Communism" where he said:

It is a great privilege to be able to be with you
tonight, because it affords me an opportunity to align
Life magazine in a very personal way with a number of
stalwart fighters—Congressman Walter Judd, Senator
Dodd, Dr. Schwarz, and many others—against the first
implacable foe our country has ever had—imperial,
aggressive Communism.

I underscore "the first implacable foe our country has
ever had" because this is a concept most Americans find
difficult to absorb.

. . . .

Never has the famous quotation from Francis Bacon
written over 350 years ago had more instant application
or current reality—"knowledge is power."

You have here with you a man who has dedicated his
life to helping disseminate that knowledge, and therefore
to helping endow our nation with that power.

That man is Dr. Fred Schwarz and, like all dedicated
men, he will be subject to over-simplified misinterpretation. Regretfully, my own magazine recently published

such an over-simplified misinterpretation. I know that you are not interested in how that happened, but I hope you will be interested in my statement that I believe we were wrong and that I am profoundly sorry.

I have read Dr. Schwarz's book *You Can Trust the Communists—To Do Exactly as They Say*, and I can think of no more appropriate way to close my remarks tonight than by quoting from Dr. Schwarz's book.

This happens to be one of the best books analyzing the Communist menace I have read. It points so skillfully to the measures which a free nation must take to win against Communism, including the importance of preserving its own freedoms and its own high moral principles to make the effort a success.

I commend this book to all of you who are here tonight and who are listening on TV.

And I want to quote briefly from its closing chapter.

The Communists are supremely confident of complete victory. They claim that their victory is assured because of the quality of character in democratic lands. They affirm that the environment generating this character is Capitalism in its dying phase. Since Capitalism is dying, it creates character without survival virtue. They are convinced that the average citizen of the Free World is so intellectually lazy and dishonest, so greedy and selfish, so intoxicated with entertainment, so consumed with his immediate problems that no matter how clear the evidence of impending doom, that evidence will never be acknowledged, and the organizational steps for survival will never be taken. We categorically reject this claim. We are not the helpless victims of our environment, doomed to destruction. The fault lies not in our environment but in ourselves. The political, judicial, educational, and cultural organizations of the free society can function only when the individual citizens have enlightened minds and are dedicated to the foundations of freedom. The basic responsibility rests on each one. Material forces alone do not determine the destinies of

men. The resources of an infinite God can change the
balance of material assets. These resources are liberated
thought the prayer, the sacrifice, and the intelligence
organizations of people filled with the love of God. Fun-
damentally, the problem is a moral and spiritual one.
The foundations of freedom must be girded with a
moral and spiritual revival. As free men humbly seek
God and present their bodies, mind, and hearts to their
country and the cause of all mankind, we may well
believe that tyranny shall not triumph and freedom shall
not perish from the earth. With fascinating parallelism
we Americans find ourselves thrust back to the days of
our founding fathers. As they strove to create our
nation, we must strive to preserve it. Most Americans
glibly remember the opening lines of the Declaration of
Independence about "life, liberty, and the pursuit of
happiness." Neither that life nor that liberty nor the
opportunity to pursue happiness would have been
achieved had it not been for the overwhelming determination of the founding fathers, expressed in their closing
words—words which we would all do well to remember
today:

And for the support of this Declaration, with a firm
reliance on the protection of Divine Providence, we
mutually pledge to each other our Lives, or Fortunes,
and our sacred Honor.

C. D. Jackson's manuscript
Reported in *The Los Angeles Times*,
October 17, 1961

During a private conversation, Mr. Jackson told me that he had
been impressed by the following passage in the last chapter of my
book, *You Can Trust the Communists (to be Communists)*.

There is always the temptation to try to form a totalitarian organization modelled on Communism. After I
had spoken at a school in Eugene, Oregon, I received
a letter from one of the students which began,

"Dr. Schwarz, you hypocrite! You came to us and you showed us the power of Communist organization, their dedication, their devotion, and their discipline. You told us how the Communist leader can sit and order every individual to do a certain task, and how the individual obeys whatever the cost. Then you start an organization with a membership fee of $10 a year, and life membership at $100. How will you ever combat them like that? Let's form an organization like that of the Communists, where we have discipline and authority and where people do what is necessary at whatever cost to themselves."

I replied that I appreciated the spirit of his letter. I did not object to his calling me a hypocrite, for I often felt that way myself. Yet I was afraid that he did not fully understand the conflict between totalitarian organization and the Christian liberty of conscience. This liberty of conscience itself should direct the individual into unselfish service to fulfill his responsibility toward God and to the preservation of that liberty for all men. Any organization that flouts this principle is anti-libertarian and anti-Christian. Discipline must be largely self-discipline; sacrifice must be voluntary, not compulsory. The mainspring of our organization must be from within the character of free citizens.

I cannot compel you to do anything in this struggle. God Himself renounced His right to compel. It depends upon voluntary choice and free will.

I also had an interview with Henry Luce, the founder and ruler of the publishing empire that included *Life, Time,* and *Fortune* magazines. I am not sure who interviewed who. In any case, our conversation was cordial. See chapter 20.

THE NEW YORK TIMES

The first articles on the Crusade published by *The New York Times* were written by Cabell Phillips. They abounded in factual errors and slanderous statements. *The Times* later acknowledged some of his errors and promised to be more accurate in the future. It kept that promise.

MINISTERIAL SLANDER

Meanwhile the campaign of slander raged. I was frequently accused of being responsible for every irresponsible statement that alleged opponents of Communism made.

In a television program from Chicago, Illinois, the respected Methodist bishop of Los Angeles, Bishop Kennedy, publicly accused me of advocating that Earl Warren, the Chief Justice of the U.S. Supreme Court, should be hanged. His statement was completely false but he refused to retract it. Here is the truth:

Following the remarkable success of the Southern California Anti-Communism School, a group of citizens decided to present a similar program with a more positive message. It would feature freedom instead of anti-Communism and be called "Project Alert."

PROJECT ALERT

They recruited some of the supporters of our Anti-Communism School to serve on the sponsoring committee and invited me to be a member. I declined as politely as I could and had no connection whatever with the project.

Project Alert was held in the Los Angeles Shrine Auditorium in December 1961. Though several of the members of the faculty of the Southern California Anti-Communism School delivered lectures, I was not one of them. Nor did I attend any session.

At that time the John Birch Society was advocating the impeachment of Earl Warren. One of the speakers at the forum, Colonel Mitchell Paige, USMC, ret., a winner of the Medal of Honor, told the audience:

> There are those today who would impeach Earl Warren, the chief justice of the United States Supreme Court. After having read some 16 or 17 of the decisions handed down by this highest court in the land, I was so appalled

> I felt that impeachment is not the proper penalty but
> rather, it appears to me, a more deserving punishment
> would be hanging.

The remark was greeted with hoots of laughter from the crowd.
At an off-stage press conference, Colonel Paige said his "hanging"
remark was rhetorical. He added, "I'm not questioning his loyalty,
but the soundness of his decisions."

School officials publicly repudiated the remark.

Later in the day, as he returned to the stage to make an apology,
he was greeted with loud applause and half of the Shrine audience
stood. He said, "I want to apologize for stating I would hang Earl
Warren. Really, it isn't my feeling that he should be hanged. Our
country is founded on sound principles, and I'm not going to try to
change them."

Press Telegram, December 14, 1961, and *The Los Angeles Times,*
December 14, 1961

The episode was widely publicized, and, astonishingly, my opponents blamed me for it. Bishop Kennedy was one of them.

I was frequently accused of "looking for a Communist under
every bed." To anyone with the slightest knowledge of my message
this was ludicrous; I constantly drew attention to Lenin's statement,
"fewer but better," and emphasized that the Communists were an
elite minority who magnified their personal power by harnessing
"social forces."

A social force is any motivating idea, emotion or grievance that
is shared by a significant number of people. The Communists
formed fronts that were allegedly devoted to the propagation of
the idea or the mitigation of the grievance. For example, one
shared idea and emotion was the "desire for peace." A shared
grievance was the existence of poverty. The Communists operated
as follows: "Find out what the people want, promise it to them,
go to work to get it for them temporarily, and enlist their support
in order to come to power over them, and install the Communist
dictatorship."

Communist fronts enabled Communists to transform many
unsuspecting people into temporary and involuntary servants.

I explained that most of those involved in a front were non-Communists and many even anti-Communists. I classified them as fellow travelers, sympathizers, pseudo-liberals, or dupes.

Recent world events testify to the validly of this message. Consider the fate of those potent organizations, the World Peace Council, the U.S. Peace Council, and the World Federation of Trade Unions. Soon after the Soviet Union disintegrated and its Communist party ceased to support them, they collapsed financially.

The hostility of one prominent Methodist minister in Los Angeles was surpassed only by his ignorance. He charged that my opposition to Communism had failed because I had not discovered and exposed a single Communist. I regarded this as a compliment. I had no desire to investigate and castigate anybody. During my career as an anti-Communist, which extends for more than fifty-five years as I write, I don't believe that I have falsely accused one person of being a Communist. My concern has been with the ideas and activities of the people who identify themselves as being Communists—people such as Marx, Engels, Lenin, Stalin, Khrushchev, Mao Tse-tung, and Gus Hall.

As far as I am aware I have been accused of falsely calling someone a Communist only once. The Reverend Alan Walker, a prominent and respected Australian Methodist minister, charged that I had accused him of being a Communist. To put the record straight, Dr. Elton Wilson and I visited Reverend Walker. Regrettably, Reverend Walker stuck to his story and refused to name my accuser.

Elton was formerly director of the Australian Christian Anti-Communism Crusade. He is one of the most intelligent and informed anti-Communists I have known, and he has a passion for truth. At an age when most men are retired, he enrolled at the University of New South Wales in Australia, and graduated as a Doctor of Philosophy.

Elton has known me well for fifty years, and he said that anyone who knows me would know that the anonymous accusation of Alan Walker was "out of character."

Not once in my entire life have I been sued.

COLLEGE PROFESSORS

Criticism and opposition from certain college professors were common. I believe that some of the hostility was motivated by pro-Communism sympathy.

Following the Southern California School of Anti-Communism, and Hollywood's Answer to Communism, I spoke to an overflow meeting of students and faculty at Stanford University and soon thereafter at the Northern California School of Anti-Communism, held in Oakland and televised over Channel 11, sponsored by the Schick Safety Razor Company.

Immediately after, I sat in the audience of a public meeting at which a number of professors and authors discussed the "dreadful" danger presented by the "radical right-wing extremists."

I enjoyed myself. I was honored to be the central object of their concern. One professor confessed to their confusion when he remarked, "We've always said that these people are paranoid, but that doesn't explain everything. It doesn't explain the fine image he can present on TV and how he can appear at Stanford as an intellectual."

STANFORD UNIVERSITY

My meeting at Stanford University had shocked them. A large crowd had gathered and the atmosphere was electric.

Following the television program, "Hollywood's Answer to Communism," an editorial in the Stanford Student newspaper had described me as an incarnation of Adolph Hitler. Pickets protested the meeting. One picket carried a large poster with a cartoon of me as a barefoot Neanderthal clad in animal skins, holding a huge club with an ominous spike, and the caption, "Dr. Dred Schwarz: author of *We Must Bust the Communists*."

After a brief introduction I sat on a stool behind the podium and began my speech. In those days I sat whenever possible as I was subject to embarrassing bouts of Paroxysmal Atrial Tachycardia (PAT).

I started off with an exposition of the Marxist doctrine of the Surplus Value of Labor and its consequences. As my message proceeded the audience began to interrupt with bursts of spontaneous applause. My daughter Rosemary, who was at the meeting, later told me that one of the girls of the opposition was in tears.

It was this kind of response that caused Professor Urban Whitaker of San Francisco State University to classify me as "the most dangerous demagogue in the United States."

During the 1960s when student rebellions were rife, I spoke to many gatherings at universities but never once did I fail to receive a courteous and respectful hearing from the students.

My nonconfrontation with Professor Herbert Marcuse, of the University of California at San Diego, will be described later. Marcuse was widely known as "the guru of the New Left."

26

....

Here Come the Books

Wholesome meats to vitiated stomach differ little
or nothing from unwholesome;
and best books to a naughty mind are not unappliable
to occasions of evil.
—JOHN MILTON, 1608–1674 (*AREOPAGITICA*)

The attacks on the Crusade in newspapers and magazines were soon followed by books.

Two of the first to appear were titled *The Far Right,* by Donald Janson and Bernard Eismann, 1963, and *The Christian Fright Peddlers,* by Brooks A. Walker, 1964. Each attempted to describe the activities of right-wing organizations and devoted a chapter to the Christian Anti-Communism Crusade and me.

THE FAR RIGHT

The chapter on the activity of the Crusade was entitled "'Enry 'Iggins of the Right." I was flattered to be compared to that devotee of the English language. It reminded me of the day a college English teacher brought his entire class to one of my lectures in order to hear my use of language.

But I disliked being classified as a right winger and despised reading that my special talent was to misinform by innuendo, and to amass a personal fortune.

The authors confused fantasy with reality. They made a number of statements, not precisely derogatory, but definitely untrue. Here are samples:

> (1) Fred Schwarz is twice a doctor: once in medicine (University of Queensland) and once in Theology (Bob Jones University).
> *The truth:* I have no degree in theology from any institution.
> (2) An Australian who has applied for U.S. citizenship, Fred Schwarz is also a psychiatrist of sorts as well as a lay preacher in the Australian Baptist Church.
> *The truth:* I have never applied for U.S. citizenship.
> (3) They quote with approval this statement from the liberal magazine *The Christian Century:* "Dr. Schwarz uses the methods of political revivalism to generate a state of mind in which people are unable to teach or learn anything."
> *The truth:* Thousands of individuals, many of them among the leaders of the world such as Ronald Reagan and President Fidel Ramos of the Philippines, will testify to what they learned from my messages.

The following passage reveals more about the mental state of the authors than it does about me:

> Although Schwarz speaks most, he says least. He talks of Christian morality and details the struggle for power within the Communist party. He is Anti-Communist, pro-American, and in favor of good as opposed to evil. He carefully avoids name calling. (page 61)

Their comment reminds me of a story about a man who visited Europe. He became bored after a few days and said, "There is nothing to see here. I was a fool to come." A European commented, "He was a fool before he came."

If the authors failed to understand my message, that reflects upon their intelligence. Maybe what they meant to say was, "He does not say any of the things we expect right-wingers to say."

Their verdict is summarized in the final sentence of their chapter:

> Schwarz is, essentially, a peddler of phrases. He has perfected the use of ambiguity. "Are those who fight racial discrimination Communists?" he was asked on one occasion. "No," he told the all-white audience, "please don't think that everyone fighting racial discrimination is a Communist." His audiences read their own meanings into his torrent of words, enjoy his showmanship, and pay him to keep up the good work.

The book contains no hint of my presentation or analysis of basic Communist doctrines such as historical and dialectical materialism, democratic centralism, and the rest. The criticism reminds me of the well-known statement by the German philosopher and poet Johann C. F. Von Schiller:

> Against the machinations of your enemies you can take defense, but against the stupidity of fools, the very gods themselves fight in vain.

THE CHRISTIAN FRIGHT PEDDLERS

Brooks R. Walker endeavored to be scrupulously fair in his book *The Christian Fright Peddlers,* and he gave credit where he believed credit was due. He wrote:

> If Schwarz misses the mark in his attack on atheism, he is nonetheless discerning when it comes to identifying one of Communism's main appeals: It has a program to change human nature. It proclaims that the old human nature will die with the passing away of bourgeois society.

As it dies, new men will emerge. No longer will there be
strife and class warfare; no longer will there be any need
for legal restraint; men will live together in peace and
freedom; an ordered society will develop without compul-
sion. Abundance, made possible by the sharing of surplus
value, will eliminate the greed of the past. Leisure time,
made possible by a fully productive economy, will enable
men to become the modern Greeks, devoting themselves
to a new birth of the arts, a renaissance in human values.

As Schwarz describes it, "There will be no need for a
police force; there will be nothing for police to do. There
will be no need for an income-tax department because
everyone working, according to his natural impulses,
gives of his best for the general well-being, and out of
the abundance thus created retains only his own personal needs. Farewell anger, lust and greed, envy, malice
and strife, pestilence and war; enter golden, companion-
able, cooperative brotherhood; mankind will live
together in the glorious day of communism that has
dawned on the earth."

Schwarz's apocalyptic description is not extreme, as
anyone will know who has read the Soviet periodicals
over the past few years or listened to American Communists who have returned recently from visits to the
U.S.S.R. The "fatherland" of Communism, it is said,
even now is moving from the phase of socialistic development to pure Communism. The machinery of the
state, the encumbrances of industrial management are
being eliminated piece by piece.

No matter where I encounter the apocalyptic vision—
whether in the writings of Fred Schwarz, in a Communist
periodical, or in a speech by an American Communist—I
find it frightening and profoundly disturbing.

Fred Schwarz sees this and sees it clearly. He perceives
the flaw in Soviet utopian idealism because his Christian
faith maintains that sinful human nature may be transformed, but only in Christian liberty. "Stand fast," said

Paul, ". . . in the liberty wherewith Christ hath made us free, and be not entangled again with the yoke of bondage."

That is the root of Schwarz's conviction.

Walker is critical of some of my contentions; for example:

(1) *My affirmation that atheism may serve as a stepping-stone to Communism.* He writes:

While atheism is an integral part of Communist philosophy, it is scarcely the touchstone of Communist morality. While Communists are committed to scientific empiricism, and some may have committed the reductionist fallacy of describing man purely in terms of his physiological makeup, not all Communists are so naive as to dispose completely of man's capacity for transcending his physiological being.

I have never said that atheism "causes" Communism. I have said that it opens the door to the acceptance of basic Marxist doctrines and thus may serve as a stepping-stone to Communism. Also, I have pointed out that it is quite possible for atheists to be fervent anti-Communists because Communism conflicts with some of their other convictions such as devotion to individual liberty. I have even advised the formation of an Atheist Anti-Communism League.

I make no apology for stressing the teaching of Lenin that "Atheism is a natural and inseparable portion of Marxism, of the theory and practice of Scientific Socialism," and I agree with the Russian author Dostoyevsky that "If there is no God anything is permissible."

(2) *My failure to see and acknowledge the good things that Communism has accomplished.* Walker writes:

Were Communism nothing but a diabolical system of evil, intent upon perpetrating one barbarism after

another, successful in the abolition of all moral principles within its boundaries and capable of exercising an
uncompromising tyranny over its proponents, it would
not be the threat it is today. It is precisely because of its
successes in raising standards of living, in furthering scientific and to a lesser extent artistic achievement, that
Communism represents an alternative to the world's
uncommitted peoples.

I have repeatedly acknowledged that most evil systems, institutions, and practices produce some desirable results but that this does
not change their evil nature. I do not think that imprisonment in a
penitentiary is conceived as partly good by the prisoner because it
provides food, clothing, shelter, and medical care; that sickness is
partly good because it may provide the sufferer with an invalid's
pension. I do not admit that the Nazi regime was less evil because it
solved the problem of German unemployment.

I have constantly taught that adding good to evil may increase the
evil. My favorite illustration is how the addition of the good bait to
the evil hook magnifies the danger to the fish. I wonder if Brooks
Walker would have made the same statements today about the
achievements and appeal of Communism. Even then, in 1964, the
flood of refugees who risked their lives to escape from the "blessings" of Communism testified to the inhuman and evil system. Such
flights continue to this day.

The events of the past seventy-eight years have confirmed my
judgment that Communism was, and is, evil.

> (3) *My failure to tell my audiences what they should
> do opened the door for real "right-wingers" to recruit,
> misinform, and misdirect.* He quotes C. D. Jackson, the
> publisher of *Life* magazine, as saying:

> Dr. Schwarz is himself well informed, and his Christ-
> ian Anti-Communism Crusade attracts much respectable
> support." [However,] . . . it also attracts people who are
> too superheated to teach and learn anything.

I have endeavored to answer this persistent charge by describing the role of a pathologist in the treatment of a disease. With Thomas Jefferson, I believed that the truth will win the battle against error if it is proclaimed. I continue to believe that.

This criticism is also a criticism of democracy, since democracy is founded upon the conviction that an informed people will be better able to choose their government wisely; and that the democratic system will enable them to change the government if they discover that their choice was unwise.

(4) *The message of the Crusade and mine is not sufficiently Christian.*

I was accustomed to the charge that you cannot mix politics and religion, that the name of the Crusade excluded all those of other faiths from the struggle against Communism. I pointed out that the name of the Anti-Defamation League of B'nai Brith did not imply that all non-Jews were excluded from the fight against defamation, and that many Jews and members of other faiths had no hesitation in cooperating with the Southern *Christian* Leadership Conference (SCLC) of Martin Luther King, Jr. I was surprised by the criticism that my message was insufficiently Christian.

Walker quotes, with apparent agreement, these words from J. Stuart Innerst, a member of the Friends Committee on National Legislation:

> I question the matter of using the term *Christianity* as descriptive of his Crusade when it preaches fear and hatred of the Communists.
>
> I don't find anything in the teaching of Jesus that warrants fear and hatred of other men. He himself lived under a totalitarian government that oppressed its people, slaughtered many of them, and enslaved many others; and yet he taught men to love the enemy and he associated with the very subversives (of his day)—that is, with the tax collectors and the stooges of Rome.

I am troubled by [the] idea of calling this a Christian
movement, especially since it doesn't give credit to the
good that Communism has actually done. Now, . . . I was
in Russia for two weeks this summer, too short [a time] to
be an expert, but I had a chance to see a great deal; and I
lived for seven years in China before Communism came
in. I know the conditions before and after because I have
read both the critical and the favorable books.

I hold no brief for Communism, but I wonder how
[Schwarz] can justify the position that he takes in talking
only about evils in Communism.

The charge that I taught fear and hatred of Communists was
false. When a pathologist teaches that smoking may lead to lung
cancer he is not teaching fear and hatred of smokers. When he
teaches that tuberculosis is infectious he is not teaching fear and
hatred of those infected.

CHURCH AND STATE

The United States has a long tradition of the separation of church
and state. This requires discretion and wisdom on the part of Christians who want their message heard by all sections of the community. Any explicit presentation of Christian doctrine in the public
schools is considered illegal by many. Jesus advised his followers,
"be wise as serpents and harmless as doves." (Matthew 10:16) I
tried to follow His teachings.

The armor of the Christian described by St. Paul describes this
ingredient, "Feet shod with the *preparation* of the gospel of peace."
Note "preparation" not presentation. (Ephesians 6)

(5) *The Communist appeal to youthful idealists.*
Walker does acknowledge that the Communists appeal
to youthful idealism. He writes:

Communist philosophy does offer an appealing, but
ultimately destructive, program for overhauling human
nature. . . .

Now, what about the appeal of Communist idealism? It is no doubt real, but scarcely a live option, at least within our western universities. Given our culture's present attitude toward Communism, it would take a very neurotic, or a very angry student, indeed, to become a Communist.

The events of the 1960s described so well in the book *The Destructive Generation,* by David Horowitz and Peter Collier, reveal the naïveté of this judgment.

(6) *My financial motivation.* On this score Walker does not criticize me but refutes my critics. He writes:

Why did Schwarz give up a successful medical practice in Australia? His more severe critics call him a "patriot for profit" and point to large earnings of the Crusade. *The New York Times* reports the Crusade's 1961 gross earnings at $1,250,000, and Schwarz declared on December 12, 1962, that gross earnings for that year would be close to $1,000,000, despite what he termed "virulent, vicious attacks" on the organization.

Midyear in 1963 Schwarz reported that, with the exception of its anti-Communism schools, the Crusade was having its "best year to date," both in terms of attendance at rallies and income.

Schwarz himself contributes generously to the Crusade, turning over all of his royalties and speaking fees (more than $140,000 in one year alone), and is careful to say that his own salary is a meager $5,000 per year, plus expenses. "I'm not boasting about this," he says. "I don't consider myself a martyr. I'm enjoying it up to the hilt."

I thank him unreservedly.

27

....

Danger on the Right

Twisted by knaves to make a trap for fools.
—RUDYARD KIPLING, 1865–1936 (*IF*)

THE BOOK *DANGER ON THE RIGHT* merits special consideration. It was written in 1964 by Arnold Forster and Benjamin R.
Epstein, two officials of the Anti-Defamation League (ADL) of B'nai
Brith. It remains an eternal disgrace to both the authors and the
organization.

The book plumbs the depths of infamy. By a process of selection
and presentation of half-truths, insinuations, and outright falsehoods, it proclaims a big lie.

It sinks far below those described by the poet Alexander Pope:

Damn with faint praise,
Assent with civil leer,
And without sneering,
Teach the rest to sneer.

The book is a colossal sneer. It illustrates what Alfred Lord Tennyson wrote:

315

That a lie which is half a truth
is ever the blackest of lies,
That a lie which is all a lie may be
met with and fought outright,
But a lie which is part a truth is
a harder matter to fight.

An authors' acknowledgement states:

> . . . this volume is the end result of a combined staff
> effort.
> Situated strategically in twenty-seven cities across the
> country, and in the national offices of the Anti-
> Defamation League in New York City, are men and
> women whose daily assignment is the accumulation of
> data about extremist movements on the American scene.

One of them was a thief. He cultivated the friendship of our office
manager, Frank Fuhr, stole some of our correspondence, and sent it
to Forster and Epstein.

CHARACTER ASSASSINATION

The objective of the chapter, "The Christian Anti-Communism
Crusade—Dr. Frederick C. Schwarz" was to malign my character
with the old charge of personal greed.

The chapter opens:

> "I am a specialist on the popularization of
> Marxism–Leninism," says Dr. Frederick C. Schwarz.
> "You can't fight Communism unless you understand it."
> And apparently you can't understand it unless you
> attend the rallies, conventions, seminars, forums, and
> "schools" promoted by the leaders of the Radical Right.
> Dr. Schwarz's own "schools of anti-Communism," for
> example. "Knowledge is power," Dr. Schwarz reminds
> us—and for the student, it is also frightening *and quite
> expensive.*

There are times when the good doctor is even more lurid than Birchers in persuading listeners *to give him generous "offerings."* Like all Radical Rightists, Schwarz disseminates fear—but he has been perhaps the most influential practitioner of that specialty, and he has had an undeniable impact on a large number of Americans. An alien in this country, he has nevertheless been "saving America" for the past twelve years, and in that time *he has been given millions of dollars* by our citizens to save our nation from Communists, Socialists, and the intellectuals. [italics added]

The false charge, "ad nauseam." Such statements as the following abound:

> . . . he is a potent force in the collection of money . . .
> Schwarz has collected more than $2,500,000 in the last few years.
> The Americans who gave Schwarz these thousands to "save America" have been given no proof that the sums went for education about Communism.

I could go on and on.

A comparable statement would be, "Arnold Forster has received more than *x*-million dollars in the last few years," when *x*-million represented the entire income of the Anti-Defamation League during that period. Would Forster regard such a statement as factual and fair if repeated in order to imply that he was using the money for personal enrichment?

Even when the authors report some of the projects on which the Crusade's income is spent, they cannot refrain from sneering and lying.

> Schwarz told *The New York Times* that in 1961 the Crusade spent $234,560 in "foreign missionary work," which included $152,615 spent in India—$58,000 for a rotary press and a building to increase the distribution

of *The Voice of Kerala,* a daily newspaper with a circulation of 29,000 which Schwarz said the Crusade had been subsidizing for nearly three years; $5,000 for an anti-Communist book distribution in Kerala; $10,000 to buy property for a home for orphan boys in Secunderabad, in Andhra State, and for the sustenance of fifty boys and their teachers.

To buy property anywhere for an orphanage is certainly a worthy undertaking, as is the feeding of orphans and those who teach them. But *how and why the cash collected to "save America from the Communist threat" is spent in distant India to house and feed orphans is puzzling.* [italics added]

That money, spent to feed, clothe, and nurture Indians, was not given to the Crusade to "save America from the Communist threat," but by loving sponsors to "adopt" needy Indian children.

I began to count the falsehoods in the chapter but gave up when I reached thirty-two.

Many of the lies are petty personal attacks that hardly merit time spent in rebuttal such as, "He rarely smiles." Ask anyone who knows me or has heard me speak.

But some of them were substantial and serious. One such was the dogmatic assertion that the Crusade was actively engaging in partisan politics. Consider this:

> He [Dr. Schwarz] more often becomes involved in the political dialogue than the spiritual.

This charge is serious, since if true, it would justify canceling the Crusade's "tax-deductible status."

After the Reuther Memorandum, IRS agents spent months investigating the Crusade's finances and found nothing that would justify declassifying it as a tax-deductible organization. Subsequent audits by IRS agents have reached the same conclusion.

Though we have opposed Communists in many countries, neither the Crusade nor I has ever endorsed a candidate or party in the United States.

The authors of *Danger on the Right* describe an incident when I allegedly endorsed Barry Goldwater for president:

> On June 26, 1963, at the Long Beach, California, Women's Club, Schwarz further involved himself in American domestic politics. During his talk a man in the audience arose and suggested throwing out of office all those liberal intellectuals so bitterly denounced by the Doctor. "We need to elect a different President!" the man shouted. "A President like Barry Goldwater!" At this the audience broke into applause, whistling and shouting its approval.
>
> Schwarz held his hands high and in a voice that could be heard above the uproar shouted, "I would say Amen! Amen! Amen!" [page 66]

Here is the true account: A question-and-answer period followed the message. One man stood up and said, "What this country needs is a moral revival!" I raised my hands and said, "I would say Amen! Amen! Amen!"

Another rose and said, "We need to elect Barry Goldwater as president." This statement drew prolonged applause.

As soon as I could make myself heard I said that we were nonpolitical and were making no political endorsements.

This was confirmed in a report published in the Communist newspaper *People's World*, January 20, 1963. They also had a representative at the meeting. He reported:

> At the June 26 meeting in Long Beach, Dr. Schwarz spoke to an all-white crowd of 250. He resents being called an "extremist" and tries to keep his pitch on a "high moral" level. But his backers, financial and in the crowds, are the same who support the other ultra-rightist movements in Southern California.
>
> When Dr. Schwarz was asked if the election of Sen. Barry Goldwater to the presidency would be the best way of "fighting communism," the Long Beach crowd

broke into applause and cheers *before the doctor had the opportunity to disavow partisan political aims.*

WHY THE ADL CHANGED ITS TUNE

The vicious attack by *Danger on the Right* contrasts starkly with a previous statement on the Crusade by an ADL official. On February 17, 1959, Theodore Freedman submitted the following report to the ADL Advisory Board, CRCs, and Rabbis.

MOTIVATION

Why did the leaders of the ADL reverse gears? Here again is the elusive and complex problem of discovering motivation. I submit the following diagnosis reluctantly; my judgment is not infallible.

I believe that the motivation for the attack by the ADL was both political and pecuniary.

POLITICAL

It is important to note the length of time between the conflicting assessments of ADL's agents. The first is dated February 17, 1959, and *Danger on the Right* was published in 1964.

During this interval the administration launched its attack upon the Crusade. I shall not repeat the story of Senator William Fulbright's memorandum and his similarity to "the Pied Piper." But Fulbright piped, and the rats followed.

It was a politically motivated attack by the administration on movements considered to be helping the Republicans. This divided people into "us" and "them."

The "us" were the fervent supporters of the Democratic Party, while the "them" were a number of "right-wing" organizations. The Christian Anti-Communism Crusade was one of "them" and therefore an enemy. The belief that the Crusade and I were on the side of the Republicans became widespread.

Central to the Fulbright attack was the false charge that the Crusade was a close ally of the John Birch Society. The evidence in sup-

TO: ADL Advisory Board, CRC's, Rabbis

FROM: Theodore Freedman

DATE: February 17, 1959

SUBJECT: Christian Anti-Communist Crusade—W. P. Strube, Jr.

During recent weeks this office has been deluged with requests for information on the above organization and individual. In view of the fact that W.P. Strube, Jr. has been making public appearances around the State and may in the future be visiting your community, this fact sheet has been prepared.

The Christian Anti-Communist Crusade was organized in Waterloo, Iowa, during the summer of 1953. Its Director and founder is Dr. Fred E. Schwarz, a psychiatrist, from Australia, who came to the United States early that year for the purpose of making an extensive lecture tour.

Since that time, Dr. Schwarz has made numerous appearances as a lecturer, has spoken on the radio and maintained contact with Washington governmental circles. On May 29, 1957, Dr. Schwarz testified before the House Committee on Un-American activities on the subject of International Communism and the necessity of a spiritual revival as the best antidote to Communism. In this context, Dr. Schwarz, who is a deeply believing Christian, puts considerable emphasis on the role of the Christian world's outlook, which in all likelihood explains the legitimate use of the adjective "Christian" in the name of the organization.

To the best of our knowledge, Dr. Schwarz has never engaged in harmful activities. As an example, one of his lecture topics is "Why Communism has attacked the Jews." On a few occasions when disreputable groups or individuals attempted to attach themselves to his coattails, he has completely ignored them.

port was that members of the John Birch Society had served as members of the sponsoring committees of our Anti-Communism Schools. Though I pointed out that numerous Democratic leaders had also served, our opponents either ignored this fact or attributed it to our skill in duplicity.

A prominent U.S. Democratic senator, Thomas Dodd, was a regular faculty member at our schools but I am unaware of any self-confessed member of the John Birch Society who served on our faculties. I repeat: I had no knowledge of the political affiliation of many of the members of the school faculties.

Many based their judgment on the false information that I was an active supporter of the Republican Party. On one occasion in 1964 a reporter phoned to ask what "we" proposed to do now that "our" candidate, Barry Goldwater, had been defeated. When I asked why he had called me, he said he knew that I was a leader in the conservative wing of the Republican Party. When I told him that I was not in the least involved in partisan politics, he was surprised and seemed bewildered. I doubt that he believed me.

I'm of the opinion that the ADL decided to "go with the flow" and thereby curry favor with the Democratic leadership. As members of the "us" team, all tactics to defeat "them" became permissible.

PECUNIARY MOTIVATION

I also believe that the attack had a pecuniary motivation. The repeated false charge that I personally received large sums of money evidences an obsession with money.

In order to carry on their work the ADL needed financial support, much of which came from the Jewish community. Potential donors needed to be convinced that the ADL was protecting them from a real and present danger. The burgeoning "Right-Wing Extremist Movement" in the United States was presented as such a danger, with the hope that this charge would fill the coffers.

It is important to note that *Danger on the Right* did not even hint that I was an anti-Semite or that the Crusade was anti-Semitic. However, since the preface states that "many Americans share the inaccurate impression that the Anti-Defamation League's sole concern is anti-Semitism," the attack by it fostered the assumption that the Crusade and I must be anti-Semitic.

The prevalence and consequences of this assumption will be discussed later.

28

....

Anti-Semitism

Yes, I am a Jew, and when the ancestors of the right honorable gentleman were brutal savages in an unknown island, mine were
priests in the temple of Solomon.
—BENJAMIN DISRAELI, 1804–1881
(REPLY TO A TAUNT BY DANIEL O'CONNELL)

I WAS CONDUCTING A RALLY in the Patriotic Hall of Los Angeles. Shortly after we began, the American Nazi Party leader, George
Lincoln Rockwell, marched down the aisle and took a seat near the
front. He was accompanied by several of his followers—all male and
muscular.

I recognized Rockwell because I had seen him on a recent television program, during which the following interchange with the program's moderator had taken place.

> MODERATOR: So you believe that New York Jews are
> worse than other Jews?
> ROCKWELL: Of course they are.
> MODERATOR: What do you propose to do with them if
> you conquer America?

323

ROCKWELL: Don't you know? We are going to gas them!

Rockwell walked away unscathed from the interview, but he was assassinated by one of his own followers soon afterward. During the question period that followed my speech at the rally, Rockwell stood up and said, "Why don't you tell the people the truth that Communism is a Jewish conspiracy?" I replied, "I don't tell the people that because it's not the truth, it is a paranoid delusion."

Although my father had become a fervent Christian he remained proud of his Jewish heritage. He often reminded us that the Jews were "God's chosen people" and taught us that Christians must love the Jews.

My record was demonstrably free from any taint of anti-Semitism. Even so, and even though the Anti-Defamation League leaders had to know this, they resolutely refused to help me refute the false charge that I was anti-Semitic when it *was* made.

On my arrival in New York in the summer of 1962, I quickly realized that the delusion that I was anti-Semitic was widespread. I sought help from individuals and organizations that professed a devotion to the truth. I thought that the Anti-Defamation League would help, since opposition to defamation was the primary reason for its existence. I wrote to Arnold Forster, and requested an interview, during which the league's representatives could question me to see if they could find any traces of anti-Semitism. To my surprise, my simple request was interpreted as an attempt to entrap the league. It was refused.

With the advantage of hindsight I believe I can explain their inexplicable conduct.

The ADL leaders knew that I was not anti-Semitic. They knew that they would be compelled to admit this if they conducted an investigation. Armed with such a verdict, I would be able to refute the charge of anti-Semitism more effectively and thereby diminish my value to them as a source of support.

One writer who never hesitated to criticize the ADL was the distinguished journalist and author, Eugene Lyons. While visiting the Soviet Union as a young journalist with socialistic convictions, he had become disillusioned by the Soviet reality. On his return to the States he wrote the books *Assignment in Utopia* (1937); *The Red Decade* (1941); and later, *Workers Paradise Lost: 50 years of Soviet Communism: a balance sheet* (1967). He became an editor of *Readers Digest,* and also served as a faculty member of our Anti-Communism Schools.

In its July 3, 1962, edition, *The National Review* published this article which contains a copy of a letter that Lyons wrote to Arnold Forster, entitled, "Does Mr. Forster Plead the Fifth?"

Does Mr. Forster Plead the Fifth?

In its June 5 and June 19 issues, NATIONAL REVIEW *commented on the attempt to smear Dr. Fred Schwarz in conjunction with his first public activities in New York City, and on the role which Mr. Arnold Forster and the Anti-Defamation League have played in that defamatory operation. Mr. Eugene Lyons, a scheduled speaker at the June 28 Anti-Communism Rally, has given us permission to publish a letter he sent to Mr. Forster:*

Dear Mr. Forster:

I have been invited to speak at the Madison Square Garden meeting organized by Dr. Fred Schwarz. I gather that the Anti-Defamation League has been attacking Dr. Schwarz. I would therefore be most grateful if you could let me know without delay what your League knows about him that I don't.

Some months ago I published an article, which I am enclosing herewith, attacking the so-called Far or Radical Right. It has, as I expected, embroiled me in argument with the Birch group. But I have no reason to believe—after making a conscientious inquiry into his career and enterprises—that Dr. Schwarz is in the same category.

In the past week I have met Dr. Schwarz personally. He also joined some of the [*Reader's*] *Digest* editors at a luncheon, in which he was thoroughly grilled on all aspects of his work. Moreover, I have questioned others who have looked into the matter.

I have found nothing that would even remotely justify the implications of the "thumbs down" by the ADL. I can only suppose, therefore, that you know something about him that nobody else seems to know. I do believe, both as a Jew and as a journalist, that you ought to share the information with me.

I feel sure that your attitude cannot be based solely on the word "Christian" in the name of his organization. On that basis, you would have to oppose the Christian Temperance societies and a thousand other enterprises including the word.

Frankly, the ADL stance in this matter is potentially dangerous in terms of anti-Semitism. Dr. Schwarz is meeting, in the great Jewish city of New York, the kind of harassment he has not met anywhere else. Millions of earnest anti-Communists are likely to misinterpret this and lay the blame at your door. I do hope to receive your answer soon.   Cordially,
June 7, 1962   EUGENE LYONS

One person who displayed knowledge, understanding, and common decency was conservative philosopher, author, and statesman William F. Buckley. I shall always be grateful for his intellectual integrity and personal courage. In his magazine, *National Review*, on June 5, 1962, and under the caption, "The Impending Smear of Fred Schwarz," he wrote:

Dr. Fred Schwarz is coming to New York, and there is to be more anxiety, more resentment, more animosity, than there was when Khrushchev came to town. The way of the anti-Communist is always hard, but the very special resentment against Schwarz has to do with his obstinate refusal to make a fool of himself. If *only* he would write a book calling Eisenhower a Communist, or

announce that the White House staff is riddled with
spies, or suggest that the Union Theological Seminary is
a Communist front, or that the ultimate loyalty of all
Catholics is suspect, or that the Jews are a treasonable
breed of men—with what relief the anti-anti-
Communists would greet the news! But no: he has been
intensively monitored over months and months, his
background has been meticulously surveyed, his financial arrangements audited; and there is no scandal to be
found. Merely the scandal of a man insisting, with
knowledge and evangelical fervor, and—how dare he!—
with a leavening sense of humor, that for all that the
danger is plain to see, the ignorance of our leaders on
the subject of Communism is outrageous and suicidal.

They could treat him with silence. But Schwarz has a
way of dealing with silence. It is hard to be silent about
an aggregation of twenty thousand people in the heart of
Sodom, listening to a man preach the necessity of sacrifice, and atonement, in behalf of survival. No, he cannot
be ignored. He must be attacked.

Dr. Schwarz arrived in New York a few weeks ago to
prepare the way for his School, which he intends to conduct at Madison Square Garden during August. As an
experienced man, he is well aware of the tendency, so
frequently remarked, to brand as anti-Semitic anyone
associated with an explicitly Christian undertaking who
is also a tough anti-Communist or conservative. Schwarz
is head of the Christian Anti-Communism Crusade.
There is, of course, no reason at all why an anti-
Communist organization cannot be Christian in character and inspiration, just so long as it does not implicitly
exclude non-Christians, Jews, Buddhists, Confucianists,
whatever, from the anti-Communist camp. It is no more
anti-Semitic to join the Christian Anti-Communism Crusade than it is anti-Christian to join, or applaud, the
American Jewish League Against Communism. But Dr.
Schwarz, aware of the automatic suspicion, decided, on

reaching New York, to have a talk with Mr. Arnold Forster, the General Counsel of the Anti-Defamation League.

An associate called on Mr. Forster. And Mr. Forster flatly refused to meet with Dr. Schwarz. On hearing this report, we at NATIONAL REVIEW found it incredible, and wrote to Mr. Forster asking whether it were true, and if so, did he care to explain why? He replied: "This is in response to your May 10 letter asking whether I have declined to meet with Dr. Fred Schwarz and, if so, why. I have no need to meet with Dr. Schwarz, nor any sense of obligation to respond as to the reason."

Well, here are the facts which might awaken Mr. Forster's elusive sense of obligation. 1) The Anti-Defamation League was founded to fight defamation. 2) Dr. Schwarz has been very widely defamed. 3) If the ADL has its ear to the ground, *i.e.,* if it is doing the job it is paid to do, and proudly insists it is doing, then it has caught the defamatory rumor that Dr. Schwarz's operation is anti-Semitic. 4) Dr. Schwarz, whether one agrees with his views on the Communist question or not, is at this moment a prominent figure on the American scene, who has a presumptive right to consult with the head of an organization engaged in arbitrating disputes of the kind that surround figures like Dr. Schwarz. And 5) Dr. Schwarz demonstrated his willingness, indeed his eagerness, to answer any questions and clear up any suspicions relating to bigotry, and to seek the ADL's expert advice on the matter of anti-Semitism. Though of dubious relevance, it adds to the irony that Dr. Schwarz is himself half-Jewish.

It looks to us as though there could be only one reason for Mr. Forster's refusal to receive Dr. Schwarz: he is, like so many other enemies of Dr. Schwarz, afraid to put himself in the position of finding out that there is nothing wrong with Schwarz. We have, at NATIONAL REVIEW, on one or two occasions, criticized the Anti-Defamation League on the grounds that it goes outside, way outside, its professional concerns, *e.g.,* in lending its considerable weight to the processes of the seculariza- tion of American education. The ADL, which is staffed by political Liberals, is notoriously unfriendly to anti- Communists of the tough stripe of Dr. Schwarz. And the high command at the ADL evidently reasoned that they would find it much more satisfying to profess ignorance about Dr. Schwarz, and therefore encourage the contin- ued circulation of invidious rumors about him, than to have to report that they had investigated him, met with him, and satisfied themselves that there was not in him the least secretion of racial or religious prejudice. We are not the first to point out that the Anti-Defamation League is highly practised in defamation. The remark, in as many words, was made by a prominent Jewish New York civil liberties lawyer, Mr. Arthur Garfield Hays, years ago.

Dr. Schwarz's New York sessions, like the earlier ones in Omaha, San Francisco and elsewhere, will not be con- ducted under a sectarian rubric. They are to be called merely the Greater New York Anti-Communism Rally and School. Dr. Schwarz has accordingly made it a point to invite prominent Jewish members of the community to serve as sponsors. But those Jews who are not terri- fied of incurring Liberal displeasure, appear to be terrified of incurring the displeasure of our old friend George Sokolsky, who on the subject of Dr. Schwarz is, apparently, obsessed. He loathes Dr. Schwarz and his operation, but appears to be incapable of making an intelligible case against him; and to a letter from NATIONAL REVIEW, asking him to state his case against Dr. Schwarz, he did not even reply. No one knows what lies behind the dark anti-Schwarzian emanations that flow out of George Sokolsky's office, even though there has been much public speculation about it. Murray Kemp- ton thinks he has the clue. "Schwarz is an Australian, and Sokolsky feels that anti-Communism is an American enterprise; he is high tariff in all things."

We don't mean to suggest it is just Jews who are smearing Fred Schwarz, by either affirmative or negative action. A passel of Protestant preachers in San Francisco, who know as little about Schwarz as they do about Communism, tore into him before he arrived there to conduct his school. And the National Catholic Welfare Conference's Father Cronin, in his celebrated pamphlet, defined and denounced, without listing their names, the extremist anti-Communists. And told the press the day of publication that he had in mind, among others, Dr. Fred Schwarz's group. However, Dr. Schwarz has never done or said a single one of the things Father Cronin labeled as extremist!

We record these events not merely because it is the job of the press to root out hypocrisy and injustice, but because we wish to put ourselves on record as opposed to the pseudo-sophisticates' view that there is no place on the American scene for anti-Communist evangelism. As a matter of fact, in America, it has been the pressure of the people, rather than of the intellectuals, that has moved our government to take whatever anti-Communist measures it has taken over the years. It is especially important that at a moment when the manicured brains of the Schlesingers and Harrimans and Rostows and Rusks are grinding out appeasement formulas on Cuba and Berlin, on Laos and Formosa, that the Fred Schwarzes get on with their job, of instructing the people in what their leaders so clearly don't know.

NATIONAL REVIEW   JUNE 5, 1962

Another courageous supporter was Rabbi Solomon Andhil Fineberg. The *Encyclopaedia Judaica,* Jerusalem, 1978, contains this biographical paragraph:

FINEBERG, SOLOMON ANDHIL (1896–), U.S.
Reform rabbi, author, and organizational leader.
Fineberg was born in Pittsburgh, Pennsylvania, and was

ordained at Hebrew Union College (1920). After serving various congregations in Pittsburgh and the New York City area, Rabbi Fineberg joined the American Jewish Committee in 1939 as community relations consultant. In that capacity he devised a successful strategy to combat anti-Semitism by persuading the press and mass media, not to publicize anti-Semitic activity, but to lay stress upon the danger to democracy and human rights in general arising from anti-Semitism. His books include *Overcoming Anti-Semitism* (1943), *Punishment without Crime* (1949), and *The Rosenberg Case* (1953). He coauthored a report for the Committee on Un-American Activities of the U.S. House of Representatives, called *Ideological Fallacies of Communism* (1957), and contributed many articles to magazines.

I first became aware of Rabbi Fineberg when I read his testimony on Communism given to, and published by, the House Committee on Un-American Activities. I called on him while I was in New York, and we became friends.

I can still remember his indignation at the treatment I was receiving from some Jewish leaders. He would say repeatedly, "It's outrageous! It's outrageous!" Toward the end of my sojourn in New York he had good news to report. He said, "We're making progress. I can now admit that I have been meeting you without risking excommunication."

29

....

Seeking Help From the Law

If the law supposes that, the law is a ass and a idiot.
—CHARLES DICKENS (*OLIVER TWIST*)

I SHALL FURTHER DESCRIBE MY visit to New York later. I now jump ahead to discuss my legal action against a newspaper for publishing a column that labeled me "One of the nation's top anti-Semites."

On April 15, 1963, the *Boston Herald* published a column by James F. Droney, which contained the following paragraph:

> On March 27 at John Hancock Hall, the Forum sponsored the appearance of Cleon Skoussen, a close associate of Fred Schwarz, *another of the nation's top anti-Semites.* [italics mine]

Since being classified as an anti-Semite was equivalent to being classified as a supporter of Adolf Hitler, I decided to take legal action.

One problem was the distance of Boston from Los Angeles, where the Crusade was based. Malcolm Champlin, the chairman of the Northern California School of Anti-Communism in 1962, was an

332

attorney and a friend, and he introduced me to a firm of attorneys in Boston.

The firm requested information and a $500 fee so that they could decide whether to accept our case. I sent the information and the fee, and they agreed to represent me. They then asked for $5,000. I sent them $5,000. The firm wrote to the newspaper and demanded a retraction. The paper refused. We were asked for a downpayment of $25,000 to enable them to initiate legal proceedings. At this point I decided to call a halt—the cost was too great.

My good friend Patrick Frawley came to the rescue. He said, "Our corporations have sponsored you on television, so an attack on you is an attack on us. Your defense is therefore a legitimate expense to protect our good name." Thereafter he took over the legal expenses. He retained the firm of Malloy, Sullivan & Sullivan, and legal action against the *Boston Herald* for publishing libel was commenced on October 1, 1968. We decided to sue the newspaper only and not James F. Droney, the columnist.

Initiation of the suit and the court hearing were five years apart, a common occurrence in legal history. In *Hamlet,* William Shakespeare names "the law's delay" as one of the justifications for suicide. During the interval, the U.S. Supreme Court delivered its verdict in the *Sullivan* case: if the plaintiff in a libel suit is a public figure, he or she must prove that the defendant showed ▄▄ "malice aforethought" before a verdict of guilty for the libel could be rendered. This decision proved to be fatal for our case.

Accompanied by our attorney Ralph Warren Sullivan (a mere coincidence), I submitted to the discovery process, during which I was questioned at great length by an attorney for the defendant. None of the information gained during this interview was used during the trial.

The case came to trial before a judge and jury on October 1, 1968. Although the verdict was for the defense, the evidence submitted during the trial exonerated me from the charge of being an anti-Semite.

The defense relied upon the *Sullivan* decisions. Nobody claimed that the statement that I was "one of the nation's top anti-Semites" was true. Its inaccuracy was implicitly acknowledged. The defense was based upon the claim that I was a public figure and that the newspaper had no malice when the offending statement was published.

I was given no opportunity to speak except to answer questions put by the attorney for the defense. The only vocabulary I needed was the word "yes." I sat and answered "yes" to a barrage of questions such as:

"Didn't *Life* magazine on such and such a date publish . . . ?"

"Didn't *The New York Times* on such a date publish . . . ?" Similar questions went on and on.

Finally, the judge ruled that I was a public figure, taking that question away from the jury.

The sole remaining question was whether the newspaper had published the article with "malice aforethought." The only evidence that we had was the newspaper's refusal to publish a retraction, but state law forbade us to inform the jury of this.

The publisher of the *Boston Herald* told the court that at the time the column was published, he had no knowledge of who I was, so malice aforethought could not have been possible.

The jury spent little time in reaching its verdict of not guilty. I agree with the character of Mr. Bumble in the novel, *Oliver Twist,* by Charles Dickens, who said, "If the law supposes that, the law is a ass and a idiot."

After the trial our attorney, Ralph W. Sullivan, had a private interview with the judge, who told him that our case could have been strengthened if I had claimed that the anti-Semitism charge had upset me so much that I had needed to go to bed and could not work. The judge added, "But there he sat, obviously enjoying every minute of it."

I have never been adept at generating sympathy; I am too combative.

The trial did teach me the valuable lesson that I should avoid legal entanglement whenever possible. I have never again been a plaintiff.

Legal action is not only extremely expensive, it also demands great expenditure of time and emotion. If I became enmeshed in legal conflicts, I would be unable to concentrate on my primary objectives—research into the pathology of Communism, education on the pathology of Communism, and preaching the gospel of Christ.

30

....

Quixotic Adventure— Journey to New York

'Twixt the optimist and pessimist
The difference is droll:
The optimist sees the doughnut
But the pessimist sees the hole.
—McLandburgh Wilson, 1915

AT THIS POINT, STILL BELIEVING that most of the attacks upon me were based on misunderstanding, and that accurate information would correct this, I set out optimistically for New York, the information capital of the nation.

I did not go alone. Our team consisted of my close colleague, the Reverend James D. Colbert, my secretary Ella Doorn, and Jim Colbert's secretary, his sister Rita Colbert. We arrived in New York in April 1962, prepared to stay for several months. I was expecting to use television to reach the people of the eastern seaboard with our message, sponsored by Patrick Frawley's corporations.

I soon experienced my first body blow. The TV station WPIX/ Channel 11, had telecast "Hollywood's Answer to Communism" to great acclaim. Jim Colbert and I arranged an interview with the

335

senior executives of that station to discuss buying television time for our New York programs.

We were given a royal welcome. The executives told us how great the reception of the Hollywood program had been, but then adamantly refused to sell us any television time. I was astonished. And angered. They tried to placate me by insisting that they were my friends! "In that case," I said, "I pray that the Lord will give us a few enemies."

In retrospect I regret my arrogance and lack of understanding. I failed to realize that they legitimately feared the loss of their license because of the Democratic administration's hostility. The forces arrayed against us were powerful indeed.

Five stations refused to sell us time. Ultimately, I was able to purchase three half-hours from WOR-TV.

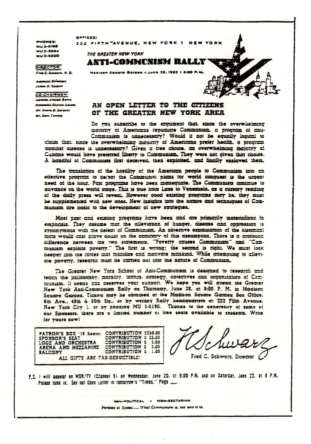

Later when I went to Washington, D.C., I was unable to purchase one minute of time on any TV station that serviced that area.

I classified our reception in New York as "boycott, bigotry, and fear." This sounded like hyperbole but it was true. The business firms that dared to support our programs were threatened with boycott; the accusations that we were right-wing extremists and anti-Semites were manifestations of bigotry; some were even afraid that the fascists were landing.

My hope was that we would be able to dispel this delusional fog with the sunshine of truth.

Our planned program in New York included two public events: a mass Anti-Communism Rally in Madison Square Garden on June 28, and an Anti-Communism School in Carnegie Hall, August 27–31. We immediately plunged into promoting these ventures.

I spoke in many smaller meetings throughout the area and sent letters to rabbis, priests, and ministers. We mailed 2,600 letters, and I prepared a series of statements on the pathology of Communism and the nature of our proposed programs as advertisements in *The New York Times*. On page 336 is a typical advertisement.

I sent the letter on page 338 to the New York rabbis.

THE NEW YORK PRESS

Our reception by the news media was not universally hostile. The *New York Daily News,* with the largest circulation of any paper in New York City, published the following editorial:

WANT TO KNOW YOUR ENEMY?

Your worst enemy, whether you are aware of the fact or not, is Communism. Communism will continue to be the whole free world's worst enemy until Communism is destroyed or made powerless.

Anybody with any sense makes it his business to learn everything he can about any enemy or enemies he has. The more you know about an enemy, the better your hope of overcoming him.

Dear Rabbi:

I am appealing to you for help in the dilemma in which I find myself. The question has arisen, "Is the existence and nature of the Christian Anti-Communism Crusade in tune with the spirit and structure of a Democratic Society?"

May I tell you a little of the history of the Christian Anti-Communism Crusade and myself. My father was born of Jewish parents in Austria. He left home when he was 12 years of age and migrated to Australia via England. He chose to become a Christian when he was about 20 years of age. He met and married my mother, Phoebe Smith, who was an English girl and a worker in the Methodist Church.

I was raised in a Christian home. When I was 17 years old, I made a personal commitment to Christian doctrine and the Christian manner of life.

My first conflicts with Communism were not primarily economic or political but were concerned with the being of God and the nature and destiny of man. I had my first debate with a Communist at the University of Queensland, Australia, in 1940.

On this foundation my opposition to Communism developed and grew. I devoted myself to a study of Communist philosophy, morality, organization, and strategy.

In 1953 the Christian Anti-Communism Crusade was formed with myself as the Executive Director. This Crusade has grown tremendously since those days.

In speaking and writing I have always repudiated completely any form of anti-Semitism and have incurred the wrath of those who have tried to identify Communism with the Jews. Our recent meetings have been picketed by the neo-Nazis who classify me as a "phony Jewish conservative" infiltrating the Gentile ranks.

In spite of this I am meeting a constant barrage of criticism because our Anti-Communism Crusade is called Christian. This is the issue on which I would like your thoughtful and sincere opinion.

Do not the dynamics of a free society encourage a multiplicity of organizations each of which unites people with a common philosophy? Do not these organizations both cooperate and compete in a field of common concern? Is this not the principle which operates in both the Jewish and Christian fraternities? Does not one centrally directed organization suggest Fascism rather than Democracy?

If it is agreed that the Christian Anti-Communism Crusade is a legitimate organization within the democratic community, would you reject an educational program of a non-political and non-sectarian nature because the organization giving the education is Christian?

These are some of the problems perplexing me at present. You would help me greatly if you would give me your opinion concerning them.

Yours very sincerely,

Fred Schwarz

Fred Schwarz
President

FCS/ed

All of which has been leading up to an earnest recommendation that you obtain, read, reread, and mayhap rereread a book called "You Can Trust the Communists (to do exactly as they say)," by Dr. Fred Schwarz; Prentice-Hall, Inc., Englewood Cliffs, N.J., 1960; 187 pages, $2.95.

About 1 million copies of this book have now got into circulation. It is to be hoped that figure may be multiplied greatly in the next few years.

Dr. Schwarz has the enemy's number from every angle: spells out in "You Can Trust the Communists" exactly why the Reds are the enemies of freedom, decency and happiness that they are; and outlines (in his last chapter, "Program for Survival") various ways in which individual citizens can get effectively into the fight to bring about a final, worldwide defeat of these enemies.

You're advised to pay no attention to some smear stuff now being circulated here against Dr. Schwarz by assorted Communists, fellow travelers, and anti-anti-Communists.

What occasions this smear campaign is the fact that Dr. Schwarz is soon (June 28) to stage one of his increasingly famous anti-Communism rallies in Madison Square Garden. This one, incidentally, has as co-chairmen Adm. Arleigh Burke, Ret.; Charles Edison, Henry B. Sargent, and Gene Tunney.

Naturally, the local friends of Moscow (and they are fairly numerous) would love to discredit Dr. Schwarz, in advance of the June 28 rally, as a crackpot right-wing extremist.

He is nothing of the kind; and his book is one of the deadliest, most level-headed and best-informed analyses of the aims and methods of the Communist enemy that we've ever been privileged to read. Again, permit us to recommend it to you, as strongly as we know how.

I was also encouraged by speaking with the unsung philosophers of New York City—the taxi drivers. I was impressed by their friendliness and common sense, unlike the intelligentsia's pretensions.

I felt that we were making progress. On June 14 *The New York Times* published an article that included the following report by Richard P. Hunt:

ANTI-COMMUNIST SAYS CITY'S HOSTILITY
IS EASING

Dr. Fred C. Schwarz, the anti-Communist lecturer, said yesterday that he was beginning to dispel "a climate that was created by misrepresentation and misinformation" about him here.

"New York is a city of bigotry, boycott and fear," he said in an interview. But he said he had made "a major breakthrough" by obtaining an offer to sell him television time for talks in advance of his rally here.

Dr. Schwarz, an Australian-born physician and former Baptist lay preacher, is the president and executive director of the Christian Anti-Communism Crusade, a nationwide organization that he says has 100,000 members. Under the sponsorship of a local committee, he is preparing to hold a Greater New York Anti-Communism Rally in Madison Square Garden on June 28.

Purposes Set Forth

The stated purposes of the rally are to "voice effective opposition to communism" and to lay plans for a school of anti-communism to be held at Carnegie Hall from Aug. 27 through 31.

In due course the rally in Madison Square Garden and the Anti-Communism School in Carnegie Hall were held. Compared to the "Southern California School of Anti-Communism" and "Hollywood's Answer to Communism," our opponents said they were dismal failures.

THE SPEAKERS

I was responsible for selecting the lecturers at our public rallies. I was commonly accused of choosing only Republican right-wing extremists, but I invited informed and articulate opponents of Communism of any political affiliation. I sent the following letter to Attorney General Robert Kennedy:

April 30, 1962

The Honorable Robert F. Kennedy
Attorney General
Department of Justice
Washington 25, D.C.

Dear Sir:

I would appreciate the privilege of a brief interview at the earliest possible moment.

The purpose of the interview would be to discuss your possible participation in an Anti-Communism Rally planned for Madison Square Garden, New York City, on June 28.

The other major speakers being presently considered are Congressman Walter Judd of Minnesota and myself.

It is desired that this rally shall be genuinely nonpolitical and nonsectarian and avoid all facets of extremism. There is a possibility of wide television coverage.

The prospective chairman for the rally is Gene Tunney.

Knowing that your association with such a rally would have many implications, I would like to meet you personally to inform you of all details including the purposes and objectives and to answer any questions.

Hoping for a favorable reply at the earliest possible moment. My present address is: Taft Hotel, New York City, New York. Phone: CI 7-4000, Ext. 1071.

Yours very sincerely,

Fred Schwarz
Director
Greater New York School of
Anti-Communism

FCS/ed

In due course I received the following reply:

Office of the Attorney General
Washington, D. C.
May 8, 1962

Fred C. Schwarz, M. D.
President
Christian Anti-Communism Crusade
c/o Taft Hotel
New York, New York

Dear Dr. Schwarz:

This is to confirm the conversation between my
Special Assistant for Public Information Ed Guthman and
Mr. James Colbert concerning the possibility of my addressing
the Anti-Communism Rally on June 28th.

I am grateful for your consideration in asking me
to participate in the program and regret that I am unable to
do so. Please express my regrets to the members of the group
and to Mr. Colbert.

Sincerely,

Attorney General

RFK:n

Jim Colbert and I met with the officers of the International Long-shoremen's Association (ILA) and invited them to nominate a speaker for the coming school. They were fervent anti-Communists and agreed to participate. For unknown reasons, the agreement lapsed. (The ILA contrasted with Harry Bridge's International Long-shoremen's and Warehousemen's Union (ILWU), which had been expelled from the AFL-CIO because of Communist orientation.)

One union official, Arthur McDowell of the Upholstery Worker's Union, was a friend and supporter. He was an intelligent anti-Communist, a faculty member at several Anti-Communism Schools, and he spoke at the Madison Square Garden Rally. Sadly, he was killed in an accident shortly after our visit to New York. His memory continues to be honored in the Art McDowell luncheons, which the fine organization, Accuracy in Media, holds in Washington, D.C.

The conservative magazine, *The National Review,* continued its valiant defense of me under the caption " 'He shall not be heard': The Anti-Defamation League." Its edition of June 19 stated:

> We wrote in the last issue of the "impending smear of Fred Schwarz," and sure enough it has impended. People in New York are going crazy trying to discredit Dr. Schwarz—unfortunately, without any help whatsoever from him, who remains innocent of every charge being leveled against him. The principal source of the campaign against him appears to be, as we predicted, the Anti-Defamation League of B'nai B'rith, which though it has failed to find a scintilla of evidence suggesting that Dr. Schwarz is anti-Semitic, is doing its level best to win converts to anti-Semitism—by arrogantly speaking, as if in the name of New York Jewry, a series of filthy and defamatory lies about him, his purposes, and his integrity.
>
> Israel Moss, director of the League, is quoted by the *Herald Tribune* as saying that the American people "have no need for the rantings of the extreme Right, the latter-day professional anti-Communists who charge as much as $250 for admission to a Madison Square Garden rally." A dollar will get you ten that Dr. Schwarz gets paid less than Moss does. The one devotes his life to spreading truths about the Communist movement; the other, if his statement as quoted by the *Tribune* is any example, makes a career out of spreading defamatory statements under the auspices of an Anti-Defamation League. Mr. Moss doesn't trouble, for instance, to say that the $250 is for a sponsors' box, seating 18, not one seat (the bulk of which are available at $1.00); that Dr. Schwarz's entire campaign is based on voluntary contributions; that the government, having examined Dr. Schwarz's records, has officially ruled that contributions to his movement are, because his movement is educational in nature, tax-exempt; that the officers of the Anti-Defamation League are no pikers at raising great

sums of dough at dinners where you pay a hundred dollars for a piece of chicken and hours of oratory about
toleration; and that in any case, it is better to be a professional anti-Communist (by the way, aren't the directors of the CIA and the FBI—and the Joint Chiefs, for
that matter—also professional anti-Communists?) than a
professional defamer.

Next day, Nathan Mironov, county commander of
the Jewish War Veterans, speaks in New Jersey: "Dr.
Schwarz may garb himself as a lamb and claim that his
organization is only an innocent educational institution, but Americans who have followed his activities
know better," says Mironov darkly. "The tenor of
Dr. Schwarz's schools has been to carry on where
McCarthyism left off, making irresponsible denunciations of innocent individuals." Mironov can't *stand*
irresponsible denunciations of innocent individuals,
and anyone who disagrees with him is a fascist and an
anti-Semite.

Next day. The Grand Wizard speaks, the same
Arnold Forster, ADL's principal spokesman, who
refused to meet with Dr. Schwarz when Schwarz asked
for a meeting at which he might answer any questions
Mr. Forster or his colleagues cared to put to him about
his background, campaign and tactics. Mr. Forster,
reports the *Tribune*, "told of an effort by Dr. Schwarz
to get the Anti-Defamation League to hold a 'formal
hearing' to prove that Dr. Schwarz was not anti-
Jewish . . . Mr. Forster refused the request because 'we
will not permit ourselves to be used in this way.' " What
way *is* the Anti-Defamation League supposed to be
used, if not to prevent and expose defamations, or get
to the bottom of charges that defamations are being
committed?

"His program [Forster went on] calls for U.S. withdrawal from the United Nations [false]. It condemns our
effective anti-Communist programs [false] such as the

Alliance for Progress [false]. It confuses many Americans by offering inane, meaningless black-and-white solutions to our most complicated problems of survival [false]. It would have Americans stand by, mute and disorganized, each man searching for Communists at home, while international Communism capitalizes the distress and starvation of the world [false]."

Mr. Arnold Forster has never given any evidence that he knows anything worth passing along about Communism, and in our lives, we can't think of anyone who turned to any of his books or pamphlets for knowledge about Communism. Dr. Schwarz, by contrast, has instilled in thousands and thousands of Americans the desire to learn something more about the enemy which continues to press successfully a war against us. "The radical Right," Mr. Forster concluded, "is not doing a very good job at fighting Communism, but is doing a damnably effective job of preaching disunity among Americans and stimulating attacks on [our] basic institutions . . ." We don't know how Dr. Schwarz is feeling—he is much more saintly than we are—but we think it's time for a little disunity concerning the proposition that the people who run the Anti-Defamation League, a basic institution in these parts, care a hang for freedom of speech and assembly, or freedom from defamation.

THE MADISON SQUARE GARDEN RALLY

In due course the Madison Square Garden Anti-Communism Rally took place. In its June 29 edition, the *New York Herald Tribune* published "At the Garden, A Battle of Isms."

> While 200 pickets stood outside Madison Square Garden last night shouting and booing at the rally against communism going on inside, those inside were busy doing some shouting and booing themselves.

About 8,000 persons showed up for the rally, the stated purpose of which was to "voice effective opposition to communism." They voiced it all right. Every time the word "communism" was mentioned there were raucus shouts and razzberries.

Meanwhile, outside, the pickets were shouting that those inside were "Fascists" and that the main speaker, Dr. Fred C. Schwarz, should be made to leave town.

There was no real disorder, however. The pickets— members of the Anti-Fascist Youth Committee and the Advanced Youth Organization—marched back and forth in the area alloted them by police and the only thing ever close to a real argument was between the two groups outside. They argued over who should march where. The police settled their problem.

The pickets called, "One, two, three, four. We don't want another war." Then they added "Five, six, seven, eight. We don't want a Fascist state."

PICKETS INVITED INSIDE

About that time Dr. Schwarz walked out of the Garden and with a police escort went over to the picket line. "Come in and learn the truth rather than be prejudiced," he called.

Most of the pickets went right on shouting, but they ran out of steam and dispersed soon after Dr. Schwarz went back inside to preside over the rally. It was sponsored by the Anti-Communist Crusade, which Dr. Schwarz directs.

Those attending paid from $1 to $250 as the price of admission. Most of those attending were in the arena area or in boxes or loges. The balconies and mezzanine were deserted.

Those inside reserved their loudest booing for a mention of the recent Supreme Court decision prohibiting the saying of prayers in public schools. They also booed at a mention of the name of Bertrand Russell and the noise reached a crescendo when a speaker said he didn't think much of the "Better Red Than Dead" philosophy.

BOOS INTO CHEERS

The boos changed to hand-clapping and cheers when speakers on the platform made predictions that communism would eventually be defeated.

Speakers included Dr. Schwarz, Herbert A. Philbrick, author and former FBI undercover agent, Eugene Lyons, a Reader's Digest editor, and Arthur G. McDowell, an official of the Upholsterers' Union.

The scene outside the rally was exciting. Policemen on horseback separated two groups of heated pickets. I visited the pickets and thanked them for providing valuable publicity for our rally. I offered to shake hands. Some did, while others appeared nonplussed.

As is customary, the reporters looked for sensational statements to quote. One was made by the Christian entertainer Pat Boone, who said:

> Many today are saying "better Red than dead"; I say exactly the reverse. I would rather see each of my four daughters, Cherry, Lindy, Debby and Laury, lined up against a wall and shot in front of my eyes, than for them to grow up in a Communist United States. I'd rather see these kids blown into heaven by an atomic bomb than taught into hell by Communists. I pray to God I'll never be faced with this awful choice.

Pat Boone was illustrating the sincerity and depth of his faith in Jesus, his Lord. His statement was consonant with that of St. Paul who said, "For me to live is Christ and to die is gain." His attitude was comparable to that of Abraham, who was prepared to trust God even if it meant the temporary sacrifice of Isaac, the miracle son whom he loved.

Nevertheless, his statement was widely misunderstood.

THE GREATER NEW YORK SCHOOL
OF ANTI-COMMUNISM

After the excitement of the rally, our preparation for the New York School of Anti-Communism was relatively peaceful and quiet.

A school differs from a rally. A school is not designed to attract a large crowd, but to instruct those eager to learn the essential nature of Communism and how it entices, trains, and directs its recruits.

The Communist wishes to transform every recruit into a social scientist who will magnify his or her personal power by discerning, harnessing, and exploiting social forces. A social force is an idea, grievance, emotion, or objective that is shared by a substantial number of people. A typical social force is the desire for peace.

The large attendance at the Southern California School of Anti-Communism was the exception, not the rule.

Many conscientious Christians were uncertain about attending our schools. They were confused by conflicting reports, some from those who had actually attended our schools, others from denominational leaders who knew nothing except the lies they had been told. For example, I received this letter from the Reverend Ralph B. Krueger of Saint Margaret's Episcopal Church:

> The Episcopal Diocese of New York officially went on record at the Convention on May 8, 1962, condemning all extremists, left and right, as not being the will of God for the Church. Your group was mentioned specifically as one of the extreme right groups to be countered and avoided.
>
> A very strong exhortation by the Bishop of the Diocese, Horace W. B. Donnegan, mentioned your group, the Schwarz School, as well as Welch's John Birch bunch, as being the kind of extremism not tolerated by the gospel.
>
> Also we have been told and I thoroughly believe it in my own conviction, to publicly denounce you and the John Birch Society as I have publicly denounced and will continue to do so, the Marxist Communists.

In my brief reply I wrote,

> I am conscious that many church authorities have condemned the work of the Christian Anti-Communism Crusade. My question is, "Was this condemnation just?" Was it based on truth and factual evidence or on prejudice and slander? I have merely asked that I be provided with the evidence concerning the faults of the Christian Anti-Communism Crusade and myself so that I can rectify these faults if possible.
>
> I had hoped that your Christian conscience would indicate a personal responsibility to discover the evidence rather than a blind submission to ecclesiastical authority.
>
> God bless you.

Before attending our New York school, one conscientious church worker wrote to Congressman Judd to enquire about me.

Who was Walter Judd? His 1990 biography, titled *Missionary for Freedom—the Life and Times of Walter Judd* and by Lee Edwards, describes him thus:

> As an outstanding legislator, brilliant orator, and anti-communist crusader, former Minnesota Congressman Walter Judd helped shape United States history in the twentieth century.
>
> His encyclopedic knowledge and eloquent voice made him a central figure in U.S. foreign affairs in the post–World War II period. In addition Judd was voted one of the most admired members of Congress by his colleagues and was seriously considered as a vice presidential candidate by two American presidents.
>
> Born in a tiny Nebraska town in 1898, Walter Judd worked his way through medical school and spent ten years in war-torn China as a medical missionary. In fact no other American has been more identified with China

than Judd, who advised presidents from Truman to Reagan and secretaries of state from Marshall to Kissinger on U.S.-Sino relations. In 1981 President Reagan awarded him the Presidential Medal of Freedom, the nation's highest civilian award, for his skills as a healer, his eloquence as a communicator, and his lifelong opposition to tyranny and support of freedom at home and abroad.

After working as a medical missionary in China where he met and treated many of the Chinese Communist leaders, Dr. Judd served ten terms in Congress as a congressman from Minnesota and then devoted his remaining years to delivering magnificent lectures to diverse audiences on the nature and objectives of Communism. He warned constantly that its threat to freedom and all Americans was "real and present."

He became a regular member of the faculty at our Anti-Communism Schools and Anti-Subversive Seminars, and he would often state that he would rather speak to these students than to the Congress of the United States.

Though not a rich man, he refused to accept any fees for speaking on behalf of the Crusade. He was a regular financial contributor, and he left a bequest to the Crusade in his will. He died in 1993 at the age of ninety-five.

The contrast between the enlightened Christian conduct of Dr. Judd and the ignorant, bigoted statements of the officials of many churches is stark, as the letter on the next page demonstrates.

After the New York School of Anti-Communism, our team returned to the head office in California. Our opponents exulted because they thought our visit had been a failure. They made much of the report that expenditure had exceeded income by $75,000. But I considered the investment worthwhile because we made significant progress in our objectives in New York City. For example:

(1) *The New York Times* stopped classifying the Crusade as "right-wing extremist" and published many straightforward reports of the nature and activities of the Crusade and me.

R H. JUDD
r., MINNESOTA

COMMITTEE:
FOREIGN AFFAIR

Congress of the United States
House of Representatives
Washington, D. C.

August 28, 1962

Mrs. H. C. Campbell
247 Christopher Street
Upper Montclair, New Jersey

Dear Mrs. Campbell:

I am sorry that I was in Minnesota when your letter came but I hope this reply will not be too late for your purposes.

With respect to Dr. Schwarz, I have seen him on several occasions in the last decade or so and have participated in three of his so-called Schools on Communism. I think he is the most astute student of Communism as a disease of the human mind and of human behavior that I have known. I wish I might have had time and opportunity to participate more in the Schools where he has been trying under great difficulty and with great misrepresentations and opposition to alert people to the malignant process that continues to spread in our own and other countries.

When stories came to my attention that there was something bad or unfavorable about Dr. Schwarz, I tried my best to get some facts. I believe in the American system of considering every man innocent until he's proved guilty. Neither from our own Government agencies nor from any of those who have passed on the smears about Dr. Schwarz have I been able to get any tangible facts on which to base a judgment. It has been most disappointing to see how many supposedly Christian leaders have engaged in the very sort of character assassination which they denounced so vehemently when they were accusing others, like Senator McCarthy, of that practice.

I have often asked the critics of Dr. Schwarz what they themselves had done to help our people understand and combat more effectively the greatest menace our country has ever faced.

Some have suggested that Dr. Schwarz did not offer anything constructive and helpful to do about Communism. This is untrue. He consistently advocates a deeper understanding of and dedication to the Christian religion and its principles as the answer to Communism. That is quite an answer!

So, until or unless something factual is developed that is derogatory, I shall continue to support Dr. Schwarz and his work and hope he may be able to reach more and more of our people, so many of whom are still slumbering as we drift into greater and greater peril.

With very best wishes,

Sincerely yours,

Walter H. Judd

At that time, the *New York Post* was biased in favor of the liberal left and its reports on us had been derogatory and sometimes malicious. One of the reports, however, was so maliciously misleading that the publisher ordered the author to apologize to me.

(2) The charges that I was an anti-Semite became muted. I have rarely been accused of this during the past thirty years. The truth will out.

(3) I made lifelong friends who have supported me and the Crusade through the years. One of these is P. Kirby, Jr., in whose home I have spent many happy hours, and these visits have enriched my life. The Kirby Foundation was a generous supporter of the Crusade for many years.

I am glad we went to New York City.

31

....

The Destructive Generation

Thou shalt not be afraid for the terror by night;
nor for the arrow that flieth by day;
Nor for the pestilence that walketh in darkness;
nor for the destruction that wasteth at noonday.
—PSALM 91:5–6

AS THE DECADE OF THE 1960s advanced, great changes took place in America. These have been chronicled accurately in the book *The Destructive Generation,* by Peter Collier and David Horowitz.

The assassinations of President John F. Kennedy, Martin Luther King, Jr., and Robert Kennedy traumatized the national psyche.

The United States' involvement in the Vietnam War led to great internal strife. The New Left was born and grew, and universities and colleges were shaken by massive student revolts. Organizations such as Students for a Democratic Society (SDS), the Black Panthers, and the Weathermen faction of Students for a Democratic Society, became household words.

The split between the Russian and Chinese Communists led to numerous Communist sects in the United States. Intellectual and physical turmoil became the order of the day.

THE THREE FACES OF REVOLUTION

In an attempt to analyze and categorize the revolutionary forces that were operating, I wrote the book *The Three Faces of Revolution*. My good friend Tom Phillips published it through his firm, Capital Hill Press, Washington, in 1972. Tom's entrepreneurial success during the past twenty years is proof that America remains the land of opportunity. He is an inspiration to many young aspiring conservative students and graduates.

In *The Three Faces of Revolution* I described three major categories of revolutionary theory and practice: (1) Communism, (2) Anarchism, and (3) Political Sensualism—the politics of sex. These tendencies sometimes competed and sometimes cooperated in a program to destroy the constitutional democracy of the United States.

1973
ANCESTRAL VOICES PROPHESYING WAR

The history of the three decades from 1960 to 1990 vindicated my diagnosis and prognosis of the character and intentions of Communism.

In my testimony given to the House Committee on Un-American Activities on May 29, 1957, I said that the Communist leaders Stalin and Mao were anticipating the world triumph of Communism by the year 1973. I had based that statement upon information provided by officials of the Republic of China that Stalin and Mao Tse-tung had agreed on that date during their meeting in Moscow in 1952.

Additional evidence is now available. Dr. Li Zhisui was Mao's personal physician from 1954 until Mao's death in 1976. In 1994 Random House published Li Zhisui's book, *The Secret Life of Chairman Mao*.

Li reports that he accompanied Mao to Moscow in November 1957 to celebrate the fortieth anniversary of the Communist conquest of Russia. He writes:

> Mao was optimistic about the future, exhilarated by the prediction he had made in his own speech. Within

fifteen years, Mao said to the assembled delegates, the Soviet Union will overtake the United States in the production of steel and other major industrial products and China will overtake Great Britain. Within fifteen years, he asserted, the material conditions in the Communist world will be transformed, their economies surpassing those of the Capitalist West. With the transformation of the material base, the whole world would be ripe for the Communist revolution.

Add fifteen years to 1957 and you get 1972.

THIRD WORLD WAR

At that time Mao was not only willing but eager to provoke a shooting war with the United States. Let me again quote from *Khrushchev Remembers,* published in 1970. Khrushchev reports that Mao assured him—

> that the atomic bomb itself was a paper tiger! "Listen, Comrade Khrushchev," he said. "All you have to do is provoke the Americans into military action, and I'll give you as many divisions as you need to crush them—a hundred, two hundred, one thousand divisions." I tried to explain to him that one or two missiles could turn all the divisions in China to dust. But he wouldn't even listen to the arguments and obviously regarded me as a coward.

MAO'S ANTI-RIGHTIST CAMPAIGN

Mao's contempt for individual life is reported by Li.

> Only three years later, in 1960, when China's foreign minister, Chen Yi, told me that half a million people had been labeled rightists, did I know that the numbers were just too large and that most of those people had been

falsely accused. What was most disturbing was that the
various work units charged with finding rightists had
been assigned a quota. Every place had to declare 5 percent of its members guilty of being rightists, whether
they really were rightists or not. Hundreds of thousands
of people had been falsely accused.

It was only later, too, that I began to understand what
it meant to be labeled a rightist, how many people lost
their jobs, were sent to labor reform camps, and died
miserable deaths. It is true that Mao did not kill his
opponents right away. But the physical and mental hard-
ship of his "reforms" often meant a tortuously slow and
painful death. Only when I was sent myself to participate in hard labor for a mere two weeks did I begin to
have an inkling of what life in the labor reform camps
was like. They could take a man who could carry only
twenty *jin* of stones and force him to carry forty, and
when his body broke and he could go no further, they
would say it was because he was a rightist. And as he lay
there shattered and broken, helpless, they would force
him to confess to his crimes and then to betray other
people. People died in those labor reform camps, where
death seemed better than Mao's reform.

I should have known. I had opportunities to know.
Mao himself had given me plenty of hints. "If we were
to add up all the landlords, rich peasants, counterrevolu-
tionaries, bad elements, and rightists, their number
would reach thirty million," he said to me one day. "If
we put them all together in one area, they would constitute a good-size nation. They could make all sorts of
trouble. But dispersed among the various party and government organs, they're just a tiny minority. Of our total
population of six hundred million people, these thirty
million are only one out of twenty. So what is there to
be afraid of? Some of our party members cannot see this
point. I've told them to just stand firm when they're
under attack. Stick it out. But some of them thought it

was disastrous to be attacked. They couldn't stand it anymore, and some of them even wanted to leave the party and join the rightists to attack us. Now we have identified all these people, and we are going to attack them."

This was the first I had heard that there were some 30 million "enemies of the people." The figure seemed enormous. But by then I knew that Mao rarely spoke without good reason, and his figure must have come from a reliable source. Later I would come to believe the figure was even higher.

I had had intimations, too, of how little the lives of his countrymen meant to Mao.

"We have so many people," he would say. "We can afford to lose a few. What difference does it make?"

Mao was a true Leninist in his attitude to life and death and was a devotee of mass action. He preferred mass killing over individual punishment.

The Soviet leader Nikita Khrushchev visited China in 1954 and was disturbed by his conversations with Mao. He returned to Moscow with foreboding about future relations between Russia and China. In *Khrushchev Remembers,* he writes:

I remember that when I came back from China in 1954 I told my comrades, "Conflict with China is inevitable." I came to this conclusion on the basis of the various remarks Mao had made.

During my visit to Peking, the atmosphere was typically Oriental. Everyone was unbelievably courteous and ingratiating, but I saw through their hypocrisy. After I had arrived, Mao and I embraced each other warmly and kissed each other on both cheeks. We used to lie around a swimming pool in Peking, chatting like the best of friends about all kinds of things. But it was all too sickeningly sweet. The atmosphere was nauseating. In addition some of the things Mao said put me on my guard. I was never exactly sure that I understood what he meant. I thought at the time that it must have been because of some special traits in the Chinese character and the Chinese way of thinking.

Khrushchev had no difficulty, however, in understanding Mao's statements about fomenting war with the United States.

NUCLEAR DETERRENCE

Did the nuclear bomb prevent a third world war at that time? Khrushchev did not object to the idea of war with the United States on moral or political grounds. His objection was that such a war could not be won.

32

....

The Soviet Union
Follows the Plan

The improvement of the understanding is for two ends:
first, for our own increase of knowledge;
secondly, to enable us to deliver and take out that knowledge
to others.
—John Locke, 1632–1704
("Thoughts Concerning Reading and Study")

THOUGH MUCH IN THIS CHAPTER has been touched upon in
other pages, some recapitulation and further comment is in order
here.

The Soviet plan for world conquest was described in chapter 8.
More sophisticated than the immediate war that Mao advocated, it
aimed to avoid nuclear destruction and allow the Communists to
enjoy the massive material wealth that Capitalism had created.

The Communist program followed the formula, "External encirclement plus demoralization plus thermonuclear blackmail lead to
progressive surrender."

As a major step toward military encirclement, the Soviet Union
installed nuclear missiles in Cuba capable of delivering an atomic
strike against the major cities on the east coast of the United States.

Their discovery by U.S. intelligence precipitated the Cuban missile crisis of 1962. President Kennedy announced to a startled nation that military action against Cuba must be taken unless the missiles were removed.

The reaction of some verged on hysteria. Linus Pauling, who twice received the Nobel Prize, said on TV, "Tomorrow we will all be dead."

During this period, the Reverend Robert H. Schuller, who had recently begun his remarkable ministry that is now headquartered in the Crystal Cathedral in Garden Grove, California, said to me, "The only people in our congregation who are not terrified are those who have heard your lecture on the dialectic."

In this lecture I had explained that the Communist philosophy, "dialectic materialism," taught that progress was achieved by a series of advances and retreats, like driving a nail into a block of wood. Each blow achieves a small advance toward the objective. I predicted that Khrushchev would act dialectically and remove the missiles. His decision to do this was announced the following day.

But the installation of the missiles did advance Communist objectives. For removing them, Khrushchev received a promise that the United States would not take military action to expel the Communist regime from Cuba and that the United States would remove nuclear missiles in Turkey.

President Kennedy had announced earlier that the presence of a Communist regime in the Western hemisphere was intolerable. After the missile crisis he became committed to tolerating the intolerable.

Khrushchev also gained credit for being a man of peace who had saved the world from nuclear destruction by removing the deadly missiles, although he had caused the danger by installing them.

This strategy of Communist "historical" progress without major war was called "peaceful coexistence." It was defined by the Communists as an "advanced form of class struggle," and it was their responsibility to lead the struggle until "the people" achieved victory over "the Imperialist enemy," the Imperialists meaning the United States and the industrialized nations of the Western world and Japan. The Soviet Union was the leader of the forces of liberation, prosperity, peace, and happiness. Large Socialist resources went into a campaign that used literature, radio, national organizations, and agents to spread this message. Though major military war was undesirable, wars of national liberation were essential.

As I traveled and lectured I displayed samples of the colorful and attractive literature that the Soviet Union and Communist China distributed, drawing special attention to their delightful children's literature that entertained while giving the message that the Communists were their friends who brought happiness and all good things.

In order to keep abreast of Communist doctrinal and strategic developments I read their esoteric literature that appealed to the mind rather than the emotions. It presented Marxist doctrines and philosophy for thinking students, with the hope that some of them would be convinced by the doctrines, dedicate their lives to the Communist Party, and become leaders in their own countries.

I urged the authorities in the United States to spend a sum equal to 1 percent of the military budget to expose the Communist lie. The Crusade did as much as we could with our limited resources to take the truth to many nations. We conducted seminars, produced and distributed literature, and supported national truth-tellers.

The founder of the Methodist Church, John Wesley, said, "The world is my parish," a motto adopted by the Crusade. Many devoted persons have embraced and served it diligently and effectively; outstanding among them are the Reverend James Colbert and Dr. John Whitehall.

THE REVEREND JAMES COLBERT

I met Jim Colbert (see chapter 9) soon after my arrival in the States in 1953. At that time he was director of Youth for Christ in Long Beach, California, a national organization recently formed by young Christian leaders, one of whom was Billy Graham. When the Crusade was formed, he became vice-president and director of missions. He later became chairman of the board also.

He has devoted much of his time to conducting anti-Communism seminars in Central and South America, Africa, and Asia. Here is an incomplete list of countries he has served: Mexico, Guatemala,

Nicaragua, El Salvador, British Honduras, Belize, Panama, Costa Rica, Venezuela, Peru, Paraguay, Argentina, Chile, and the Dominican Republic in the Western hemisphere; Nigeria, Ghana, Kenya, Tanzania, Zambia, Zimbabwe, and South Africa in Africa; and India, Taiwan, Korea, and Japan in Asia.

The following clips from Jim Colbert's reports are selected from hundreds:

> One of the first things that my host in Nigeria, Evangelist N. C. Joseph, said to me was, "Since your first visit to Nigeria, the fires of anti-Communism have been burning and we are winning."
>
> *February–March 1988*

> Clark Bowers accompanied me to Nigeria. When Clark witnessed the enthusiastic response of the pastors and people in Nigeria and how they commit themselves to the struggle, he told me, "I have been somewhat cynical about our chances against Communism, but since coming to Nigeria I can see how one man can make a difference in these countries. The people accept your message without question. This is the way to go."
>
> *February–March 1988*

> Our first seminar was at the University of Arts and Sciences at Oyo, Nigeria. My African colleagues and I seemed to sense a spirit of excitement and anticipation emanating from the crowd. Many remembered our seminar there last year when the professors who were serving as leaders of the Nigerian-Soviet Union Friendship Association (a Communist front) resigned from the Association en masse after the seminar.
>
> *January–February 19, 1990*

God gave Jim a tender heart; appeals for help never fail to move him to action. His Christian faith is inspiring.

Wherever he goes he meets with statesmen, educators, news moguls, ministers, and students, often facing danger with courage and serenity. After being with Jim in many countries, Clark Bowers wrote in 1995, "Give my very best personal regards to the most humble and courageous man I know, Jim Colbert."

DR. JOHN WHITEHALL

As I said earlier, Lillian and I have always been proud to claim John Whitehall as our foster son; John and our natural son John Schwarz were like twins.

John Whitehall became a medical doctor, a serious student of Communism, and an active anti-Communist crusader. Like Jim, John never flinched in the face of danger.

In 1975 in East Timor, a colony in the Portuguese empire, a revolution broke out. The Portuguese government evacuated their officials and troops, leaving the indigenous revolutionary forces to fight among themselves. For some time all that the outside world knew about Timor was that a pall of smoke enveloped the island.

John Whitehall organized an expedition to take medical services to the island. On landing and finding many wounded needing urgent attention, he performed life-saving surgery on many patients from both sides in the conflict.

John and his wife Elsie spent time in Vietnam under the aegis of the World Council of Churches, but they soon became disillusioned with the policies and activities of the Council and left. Later, John served at a missionary hospital in South Africa.

He continued his study of Communist doctrines and became increasingly active as a writer and lecturer. He represented the Crusade in Mexico and Canada and was frequently a member of the faculty of our Anti-Communism Schools.

He became director of the Pacific Christian Anti-Communism Crusade. His work in the Philippines was so effective that the New People's Army (NPA) of the Philippine Communist Party placed him on their list for assassination.

In order to cope with the needs of his growing family, John returned to Australia in 1990 and resumed his pediatric medical practice. He and Elsie continued their Christian service.

THE MENACE OF SDI

The paradoxical situation arose that transformed the weapons of total destruction into the guardians of peace. Logically, the certainty of mutual destruction would be abolished if either side obtained an effective defense against nuclear weapons, which explains the opposition of the Soviet Communists and also the opposition of many non-Communists in the United States to the Strategic Defense Initiative (SDI). Gorbachev wrote:

> Of course, our people are alarmed by the Strategic Defense Initiative. We have said this more than once. But maybe they are merely trying to intimidate us again? Perhaps it is better to stop fearing SDI?
>
> Indifference was certainly inadmissible. We saw that although millions of Americans, including prominent political and public leaders, ordinary people, scientists, religious leaders, and school and university students, were against SDI and nuclear tests, some quarters in the United States had gone crazy over the Star Wars program. This was all the more dangerous because it ensued directly from a rapid militarization of political thought. And yet it was necessary to get rid of the impression about us for which we were not responsible. They think that if the USSR is afraid of SDI, it should be intimidated with SDI morally, economically, politically and militarily. This explains the great stress on SDI, the aim being to exhaust us. So, we have decided to say: yes, we are against SDI, because we are for complete elimination of nuclear weapons and because SDI makes the world ever more unstable. But for us the issue involves responsibility rather than fear, because the consequences would be unpredictable. Instead of promoting security, SDI destroys the remnants of what might still serve security.
>
> Speaking in Togliatti, I decided to say once again that our response to SDI would be effective. The United States hopes that we will develop similar systems, so it

can get ahead of us technologically and take advantage of its technological superiority. But we, the Soviet leadership, know that there is nothing which the US could achieve that our scientists and engineers could not. A tenth of the US investments would be enough to create a counter-system to frustrate SDI.

Gorbachev recognized a trap and decided to fall into it.

Actually, the Soviet plan for the conquest of the United States did not require vast nuclear destruction. The role of nuclear weapons was to make nuclear war unthinkable while the Communist forces expanded their worldwide power by adding country after country to the ranks of anti-Imperialists through wars of *national* liberation. By this process, the forces of Communism would become overwhelming and a series of accommodations would ultimately result in Soviet hegemony—the process I named "progressive surrender."

During the 1960s and the 1970s this program made great progress. Anticolonial and anti-Imperialist wars of national liberation transformed many countries of Asia, Africa, and Latin America into willing or unconscious allies of Communism. It finally failed because the conditions of disunity, economic exhaustion, and corruption that Marxists believed would develop in the Capitalist countries developed instead in the Socialist countries, and these finally destroyed both the Soviet empire and the Soviet Union itself.

Some quotations from Gorbachev's *Perestroika* are illuminating, and not entirely consistent. The following excerpts are self-explanatory.

He wrote:

I shall repeat that as far as the United States foreign policy is concerned, it is based on at least two delusions. The first is the belief that the economic system of the Soviet Union is about to crumble and that the USSR will not succeed in restructuring. The second is calculated on Western superiority in equipment and technology and, eventually, in the military field. These illusions nourish a policy geared toward exhausting socialism through the arms race, so as to dictate terms later. Such is the scheme; it is naive.

History has proved that it was Gorbachev who harbored the delusions. In the first chapter of his 1987 book *Perestroika,* he described the true situation in the Soviet Union.

> Analyzing the situation, we first discovered a slowing economic growth. In the last fifteen years the national income growth rates had declined by more than half and by the beginning of the eighties had fallen to a level close to economic stagnation. (page 15)
>
> As time went on, material resources became harder to get and more expensive. On the other hand, the expensive methods of fixed capital expansion resulted in an artificial shortage of manpower. In an attempt to rectify the situation somehow, large, unjustified, i.e., in fact unearned, bonuses began to be paid and all kinds of undeserved incentives introduced under the pressure of this shortage, and that led, at a later stage, to the practice of padding reports merely for gain. Parasitical attitudes were on the rise, the prestige of conscientious and high-quality labor began to diminish and a "wage-leveling" mentality was becoming widespread. The imbalance between the measure of work and the measure of consumption, which had become something like the linchpin of the braking mechanism, not only obstructed the growth of labor productivity, but led to the distortion of the principle of social justice.
>
> So the inertia of extensive economic development was leading to an economic deadlock and stagnation. (page 20)
>
> We failed to use to the full the potential of socialism to meet the growing requirements in housing, in quality and sometimes quantity of foodstuffs, in the proper organization of the work of transport, in health services, in education and in tackling other problems which, naturally, arose in the course of society's development.

An absurd situation was developing. The Soviet Union, the world's biggest producer of steel, raw materials, fuel and energy, has shortfalls in them due to wasteful or inefficient use. One of the biggest producers of grain for food, it nevertheless has to buy millions of tons of grain a year for fodder. We have the largest number of doctors and hospital beds per thousand of the population and, at the same time, there are glaring shortcomings in our health services. Our rockets can find Halley's comet and fly to Venus with amazing accuracy, but side by side with these scientific and technological triumphs is an obvious lack of efficiency in using scientific achievements for economic needs, and many Soviet household appliances are of poor quality.

This, unfortunately, is not all. A gradual erosion of the ideological and moral values of our people began. (page 21)

Thus economic deterioration was correlated with, or caused by, an accompanying moral degeneration.

Eulogizing and servility were encouraged; the needs and opinions of ordinary working people, of the public at large, were ignored. In the social sciences scholastic theorization was encouraged and developed, but creative thinking was driven out from the social sciences, and superfluous and voluntarist assessments and judgments were declared indisputable truths. Scientific, theoretical and other discussions, which are indispensable for the development of thought and for creative endeavor, were emasculated. Similar negative tendencies also affected culture, the arts and journalism, as well as the teaching process and medicine, where mediocrity, formalism and loud eulogizing surfaced, too.

The presentation of a "problem-free" reality backfired: a breach had formed between word and deed, which bred public passivity and disbelief in the slogans

being proclaimed. It was only natural that this situation
resulted in a credibility gap: everything that was proclaimed from the rostrums and printed in newspapers
and textbooks was put in question. Decay began in public morals; the great feeling of solidarity with each other
that was forged during the heroic times of the Revolution, the first five-year plans, the Great Patriotic War
and postwar rehabilitation was weakening; alcoholism,
drug addiction and crime were growing; and the pene-
tration of the stereotypes of mass culture alien to us,
which bred vulgarity and low tastes and brought about
ideological barrenness increased. (pages 21, 22)

This deterioration was evident throughout the entire ranks of the
Communist Party, including the supreme leadership.

At a certain stage this made for a poorer performance
by the Politburo and the Secretariat of the CPSU Central
Committee, by the government and throughout the
entire Central Committee and the Party apparatus, for
that matter.
Political flirtation and mass distribution of awards,
titles and bonuses often replaced genuine concern for the
people, for their living and working conditions, for a
favorable social atmosphere. An atmosphere emerged of
"everything goes," and fewer and fewer demands were
made on discipline and responsibility. Attempts were
made to cover it all up with pompous campaigns and
undertakings and celebrations of numerous anniversaries
centrally and locally. The world of day-to-day realities
and the world of feigned prosperity were diverging more
and more. (page 22)

These quotations from *Perestroika* are sufficient to show that the
process that led to the sudden collapse of the Soviet Union was
almost the mirror image of its projections for the collapse of the
United States—external encirclement, internal demoralization, and
nuclear blackmail.

Gorbachev sought to reform the Communist Party of the Soviet Union, not destroy it. He was like a technician who, polishing a huge rough diamond, shatters it in the process.

The collapse of Communism in Eastern Europe and the Soviet Union could be called "The revenge of human nature."

33

....

Freud to the Rescue

Progress beyond the primal horde—i.e., civilization—
presupposes guilt feelings: it introjects into the individuals,
and thus sustains, the principal prohibitions, constraints,
and delays in gratification on which civilization depends.
—HERBERT MARCUSE (*EROS AND CIVILIZATION*)

DURING THE 1960s, A STRANGE phenomenon that became
known as the New Left developed on U.S. campuses. This movement incorporated many of the ideas of Herbert Marcuse, "The
guru of the New Left."

Following the rise of Hitler, Marcuse left Germany and sought
refuge in the United States, where he taught at various universities
and finally at the University of California at San Diego, and directed
the graduate studies of the radical Communist Angela Davis, among
others.

Marcuse was a Marxist who was enamored with revolution. He
regretted that the American working class was failing to fulfill its
"revolutionary duty" to overthrow Capitalism. He blamed this on
the development of a "false consciousness" in the workers due to the
material blessings such as homes, cars, and television sets that Cap-

italism had provided. These riches were made possible because a "welfare through warfare" state existed in industrial countries.

Marcuse believed that this state should be overthrown. How? He turned to the teachings of Sigmund Freud, the founder of psycho-analysis, for assistance, and sought to deenergize capitalist society through a "sexual revolution."

Freud taught that two basic instincts provide the energy to sustain life and society—the sex instinct and the death instinct, "thanatos." The former provides the constructive energy of society, the latter its destructive energy.

The energy used in construction is sublimated sexual energy. This is made available by restricting sexual indulgence to "monogamic patriarchal sex," or heterosexual intercourse within marriage, while other channels for the expenditure of sexual energy are blocked. The residual potential energy can be used for constructive purposes. To the faithful Freudian, the statement "Sex built the Boulder Dam" rings true.

Marcuse advocated the "resexualization of the human body" so that numerous areas would be used for erotic purposes. By expending the bulk of sexual energy in sexual activity, the supply for constructive labor would lessen and capitalist society would thus be deenergized.

A San Diego woman audited one of Marcuse's classes and accused him of promoting sexual promiscuity. He replied:

"Madame, you do not understand. What I do is much worse. I am teaching the political consequences of the Sexual Revolution."

In the political preface to his seminal book *Eros and Civilization*, published in 1966, Marcuse wrote:

> It was the thesis of *Eros and Civilization*, more fully developed in my *One Dimensional Man*, that man could avoid the fate of a Welfare-Through-Warfare State only by achieving a new starting point where he could reconstruct the productive apparatus without that "inner-worldly asceticism" which provided the mental basis for domination and exploration. "Polymorphous sexuality" was the term which I used to indicate that the new direction of progress would depend completely on the opportunity to activate repressed or arrested *organic,* biological needs; to make the human body *an instrument of pleasure rather than labor.*
>
> *Eros and Civilization*

This vision of Marcuse has been realized in the sexual revolution, which has contributed to heterosexual and homosexual promiscuity, widespread illegitimacy, the breakdown of the family, massive welfare programs, and of course the AIDS epidemic.

The harvest of Marcuse's teaching can be seen in the centers of such cities as Washington, D.C., Los Angeles, and Detroit.

In due course an opportunity came for a confrontation with Marcuse. On January 2, 1970, a letter from the Extension Department of the University of California at San Diego invited me to participate in a debate with Professor Marcuse. The debate was to be part of a course entitled, "Conservative and Traditional Views on Contemporary Issues." I accepted.

On March 13, 1970, the *Triton Times*, the San Diego campus student newspaper, published the following letter by Herbert Marcuse:

> I strongly protest against the university sponsorship of Dr. Fred Schwarz in the course 139X of the Extension Division.

Dr. Schwarz is the chief of the so-called "Christian Anti-Communism Crusade." The publication *Danger on the Right*, by Arnold Forster and Benjamin R. Epstein (1964), sponsored by the Anti-Defamation League of B'nai Brith, devotes a whole chapter to Dr. Schwarz, to which I refer for documentation. It presents him as a hate-monger and rabble rouser of apparently hysterical stature. The same chapter also reports on the way his Crusade is financed. I was told that Dr. Schwarz intends to attack me, and I was asked whether I would appear at his lecture. I like to be attacked if my critics have read and, preferably, understood my books. This does not seem to be the case of Dr. Schwarz, as shown by his "exegesis" of what he thinks is my philosophy, or that of Marx and Freud. I therefore declined the invitation.

I consider the appearance of Dr. Schwarz in a university course an insult to the intelligence of any serious audience, a mockery of genuine education, and a mockery of conservative thought.

The *Triton Times* published my reply on March 18, 1970. It is printed in *The Three Faces of Revolution* (pages 176–177):

Dr. Marcuse appears to hold his colleagues and the students at the University of California at San Diego in low esteem. He would protect them from the danger of hearing me lecture. He does not think they are capable of recognizing a "hate-monger and rabble-rouser of apparently hysterical stature" and making their own judgment. In his letter to Dr. Martin N. Chamberlain—director, University Extension, USCD, published in your edition of March 13—he strongly protests that I am to deliver one lecture entitled "A Rebuttal to the Left" in the series "Conservative and Traditional Views on Contemporary Issues."

If everything Dr. Marcuse says about me in his letter were true (and much of it is false), it would still indicate that I represent a significant influence meriting study. The fact that the book *Danger on the Right* by Arnold Forster and Benjamin Epstein, which is sponsored by the Anti-Defamation League of B'nai Brith, devotes a whole chapter to me, indicates this. In passing, I mention that this chapter contains 32 errors of fact.

I have read the available books of Herbert Marcuse. These include: *Reason and Revolution, Negations, Soviet Marxism, Eros and Civilization, One Dimensional Man,* and an *Essay on Liberation.* I have also read several essays and articles written by Dr. Marcuse. I do not claim to have understood all that he has written. I sincerely doubt if Herbert Marcuse has done this. I do claim that I have understood sufficient to justify comment and criticism. The extent of my understanding I leave to the verdict of those who hear the lecture.

I intend to discuss the message of Herbert Marcuse on the basis of the books he has written himself and not on those of his enemies.

Herbert Marcuse's letter provoked considerable interest in the editorial pages of many newspapers, which stimulated interest in the program scheduled for April 2, 1970.

Harold Keen, news director of a San Diego TV station, invited me to appear for an interview on his "Encounter" program. I accepted.

During the interview, March 18, 1970, Keen said, "Herbert Marcuse has accused you of being a hate-monger and a rabble-rouser of apparently hysterical stature. Are you a hate-monger?"

"I certainly do seem to arouse some people," I said. "I appear to have aroused Herbert Marcuse. Whether that makes me a rabble-rouser is a matter of opinion. As for being a hate-monger, I am too happy to hate. God and life have been good to me. You cannot hate while you're happy."

As the lecture drew near, tensions rose. Rumors of demonstrations circulated. The big question was, "Will there be violence?"

Two hundred "radical" students gathered outside the Scripps Auditorium where the session was to be held. They were not protesting my appearance, but rather their exclusion from the lecture. This was an official university function, and an admittance fee of $4 had been set by the university. The students outside claimed they could not afford it. I ended up saying that the Christian Anti-Communism Crusade would pay the $4 fee for each student, and forty-four were admitted.

Behavior during the lecture was perfect. Following the lecture, all questions were pertinent and searching. There was no evident hostility from the students, though there was some from adults.

One adult, whom I assumed to be a faculty member, regretted that no one was at the meeting to speak up for Herbert Marcuse. Who was to blame for that?

The final question caused considerable consternation. A young man rose and asked, "Fred, are you against f---ing?" A shocked hush came over the audience. In those days the word was unspeakable in respectable, especially mixed, company. The chairman refused to accept his question, and a father in the audience said to me later, "If my daughter had been there I would have knocked him down." Another said he wanted to sue the university.

I rose and pointed out that we had just witnessed an application of the teaching of Marcuse on the uses of "verbal violence" or obscenity. He taught that one big problem that confronted young idealistic revolutionaries was the danger of being co-opted by representatives of Capitalism and transformed from "revolutionaries" into "reformers." When this danger became evident the discourse could be interrupted by using obscenity.

The audience clapped and cheered, including the young man who had asked the question.

34

....

Bring on the Clowns

A vile conceit in pompous words expressed
Is like a clown in regal purple dressed.
—ALEXANDER POPE (*ESSAY ON CRITICISM*)

IT'S HARD TO IMAGINE A circus without its clowns. The "Circus Maximus Slanderous" featured many acts of serious character assassination during the 1960s, and some that were clownish. These have continued until recent times. The magazine *The Humanist* featured an article in its September/October 1992 edition that is worthy of *Mad* magazine. It is entitled, "The Great Right Snark Hunt," and it states:

> In the late 1950s and early 1960s, a network of nativist anti-communists spread the gospel of the Red menace through books, magazine articles, and workshops. Perhaps the most influential leader of this movement was Dr. Fred Schwarz and his California-based Christian Anti-Communist Crusade. A tireless lecturer, Schwarz wrote *You Can Trust the Communists (to be Communists)* in 1960; it sold over one million copies and soon became the secular Bible of the nativists.

As I read this I was flattered but puzzled: flattered to learn that I was the most influential leader of a movement and that my book was its Bible, but puzzled because I had no idea who the "nativists" were. American history is not a staple in Australian schools.

I consulted various dictionaries, and all I learned was that "nativists" were dedicated to preserving the rights of native-born Americans from the threat of immigrants.

I remained puzzled, for I am an Australian whose green card certifies that I am an immigrant. Apparently I was considered by the author to be an immigrant leading an anti-immigrant movement in the United States. This seemed unusual to say the least.

The author was identified as Chip Berlet, an analyst at Political Research Associates. The information about him in the article was limited to the *Nation, In These Times,* the *Utne Reader,* and the *Progressive.* These magazines leaned to the left, and it was reasonable to assume that he shared their philosophy.

How did he reach the conclusion that my book "became the secular Bible of the nativists"? It contains no discussion of problems associated with immigration. What it does is analyses the pathological nature of Communist doctrines, organizations, practices, and objectives and dares to make a prognosis of future Communist conduct.

It is true that the message of the book conflicts with the delusional convictions and hopes of those who believe that Communism is benign. These delusions were not uncommon in academic circles in bygone years and some linger on. One leading academic, the historian Eugene Genovese, confessed his delusions and consequent harmful activities in the April 17, 1995, edition of the magazine *The New Republic.* In a review of the book *The Age of Extremes, A History of the World, 1914–1991,"* by the noted historian Eric Hobsbawm, Genovese wrote:

> Many of us who supported the socialist bloc to the
> bitter end believed for a long time that the political
> Byzantinism, mass murders, and bureaucratic rigidities
> of socialism would be overcome, that these horrors were
> all that was keeping capitalism afloat. We overestimated

the weaknesses of capitalism and we underestimated the weaknesses of socialism. In effect, we remained convinced that capitalism could not solve its problems, but that socialism would solve its own. But those latter problems were not passing, they were intrinsic. And so our blunder, as blunders go, was a beaut.

Does Berlet believe that Genovese has become a "snark hunter," the term the author uses to identify anti-Communists? It only reveals the author's conviction that the Communist danger never existed. This is comparable to believing that the Nazi danger never existed. Berlet will surely resent being likened to those who belittle or deny the hideous crimes perpetrated during the holocaust, but his statements justify the comparison.

An explanation of why I have never applied to become an American citizen is appropriate at this juncture. To be an American citizen would be a great honor, and I have considered it. Why have I not done so?

I was born, nurtured, and educated in Australia, and my roots there are deep. A substantial part of my motivation for seeking to expose the dangers of Communism to the American people was to contribute to the security of Australia if the Communist plan to conquer all Southeast Asia should succeed. As reported previously, my wife Lillian decided to educate our children in Australia and all our family is based there. I would have been proud to have joint citizenship in Australia and the United States but no appropriate opportunity to seek this ever arose.

Has my continuing Australian citizenship been a handicap? I do not believe so. I have been overwhelmed by the hospitality and acceptance of the vast majority of American citizens with whom I have come in contact. They have judged the message rather than the messenger. Occasionally I have met traces of xenophobia. Once or twice when I have been a guest on a talk show, a caller has advised me to "go back to Australia where you belong, and stop interfering in the internal affairs of the United States." I have never had to reply. Supporters have always rushed to my defense and assured me that I am most welcome here. The United States has a hospitable heart, and I will be eternally grateful.

Finally, on the article: The author Berlet alleges the existence of a vast "nativist" conspiracy, a major menace. He identifies anti-Communism with "nativism." He states, "In the late 1950s and early 1960s, a network of nativist anti-Communists spread the gospel of the Red Menace through books, magazine articles, and workshops . . . The Goldwater nomination was the high point for the resurgent nativists in the 1960s."

Berlet claims that an exploitable paranoid strain exists in America. He may be right. If he is serious in his quest to find a believer in a vast paranoid conspiracy, a look into a mirror would guarantee success.

35

·······················

Class Warfare in the U.S.A. and Anti-Subversive Seminars

And the mind's evil lusts and deadly war
lie at the threshold of hell.
—VIRGIL (*THE AENEID*)

A little learning is a dangerous thing.
—ALEXANDER POPE

THE EXPECTATIONS OF THE COMMUNIST leaders that internal forces in America would develop and ultimately lead to the overthrow of the government seemed to be approaching fulfillment during the 1960s and early 1970s. The Vietnam War was generating forces of internal conflict that were tearing asunder the fabric of national unity. These forces included the Weathermen faction of Students for a Democratic Society and the Black Panthers. Both accepted the Leninist doctrine of Imperialism and set out to make the United States ungovernable.

The Weathermen summarized the Leninist doctrine of Imperialism in their official document, "You Don't Need a Weatherman to Know Which Way the Wind Blows." The title was inspired by a Bob Dylan song.

380

We are within the heartland of a worldwide monster, a country so rich from its worldwide plunder that even the crumbs doled out to the enslaved masses within its borders provide for material existence very much above the conditions of the masses of people of the world. The U.S. empire, as a worldwide system, channels wealth, based upon the labor and resources of the rest of the world, into the United States. The relative affluence existing in the United States is directly dependent upon the labor and natural resources of the Vietnamese, the Angolans, the Bolivians, and the rest of the people of the Third World. All the United Airlines Astrojets, all the Holiday Inns, all Hertz's automobiles, your television set, car, and wardrobe already belong, to a large degree, to the people of the rest of the world.

> Harold Jacobs, ed., *Weatherman*
> (Berkeley, Ramparts Press, 1970)

They set out to "Bring the War Home."
Giving a report on terroristic activity at hearings before a subcommittee of the committee on the Judiciary of the United States Senate, in 1974, I said:

> Those who became Weathermen believed this so sincerely that they became articulate and active enemies of their own country and dedicated their lives to violent overthrow of the capitalist system. They felt they must engage in criminal activity.
>
> To many American citizens this Weatherman statement appears ridiculous. Unfortunately, it does not appear ridiculous to many university students. Recently I traveled by bus from New York to Philadelphia. A student from the University of Pennsylvania sat beside me. We discussed revolutionary activity on the university campus, and he gave no indication of being a radical. However, I quoted the above Weatherman description of

the United States of America and his reply startled me:
"What's wrong with that?"

(Hearings, U.S. Government Printing Office,
Part 3, July 5, 1975)

THE BLACK PANTHERS

The Black Panther Party was formed by Huey Newton and Bobby Seale in Oakland, California, in 1966. Under the inspiration of the statement of the Chinese Communist leader, Mao Tse-tung, that "political power grows out of the barrel of a gun," the Black Panthers picked up the gun. A favorite slogan of Newton was, "The Red Book and what else? The gun!"

The American psyche was wounded, and disorder prevailed. Destructive forces were rampant on campuses of major universities, in the black ghettos of the central cities, and in numerous public demonstrations.

Were the Black Panthers Communist? According to their leader, Huey Newton, the party certainly was. On November 19, 1970, in a speech at Boston College, he said, "The Black Panther Party is a Marxist–Leninist party because we follow the dialectical method and we integrate theory with practice." (*The Black Panther,* January 23, 1971)

But the prevailing disorder of the late 1960s and early 1970s was not restricted to one or two radical sects. The disruption made it difficult to hold any mass rallies. Even many high schools stopped holding public assemblies.

This brought about changes in the type of meetings we held. We now directed our efforts to reaching the students in universities and colleges, and to gatherings at dinner meetings.

Schools of Anti-Communism were replaced by Anti-Subversive Seminars. Special efforts were made to recruit college and university students through "scholarships" which provided them with a minimal sum for their accommodation and food in the hotels in which the seminars were held.

We conducted many of these seminars in Washington, D.C., and some who attended have since come to occupy influential positions in America's national life.

In arranging these seminars we often cooperated with Young Americans for Freedom, a student organization.

The accompanying cartoon indicates our Anti-Communism Seminars were not always praised. This cartoon appeared in the November 1972 in *Coast,* a magazine that catered to the rock-music crowd. The author of the text was a young man, Fred Setterberg, who introduced himself to me as a reporter for the *Daily Californian* at the University of California at Berkeley. I considered it rather flattering that he had to resort to falsehood in order to be derogatory. His statement that I raised a lot of money at the seminar was completely untrue. We dispersed money via scholarships to those who attended, including Fred Setterberg. I was disappointed because I liked Fred and thought he had journalistic integrity. I sent him this letter:

> Dear Fred:
>
> You know and I know that your statement, "He raised a lot of money" is a lie. It puzzles me that you found it necessary to lie. Did the editor of the magazine demand that you make this statement? Maybe he inserted it. If this is the case, you have my deep sympathy.
>
> If you did betray journalistic ethics by lying, repentance will still lead to forgiveness. I offer you my friendship.
>
> With Christian love, Fred Schwarz

THE NEWSLETTER

The Crusade newsletter was published twice each month to provide accurate, up-to-date, documented evidence of Communist doctrines, organizations, plans, and activities. Its main source was the copious literature published by the Communists themselves.

To obtain this information I subscribed to a large number of Communist magazines which I read critically. I published statements verbatim from official Communist sources whenever I considered them significant. Trustworthy information, not sensation, was the objective. No charge was made for the newsletter.

While I attempted to provide perspective and analysis to the information presented, I tried to distinguish between evidence and personal opinion. I asked no one to accept a conclusion based solely

upon my unsubstantiated word. I regularly revealed my sources and frequently pointed out that I had no access to secret information derived from espionage.

The mailing list for our newsletter consisted of two categories— our family list and our missionary list.

SOME OF THE COMMUNIST PERIODICALS
DISTRIBUTED IN THE U.S.A.

On the missionary list were individuals and organizations that we hoped could and would profit from the newsletter's information. These included public and college libraries, editors and columnists of newspapers, program directors of radio and television stations, and every member of the U.S. Congress as well as the president and his administrative leaders.

The family list consisted of those who asked to receive the newsletter. Most of these were supporters but some were critics.

We requested financial support from those on the family list so that our free distribution could continue and the many worldwide activities of the Crusade could be maintained.

The family list also received a cover letter that contained information about Crusade activities along with a financial appeal. From time to time I included personal information about the Schwarz family, and this was a regular feature of the Christmas edition.

During the destructive era of the 1960s and 1970s the Crusade work continued to be effective despite decreased publicity. Though public meetings were conducted, attending numbers were smaller. My role resembled that of the "circuit riders" of early U.S. history, but my horse was the airplane.

The Crusade's supporters were scattered throughout the nation. I regularly visited cities such as Washington, D.C., New York, Chicago, Milwaukee, Indianapolis, Columbus (Ohio), Cincinnati, Dallas, Houston, St. Louis, Phoenix, San Diego, San Francisco, Portland, Seattle, and, of course, Los Angeles, to meet with Crusade family members and potential recruits.

I depended upon the cooperation of an unselfish and unpaid Crusade representative in each city; a volunteer and personal friend. When I decided that the time was ripe I would call my friend and ask that a suitable venue for a meeting be selected on a given date. It was usually a hotel or motel where we could hold a dinner and meeting. I then sent a letter to all on our mailing list who lived within about fifty miles of the meeting location. I announced the subject on which I would speak and invited them to come and bring friends. I enclosed a card, addressed to the Crusade representative, with which they could make reservations.

Those attending paid for their own dinner. Those who were unable to attend the dinner were invited to come to the lecture.

I usually spoke for about an hour and a half, following which an offering was taken while I answered questions. The total amount in the offering was announced.

There were those who frequently criticized me for speaking too long, including my wife Lillian. On one occasion, in Chicago, the businessman who was to chair the meeting, aided by Lillian, pleaded that I limit my message to one hour. I yielded, kept my promise, and felt smug.

Then came this note with the offering of one guest. "When we come a considerable distance at considerable personal inconvenience to hear you speak, we do not expect you to limit yourself to one hour." I proudly showed the note to the chairman and Lillian. As I remember, Lillian's said, "There's one nut in every crowd!"

I will never cease to be grateful to those unsung and unpaid heroes who made these meetings possible. I refrain from mentioning names since they are so many.

These meetings were a major source of the income that was essential to maintaining the Crusade. However limited their financial resources, these people were actually major financial contributors.

Many times I have heard someone say, "I wish I could give you a million dollars." One man who succeeded was Dr. Roger Congdon. He was professor of Bible at Multnomah College in Portland, Oregon, and also served as pastor of a small Baptist Church during the weekends.

Dr. Congdon and his wife were the parents of thirteen children. He once told me that his income would have been greater had he simply gone on welfare.

When I wanted to hold a meeting in Portland, Oregon, I called Dr. Congdon. He responded enthusiastically, selected a location, accepted reservations, and along with his charming and amazingly youthful wife served as host and hostess.

I became aware of one man who attended the meetings regularly. He invariably sat at the very front and held a hand to his ear during the address. He would remain for a personal chat when the meeting was over, and I discovered he had a delightful sense of humor. He always had a twinkle in his eye and a joke to tell. He regularly contributed $1,000 to the offering. His name was Harry Casey, and we became friends.

He told me how he and his brother James had left school at the age of about eleven to deliver parcels and packages by bicycle. This work had grown, and it became United Parcel Service (UPS), of which his brother was chairman. Harry would quote with pride the current statistics of UPS. Harry himself owned and operated a Ford agency.

The time came when he told me that his brother James was terminally ill in a nursing home in Seattle, Washington; James Casey died at the age of ninety-five.

My secretary, Ella Doorn, received a phone call from Harry soon after his brother's death. He asked, "What's the biggest check the Crusade has ever received?" She answered, "$50,000." He said, "I want to beat that." Shortly thereafter his personal check for $100,000 came. It was the first of many such checks that he gave during the following twenty years.

Harry was a widower with children, grandchildren, and great-grandchildren to whom he was devoted. A birthday party in his honor was held each July in the Athletic Club of Portland, Oregon.

One day he asked me, "How can I get you to come to my birthday party?" I said, "Try inviting me." He did, and after that I attended his party each year until he died.

At each of his birthday parties he made a speech which always included a joke. Here is one I remember:

> The professor stood before the class and said, "The USA is bordered to the north by Canada; to the south by Mexico; to the east by the Atlantic Ocean; and to the west by the Pacific Ocean. How old am I?"
>
> After some minutes of silence one student raised his hand and replied, "Forty-six years, sir."
>
> "Exactly right," said the professor. "Now will you tell the class the logical steps by which you reached that conclusion?"
>
> "It was very simple," said the student. "I have a brother who is twenty-three, and he's a half-wit."

Harry combined great generosity with a devotion to thrift. Although increasingly deaf, he always answered the phone personally. On one occasion when I called him he asked, "Do you need any money?" "We certainly do," I replied. He said, "I will send you twenty-five." This meant $25,000. Then, "You didn't call person-to-person, did you?" Why spend the extra money for a personal call when he always answered personally?

He once asked me, "What percentage of the Crusade income is spent on fund-raising? I hope it is not more than 20 percent." He was clearly pleased when I told him that it was between 3 and 4 percent.

All gifts from Harry Casey have been personal. Harry remained "young at heart" despite his chronological age. And he had a poetic soul. Some poets became old while their years were few. One was Lord Byron who wrote:

> There's not a joy the world can give like that it takes away,
> When the glow of early thought declines in feeling's dull
>   decay;
> 'Tis not on youth's smooth cheek the blush alone, which
>   fades so fast,
> But the tender bloom of heart is gone, ere youth itself be
>   past.

> Then the mortal coldness of the soul itself comes down;
> It cannot feel for others' woes, it dare not dream its own;
> That heavy chill has frozen o'er the fountain of our tears,
> And though the eye may sparkle still, 'tis where the ice
>   appears.

> Oh could I feel as I have felt—or be what I have been,
> Or weep as I could once have wept o'er many a vanished
>   scene;
> As springs in deserts found seem sweet, all brackish though
>   they be,
> So, midst the wither'd waste of life, those tears would flow
>   to me.

Harry was an Irish Catholic. He loved his family, his Church, and his country. I believe he also loved the Crusade. He personified the teaching of Jesus, "It is better to give than to receive."

One day, Dana Rohrabacher, a speechwriter for the president, called me asking how he could get in touch with Harry because the president wanted to relate how he and his brother illustrated what a great land of opportunity America is. The president gave the speech and conferred an award on Harry, who was delighted.

On January 11, 1990, Lillian and I celebrated our fiftieth wedding anniversary in the Beverly Wilshire Hotel of Los Angeles. All our children, their spouses, and our grandchildren made the long journey from Australia to attend the festivities. Our hearts glowed with pride as they graced the platform.

Harry willingly accepted the position of honorary chairman of the celebration. He flew from Portland, Oregon, with his son Paul and some of his grandchildren. Although he was ninety-nine years old and unable to hear, he occupied a seat of honor for four hours without a word of complaint. He was truly a great friend.

It was a sad day that brought the news that Harry had died at 102 years of age. His son Paul called with the news.

He had established a family trust and had designated two and one-half percent of it for the Crusade. I attended his funeral with a sadness that was mingled with joy. We Christians do not sorrow as do those who are without hope. We believe the promise of Jesus, "I go to prepare a place for you that where I am there you may be also." (John 14) The friendship and generous support which Harry gave was made possible by Dr. Roger Congdon, whose own income would have been larger had he substituted welfare for work. Dr. Congdon was like the small boy who provided the loaves and fishes with which Jesus fed the multitude.

Thousands have been nurtured and fed physically and spiritually due to Roger Congdon and Harry Casey. Never say, "I can do nothing!" since truly "Great oaks from little acorns grow."

36

....

The Vietnam War

Revolutionary war is an antitoxin which
not only eliminates the enemy's poison
but also purges us of our own filth.
—MAO TSE-TUNG (*QUOTATIONS*) 1967, P. 60

FROM THE CONCLUSION OF THE Second World War in 1945
until the smashing of the Berlin Wall in 1989, the "Cold War" raged.

Who started the Cold War? Historians disagree on the answer.
Some blame Joseph Stalin, while others indict the United States. An
enlightened Marxist–Leninist would reply: "History did."

Marx and Engels began their *Manifesto of the Communist Party*
with the categorical affirmation: "The history of all hitherto existing
societies is the history of Class Struggle." They believed they had
discovered the contemporary Class Struggle between the forces of
Capital and Labor; between the Bourgeoisie and the Proletariat.
They also believed that this struggle could be terminated only by the
victory of the proletariat.

The Communists who ruled the Soviet Union believed that history had appointed them to lead the proletarian forces in the truce-
less worldwide Class Struggle. The "Cold War" was the name given

391

to this struggle during the years 1945 to 1989. The war was called "cold" because it did not involve major military conflict, with the use of nuclear weapons, between the leading combatants, the United States and the Soviet Union.

The Communists believed that such a "hot" conflict should be avoided because of the destructive power of nuclear weapons. They were convinced that the Cold War could be won without nuclear conflict.

The name given to this phase of the Class Struggle was "peaceful coexistence," which the Communists defined as a "specific form of Class Struggle." (*Perestroika,* page 147)

Many subordinate "hot" wars, however, were to be waged as part of the "Cold War." These were primarily wars of national liberation that would lead to the "encirclement of the cities by the countryside," meaning the encirclement of the Capitalist countries by the forces of the Communist empire. This encirclement would gradually weaken the Capitalist countries and encourage the creation of revolutionary forces within them. The combination of encirclement and demoralization would eventually lead to the capitulation of the United States and its allies, and the triumph of world Communism. I used the formula, "External encirclement plus internal demoralization plus thermonuclear blackmail lead to progressive surrender," to present their conviction and the strategy based upon it.

This Communist strategy was perceived and understood, however dimly, by the U.S. authorities, and it provided a rationale for opposition to any enlargement of the encircling Communist forces. This realization led to U.S. involvement in the Vietnam War.

The Vietnam War was one battle in the universal class war. President Kennedy and his advisers understood that the Communist conquest of Southeast Asia would be a major advance in encircling the United States and that it should therefore be resisted. The Communist conquest of Vietnam would lead to a chain of events that would finally add all of Southeast Asia to the Communist empire. This was called "the domino theory."

These convictions led to the dispatch of the U.S. military to aid the Vietnamese who were resisting the conquest of South Vietnam by the Communist armies of the north led by Ho Chi Minh.

One of the main architects of this policy, former Secretary of Defense Robert McNamara, with benefit of hindsight, published the book *In Retrospect* in 1995. In this book he declared that U.S. involvement in the Vietnam War was terribly wrong and that it led to inevitable defeat and humiliation. Is this true, half true, or false?

Shakespeare wrote:

> There is a tide in the affairs of men,
> Which, taken at the flood, leads on to fortune;
> Omitted, all the voyage of their life
> Is bound in shallows and in miseries.
> (Julius Caesar IV. iii)

Despite the defeat of the U.S. forces and the fall of Vietnam to the Communists, the loss was not total. The Communists had been prevented from seizing Southeast Asia when the tide was "at the flood." One immensely important asset, time, had been won.

While the war was being waged, major changes were taking place on the world stage. These eventually led to the ultimate defeat of the Communist strategy of encirclement.

Two of these changes were:

(1) The development of destructive forces within the Communist empire. In the Soviet Union, these forces led to the conditions described by Gorbachev in his book *Perestroika* (see chapter 33). The conditions included economic deterioration throughout the Soviet Empire and pervasive corruption within the ranks of the Communist Party of the Soviet Union (CPSU).

(2) The time gained was utilized by President Ronald Reagan to strengthen the military forces of the United States.

These developments caused Gorbachev to conceive and enact the programs of *perestroika* and *glasnost* and, subsequently, to renounce Soviet leadership of the proletarian forces in the Class War. This abdication was formalized by a change in the definition of peaceful coexistence. In *Perestroika,* Gorbachev reported:

Changes were introduced in the spirit of the new out-look into the new edition of the CPSU Program adopted by the 27th Party Congress. Specifically we *deemed it no longer possible to retain in it the definition of peaceful coexistence of states with different social systems as a "specific form of Class Struggle.* [italics added]

These changes led to the disintegration of the Soviet Union itself.

Thus while the battle represented by the Vietnam War appeared to be lost, it nevertheless contributed to the final victory of the United States in the Class War. The soldiers who died in Vietnam did not die in vain.

37

....

The Evil Empire

One man with a dream, at pleasure,
Shall go forth and conquer a crown;
And three with a new song's measure
Can trample an empire down.
—Arthur William Edgar O'Shaughnessy, 1844–1881 (Ode)

THE UNION OF SOVIET SOCIALIST Republics was an empire in substance if not in name. President Reagan created considerable controversy when he called it "the evil empire" in a speech he gave to the National Association of Evangelicals on March 8, 1983. Some regarded this as unnecessarily provocative, never mind that the USSR propaganda had termed the United States an empire of evil many thousands of times.

From 1917 until 1987, the date of the renunciation of class struggle, the Soviet empire grew. It was held together by the doctrine that, once the Communist Party had conquered any country, Communist authority became irreversible. If the people of that country sought to overthrow the Communist dictatorship, the military power of the Soviet Union would be used to maintain the party in power.

395

This policy—of supporting the Communist quest for power in other countries, and maintaining that power once achieved—was announced by Lenin when, in 1919, he established the Comintern, commonly called the Communist International. Leonid Brezhnev merely formalized it when he proclaimed the "Brezhnev Doctrine" after the Soviet occupation of Czechoslovakia in 1968. It was acknowledged by President Chernenko when he stated that the CPSU had always obeyed Lenin's instruction that the needs of the world revolution must take precedence over the needs of the Soviet Union, however great these needs might be.

ECONOMIC STRAINS UPON THE SOVIET UNION

This policy placed great strains upon both the military and economic strength of the Soviet Union. It led to the invasion of Hungary by Soviet military forces when the Hungarian people overthrew their Communist rulers in 1956, to a similar invasion of Czechoslovakia in 1968, and to the fatal attempt to reimpose Soviet rule in Afghanistan in 1979. It also drained the Soviet treasury, as funds had to be found to support Communist dictatorships and parties worldwide. Thus Castro and the Communists were kept in power, as Castro frequently acknowledged, by a massive Soviet subsidy variously estimated as from five million to twelve million dollars a day.

The U.S. Communist Party under the leadership of Gus Hall received millions of dollars annually. In addition, a vast network of international organizations such as the World Peace Council (WPC) and the World Federation of Trade Unions (WFTU) were supported. This worldwide propaganda campaign cost a fortune. So did the worldwide espionage program.

The enormous demands upon the Soviet treasury became unsupportable and contributed to the changes introduced by Gorbachev and the collapse of the Soviet Union.

Meanwhile a controversy raged in U.S. academic and political circles over whether the expansionism of the Soviet empire was primarily due to Communist doctrine or Russian Imperialism. I contended, and continue to contend, that Communist doctrine was the primary motivation, hence my identifying the Communist formula for the conquest of the United States: "External encirclement plus internal demoralization plus thermonuclear blackmail lead to progressive surrender."

The military and economic policies of Ronald Reagan also imposed great strains on the economic resources of the Soviet Union. Gorbachev acknowledged as much in his book *Perestroika:*

> I shall repeat that as far as United States foreign pol-
> icy is concerned, it is based on at least two delusions.
> The first is the belief that the economic system of the
> Soviet Union is about to crumble and that the USSR will
> not succeed in restructuring. The second is calculated on
> Western superiority in equipment and technology and,
> eventually, in the military field. These illusions nourish a
> policy geared toward exhausting Socialism through the
> arms race, so as to dictate terms later. Such is the
> scheme; it is naive.

Gorbachev called the U.S. policy delusional, but history confirms that he was the one with the delusions.

The policies of *perestroika, glasnost,* and democratization weakened the power of the CPSU. I do not believe Gorbachev intended this. If Communists were sufficiently dedicated and efficient, he believed the Soviet people would accept Communist leadership gladly. But he did weaken the formal links between the party and the government, and the results were disastrous.

There was little organized resistance within the party to the policies of Gorbachev. This was due to the application of the Leninist doctrine of "Democratic Centralism." This affirmed that decisions made by higher organizations of the party must be accepted and obeyed by all members below. The highest organizations of the party were the Central Committee and its Politburo. Those who occupied positions in them had risen through the ranks and become accustomed to submission and obedience. Gorbachev was the first secretary, the chosen leader of the party. Since the party was believed to be history's executive, his prestige and authority were enormous. He controlled the agenda of meetings of the Politburo and the activities of disciplinary party organizations such as the KGB and the army.

Meetings of the Politburo were secret. Nevertheless it was widely believed in the Western world that factions existed within the Politburo and that opposition to Gorbachev was led by a Marxist fundamentalist named Yegor Ligachev. However, Ligachev said later that he could not remember one meeting of the Politburo in which the voting for the Gorbachev reforms had not been unanimous.

Some Communists believed that the reforms of Gorbachev were not proceeding quickly enough. Boris Yeltsin, prominent in the Moscow Communist Organization, was one such critic. He gained public popularity protesting the excessive personal privileges that party members continued to enjoy, and he identified with the people by traveling by bus and subway instead of by limousine. Because he dared to criticize Gorbachev, he was reprimanded and demoted. He was revenged later when he humiliated Gorbachev before the Supreme Soviet after Gorbachev's release from captivity, following the abortive "coup" of August 1991.

The reforms of Gorbachev strengthened the power of the Supreme Soviet, roughly similar to the Congress of the United States, and weakened the power of the Communist Party, which could be compared to the presidency. These comparisons are confusing because the headquarters of the Supreme Soviet was known as the "White House."

THE CAPTIVE HORSE BOLTS

The situation in the Soviet Union prior to the reforms of Gorbachev can be likened to those of a horse kept on a short tether. This made its range of movement extremely limited and its food scarce, as it had an extremely small area on which to forage. Consequently, it was unhappy and inwardly rebellious.

The owner thought that the horse would be more content if he lengthened the tether so that it could move more freely and enjoy more nourishment. He overlooked the fact that the basic desire of the horse was to be free and that any lengthening of the tether would enable him to gain momentum and possibly break the tether. Gorbachev lengthened the tether, and the ungrateful horse bolted.

One important force that contributed to the overthrow of Communism in the Soviet Union was nationalism. According to Karl

Marx, this force was a creation of Capitalism and did not exist for the working class. How wrong he was, and is.

The Soviet Union was sometimes called "a Prison House of Nations." The countries of Eastern Europe ruled by Communists, among them Poland, Hungary, Czechoslovakia, Rumania, Bulgaria, and East Germany, along with the Baltic countries of Lithuania, Latvia, and Estonia, were known as the "captive nations."

Nationalism was a major factor in delivering the captive nations from their bondage. It also contributed greatly to the disintegration of the Soviet Union. Today, it threatens to destroy the national unity of Russia itself as many internal ethnic groups struggle for independence. The civil war in Chechnya is an example of this.

The avalanche of change set in motion by Gorbachev's reforms smashed the walls that had imprisoned the Soviet people. The security of prison life with its provision of basic food and shelter was lost. The possibility of unemployment replaced the economic security of the slave. Some complained, "Formerly we had misery and security; now we have only misery." Crime, which had been kept in check to some degree by the Communist rulers, became rampant.

The immediate results of freedom included anxiety as well as opportunity. Inflation was rife. The soldiers returning from the outposts of the empire found increasing difficulty in finding living quarters. Russians living in newly independent republics were often regarded as colonists and were threatened or persecuted. It seemed that anarchy was replacing tyranny.

Not surprisingly many of the leaders in the disintegrating institutions thought that it was imperative to restore order and discipline.

This resulted in a coup. The conspirators, led by Gennadi Yanayev, included the head of the KGB, the Ministry of the Interior (the police), the defense minister, and leading members of the old party apparatus. On August 19, 1991, they kidnapped the vacationing Gorbachev, placed him under house arrest, and demanded that he join them and restore authoritarian rule in Russia.

Gorbachev refused to join the coup leaders, though some remain convinced that he had either consciously or unconsciously encouraged the plotters.

The coup leaders sent military forces to seize the Soviet White House, where the Supreme Soviet was in session. Yeltsin led the opposition and rallied support while standing on a defensive tank. A regiment of the military remained loyal to the Supreme Soviet and resisted. The determination of the coup leaders wavered, and they released Gorbachev and surrendered. The coup had lasted only three days.

Gorbachev did not return to the Supreme Soviet as a hero. He was humiliated, and took orders from Yeltsin. The true hero of the victory was Yeltsin, who had headed the resistance from the beginning.

As a result of the coup, the Communist Party was declared an illegal organization and its property was confiscated. Gorbachev lost his position and power. He resigned on December 25, conceding that the USSR no longer existed.

The Supreme Soviet, or Parliament, became the recognized authority even though it had been elected when the Communist Party was in power. New elections were held, and constitutional changes took place. Yeltsin was elected president. It seemed that Gorbachev's day was done.

38

....

The Cold War

Sleepe after toyle, port after stormie seas,
Ease after warre, death after life, does greatly please.
—EDMUND SPENSER (*THE FAERIE QUEENE*)

THE "COLD WAR" CAME TO an abrupt end in 1989. It is difficult to give a precise date for the end of the "war." Some would
choose the destruction of the Berlin Wall; others would select the
day on which the Soviet Union was abolished.

My personal choice for a specific date would be when the
Twenty-seventh Congress of the Communist Party of the Soviet
Union renounced the definition that the peaceful coexistence of
states with different social systems was a "specific form of Class
Struggle"—June 28 to July 1, 1985. This was a renunciation of the
Class War which had become known as the Cold War.

Gorbachev describes the rationale for the change thus:

> In developing our philosophy of peace, we have taken
> a new look at the interdependence of war and revolution.
> In the past, war often served to detonate revolution. One
> may recall the Paris Commune which came as an echo of

401

the Franco–Prussian war, or the 1905 Russian Revolution triggered by the Russo–Japanese war. The First World War provoked a real revolutionary storm which culminated in the October Revolution in our country. The Second World War evoked a fresh wave of revolutions in Eastern Europe and Asia, as well as a powerful anti-colonial revolution.

All this served to reinforce the Marxist–Leninist logic that imperialism inevitably generates major armed confrontations, while the latter naturally creates a "critical mass" of social discontent and a revolutionary situation in a number of countries. Hence a forecast which was long adhered to in our country: a third world war, if unleashed by imperialism, would lead to new social upheavals which would finish off the capitalist system for good, and this would spell global peace.

But when the conditions radically changed so that the only result of nuclear war could be universal destruction, we drew a conclusion about the disappearance of the cause-and-effect relationship between war and revolution. The prospects of social progress "coincided" with the prospects of the prevention of nuclear war. At the 27th CPSU Congress we clearly "divorced" the revolution and war themes, excluding from the new edition of the Party Program the following two phrases: "Should the imperialist aggressors nevertheless venture to start a new world war, the peoples will no longer tolerate a system which drags them into devastating wars. They will sweep imperialism away and bury it." This provision admitting, in theory, the possibility of a new world war was removed as not corresponding to the realities of the nuclear era.

Perestroika

No longer would the advent of a "hot war" be regarded as the dawn of "world Socialism." This basic ideological change was due in large measure to the economic, social, and cultural realities that existed within the Soviet Union. Instead of the creation of economic abundance, civil harmony, and individual perfection, as Marxist–Leninist theory had predicted, the reality was widespread poverty, environmental degeneration, corruption, criminality, and alcoholism. These latter characteristics had become common, if not dominant, within the Communist Party itself.

The conditions for the overthrow of Communism existed, but the precise mechanism by which it came to pass continue to confuse many.

The Communist Party was the de facto government of the Soviet Union but it was not the de jure government. How could this be?

The relationship between the party and the Soviet state can be illustrated by Lenin's description of how the party ruled the labor unions. He described this in his book, *Left Wing Communism—an Infantile Disorder,* when he wrote:

> In its work, the party relies directly on the *trade unions,* which, at present, according to the data of the last congress (April 1920), have over 4,000,000 members, and which are formally *nonparty.* Actually, all the directing bodies of the vast majority of the unions, and primarily, of course, of the all-Russian general trade union centre or bureau (the All-Russian Central Council of Trade Unions), consist of Communists and carry out all the directives of the party. [italics added]
> *Selected Works of Lenin,* Moscow, vol. II, part 2

This principle applied to the entire government of the Soviet Union. The nominal governmental authorities were the Soviets, the elected bodies comparable to national, state, and local administrations in democratic countries. However, the control of these bodies was ensured by Communist Party control of elections. The party chose all the candidates who could be elected; in most instances, only one candidate. One of the revolutionary changes introduced by the Twenty-seventh Congress of the CPSU was "the listing of more candidates in the ballots than there are seats to be filled."

While favorably assessing the experience accumulated
in this field since the 27th Congress of the CPSU, the
Conference deems it necessary to go further and ensure
unlimited nomination of candidacies, their free and
extensive discussion, the listing of more candidates in
their ballots than there are seats to be filled, strict obser-
vance of a democratic electoral procedure, regular
reports by deputies on their work, and a real mechanism
for their recall.

Documents and Materials, Gorbachev, page 132

Gorbachev also stresses:

The principle that all Communists in executive posts
are to report and be fully answerable to the primary
party organizations must be observed consistently;
efforts should be undertaken to have every executive
maintain close links with the masses, set an example of
competence, hard-working dedication, modesty, accessi-
bility and respect for people.

Ibid, page 145

The party itself was organized and controlled by the Leninist doctrine of democratic centralism. Thus by placing its members in all
elected and nominated government positions, and by controlling
their ideas and actions, the party became the monopolistic de facto
government in every sphere of national life.

Gorbachev recognized that the sacrificial devotion of individual
party members had deteriorated and had become replaced by selfishness. They had "lost their first love." He set in motion a pseudo-
religious revival campaign which, like most such campaigns, was
limited and temporary in its success. Gorbachev laments:

There is a lack of due determination in carrying out
the decisions of the 27th CPSU Congress and the Plenary
Meetings of the CPSU Central Committee held in January and June 1987. New democratic methods of leader-

ship, openness, and glasnost find it hard to make their
way, coming up against conservatism, inertia and dog-
matism in thinking and acting. The attitude to work, to
the practical implementation of tasks has not yet duly
changed in various section of society, including work
collectives. Conscientious performance of duties has not
yet become an accepted standard. Labor discipline falls
short of the demands of perestroika. All this affects the
end results of work being done.

There are still many functionaries in every area of
public, state, and economic activities who cannot, or do
not want to, part with the command style of administration, who respond painfully to new developments.

Ibid, page 121

Gorbachev sought to reform, not destroy, the party. He wanted to
strengthen it. He wrote:

The wish to see the party still stronger has resounded
here most passionately and resolutely. This can only be
welcomed, and I think all of us are pleased. As put down
in its resolution, the Conference demanded that our party
should in every respect be a Leninist party not only in
content but also in its methods. In other words, it must
renounce command-style methods once and for all, and
conduct its policy by means of organizational, personnel,
and ideological work in strict conformity with Soviet
laws and the democratic principles of society.

There should be no duplication of the work of state
bodies. There should be no dictating to trade unions, the
YCL, and other public organizations, or to the unions of
writers, artists, etc. Does this mean that the Party's leading role can weaken? Doubts of that kind have, indeed,
been expressed. As I see it, the Conference gave a sufficiently clear and convincing answer: no, the party's leading role cannot weaken. As the ruling party, it has all the
requisite levers to implement its leading role. And the

most important lever of all are the 20 million Communists carrying out the party's political line in all areas of
life.

Ibid, page 107

The changes that Gorbachev instituted—*perestroika, glasnost,*
and democratization—were like someone removing a boulder and
thereby unleashing an avalanche. This avalanche swept Gorbachev
from power, and destroyed, at least temporarily, the Communist
Party of the Soviet Union and the Soviet Union itself.

The saga of the life of Gorbachev, however, is not yet complete.
Much remains to be written.

39

....

Inside the Chinese Communist Mind

EVERY DOCTOR KNOWS THAT CONDITIONS which exist at present will not necessarily remain the same in the future. This is why a responsible physician, after examining present conditions in the patient, endeavors to predict probable future developments before prescribing treatment. The probable future is called the prognosis.

When considering Communism in China, it is vitally important to consider the prognosis. Today, Capitalism prevails in the economic realm, while Communist dictatorship retains political power. What will the future be?

One favorite Communist saying is, "The only constant is change," and it is important to discover what changes the Communist leadership may have in mind. A unique opportunity for insight into the Chinese Communist mind is provided by recent discussions between the highest level of Chinese Communist leaders and the first official Republican Party delegation led by American Ambassador Faith Whittlesey. These discussions took place in the great hall of China from April 26 to May 14, 1994. Dr. Clark Bowers was a member of the U.S. delegation, and the following is a record of some of the questions he asked Mo Xiusong, vice-chairman of the Chinese People's Political Consultative Conference, and the answers:

CLARK: Is the long-term goal of the Communist Party of China still world Communism?

MR. MO: *Yes, of course, that is the reason we exist. However, the road to Communism may take well over a hundred years and the transition doesn't have to be violent.*

CLARK: Do you believe that it is possible for a revolutionary to be violent?

MR. MO: *No. It is the counter-revolutionary who commits acts of violence as he tries to work against peace and history's will.*

CLARK: Is it possible to reach your goal of world Communism while any of the bourgeois or their economic environment still exist?

MR. MO: *No, that would be against the laws of science.*

CLARK: How do you define "Peaceful Coexistence?"

MR. MO: *Reaching our goal of peace through any means short of open conflict.*

CLARK: When you use the word peace, do you mean final peace that would end the conflict between the classes?

MR. MO: *Since the beginning of history, the world has passed through its stages by the conflictional process of the dialectic. As members of the Communist Party, we work for the cessation of conflict through the final revolution of thesis and antithesis which will take place under Communism.*

CLARK: Where in Marxist thought is it explained how this final resolution takes place?

MR. MO: *It is not clear from Marx's writings how this takes place.*

CLARK: What is the PRC's position regarding the West's view of human rights?

MR. MO: *We believe there are many human rights, and human economic rights are currently of the greatest concern to the people of China. The rampant individual-*

*ism of the West will be the source of its downfall. In our
tradition we place a much greater emphasis on the group
than on the individual.*

CLARK: There are many reports in the West regarding
the persecution of religious people in China. Does the
atheist leadership of the PRC officially recognize the
rights of religious freedom?

MR. MO: *The freedom of religious belief is guaranteed in our constitution, and there are many churches
and monasteries in our country.*

CLARK: Is the concept of religious practice part of
your right of religious belief, and do members of the
Communist Party also have the right to believe in God?

MR. MO: *First, you must realize that membership in
the Communist Party is very demanding and is only for
the disciplined few. If one chooses to join the party, they
must understand and believe in the scientific laws of
Socialism. The first of these scientific laws is atheism. If
a party member chooses to believe in religious supersti-
tion, he is free to leave the party. As far as religious practice is concerned, the people of China may participate in
any of the state's registered places of worship. In 1950
the party created the Catholic Patriotic Association to
govern Catholics and the Three Self-Patriotic Movement
to oversee Protestants. These organizations were needed
to cut off the foreign control of religion and to regulate
it internally. Historically, there have been those who
have tried to destabilize the country of China through
illegal religious organization and practice. This will not
be allowed.*

CLARK: As part of your reform, do you even desire to
ever allow for anti-Socialist political parties?

MR. MO: *No, that would be unconstitutional.*

CLARK: Do you have any desire to change this part of
the constitution?

MR. MO: *No, the people wouldn't support it.*

CLARK: Who speaks for the people of China?

MR. MO: *The Communist Party of China acts on behalf of the workers of China. We are their mind.*

CLARK: How do you justify economic reform which seems to be at odds with your socialist stage of development?

MR. MO: *We need to have more of a commodity at this stage because we did not go through a proper stage of Capitalism after our feudal stage. We also are experimenting with private ownership of the means of production tempered by public ownership of private property. Additionally, we are currently dealing with the questions of whether the means of production is a commodity in and of itself. We believe that in the past we overemphasized the form of the relationship of production within society. Lenin's New Economic Policy has much to offer in this regard.*

CLARK: What lessons have the PRC learned from the collapse of the Soviet Union?

MR. MO: *The historical miscalculations of Gorbachev led to an unbridled chaos that tore the social fabric of the USSR apart. We opposed a similar destabilization in Tiananmen Square in 1989, and history has vindicated our leadership by the economic and political stability that has followed.*

The more Communism appears to change, the more it remains the same. This is illustrated by the answers Clark Bowers received to the questions he asked. They testify that the Chinese Communists continue to be guided by the example and teachings of Lenin.

The first question by Clark was: *"Is the long-term goal of the Communist Party of China still world Communism?"* The answer was a categorical: *"Yes, of course, that is the reason we exist."*

COMMUNIST SEMANTIC GYMNASTICS

The answer to Clark's second question opens a window through which the semantic gymnastics of the Communists can be observed.

Clark asked: *"Do you believe that it is possible for a revolutionary to be violent?"* This time the answer is a categorical *no*. It is accompanied by the statement: *"It is the counter-revolutionary who commits acts of violence."*

In the light of the record of the unbridled violence which the Communists have used during their ascent to power in various countries, and the brutal murder of countless millions while in power, this statement seems to surpass the highest peak in the towering range of Communist absurdity. Nonetheless, it is consistent with Leninist doctrine and morality and is an example of Communist "situation ethics."

Lenin stated, *"Communist morality is determined by the exigencies of the class struggle."* The basic Marxist doctrine is derived from the conviction that a state of warfare exists between the proletariat (workers) and the bourgeois (middle-class owners of property), and that history has ordained that this warfare will end with proletarian (Communist) control of all mankind. Consequently, any action which advances Communist conquest is good.

Applying this to the period of class struggle, it follows that actions, even shooting, looting, and mass murder, are benign if they advance the cause of Communism. They are therefore nonviolent acts. Only acts that delay Communist conquest can possibly be violent.

According to Communist doctrine, when the Communists control the whole world, universal peace will prevail. Therefore, they take peaceful guns and put peaceful bullets into the brains of their warmongering opponents and thereby provide them with a peaceful death, after which they inter them in peaceful mass graves.

THE PARTY IS THE MIND OF THE WORKERS

The Leninist concept of the nature and role of the Communist Party still lives in the minds of the Communist rulers of China. The Chinese spokesmen explained to Clark that *"membership in the Communist Party is very demanding and is only for the disciplined few."* When asked, *"What then gives the Communists the right to speak for and rule over the people of China?"* Mr. Mo answered with his statement: *"The Communist Party of China acts on behalf of the workers of China. We are their mind."*

Again, this is pure Leninism. The statement: *"The Communist Party is the mind, the morals, and the conscience of our epoch"* adorned the building in Moscow that served as the former headquarters of the Communist Party of the Soviet Union.

"ATHEISM IS THE FIRST SCIENTIFIC LAW"

The Chinese Communist attitude to religion is also Leninist. Religion is tolerated among the uninformed masses, but it is not permitted for members of the Communist Party. After stating that *"The freedom of religious belief is guaranteed in our constitution . . . ,"* Mr. Mo states, *"If one chooses to join the party, they must understand and believe in the scientific laws of Socialism. The first of these scientific laws is atheism."*

Mr. Mo justifies the slaughter by the Chinese military to disperse the protesting students and workers in Tiananmen Square in 1989 by claiming that it prevented a destabilization similar to that which tore the social fabric of the USSR apart and created unbridled chaos. It was therefore nonviolent.

That military action illustrates the helplessness of a large protesting demonstration if unarmed protestors are attacked by modern military weapons such as machine-gunning planes and marauding tanks. Therefore, to defeat a popular insurrection, the tyrants must have a supply of modern weapons at their disposal, and soldiers who are willing to obey the orders to use them.

The master revolutionary strategist, Lenin, stated that a breakdown in the will of armed rulers was necessary for the success of a revolution. Weapons are useless if authorities lack the will to give the orders to the soldiers who must use them. It is therefore necessary to demoralize the rulers, and subvert the soldiers, if the revolution is to succeed.

The prospect that the Chinese Communists, in the foreseeable future, will possess massive military and economic might, along with Leninist doctrines and will, is alarming. Only those conscious and unconscious Marxists, who believe that economic conditions create all ideas and institutions, can be complacent.

David Schwarz with soldiers who have stopped a bus in the Philippines to check for guerrillas of the New Peoples' Army.

How the Philippine Communists of the New People's Army treated a Sunday school.

With America's Great Lady—Phyllis Schlafly.

With Ronald Reagan.

With Reed Irvine, Joe Goulden, and Clark Bowers in an Accuracy in Media television program.

Norm Walker (far left) and Dr. John Whitehall next to President Ramos of the Philippines. The president kept the book, "You Can Trust the Communists (to be Communists)" on his table when he was chief of staff of the Philippines Army.

Triple Celebration Banquet

In Honor Of
Dr. and Mrs. Fred Schwarz

- *50th Wedding Anniversary*
- *Dr. Schwarz's 77th Birthday*
- *His 40 Years of Leadership for Freedom*

January 11, 1990

Beverly Wilshire Hotel
9500 Wilshire Boulevard
Beverly Hills, California

★

Sponsored by the
Family and Friends of Dr. and Mrs. Schwarz
in association with the
C.A.C.C.

A bird's-eye view of the triple decked head table at the Triple Celebration Banquet, which took place in the Beverly Wilshire Hotel on January 11, 1990.

Sweeter as the years roll by.

The Honorable Max Bushby, O.B.E., and his wife Elaine.

Mr. Harry Casey, aged 99 years, and his son Paul. Harry served as honorable chairman of the triple banquet. Accompanied by his grandchildren, he and his son flew in from Portland, Oregon.

Plaques presented by the county and city of Los Angeles are held high.

Dale Evans speaking, encouraged by her smiling husband Roy Rogers. Others on the platform also spoke. Left to right: Supervisor Mike Antonovich, Congressman Dana Rohrabacher, Congressman Robert Dornan, and Reid Irvine of Accuracy in Media.

Patrick J. Frawley, Chairman.

Keynote speaker, red-haired grandson Benjamin Esler, who stole the show. He is supported by his cousins, right to left: Jane Schwarz (now M.D.), Nicole Esler, and Penny Schwarz, who also spoke.

Loving granddaughters Sarah Schwarz and Katherine Harris.

Clark asked if they considered the present situation in China to be a stage of "Negation." Without hesitation they agreed that it was. He then asked, *"When do you anticipate 'the Negation of the Negation?'"* This question seemed to cause great consternation. A spirited discussion among the Chinese, in Chinese, resulted. After a considerable time, their spokesman acknowledged that they did not know. He also added that in twenty years of discussion with American leaders, he had never been asked such a question.

"Dialectical materialism" contends that progress proceeds by a series of sudden reversals of direction known as "negations." Each "negation" is subsequently followed by a "negation of the negation." This may be exemplified by the procedure of driving a nail.

Abrupt changes in Chinese policies and programs will take place whenever the Communist leaders consider the time to be ripe. This should never be forgotten.

If the present economic system, known as "Socialistic Market Economic Structure," continues in China, along with the monopoly of political power by the Communist Party, there will be phenomenal growth in material resources, including modern weapons. An editorial in the November 17, 1995, edition of the prestigious magazine *Science* states:

> China has a minimum of half a million scientists and engineers engaged in research and development (R&D), with thousands of outstanding Western-trained researchers returning every year. More than 6,000 libraries and information centers boast scientific databases, and another 25,000 provide "integrated technical services" in specialized areas from the earth sciences to engineering. Several billion dollars in government funding is going to R&D in an economy where the salary of a full-fledged researcher may be as little as $1,400 a year.

Caveat emptor . . .

40

....

Communism and Morality

Myself when young did eagerly frequent
Doctor and Saint, and heard great argument
About it and about: but evermore
Came out by the same door where in I went.
—OMAR KHAYYÁM (*THE RUBÁIYÁT*), FITZGERALD

ONE OF THE QUESTIONS THAT stimulated great argument during my youth was, "Does heredity or environment play the greater role in the formation of human character?"

This question still causes controversy, as shown by the reaction to the book, *The Bell Curve: Intelligence and Class Structure in American Life,* by Charles Murray and Richard J. Herrnstein.

The discovery of genes is relatively recent, and many believe it has tipped the balance in favor of heredity. The authors of *The Bell Curve* contend that scientific experiments have confirmed that two-thirds of cognitive ability, commonly called intelligence, is due to genes, and one-third to environmental experience.

My youthful answer to the question was to pose another one. "Which has the greater influence on the area of a rectangle, the length or the breadth?" The obvious answer is "both." The area is a product, not a sum. It is not either/or.

414

A comparable question is: "Do ideas or experiences play the greater role in determining the choice to become a Communist?" The answer of Karl Marx to this question is experiences, since ideas are generated by experiences. The *Manifesto* states:

> Does it require deep intuition to comprehend that man's ideas, views and conceptions, in one word, man's consciousness, changes with every change in the conditions of his material existence, in his social relations and in his social life?
>
> What else does the history of ideas prove, than that intellectual production changes its character in proportion as material production is changed? The ruling ideas of each age have ever been the ideas of its ruling class.
>
> When people speak of ideas that revolutionize society, they do not but express the fact, that within the old society, the elements of a new one have been created, and that the dissolution of the old ideas keeps even pace with the dissolution of the old conditions of existence.
>
> *Manifesto of the Communist Party*
> (Progress Publishers, Moscow,
> 1888 edition reprint, page 72)

This conviction led to the formation of his theories concerning class, class consciousness, class conflict, and the inevitable birth of Socialism from the womb of a decaying Capitalism.

I have known a number of Communists. My own judgment, for what it's worth, is that the etiology of their embrace of Communism varies considerably. For some it is primarily an intellectual choice, while for others it is an emotional reaction.

Frederick Vanderbilt Field, an American child of wealth and privilege, became a Communist. In his book *From Right to Left,* he states that he chose to become a Communist because he believed that Capitalism inevitably led to Imperialism.

Others have become Communists after being involved in strike activity during which they suffered considerably. This generated a sense of community with the leaders of the strike who were Communists, and some of the strikers were seduced by the ideas which provided a rationale for the suffering they were experiencing for "the cause." They enlisted in what Stalin described as the "army of the great proletarian strategist, the army of Comrade Lenin."

Certain environments such as poverty, injustice, and oppression create fertile soil for the germination and growth of Communist ideas. This has led some to conclude that poverty, injustice, and oppression cause Communism. If this were so, the world would have been Communist centuries ago, as these conditions have existed throughout recorded history.

Thus a study of the pathology of Communism demands attention to both ideas and experiences. Consideration must be given to the role morality plays in Communist recruitment and conduct.

I have always taught that an immoral environment fosters Communist development. Consequently, I directed attention to such issues as the family breakdown, sexual promiscuity, abortion, homosexuality, the death penalty, and the AIDS epidemic.

Some have considered this a departure from the primary objective of diagnosing and reporting the pathology of Communism. To me it has been and is an essential element in the quest to attain that objective.

What is morality? Many philosophers have attempted to define it. *Random House Dictionary* defines it as "conformity to the rules of right conduct; moral or virtuous conduct." It defines "morals" as "principles or habits with respect to right or wrong conduct." These definitions assume that right and wrong are knowable and known.

Throughout history various moral codes have been devised to promote moral conduct.

Hippocrates, a Greek physician who lived about 450 B.C., devised the Hippocratic oath, which has guided physicians through the centuries so that their conduct would be ethical and moral.

The Hippocratic oath includes the following:

> I will follow that method of treatment which, according to my ability and judgment, I consider for the benefit of my patients, and abstain from whatever is deleterious and mischievous. I will give no deadly medicine to anyone

if asked, nor suggest any such counsel; furthermore, I will not give to a woman an instrument to produce abortion.

With purity and with holiness I will pass my life and practice my art. I will not cut a person who is suffering from a stone, but will leave this to be done by practitioners of this work. Into whatever houses I enter I will go into them for the benefits of the sick and will abstain from every voluntary form of mischief and corruption; and further from the seduction of females or males, bond or free.

Whatever, in connection with my professional practice, or not in connection with it, I may see or hear in the lives of men which ought not to be spoken abroad I will not divulge, as reckoning that all such should be kept secret.

While I continue to keep this oath unviolated may it be granted to me to enjoy life and practice the art, respected by all men at all times, but should I trespass and violate this oath, may the reverse be my lot.

World Book Encyclopedia

The Bible reports how God gave Moses the Ten Commandments as a guide to righteous behavior. These commandments have guided millions through the ages.

Jesus emphasized the Golden Rule—"Do unto others as you would that they should do unto you."

In addition, the wisdom of the ages has been encapsulated in what are commonly known as proverbs.

Rudyard Kipling called these codes and proverbs "The Gods of the Copybook Headings," and described, with prophetic insight, what happens when they are scorned and rejected.

On the first Feminian Sandstones we were promised the
  Fuller Life
(Which started by loving our neighbor and ended by
  loving his wife)

Till our women had no more children and the men lost
    reason and faith,
And the Gods of the Copybook Headings said: "*The wages
    of sin is death.*"

As it will be in the future, it was at the birth of Man—
There are only four things certain since Social Progress
    began—
That the Dog returns to his Vomit and the Sow returns
    to her mire,
And the burnt Fool's bandaged finger goes wobbling back
    to the Fire;
And that after this is accomplished, and the brave new
    world begins,
When all men are paid for existing and no man must pay
    for his sins,
As surely as Water will wet us, as surely as Fire will burn,
The Gods of the Copybook Headings with terror and
    slaughter return!

Is it superstitious to regard this verse as a prophetic interpretation of the AIDS epidemic in the United States?

And Communism has its moral code. Lenin announced it when he wrote, "Proletarian morality is determined by the exigencies of the Class Struggle." In application, this meant that any action that favored proletarian advance in the Class Struggle was good and that hindered it was bad; any statement that led to the advancement of Communism automatically became true.

The name of the organization I founded is the Christian Anti-Communism Crusade, and we believe that the apostle James discerned an essential ingredient of Christian morality when he wrote:

Religion that God our Father accepts as pure and
faultless is this: to look after orphans and widows in
their distress and to keep oneself from being polluted by
the world.

                                          (James 1:27, NIV)

Because of the symbiotic relationship between Communism and morality—or immorality—I have devoted considerable attention to moral questions during latter years.

MORAL CONSIDERATIONS

It is now widely recognized that illegitimacy and the breakdown of the family are responsible for much of the social pathology that is threatening the existence of free society. I became aware of this after reading the writings of Daniel Moynihan, George Gilder, and Herbert Marcuse. The activities of such groups as the radical Weathermen confirmed the reality of the threat, and I have been writing about it consistently during the past thirty years.

Any description of the pathology of Communism would be incomplete without reference to the environmental consequences of sexual promiscuity, drug intoxication, family disintegration, the sanctification of sodomy, the exaltation of selfishness, and the devaluation of life.

41

....

Consequences of Immorality

On the first Feminian Sandstones we were promised
the Fuller Life
(Which started by loving our neighbor and ended
by loving his wife)
Till our women had no more children
and the men lost reason and faith,
And the Gods of the Copybook Headings said:
"The Wages of Sin is Death."
—RUDYARD KIPLING

SEX

In the book of Genesis, the Bible informs us that after making man and woman in His own image, God said to them, "Be fruitful and multiply and fill the earth and subdue it."

The fulfillment of this mandate was made possible by the existence of two basic human instincts, the sex instinct and the maternal instinct. The former assured that an adequate number of offspring would be conceived and born, while the second assured that newborn babies would be nurtured so that they could survive. Both of these instincts are present and powerful in the majority of women.

Each organ of the human body has both structure and function. Structure is the theme of Anatomy while function is the theme of Physiology. When structure and function are in harmony the usual result is health and pleasure. When there is disjunction between them, pathology exists.

REPRODUCTION

One of the basic features of human life is reproduction. To secure this a complex mechanism has been created involving both anatomy and physiology.

The female body is built so that it can reproduce offspring. An essential element of the reproductive apparatus is a canal into which the spermatozoa which are necessary to fertilize the ovum or egg may be introduced and through which the developed babe may enter the world. The male possesses the appropriate organ, the erectile penis, to inject the seminal fluid, which contains the spermatozoa.

Both male and female bodies contain another canal into which enters the food that is needed to provide energy for human activity and to create and replenish tissue. The food is digested as it passes through this canal, and the toxic residue of the digested food is excreted from it. This tube is known as the alimentary canal, and it terminates in the rectum and anus.

The primary purpose of the vagina is reproduction, while that of the anus is excretion.

As noted earlier, when structure and function are in harmony the result is usually health and pleasure. When organs are used for functions for which they are not designed, the result is often disease and pain.

The anus and rectum are the sewers of the human body. The excretory end products of digestion pass through them and contaminate them. Fecal remnants invariably remain.

The excretory products of digestion are toxic. They provide a habitat for organisms that cause infectious diseases. Consequently, if raw sewage, containing infectious excreta, reaches recreational waters in rivers, lakes, or seas, swimmers are legally denied the use of those waters until the danger of infection has passed. Sewers do not constitute appropriate playgrounds.

Some homosexuals find pleasure in the practice of anal intercourse, known as sodomy. This is comparable to swimming in water containing raw sewage. Indulgence in this conduct often causes debilitating and deadly diseases. It is claimed that these diseases can be avoided by the practice of "safe sex."

The term "safe sex" has become a synonym for sexual intercourse using a condom.

A condom is a thin sheath which is worn over the erect penis so that it forms a barrier between seminal fluid and the vagina during heterosexual intercourse, or the rectum and anus during anal intercourse. The cellular lining of the vagina is designed to resist the pressure exerted by the penis but the lining of the anus and rectum is not.

The condom is used to prevent the possibility of pregnancy or disease.

The condom is normally worn by the male, but recently a female condom has been designed. Most condoms are made of thin rubber or latex but about 5 percent are made from lamb membrane.

How much safety does a condom confer? The dangers are twofold. One is due to the rupture of the condom during intercourse and the other to the passage of a virus through tiny holes or pores. The former is more common with latex or rubber condoms, while the second derives from the use of the lamb membrane condom.

The March 1989 edition of the magazine *Consumer Reports* gives the results of extensive tests on the reliability of condoms. Here are some of the findings:

> When we asked readers, about one in four said that a condom has broken in the past year.
>
> Anal intercourse, one of the riskiest activities for contracting AIDS, is also one of the most punishing for a condom.
>
> Scientists also gauge the condom's effectiveness as a contraceptive. For condom users failure rates have ranged from roughly 5 percent to 15 percent.

This record does not justify the term "safe sex." Some now refer to "safer sex," which is more realistic but not encouraging. A *Consumer Reports* May 1995 article, "How reliable are condoms?," gives substantially the same message as the 1989 article.

Since the consequences of infection with the AIDS virus are so deadly, the risks associated with promiscuous sex are unacceptable.

The May 1995 article reports that condoms made from lamb membrane, called skins, are stronger, so the risk of rupture is less. This advantage, however, is nullified because lamb membrane is porous.

Genuine safe sex is practiced in faithful, uninfected monogamy.

The following parable on "Sodomic Swimming" illustrates the dilemma:

> The waters of the lake sparkled in the sunlight, and the high school students, on a class outing, gazed at them with eager eyes. The day was hot and steamy, and they longed to plunge into the lake's cooling embrace. But they had just heard the doleful news that the lake was closed to swimmers because a discharge of raw sewage had polluted the waters and made them vehicles for the transmission of disease. Their genes cried out in protest and urged them to take the risk of a refreshing swim.
>
> One of the accompanying teachers said, "You know what young people are like. It is almost certain that some of them will yield to their desires and plunge into the waters. We have a duty to protect them. We must urge them, if they do swim, to make sure that it is 'safe' swimming, by wearing a wet suit, rubber boots, rubber gloves, and to refrain from immersing their heads in the water."
>
> Another teacher replied, "Surely we must insist that they learn to exercise self-control. Swimming must be prohibited, not tolerated."
>
> The first teacher sneered, "Keep your fanatical, religious ideas to yourself. Don't try to foist your ideas on

others. You want the students to abide by your values.
You are trying to apply the principle, 'Do unto others as
you would wish them to do unto you.' The man who
taught that was a religious leader, and mixing religion
with education is unconstitutional.' "

CACC Newsletter, May 1994

The diseases that result from the practice of sodomy have been
described by Mirko D. Grmek, M.D., Ph.D., in his authoritative
book, *History of AIDS*. Describing homosexual practice in America
in the 1970s and 1980s, he wrote:

> Studies showed that most American homosexuals liv-
> ing in large cities had several dozen sex partners each
> year; mean figures of eighty to one hundred partners
> were not rare, and some mounted into hundreds. About
> 10 percent of homosexuals interviewed had had sexual
> contact with over five hundred persons during their
> lives. *In medical terms the almost immediate result was
> an increase in the "classic" sexually transmitted diseases,
> notably syphilis and gonorrhea; of certain viral diseases,
> such as hepatitis, herpes, and cytomegalovirus; and
> intestinal parasites, such as amebiasis. Skin disorders of
> an otherwise relatively rare nature, and chronic diar-
> rhea, became the daily lot of homosexuals.* The rise in
> these disorders preceded the AIDS outbreak, and already
> indicated the point at which the epidemiologic situation
> was ready to explode. In San Francisco's Castro district
> and New York's Greenwich Village, the spread of AIDS
> in 1981–1982 was catastrophically faster than anywhere
> else in the Western world. It was thus in the crowded
> ranks of the American homosexual community that the
> AIDS virus finally passed the point of no return in its
> epidemic spread. [italics added]

I published an article captioned, "It's the Diseases—Stupid," in
our April 1994 newsletter. I quoted this statement by Dr. Grmek.

The article stimulated the following critical letter from R. W. Schumacher of Oregon (CACC Newsletter, September 1, 1994, page 5):

Dear Fred:

Ordinarily I do not spend my time responding to newsletters. However, one of your crusaders left your April 1 issue on my porch. If an anonymous stranger expects me to read your material, then I will exercise my right to respond.

Your article titled "It's the Diseases—Stupid" is so full of false assumptions and illogical conclusions that I scarcely know where to begin. First, you are using your status as M.D. to make people think you are an expert on the subject. You might know diseases, but you are short on logic and on understanding of human behavior.

Your sentence tying sodomy to gay rights issues ignores two simple facts: Not all homosexuals engage in anal sex, and many heterosexuals do. And yes, I did notice that you always used the fundamentalist hot-button word "sodomy" instead of using professional medical language. If you insist on using that term, maybe you should re-read the story of Sodom. You'll find references to homosexual and heterosexual rape, and you'll find that Lot's wife gets turned to salt for gawking while her husband gets away with incest. So maybe sodomy should be defined as incest, since it is the only consenting sex in the story.

The quote from Mirko Grmek, which is used to *blame* homosexuals for the beginnings of AIDS in America, conveniently overlooks the fact that in much of the world, the disease is spread mostly by heterosexuals. The obvious conclusion, based on your own statement that actions which spread disease should be illegal, is that heterosexual conduct must be banned. Yet your article focused entirely on homosexual conduct. May I suggest you correct this oversight in your next issue?

And by the way, virtually all of the people who had the wild sex lives Grmek described, are now dead. To someone considering a similar lifestyle, that is far more sobering than some law in the books. That's where human behavior comes into the picture. Sodomy laws have never stopped people from having the type of sex they prefer, nor have they prevented people from being homosexual. A few unfortunate individuals have had their lives ruined by selective enforcement of a largely unenforceable law; otherwise the laws have had little effect. Compare that with the education campaigns which encourage people to delay having sex, and to practice safe sex. Far more men and women have changed their behavior because of education than because of laws.

Finally, what does all this talk of "sodomy" have to do with communism anyway? The Soviet Union had severe penalties for male homosexuals (they apparently didn't feel threatened by lesbians). Soon after the Soviet Union broke apart, Russia repealed the old anti-homosexual laws. Isn't it a bit ironic that they realized that part of the process of freedom is to allow citizens to be themselves—gay or straight—while in the United States there are people who wish to take this right away?

Sincerely,

R. W. Schumacher, Oregon

Dear Mr. Schumacher,

I thank the anonymous stranger who introduced you to my newsletter, and I thank you for your response. I have read it several times with great interest and concern.

I was challenged by your statement that *"Your article titled 'It's the Diseases—Stupid' is so full of false assumptions and illogical conclusions,"* and looked for your evidence to support this accusation. After repeated readings of your epistle, I am unable to find any of the *"false assumptions and illogical conclusions"* to which you refer. Surely you should be able to quote at least one of them.

You make a number of general statements which are true, but irrelevant. For example, you state: *"Not all homosexuals engage in anal sex, and many heterosexuals do."* I do not question that this statement is true, but it is comparable to the statement, *"Not all birds fly, and many fishes do."* I believe that most individuals would nevertheless rightly regard flight as a characteristic of birds rather than fish.

You criticize my use of the word "sodomy" to describe anal sex. *Webster's Dictionary* defines sodomy as, *"Any sexual intercourse regarded as abnormal, as between persons of the same sex, especially males, or between a person and an animal."* The *World Book Dictionary* gives virtually the same definition.

You endeavor to refute my presentation of the evidence presented by the world authority, Mirko Grmek, in his book *The History of AIDS,* that homosexual conduct caused the AIDS epidemic in America, by pointing out that the disease is spread mostly by heterosexuals, in some other countries. Your statement is true concerning some other countries, but does not refute the overwhelming evidence that homosexual conduct caused the epidemic in America.

Your comment, *"Virtually all of the people, who had the wild sex lives Grmek described, are now dead,"* sustains my conclusion that homosexual conduct is deadly.

The evidence, which proves the homosexual origin of the American AIDS epidemic, is presented by Randy Shilts, in his book, *And the Band Played On.* Shilts was a self-confessed homosexual and a supporter of "gay rights." Sadly, he has died from AIDS since writing his book.

With journalistic integrity, Shiltz reports the conduct of the homosexual airline steward, Gaetan Dugas. (Please note that GRID was the early name for AIDS.)

"Gaetan could be connected to nine of the first nine-teen cases of GRID in Los Angeles, twenty-two in New York City, and nine patients in eight other North American cities."

"A CDC statistician calculated the odds on whether it could be coincidental that 40 of the first 248 gay men to get GRID might all have had sex either with the same man or with men sexually linked to him. The statistician figured that the chance did not approach zero—it was zero."

The statistical evidence that Gaetan Dugas was the source of the AIDS epidemic in America is overwhelming. How he contracted AIDS is unknown.

Education and law are not exclusive alternatives. Laws are great educators. I draw your attention to the role the laws have played in persuading many people to buckle-up when they drive an automobile. Most of my acquaintances had failed to do this when education, unassisted by law, attempted to persuade them to use seat belts. Since the law made the wearing of seat belts compulsory, most of them buckle-up automatically.

Would you deny that the anus and rectum are the sewers of the human body, and that, as such, they are contaminated by raw sewage? Do you deny that contact with raw sewage may cause disease, and that the closing of beaches, which are contaminated by raw sewage, is legitimate?

If sodomy were outlawed, it would be impermissible to teach in schools that it is natural and permissible. The major method for the spread of AIDS would be impeded, though not stopped completely.

You ask, *"What does 'sodomy' have to do with Communism?"* That is similar to asking, "What did swamps have to do with malaria?" Swamps provided the habitat for mosquitoes which carried the malarial parasites and transmitted them to humans. Moral degeneracy creates the habitat in which Marxist ideas and Communist activists can flourish and recruit.

I again thank you for your well-written and thought-provoking letter, and ask you to provide specifics of any "false assumptions and illogical conclusions" which, according to your letter, abound in my article.

With Christian love,
Fred Schwarz, M.D.

I am still awaiting a response.

The sex instinct is powerful and creative. It is the dynamic which provides the continuity of human life. When used intelligently and appropriately it is a source of great pleasure and it enriches life and art. When misused it can cause suffering, disease, and death.

The provision of parameters for indulgence in sexual activity has been essential for the progress of civilization. Control of sexuality and morality have been inextricably intermingled.

Sex education which ignores moral parameters has been a failure; it is like teaching adolescents the use of firearms without any reference to necessary restraints upon their use. Such amoral sex education has exacerbated the problems it promised to eliminate. It has been sold to parents as a means of reducing illegitimacy and sexually transmitted diseases but has been accompanied by a deplorable increase in their prevalence. While correlation does not always indicate causation, the constant association of two developments is suggestive of a causal relationship.

THE CULTURE WAR

During recent decades a war against traditional morality and culture has raged in America. Those who recognized the existence of this war and warned of its consequences have received the treatment usually given to prophets. They have been ridiculed and condemned.

Pat Buchanan was excoriated in the press and the academy when he stated in his address to the 1992 Republican Convention, "There is a religious war going on. We must take back our cities, and take back our culture, and take back our country."

Evidence of the existence of the culture war abounds. William Bennett, former secretary of education, distinguished fellow in Cultural Policies Studies, and author of the best-selling *Book of Virtues,* published a report on the casualties caused by the culture war, entitled: "The Index of Leading Cultural Indicators."

In the introduction, Bennett states:

> "Since 1960, population has increased 41 percent; the Gross Domestic product has nearly tripled; and total social spending by all levels of government (measured in constant 1990 dollars) has risen from $143.73 billion to $787.0 billion—more than a five-fold increase. Inflation-adjusted spending on welfare has increased 630 percent and inflation-adjusted spending on education has increased 225 percent . . .

> "But during the same 30-year period there has been a 560 percent increase in violent crime; more than a 400 percent increase in illegitimate births; a quadrupling in divorce rates; a tripling of the percentage of children living in single parent homes; more than a 200 percent increase in the teenage suicide rate; and a drop of almost 80 points in the S.A.T. scores. Modern-day social pathologies, at least great parts of them, have gotten worse. They seem impervious to government spending on their alleviation, even very large amounts of spending . . .

> "A disturbing and telling sign of the declining condition among the young is the result of an on-going teacher survey. Over the years teachers have been asked to identify the top problems in America's public schools. In 1940 teachers identified talking out of turn; chewing gum; making noise; running in halls; cutting in line; dress code infractions; and littering. When asked the same question in 1990, teachers identified drug abuse; alcohol abuse; pregnancy; suicide; rape; robbery; and assault . . .

> "Our social and civic institutions—families, churches, schools, neighborhoods and civic associations—have traditionally taken on the responsibility for providing our

children with love and order; discipline and self-control; compassion and tolerance; civility and respect for legitimate authority; fidelity and honesty.

These responsibilities, replicated through the generations, are among the constitutive acts of civilization. When these institutions fail, others may need to step in. But government, even at its best, can never be more than an auxiliary in the development of a free people's moral disposition and character.

"The social regression of the last 30 years is due in large part to the enfeebled state of our social institutions and their failure to carry out a critical and time-honored task: the moral education of the young. We desperately need to recover a sense of the fundamental purpose of education which is to engage in the architecture of souls. When a self-governing society ignores this responsibility, then, as this document demonstrates, it does so at its peril." [italics added]

THE ONSET OF AIDS

Aware of the relationship between demoralization and Communism, and considering AIDS one of the casualties of the Culture War, I have tried to read the copious literature on AIDS which has proliferated during the past fifteen years. I have tried to understand technical articles such as those published in *Science* magazine but confess that I lack the genetic knowledge necessary to grasp all the intricacies of viral proliferation and mutation involved. I have devoured the literature on the subject which is written for the general public, and the Crusade has distributed widely and freely such books as *The AIDS Cover-Up*, by Gene Antonio; *AIDS, The Unnecessary Epidemic,* by Dr. Stanley Monteith; and *AIDS! What the Government Isn't Telling You,* by Dr. Lorraine Day.

What caused the AIDS epidemic in the United States? As previously noted it began with the homosexual activity of one person, Gaetan Dugas. How did he contract AIDS? The answer is, "We do not know."

Many theories have been advanced to account for the existence of the HIV virus. Some believe it originated in Africa, maybe as a mutation of a virus that existed in monkeys. Others allege that it was genetically engineered, usually for nefarious purposes. The Communists blamed the CIA, and others claim that it was engineered for racial genocide. Paranoia knows few restraints.

I developed my own theory concerning the origin of the AIDS epidemic, and I published this theory in a February 1, 1986, newsletter. I wrote:

THE ORIGIN OF AIDS

Where did the AIDS virus come from? Why has the epidemic of AIDS appeared at this time? No one knows the answers to these questions, but several theories are current. Some believe that the virus recently appeared in Africa due to a change in the genes of a monkey virus that caused it to become pathogenic to the human species. Others believe that it is God's judgment upon the nation for the glorification of the sin of sodomy.

I suggest the possibility that the AIDS virus has been in existence for an indefinite period and that the AIDS epidemic is the result of the development of conditions that facilitate its spread. These conditions are the direct result of the legality, respectability and growth of the homosexual movement.

An analogy may help. How long has the atom bomb menaced mankind? Since 1945. Former generations knew nothing of the possibility of such a bomb.

The radioactive elements that can create an atom bomb have been in existence since the dawn of history, but they did not explode, because they were dispersed widely. An atom bomb was created when scattered fissionable material was collected and brought together in one place so that the quantity was large enough to exceed the critical mass.

Homosexuality and homosexuals have likewise existed since the dawn of history. The Bible records, discusses, and condemns homosexual conduct. However, homosexuals were scattered and "in the closet." Their activities were illegal, classified as diseased by the medical profession, and declared sinful by the church.

Then came the "Homosexual Revolution." Thousands of homosexuals were gathered in one place. They became a political force courted by politicians. Mayors and governors joined in celebrating the liberation of homosexuality by declaring "Gay Pride Week." Homosexual conduct increased exponentially.

The proliferation of homosexual conduct is illustrated by the establishment of temples to sodomy euphemistically called bathhouses. A description of the inside of one of these bathhouses was published in the December 2 edition of the magazine, *The New Republic*. It was captioned "Inside a Bathhouse" and was written by Philip Weiss. Here are extracts from his report:

The New St. Marks Baths is housed in a five-story brick building that is painted black and has steel shuttering over the windows. A plaque says it was the site of the last New York City home of James Fenimore Cooper. I walked past its doors twice, rethinking my plans, then went in and up an old marble-tiled staircase to a caged admission booth . . .

Until I got to the third floor I did not realize how many men were in the building. A black steel staircase, lit by red light bulbs, took me up to a narrow doorway that opened on a dark warren of rooms that was teeming with men in towels. They passed up and down the cramped corridors between the cubicles—53 cubicles on the floor under red light, each room large enough for a raised pallet and a bit of floor space, each with a large black number on the door . . .

Many occupants of the cubicles had arranged themselves on their beds with their doors open. Body language: most were on their backs, naked or decorated with the towel, eyeing the doorway; others lay on their stomachs but peered back over their shoulders at the door. The traffic in the passageways sometimes bottle-necked when a man leaned into a doorway to examine the candidate more closely . . .

But men were constantly being rejected, not chosen, which is why the place was so silent, so thick with long-ing and dread. Sometimes I could see the clients' desper-ation in their faces as they stared up from the pillows, their elbows hoochie-koochied behind their heads. The silent bargaining appeared to be frank, withering even: at one cubicle, two men crowded into the doorway and bent forward to consider the object flintily . . .

There were 53 cubicles on the fourth floor as well—I guessed there were about 200 men in the bathhouse. The place is open 24 hours a day, seven days a week. Although it was a Saturday night, the busiest time, I had some feeling of the absolute similarity of one hour there to any other hour.

Four years later I was encouraged on reading a statement by the world authority Mirko D. Grmek in his definitive book, *History of AIDS,* published in 1990. In the introduction he wrote:

The AIDS virus is extremely variable. It had once been controlled by natural selection favoring less virulent strains. Social factors enlarged its routes of transmission and allowed it to break through a sort of critical thresh-old that had previously limited its expansion. A profound analogy exists between the process by which the AIDS epidemic came into being and one which, by exceeding a critical mass, touches off an atom bomb; or one which, on an individual level, causes a cancer to break through the equilibrium between the forces of immunological control and those of inevitable, incessant cellular errors.

I have kept abreast of the controversies that are raging concerning the origin of the AIDS epidemic and the best way to prevent and treat AIDS, and have reached some conclusions:

(1) AIDS is a deadly disease which is causing increasing suffering and death.

(2) Every possible effort should be made to find a vaccine to provide immunity against infection with AIDS, and medications which will cure those already infected.

(3) AIDS should be treated primarily as an infectious disease. The methods which have proved effective in the control of other infective diseases should be utilized against AIDS. These methods include:

a. Discovery of the location of the infective agent. This requires widespread testing. Ideally, testing for infection with the HIV virus should be universal and mandatory.

b. Laws to prevent the transfer of the infective agent to the uninfected should be passed and enforced.

c. An educational program to teach how AIDS is contracted and spread should be continuous. One effective means of education is the enactment of appropriate laws. Laws are great educators. As St. Paul said, "The law is a schoolmaster."

(4) The protection of health and life should take precedence over the right of individual privacy. The right to live is a basic civil right.

Unfortunately, the procedures that have effectively prevented the spread of other infectious diseases have not been applied to the treatment of AIDS. It has been treated as a civil rights problem instead of a health problem. Those in danger of contracting AIDS have often not been warned of the danger. In many instances:

(1) Doctors have not had the legal right to inform the spouse that the sexual partner is infected with the HIV virus. As a consequence many wives have contracted the disease.

(2) It has been impermissible to inform mothers that their babies test positive for the HIV virus.

(3) Prostitutes who are known to be infected with the HIV virus are legally entitled to continue to practice their profession.

(4) Health workers such as doctors, dentists, and nurses are kept unaware of the infective status of their patients, and vice versa.

This results from the pervasive legal requirement that testing for HIV status must be voluntary. Only in rare and specific cases can it be mandatory.

The consequences of this devotion to "privacy" is that the majority of those who are infected by the AIDS virus, and who are potentially infectious to others, are unaware of their condition. They are robbed of the opportunity to seek treatment which may delay the onset of AIDS symptoms. They lack incentive to avoid conduct that may infect others.

No other infectious disease in modern history has been treated in this way. Consider the treatment of tuberculosis. Testing has often been mandatory, and the health authorities have been notified of the results. In many instances testing for infection with syphilis has been mandatory in order to gain a marriage certificate. When a person was known to be infected, the health authorities were notified so that contacts could be traced.

As I returned by air to Australia recently, I was compelled to complete an immigration form which asked if I was suffering from tuberculosis, but there were no questions concerning my AIDS status.

The consequence of this lack of knowledge leads to further infection and suffering. A recent happening in Australia illustrates this.

Many doctors in Australia remove small skin lesions in their offices, using local anesthetic.

One morning five patients underwent this procedure in the office of an Australian doctor. The patients were unknown to each other and went their separate ways following the minor surgery, which appeared to have been satisfactory.

One of those patients was a woman in her forties. Some considerable time later she volunteered to give blood for the blood bank. She was tested for the AIDS virus, and to her astonishment and horror the results were positive. The appropriate authorities told her that these were the only possibilities for infection: (1) sexual activity, (2) blood transfusion, (3) injection with infected needles used to inject illegal drugs, and (4) becoming infected as a baby following birth to an infected mother.

She insisted that she could not have contracted the infection in any of these ways but was not believed by the health authorities. They suspected that she was hiding some illicit sexual activity.

The woman kept searching, and she recalled her visit to the doctor. Tests were conducted, and it was discovered that one of the patients who had undergone minor surgery in the doctor's office that morning had been infected with the AIDS virus, and all the others had contracted the infection.

The first patient was a young man who was unaware that he was HIV-positive at the time of surgery. He subsequently died from AIDS.

Another patient was a woman in her seventies who had also died. The remaining three patients are HIV-positive, and DNA tests indicate that their infection was derived from the same source. The doctor remains negative.

It is widely believed that this is what happened:

The nursing staff prepared sterilized towels, sterilized syringes and needles, sterile anesthetic, and sterile gloves. The local anesthetic was in a sterile solution in a rubber-stopped bottle.

The doctor inserted a sterilized needle through the sterilized rubber, withdrew a portion of the anesthetic into the sterilized syringe, and injected it into the patient. He placed the syringe, with the needle attached, on a sterile towel.

During the surgical procedure the patient began to feel pain, so more anesthetic was needed. The doctor inserted the needle attached to the syringe into the anesthetic solution. Since the needle had been inserted previously into the patient it contained minute traces of blood. This infected the contents of the bottle. When anesthetic was withdrawn for the following patients, it contained the HIV virus and infected all who received it.

Please note: These infections were discovered only because one of the patients attempted to donate blood. Similar events may have taken place and remain undiscovered.

The doctor denies everything. But it has now become the practice to use a fresh sealed ampule of anesthetic with a fresh sterile syringe and needle for each injection.

Countless tragedies have resulted from the unknown and unknowable status of those infected and infective with the AIDS virus. The dying and the dead cry out, "Test! test! test! and notify potential victims and the health authorities of the results."

THE ORIGIN OF HOMOSEXUALITY

"But aren't homosexuals born that way?"

This question is often asked by those seeking a rationale for sodomic conduct.

Again I must say, "I don't know." I lack the scientific knowledge necessary to answer this question dogmatically. My opinion, for what it is worth, is that both nature and choice are contributing factors.

What I affirm with conviction is that the question is essentially irrelevant. Modern science tells us that the human genome contains close to 100,000 genes, and thousands of scientists are working assiduously to "map" the genome, to classify each gene. Attempts are also being made to discover the function of each gene.

Each gene has a specific function. The gene may create a definite pattern of conduct, but it is more likely to provide a "tendency" to conform to that pattern. With so many genes it is likely that one is involved in most forms of conduct. The press frequently reports that a gene has been found that indicates susceptibility to alcoholism, breast cancer, or some other common human condition.

Consider a man who is arrested for drunk driving. Is he entitled to plead that he is merely fulfilling the demands of his genetic nature since he has been born with a natural desire for both motion and alcohol?

The old excuse, "The devil made me do it!" has now become, "The genes made me do it!"

We are born with many antisocial impulses, and civilization depends upon their control. Some people are born with a tendency to sudden anger. Does this give them the right to assault others whenever they feel the urge? Every rapist could plead that he is born with strong sexual and aggressive instincts. Does this justify his indulgence in rape?

Civil society is possible only when such "natural" urges are controlled. If yielding to such urges harms others, the conduct is antisocial. It should also be illegal.

We often hear the cliche, "You can't legislate morality." Some claim that attempts to do this breach the constitutional mandate: the separation of church and state. What nonsense!

It is true that murder is an immoral act. One of the Ten Commandments is, "Thou shalt not kill." Is the law that forbids and penalizes murder therefore unconstitutional? Morality, ethics, and legality are inextricably intertwined in civil society.

When conduct destroys others it is not enough merely to classify it as immoral. It should also be illegal.

The indulgence in sodomy has destroyed the health and lives of thousands of Americans. The primary victims are those who have voluntarily indulged in sodomy, but many innocents have also been penalized.

The AIDS epidemic is like a fire that destroys the arsonists and all in its path—uninformed wives of bisexual husbands who have contracted AIDS through the practice of sodomy, recipients of blood transfusions, hemophiliacs, babies born to infected mothers, and others.

Measures to prevent such infections in the future are desirable and should be legal. This means that each individual should know whether he or she is a potential source of infection to others. Sources of infection should be discovered and controlled. Actions which subject others to serious risks should be forbidden by law despite any genetic involvement in their motivation.

An ancient proverb says, "It's remarkable how easy it is to keep your temper when the other man is much bigger than you are."

Few acts of rape are committed in broad daylight in front of a police station.

42

....

Love of Life and the Death Penalty

Not in entire forgetfulness,
And not in utter nakedness,
But trailing clouds of glory do we come
From God, who is our home . . .
—WILLIAM WORDSWORTH, 1770–1850
(*INTIMATIONS OF IMMORTALITY*)

HOW MUCH LIFE WILL IT save? This is the question that must be asked by a physician or surgeon when considering whether a medical or surgical procedure is justified.

Other important questions are, "What will be the quality of the life that will be preserved?" and "Is this life worth saving?"

Is a person in a coma, with no hope of recovery, really alive? Breathing is an essential element of life but it is only one component. Can real life exist without consciousness or the reasonable prospect of regaining consciousness?

Answers to these questions are controversial, and sometimes a definitive answer is difficult, if not impossible, to discern. Nevertheless, answers can usually be rationally determined, and these can help us form some guiding principles.

440

Lawmakers should keep in mind that, as Justice Oliver Wendell Holmes, Jr., said, "hard cases make bad law." Should laws be enacted that favor a few and penalize many?

Many questions must be asked and answered when considering life-and-death issues such as abortion and the death penalty.

Personally, I am guided by my answer to the question, "How do we preserve the maximum life possible?" I am aware that situations do arise where some killing is inevitable. In this sinful world some people will commit murder whatever the laws. There will be victims, and the objective is to reduce their number to a minimum.

THE DEATH PENALTY

Guided by the principle that life is precious, I support the death penalty. I believe this will save life. I believe that the death penalty is a deterrent to murder, although it is difficult to prove this by available statistics. It has been said that "figures can't lie but liars can figure," and figures are readily available to indicate that the death penalty is, or is not, a deterrent to murder. A natural tendency exists to select the figures that sustain the conclusion already reached.

Common sense does tell me that fear of the death penalty does indeed deter murder in some cases. This is reinforced by the efforts of most convicted murderers to delay or prevent execution. But this belief is not my prime reason for my support of the death penalty. My main support for it is based upon overwhelming evidence that it preserves more lives than it ends. Dead men lose their power to kill, and an executed murderer cannot kill again.

Many cases of serial murderers are on record. Once a person has murdered it is possible that he or she may kill again. Many murderers, released after serving prison sentences and presumed rehabilitated, have killed again.

Opponents of the death penalty may argue, "Since the death penalty brutalizes society it would be better to confine murderers for the rest of their lives without the possibility of parole."

This has two problems:

(1) While such a sentence may be pronounced, it is impossible to enforce. Present sentences do not limit the

powers of future governors and other authorities who may grant clemency. Prisons are crowded with inmates and overcrowding constantly grows worse. Building more and bigger prisons is not always possible. Therefore, the pressure to release even violent criminals grows.

(2) Convicted murderers may kill again—prisoners or guards—while in prison. They have little or nothing to lose.

It is sadly true that some innocents have been convicted of murder and executed. This is appalling. Nevertheless, the available evidence suggests to me that the number executed due to false conviction is less than those who have been killed by released murderers.

A Long Beach, California, *Press-Telegram* article dated August 19, 1995, article reported: "Crowd cheers as jurors ask death for serial killer." A forty-five-year-old man was convicted of murdering twelve women during a two-year campaign of terror. A sister of one victim said, "Now I know that he'll never be able to hurt another person. As long as he can't hurt anyone else, then my sister didn't die in vain." The prosecutor said: "[He] is no longer a member of the human race. By the nature of the crimes he has committed for twenty-two years, he has no heart, he has no soul and, by God, he has no conscience."

INCENTIVE

The assurance that execution isn't possible encourages criminals to kill witnesses who could testify against them. Whenever there is no possibility of a substantial increase in the penalty if the criminals add murder to kidnapping and/or rape, the incentive to murder will be strong since the likelihood of conviction is decreased if the witnesses are eliminated. Nothing to fear and much to gain from additional murder provides a powerful incentive.

This is particularly true in the case of rapists. Often the rapist is known to the victim. Once the rapist's passion has spent itself, he thinks of self-preservation. She can identify him. He must dispose of her. This accounts for the numerous instances where little girls are strangled after being raped.

An example of how the absence of the death penalty gave an incentive for murder is the experience of a beauty queen in Australia who was brutalized, gang-raped, and then murdered.

Anita Cobby was working as a nurse in a hospital in the heart of Sydney. After work one Sunday evening in February 1986, she traveled by train to Blacktown, a Western Suburbs station. It was 9 P.M.

While she walked toward her home a gang of young hoodlums seized her, dragged her screaming into a car, and sped off to a deserted field several miles away. They proceeded to brutalize and rape her.

Their passion spent, the gang held a meeting to decide what they should do with her. One of them pointed out that the punishment for the rape and torture they had inflicted would not be increased substantially if they killed her, but the probability of their being caught would be diminished if she were not alive to identify them. Thereupon they strangled her.

After trial and conviction the judge ruled that they should never be released. Nevertheless, appeals for their release are now before the courts and the outcome is uncertain.

The paradoxical conclusion is inescapable that the appropriate execution of certain murderers saves lives and that it is therefore just and compassionate.

43

....

Abortion

An infant crying in the night
An infant crying for the light
And with no language but a cry.
—ALFRED LORD TENNYSON (*IN MEMORIAM*, LIV)

BORN WITHOUT A CHANCE

A SQUALID VILLAGE set in wintry mud.
A hub-deep oxcart slowly groans and creaks.
A horseman hails and halts. He shifts his cud
And speaks:

   "Well, did you hear? Tom Lincoln's wife today.
The devil's luck for folk as poor as they!
   Poor Tom! poor Nance!
Poor youngun born without a chance!

"A baby in that Godforsaken den,
That worse than cattle pen!
Well, what are they but cattle? Cattle? Tut!
A critter is beef, hide and tallow, but

444

Who'd swap one for the critters of that hut?
   White trash! small fry!
Whose only instincts are to multiply!
   They're good at that,
And so, today, God wot! another brat!

"Another squawking, squalling, red-faced good-for-naught
Spilled on the world, heaven only knows for what.
   Better if he were black,
For then he'd have a shirt upon his back,
And something in his belly, as he grows.
More than he's like to have, as I suppose.
   Yet there be those
Who claim 'equality' for this new brat,
   And that damned democrat
Who squats today where Washington once sat,
He'd have it that this Lincoln cub might be
Of even value in the world with you and me!

"Yes, Jefferson, Tom Jefferson, who but he?
Who even hints that black men should be free.
That featherheaded fool would tell you maybe
A president might lie in this new baby!
In this new squawker born without a rag
To hide himself! Good God, it makes me gag!
   This human spawn
Born for the world to wipe its feet upon
   A few years hence, but now
More helpless than the litter of a sow,
And— Oh, well! send the womenfolks to see to Nance.

"Poor little devil born without a chance!"
EDMUND VANCE COOKE

I SAW MY FIRST ABORTION when I was a medical student in
1943 at the Brisbane General Hospital.

The Privy Council of England, which served as the Supreme Court of countries in the British empire at the time, had recently ruled that an abortion was permissible if the continuation of the pregnancy threatened the physical or mental health of the mother. The superintendent of the hospital decided to terminate the pregnancy of a fifteen-year-old girl who had been raped about six months previously. Since she was crying it was judged that her mental health was in danger.

In those days, abortion was not regarded lightly. In medical circles abortionists were looked on as the scum of the earth.

A group of medical students was granted the opportunity to witness the procedure. I was one of them. Since the pregnancy had existed for six months, the baby—no one referred to it as a fetus—was deemed too large for vaginal extraction, so a Caesarean section was performed.

We watched as the surgeon incised the abdomen and the uterus and removed the writhing, crying child. He handed it to an attendant to dispose of it in the trash.

Since that day I have never doubted that an abortion terminates a human life. It kills a baby. Whatever adjectives such as "potential" or "developing" may be added to qualify that life, they do not hide the fact that it is human. Since the baby exists, it is a "being"; since it is alive, it is a "living being"; since its life is human, it is a "living human being." Every abortion kills a living human being.

I find it difficult to express the contempt I feel for the intellectual dishonesty of those who discuss the problem of abortion without giving any consideration to the central fact that it kills a human being. I use terms "baby" and "human" advisedly. Names are important, which is why those who support the right to kill the unborn child usually refer to it as a fetus.

Can you imagine an expectant mother saying to a three-year-old child playing on her lap, "Be careful or you might hurt the fetus"? In popular speech the word "fetus" is usually reserved for a baby who is about to be aborted.

In some circumstances the termination of human life is justified. Self-defense is one of them, but the threat to life must be real and imminent before killing is legitimate.

No one I know argues that killing a human being is justified because he or she causes mental stress; or that such a decision should be entrusted to the victim and her psychiatrist. To justify killing, the threat must be physical.

Hopefully, the days are gone when someone powerful could dispose of the life of another casually. Such power did exist in the past. The famous poem, "My Last Duchess," by Robert Browning, relates how the duke of Ferrara disposed of his duchess because she smiled too easily. It also reveals that this same duke was a lover of art. His former wife became part of his art collection. This has present relevance, as I have little doubt that some abortionists are connoisseurs of art.

MY LAST DUCHESS
FERRARA

This famous monologue owes its inspiration to Browning's first trip to Italy in 1834. The hardness and cruelty of the Renaissance under its surface richness and polish is personified in the figure of the duke of Ferrara. He is showing the portrait of his late wife, whom he had quietly done away with, to an intermediary sent by the father of the girl he expects to marry.

That's my last Duchess painted on the wall,
Looking as if she were alive. I call
That piece a wonder, now: Frà Pandolf's hands
Worked busily a day, and there she stands.
Will 't please you sit and look at her? I said
"Frà Pandolf" by design, for never read
Strangers like you that pictured countenance,
The depth and passion of its earnest glance,
But to myself they turned (since none puts by
The curtain I have drawn for you, but I)
And seemed as they would ask me, if they durst,
How such a glance came there; so, not the first
Are you to turn and ask thus. Sir, 't was not
Her husband's presence only, called that spot

Of joy into the Duchess' cheek: perhaps
Frà Pandolf chanced to say "Her mantle laps
Over my lady's wrist too much," or "Paint
Must never hope to reproduce the faint
Half-flush that dies along her throat": such stuff
Was courtesy, she thought, and cause enough
For calling up that spot of joy. She had
A heart—how shall I say?—too soon made glad,
Too easily impressed; she liked whate'er
She looked on, and her looks went everywhere.
Sir, 't was all one! My favour at her breast,
The dropping of the daylight in the West,
The bough of cherries some officious fool
Broke in the orchard for her, the white mule
She rode with round the terrace—all and each
Would draw from her alike the approving speech,
Or blush, at least. She thanked men,—good! but thanked
Somehow—I know not how—as if she ranked
My gift of a nine-hundred-years-old name
With anybody's gift. Who 'd stoop to blame
This sort of trifling? Even had you skill
In speech—(which I have not)—to make your will
Quite clear to such an one, and say, "Just this
Or that in you disgusts me; here you miss,
Or there exceed the mark"—and if she let
Herself be lessoned so, nor plainly set
Her wits to yours, forsooth, and made excuse,
—E'en then would be some stooping; and I choose
Never to stoop. Oh sir, she smiled, no doubt,
Whene'er I passed her; but who passed without
Much the same smile? This grew; I gave commands;
Then all smiles stopped together. There she stands
As if alive. Will 't please you rise? We 'll meet
The company below, then. I repeat,
The Count your master's known munificence
Is ample warrant that no just pretence
Of mine for dowry will be disallowed;

Though his fair daughter's self, as I avowed
At starting, is my object. Nay, we'll go
Together down, sir! Notice Neptune, though,
Taming a sea-horse, thought a rarity,
Which Claus of Innsbruck cast in bronze for me!

President Clinton said that abortion should be "safe, legal, and rare." This is one of the most callous statements I have ever heard. To quote Shakespeare, somewhat out of context, it is "a tale told by an idiot, full of sound and fury, signifying nothing." Actually, it signifies something appalling. It is impossible for an abortion to be safe for the baby involved. And the present state of the law guarantees that abortion will not be rare. The reported one-and-a-half million babies aborted in the United States each year demonstrates how "rare" it is.

QUALITY OF LIFE

Another rationalization used to justify abortion is that the life of the expected child would not be worth living. History refutes this argument. The poem describing Abraham Lincoln at birth is eloquent. Another example is described in "Listen to the Music of the Night," by Paul Harvey.

LISTEN TO THE MUSIC OF THE NIGHT

NOVEMBER 5—When communists invaded South Korea in 1950, there was carnage in many villages below the 38th parallel.

One of the enemy bombs found the village home of a tiny 3-year-old girl named Kim. Scores of villagers died that day. She was among the few to be spared—though the bomb blast left her grievously wounded.

Girl babies were more a liability than an asset to impoverished Korean families anyway. So, a short time later—the war still raging—Kim's father, frustrated by his inability to feed his children, took this one down to the river to drown her.

HE HAD ALREADY drowned another baby daughter, but this time, the child's mother interceded. She came running and screaming, refusing to allow her baby Kim to be disposed of this way.

After much discussion, the desperate father relented and took the child to an orphanage in Taigu.

It was there that she was nursed back to health, and it was there that the child learned to sing. Soon, she was soloist in the orphanage church services.

When Kim was 10, she was adopted by the George Wickes family of Dayton, Ind. Now, Kim had an American home and an American name: Kim Wickes.

In return, she has rewarded us all.

An outstanding student, she graduated first from Wheaton College and then from the Indiana School of Music. She won a scholarship to the Vienna Institute of Music and studied under Frau Ludwig in Europe.

And, in the years since, Kim Wickes has brought audiences to their feet in Europe, Malaysia and Hong Kong. She's been to Israel 11 times. She received a triumphant welcome home to Korea.

When she soloed with the Billy Graham Crusade in the Hollywood Bowl, the evangelist called it "some of the best music the Hollywood Bowl has ever heard!"

And as she inspired him, his message convinced her. Now a Christian with concerts, recordings, and radio and TV performances, Kim Wickes has entertained and motivated uncountable millions on every continent.

WE WHO HAVE HEARD her in person have heard vocal music with the delicacy of bird song and with the might and majesty of a heavenly host of angels.

Listeners may come and go, hearing and heeding her Christian message, and yet not know what I have related about the child of Korea—whose father sought to drown her as "useless" at the age of 3.

And who, from the enemy bombardment of her village, was sentenced to a lifetime of sightlessness.

It is music of the night that is now turning on lights
all over the world.

Paul Harvey
Copyright 1994 Creators Syndicate, Inc.

OVERPOPULATION

What about protection of the planet from the ravages caused by
overpopulation? Many contend that this requires abortion on a
large scale. This has led to the Chinese Communist policy of compulsory abortion for a second child.

It is noteworthy that those who advocate radical measures to
limit the growth of world population exclude themselves from those
who should be culled.

During an Anti-Subversive Seminar in Washington, D.C., speaking with tongue-in-cheek, I proposed the following solution to the
problem of overpopulation:

> In this life we should share the wealth. It is intolerable
> that some people enjoy fabulous wealth while others live
> in dire poverty.
>
> Life itself is the greatest form of wealth. It is outra-
> geous that some enjoy many years extending into old
> age while others are terminated before birth.
>
> The development of the computer has made it possi-
> ble to rectify this injustice. We can now create a desir-
> able balance between the resources of the earth and the
> ideal population. Put the computers to work and calcu-
> late what the population should be and the amount of
> life that should be allotted to each person. For the sake
> of argument let's assume that the just quantity of life per
> person should be fifty-five years. Instead of killing the
> unborn, each one reaching the just limit should submit
> to life termination in the most humane way conceivable.

After the lecture a distinguished legal scholar approached me. He
said, "I am convinced by the logic and justice of your proposed solu-

tion for overpopulation. I have one problem with it. You set the quantity of permissible life too low. I am nearing fifty-five."

SELFISHNESS

Many find arguments based upon convenience and pleasure more convincing than arguments based upon reason, logic, and justice. To them, the most powerful argument is, "I want to do this." They welcome rationalizations that calm any pangs of conscience—hence, the canonization of choice.

Sometimes a pregnancy is inflicted upon a woman and causes great suffering. This is certainly true in respect to rape or incest. In rare instances the pregnancy threatens the life of the mother. These are the "hard cases" which, in the words of Supreme Court Justice Oliver Wendell Holmes, Jr., make "bad law."

When the mother's life is genuinely threatened, the issue of self-defense exists. It is widely acknowledged that killing in this instance is justified.

But the problems that ensue from rape and incest have no ideal solutions. The victim has suffered greatly and is not responsible for her pregnant condition. Is it fair that her suffering continue for another nine months?

On the other hand, the baby is not responsible for the crime, either. Should the baby be punished by undergoing execution?

This dilemma opens the door for advocates of permissive abortion to justify killing babies who are not the result of rape or incest and who do not threaten the life of the mother. Abortions due to rape or incest account for only 2 percent of the abortions performed legally in the United States each year.

The sincerity of those who use this argument can be tested by their response to the following suggested compromise:

"If the law makes an exception and permits abortion when the pregnancy is due to rape or incest, will you agree to a law protecting the lives of other unborn babies?"

The scornful refusal of many who insist on the right to choose to kill the unborn at a whim is eloquent.

A MORAL DILEMMA

Those who believe that life is precious from conception and should be preserved are also often confronted with a dilemma. Should they accept and support legislation that saves some babies but not all? If they do, will it be a betrayal of principle or a life-saving act?

The biblical account of Solomon's dilemma when he was confronted by two women who claimed to be mothers of the same baby and his solution offer guidance. The one who put the interests of the baby above her own interest and well-being was the real mother. When considering abortion, the well-being of the baby should never be ignored.

44

....

The Canonization of Gorbachev

Why, man, he doth bestride the narrow world
Like a Colossus; and we petty men
Walk under his huge legs, and peep about
To find ourselves dishonorable graves.
Men at some time are masters of their fates:
The fault, dear Brutus, is not in our stars,
But in ourselves, that we are underlings.
—SHAKESPEARE, *JULIUS CAESAR*

AFTER BEING HUMILIATED BY BORIS Yeltsin and losing his powerful positions as president of the Soviet Union and secretary of the Communist Party of the Soviet Union, Gorbachev did not fade gracefully into the sunset. What he lost in Russia he gained in the United States. He remains a major player on the world stage. He became chairman of the International Institute for Social, Economic, and Political Studies in Moscow; chairman of the International Green Cross; and honorary chairman of the Gorbachev Foundation/USA in 1992.

The Gorbachev Foundation convened, and Gorbachev chaired a State of the World Forum, which was held in San Francisco, Cali-

454

fornia, from September 27 to October 1, 1995. He recruited many of the leaders of the world to serve as co-chairs, fellows, and participants. The co-chairs were:

Askar Akaev *President, Kyrgyzstan* Oscar Arias *President, Costa Rica (1986–1990)*

James A. Baker, III *US Secretary of State (1989–1992)*

Tansu Ciller *Prime Minister, Republic of Turkey* Ruud Lubbers *Prime Minister, The Netherlands (1982–1994)*

Thabo Mbeki *Deputy Executive President, Republic of South Africa*

Rigoberta Menchú Tum *Nobel Peace Prize Laureate (1992)*

Yasuhiro Nakasone *Prime Minister, Japan (1982–1987)*

George Shultz *US Secretary of State (1982–1989)*

Maurice Strong *Chairman, Earth Council*

Ted Turner *Chairman, Turner Broadcasting System, Inc.*

Desmond Tutu *Archbishop of Cape Town, South Africa*

Fellows and participants included many of the most powerful and wealthy men and women in the world:

Dwayne Andreas *Chairman and CEO Archer Daniels Midland Co.*

Oscar Arias *President, Costa Rica (1986–1990)*

Kurt Biedenkopf *Premier of Saxony, Federal Republic of Germany*

Zbigniew Brzezinski *National Security Advisor to the President (1976–1980)*

George Bush *President of the United States (1989–1993)*

Alan Cranston *U.S. Senator (1968–1992)*

Mario Cuomo *Governor of New York*

John Denver *Musician*

Sonia Gandhi *Founder, Rajiv Gandhi Foundation*

Thomas Graham *Senior Program Advisor, The Rockefeller Foundation*

Vaclav Havel *President of the Czech Republic (taped message)*

Theodore Hesburgh *President, University of Notre Dame (1952–1987)*
Samuel Huntingdon *Professor, Harvard University*
Max Kampelman *Attorney, former U.S. Arms Control Ambassador*
Amory Lovins *President, Rocky Mountain Institute*
Ruud Lubbers *Prime Minister of the Netherlands (1982–1994)*
David Packard *Founder, Hewlett-Packard Corporation*
Carl Sagan *Astronomer, Author, Cornell University*
George Schultz *Secretary of State of the United States (1982–1989)*
Margaret Thatcher *Prime Minister, United Kingdom (1979–1990)*
Ted Turner *Chairman of the Board, Turner Broadcasting Systems, Inc.*
Desmond Tutu *Archbishop of Cape Town; Nobel Peace Prize Laureate, 1984 (via satellite)*

FINANCIAL SUPPORT

The forum was a project of the Gorbachev Foundation, a 503(c)(3) organization, and therefore tax-deductible.

In addition to a fee of $5,000 for many of those attending, the forum received many major contributions up to $250,000.

THE FORUM

My dear friend and protogé, Clark Bowers, Ph.D., distinguished visiting fellow at Harvard University, was elected a delegate to the forum.

He gave his impression of it as a "merging of the ideas of the New Age and the New Left." There were, however, a few discordant voices as shown by the statements of Margaret Thatcher and George Bush in the final session with Mikhail Gorbachev, which was moderated by Bernard Shaw, an anchor man for CNN:

GORBACHEV: History shows optimism for new great leaders within a democratic framework.

THATCHER: The speed of the USSR's breakup surprised us. This move away from Communism without any experience can be shocking. The most important elements that must be applied to the former USSR are (1) most importantly, rule of law, (2) real private property for the average citizen, (3) a market economy, and (4) developing a moral social community of people.

GORBACHEV: We have missed some important opportunities following the post Cold War Era. Now that the arms race is mainly over, economic issues and national identity become more important. The world is at a watershed. We must change international relations for a new world. A new world that includes dramatic current problems and equally dramatic future problems.

BUSH: In Desert Storm the world saw that the UN can have an important role in setting up law of order and protection against aggression. However, the UN still is very limited and cannot solve all of our problems. We need NATO and bilateral relations with key countries as well. And the U.S. has a disproportionate responsibility to lead the way.

THATCHER: Still it must be noted that it was the U.S. that passed all the resolutions in the UN and did all the main fighting under George Bush's general leadership. Bosnia should have never been under UN authority. Nation states must do all the fighting.

GORBACHEV: We have squandered most of the momentum gained during our teamwork together against Iraq. I think the UN is more important today than ever. The fact that the USSR and China agreed during the Gulf War is an even more important development even though we didn't lead or fight. Bosnia is a failure. It was an example of some countries trying to get tactical gains for prestige and power purposes. This is wrong and must be stopped. Additionally, you should never expand NATO.

THATCHER: It is a mistake to run any of the military operations through the UN. With NATO having to tell the UN when and where the air strikes will be, it is like telling your enemy what you are going to do and when you are going to do it. This is crazy. We must not treat all countries the same because of vast differences in human rights and global ambitions, etc. If anything, the UN should be used more for famine relief but not warfare.

GORBACHEV: I strongly disagree! You cannot convince the millions of TV viewers that are watching us today that now is not the time for more UN growth and involvement including global security. Our goal is to unite the world and prevent conflict. International relations cannot be based on a few special countries' interests. We will not allow any global policeman country. I will never accept a smaller role for the UN, and the U.S. role is not to be global policeman. The U.S. people applaud me all over the country when I tell them this. Still, the U.S. should be present helping out other countries economically.

THATCHER: The fact is, Mikhail, that the U.S. saved Kuwait alone without the United Nations, and if the U.S. had not acted as global policeman, Iraq would control 60 percent of the world's oil today and be continuing their expansion into biological, chemical, and nuclear weapons.

BUSH: I agree people in the U.S. don't want the U.S. as world policeman but fundamentalism, nuclear proliferation, drugs, terrorism, etc., cannot be controlled by the UN. The leadership must be taken by the major powers. The U.S. has a moral obligation to help guarantee peace because of our democracy and our very clear human rights record.

GORBACHEV: Other powers will not allow themselves to be second powers. Don't think that India, China, or Russia will take second place on any matters to the U.S.

BUSH: The UN needs change, but it cannot be a substitute for the nation state. The U.S. cannot pull back, we must use our influence in diplomacy to continue to push for human rights in China and in many other parts of the world.

BERNARD: China may invade Taiwan. If this should happen, should we intervene militarily?

BUSH: We want to prevent it and we believe that reunification should be peaceful. We want to push China toward a peaceful solution. However, I will not discuss the possibility of a military confrontation.

THATCHER: You cannot introduce economic freedom without it eventually leading to political freedom. I hope this will happen in China.

BERNARD: Are we making technology a god at the expense of the human spirit, culture, and religion?

THATCHER: No. Science is completely neutral and has been used for good and evil historically. The question is how humans use it.

GORBACHEV: Yes. The twentieth century had great technological advances, and we should notice that it also was the most cruel century in history.

BUSH: I support technology, and I believe it should be used as it has been in the past to benefit millions of others.

BERNARD: Have we pillaged the planet with too much industry, environmental, and nuclear waste?

THATCHER: I want to be very clear in stating that historically, countries do not succeed based on natural resources. Look at Russia for example; they should be the wealthiest country on earth. They have more of everything in the area of natural resources. The reason they are so poor is because of their system. And that system has also brought the worst environmental record in history. The key to success is countries with true free enterprise and strict rule of law that have developed property rights. Look at Japan and Taiwan among many others. They are countries with very little natural resources that are far more productive per capita than Russia. Developing countries have no right to point to the West and tell us we owe them more money so they can be successful.

GORBACHEV'S BOOK

The patriarch Job laments, "Oh . . . that mine adversary had written a book." (Job 31:35)

Gorbachev has obliged with a book entitled *The Search for a New Beginning—Developing a New World Order.* A copy of the preliminary text was distributed as part of the publicity for the forum. It opened with this alarming account of the danger of the nuclear bomb.

> My personal situation and experiences as the president of the former Soviet Union have provided me with insight into an unimaginable terror that has been shared by only a few individuals on this planet. In my hands there rested the sheer raw power to unleash nuclear weapons on the world and destroy human life. For seven years this power was never more than a few feet away.
>
> At all hours of the day and night, wherever I went, whatever I did, awake or asleep, some military aide was nearby, holding at the ready that infamous black box containing the nuclear codes that became the dark and evil emblem of our tortured nuclear age.
>
> I was haunted by the constant awareness that I might be required to calculate and decide in an instant of time whether some kind of nuclear action might be required in response to a real or imagined or mistaken attack perceived to be under way against my country. I know this nightmare was shared equally by Ronald Reagan and George Bush when they were president.
>
> The ultimate absurdity of relying on nuclear weapons was dramatically revealed to me, and I am sure to President Bush as well, when we met in Washington in the summer of 1990.
>
> During that visit, we shared a helicopter ride together to Camp David. Near President Bush sat a military aide

with the nuclear codes enabling him to destroy the
Soviet Union. Near me sat my military aide with the
codes required to destroy the United States. Yet President Bush and I sat together on that small helicopter
talking about peace. Neither of us planned to ever use
the awesome power we each possessed. Yet we possessed
it. And we both knew how ordinary and fallible we both
were.

This statement explains the concern of many of the participants in
the forum. They are justifiably frightened. An appropriate name for
the conference would have been "A gathering of frightened men."
It calls to mind the prophetic words of Jesus:

And there shall be signs in the sun, and in the moon,
and in the stars; and upon earth distress of nations, with
perplexity; the sea and the waves roaring; Men's hearts
failing them for fear, and for looking after those things
which are coming on the earth: for the powers of heaven
shall be shaken. (Luke 21:25–26)

Jesus followed this prophecy with this word of hope and
deliverance:

And when these things begin to come to pass, then
look up, and lift up your heads; for your redemption
draweth nigh. (Verse 28)

Gorbachev's book contains a wish list of desirable ends with no
indication of how they can be attained. It exemplifies the proverb,
"If wishes were horses then beggars could ride." Another appropriate name for the forum would have been, "Beggars on Horseback."
Most of the wishes were statements of truths which have been
taught in Sunday Schools for generations, such as:

The roots of the current crisis of civilization lie within
humanity itself . . . *Only by renouncing selfishness and*

attempts to outsmart one another to gain advantage at
the expense of others can we hope to ensure the survival
of humankind and the further development of our civilization. (pages 15–16) [italics in original]

Tell that to the genes. The desire to eliminate selfishness from
human nature is as old as history. The monstrous crimes of Stalin,
Mao, and Pol Pot were based upon a conviction that selfishness
could be eliminated from human nature by creating a perfect economic system.

We have suddenly become like careless children
whose vigor and activity far exceed the development of
their morality and consciousness. (page 20)

What's so sudden about this? Consider the numerous wars
throughout history.

The wealth of some means the poverty of others.
(page 22)

And in many instances, the enrichment of some means the enrichment of others. Consider the enrichment of the pharmaceutical companies that discover, manufacture, and distribute life-saving drugs.

In the final analysis the main source of our troubles is
not outside, but within us, in our attitudes toward one
another, toward society and nature. All the rest derives
from that. We must therefore first change ourselves,
through education and multidisciplinary, world-wide,
and cross generational interaction.
And having changed ourselves, we must come
together in all our diversity to build a new world.
(pages 74–75)

Who can quarrel with that? Jesus said:

But those things which proceed out of the mouth
come forth from the heart; and they defile the man. For
out of the heart proceed evil thoughts, murders, adulter-
ies, fornications, thefts, false witness, blasphemies.
(Matthew 15:18–19)

Is Gorbachev still a Marxist–Leninist? How much of the basic
ideas that guided him during his ascent in the Communist apparatus
does he retain?

Gorbachev provides an answer in his reply to Clark Bowers at the
forum:

> CLARK BOWERS: Mr. Gorbachev, you made it quite
> clear in your book *Perestroika* that your solution for the
> problems of the USSR was not to abandon the Marx-
> ist–Leninist course but rather to adapt it to modern
> times, and interpret it more accurately. Do you still, gen-
> erally, believe that the way for the world to perfect
> human nature is by eliminating the corrupting influence
> of the capitalist economic environment or do you now
> disagree with what you wrote in *Perestroika?*
> MIKHAIL GORBACHEV: My general beliefs have not
> changed. Yet, in the past, the way in which those beliefs
> have been interpreted, applied to diverse cultures and
> forced along by man, instead of History, has been awful.

Try as I may, I cannot fully understand his second sentence. I
agree that the way in which his ideas have been applied has been
awful, but how does he separate the role of man from history? Is history not a record of the activities of mankind? Does he identify an
agency called History as one that can operate independently of the
activities of men and women? Is this not a deification of History; the
creation of a god?

I once watched and listened carefully as Gorbachev and Yeltsin
answered questions on a television program. Gorbachev stated categorically that he was an atheist, while Yeltsin said he was now seeking to discover if God existed.

Has Gorbachev changed? He now states that certain "extras" must be added to the beliefs of Marxism–Leninism. He believes that a "spiritual" vacuum exists and that a way must be found to fill it.

When Clark Bowers asked, "How can dialectical materialism be compatible with any form of spiritualism, since by definition materialism means that there is nothing in the universe except matter in motion?" Gorbachev answered:

> This is a very complex matter, and I do not think that it is productive toward our goals here to use such antiquated language to divide us. Our goal is to focus on similarity and to build a supranational basis and a *global civilization* for keeping the peace.

This was a polite way of saying "shut up!"

What are the additional ideas which have been added to Gorbachev's Marxism–Leninism? A careful reading of his book and careful attention to his statements reveal elements of pantheism, Hinduism, environmentalism, and the superstitions of the New Age. I venture to suggest that the greatest of his ideas is Marxism–Leninism.

DEMOCRACY

> *The Holocaust should be a reminder about the dangers in democracy,* about the imperfections of existing democratic systems, and about the special responsibility of all those who are committed to democracy, not just in words, but in deeds. (page 41)

Gorbachev advocates a New World order in which national sovereignty will be subordinate to a central world authority. This would mean the abandonment of the American birthright, its sovereignty.

A stepping-stone to this objective is submission of U.S. authority to the institutions of the United Nations. This would lead to further erosion of individual liberty.

Does Gorbachev have ambitions to become leader of an international government which rules the entire globe? Suspicion of this may appear paranoiac, but justified.

FAITH

If something should be, then it must be. This seems to be the faith of Gorbachev. His axioms are, "what should be, must be," and "what must be, will be." How the desirable is to be translated into the achievable, and the achievable translated into the achieved is not specified.

His attitude reminds me of the radiant assurance of the young Communists I met in my youth who were intoxicated by the vision of the new man and the New World that was in gestation in the Soviet Union. What a wonderful world that would be! The vision justified all measures needed to fulfill it.

Gorbachev presents his vision:

> *The time has come to choose a new direction of global development, to opt for a new civilization.* Today we can only chart its most general outlines. It is a civilization that rules out confrontational approaches. Economic, political, class, interethnic, or ideological wars will have to be abolished. The use of force as a political tool will have to be rejected. Cooperation will gradually supplant competition. It will be a civilization of mutual tolerance, with cultures and nations becoming increasingly open-minded and diversity understood and used as a factor of progress. And, first and foremost, it will be a civilization that assures harmony and creative coexistence between humanity and the rest of nature.

I would not have been surprised if he had added:

The state shall wither away, universal harmony shall prevail along with total abundance and the rule shall be—

"From each according to his ability; to each according to his need."

Marxism–Leninism lives.

45

....

Cloud of Witnesses

Seeing we also are compassed about with so great a cloud
of witnesses, let us lay aside every weight, and the sin
which doth so easily beset us, and let us run with
patience the race that is set before us.
—HEBREWS 12:1

FROM THE START, I HAVE emphasized Communist thought.
Their actions were guided by their thoughts. One of my favorite biblical texts says, "As a man thinketh in his heart, so is he." (Proverbs
23:7)

In order to discover the basic beliefs of the Communists, and their
resulting Communist conduct, I consistently researched Communist
thinking. I studied much of the copious Communist literature that
flowed in a constant stream. Knowledge of their thoughts provided
a basis for understanding their past and present actions, and pre-
dicting their future conduct. In order to present this knowledge in
words that could be understood, I frequently used analogies. Many
who were already active in the battle against Communism used the
information. Others were stimulated to devote their lives to the
defeat of Communist aggression. The number is legion.

466

I submit a few names from among those who acknowledge having received a measure of enlightenment.

RONALD REAGAN

I did not convert Ronald Reagan to anti-Communism. The Communists had already done this. As president of the Screen Actors Guild he had discerned their duplicity and been subjected to their venomous attacks. He attended the Southern California School of Anti-Communism, held in Los Angeles on August 28 to September 1, 1961, and expressed appreciation for the clarity of the messages exposing the pathological nature of Communist doctrines.

I take pride in recounting that the man who later became president of the United States, and who enacted programs that led to the downfall of the Soviet Communism, once served as a substitute speaker for me. It was in 1962 when he was a lecturer sponsored by the General Electric Corporation. I was scheduled to speak at a luncheon in Omaha, Nebraska, but bad weather delayed my arrival. The meeting was chaired by the mayor of Omaha, and Ronald Reagan held the fort until I arrived.

I due course he became president of the United States of America, and the rest is history. His outstanding role in formulating the programs that led to the downfall of Soviet Communism is undeniable. His place in the pantheon of history is secure.

The influence of my message on his thoughts, statements, and programs was both direct and indirect. The indirect influence resulted from our numerous Schools of Anti-Communism and Anti-Subversive Seminars. In due course many of the students came to occupy responsible positions in government, education, and religion.

Three of them became speechwriters for President Reagan. They were Dana Rohrabacher, Tony Dolan, and Jack Wells.

President Reagan was a great orator. Two of his outstanding speeches were to the British Parliament and to the National Association of Evangelicals in Fort Lauderdale, or the "Evil Empire" speech.

I congratulated Tony Dolan, the speechwriter who helped prepare these speeches, and he replied, "You should have liked it. I took it all from you." He sent me a copy of the "Evil Empire" speech with this note: "I thought you might like to see the oak tree that has grown from the acorn which you planted so many years ago."

As the Bible says, "Cast thy bread upon the waters: for thou shalt find it after many days." (Ecclesiastes 11:1)

The same thought is expressed in Henry Wadsworth Longfellow's poem, "The Arrow and the Song":

I shot an arrow into the air,
It fell to earth I knew not where;
For, so swiftly it flew, the sight
Could not follow it in its flight.

I breathed a song into the air,
It fell to earth, I knew not where;
For who has sight so keen and strong,
That it can follow the flight of a song.

Long, long afterward, in an oak
I found the arrow, still unbroke;
And the song, from beginning to end,
I found again in the heart of a friend.

As previously noted, on January 11, 1990, Lillian and I celebrated our golden wedding anniversary in the Ballroom of the Beverly Wilshire Hotel in Los Angeles. We heard messages from President Reagan, Bill Buckley, Roy Rogers and Dale Evans, Congressman Bob Dornan, Congressman Dana Rohrabacher, Supervisor Mike Antonovitch, Reed Irvine, Eleanor Schlafly, and numerous others.

Our son John has never been a public speaker. He takes after his mother and excels in private conversation. He surprised me by asking if he could be the speaker on behalf of the family.

In his speech he told me something I had not fully realized. He said how much he had missed my presence during his adolescent years and how he had wondered if my absence due to my work as an Anti-Communist Crusader was really justified. He proceeded to say that the harvest reaped proved beyond question that it had been well worthwhile.

He is passionately devoted to his own family and still takes time off from his exceedingly busy medical practice to tutor his children as they confront their examinations.

Did the years spent in analyzing Communist doctrines and deeds, and publishing the results, make a contribution to the termination of the Cold War? Many whose judgment I respect claim that my influence has been significant indeed. I hope this is so.

The Communists in the Soviet Union were aware of the existence and activity of the Crusade, as can be seen by their publication of the following cartoon in the December 1964 edition of the Soviet magazine, *Science and Religion,* their government's "monthly popular atheist journal."

I can say truthfully that I did discern the existence of the forces that would lead to the collapse of Communism in the Soviet Union and wrote this prediction in our May 2, 1968, Crusade newsletter:

> Today Communism is powerful and aggressive. It is stronger numerically, militarily, economically, propagandistically, and subversively than any comparable movement in human history. It has delivered shattering blows against the free world during the past 50 years. An objective analysis of the historic record would indicate that it is winning the battle for world conquest. However, today Communism is suffering from an internal hemorrhage that will progressively weaken it so that, if

"Schwarz bellowing anti-communism"   "Schwarz onward into battle"   "Schwarz worshiping and praying to the atom bomb"   "Frawley paying off Schwarz for a job well done"

the free world can survive the next few years, the future
is radiant with hope.

Nevertheless, I did not expect the collapse to come so quickly and
suddenly, and I was surprised when it did happen.

There is a natural tendency to identify correlation with causation.
This tendency is expressed by the Latin phrase, *post hoc ergo
propter hoc,* which translates, "after this, therefore on account of
this." Correlation does not necessarily prove causation, but consistent correlation of two events suggests that a causal relationship
exists. This is the basis of empirical science. For example, the regular rising of the sun over the horizon correlates with the increase of
daylight so it is reasonable to believe that the latter is caused by the
former.

I venture to believe that my absence from home, to which our son
John referred when he spoke at our Golden Wedding Anniversary
celebration, did contribute to the end of the Cold War.

This assurance gives an encouragement to individual activity
against an apparently overwhelming and invincible force.

I am only one, but I am one,
I cannot do everything, but I can do something.
That which I can do I should do;
And that which I should do, by the grace of God,
I will do.   (Anon)

The poet Arthur Hugh Clough (1819–1861) wrote:

Say not, the struggle naught availeth,
The labor and the wounds are vain,
The enemy faints not, nor faileth,
And as things have been they remain.

For while the tired waves, vainly breaking,
Seem here no painful inch to gain,
Far back, through creeks and inlets making
Comes silent, flooding in, the main.

And not by eastern windows only,
When daylight comes, comes in the light;
In front, the sun climbs slow, how slowly,
But westward, look, the land is bright.

As St. Paul exhorts, "And let us not be weary in well-doing: for in due season we shall reap if we faint not." (Galatians 6:9)

Despite the shattering of the Berlin Wall and the dissolution of the Soviet Union, I did not join the chorus that "Communism is dead." I did not "fold my tent and steal away."

I was aware that Communism had been declared dead previously, only to rise again with greater menace. Examples: The announcement by the leading newspapers of the world in 1921 that Communism was dead when Lenin restored economic procedures in the Soviet Union by his New Economic Policy; Chiang Kai-Shek's allegedly defeat of the armies of Mao Tse-tung in China in 1934 when Mao led the remnants of those armies on the Long March to a haven in Yenan. I also knew that Jesus told the parable:

> When the unclean spirit is gone out of a man, he
> walketh through dry places, seeking rest, and findeth
> none. Then he saith, I will return into my house from
> whence I came out; and when he is come, he findeth it
> empty, swept, and garnished. Then goeth he, and taketh
> with himself seven other spirits more wicked than him-
> self, and they enter in and dwell there: and the last state
> of that man is worse than the first. Even so shall it be
> also unto this wicked generation.
>
> (Matthew 12:43–45)

I knew that the Communists were guided by the philosophy of dialectical materialism, which taught that progress proceeded by ebb and flow; that the objective was to be reached by a process similar to the rise and fall of the hammer. I was also well aware that the forces that the Communists harnessed in their quest for power continued to exist and that the ideas that motivated and directed the Communists endured.

Consequently, I continued to publish the Crusade newsletter and introduced a new regular feature captioned, "The Lively Communist Corpse," which reported the continuing activities of the Communists both in the United States and worldwide.

A paradoxical situation developed in the United States. The Communist Party USA suffered severe blows which many considered lethal. The Soviet subsidy of millions of dollars ceased, and internal dissension within the ranks caused the expulsion of many leading lifelong Communists such as Herbert Aptheker and Angela Davis. Nevertheless, the Communist Party USA, under the leadership of Gus Hall, is making remarkable progress and is recruiting and growing rapidly. Numerous Communist sects survive and publish, including several Trotskyist groups. The fanatical followers of Stalin and Mao continue to publish the *Revolutionary Worker,* idolize Abilmael Guzman (the imprisoned leader of the murderous Communist Party of Peru, the Shining Path), and to support terroristic violence throughout the United States and the world.

Meanwhile the Communists continue to rule China, to conduct nuclear explosions in search of more effective nuclear weapons, to establish military power in the Spratly Islands, to threaten Taiwan as they project missiles nearby, and to expand their economic and military power as they continue on their long march toward their announced objective—the establishment of world Communism.

North Korea continues its quest for nuclear weapons under the guidance of its Communist dictatorship.

The semipenitent Gorbachev gains the support of many world leaders who are profoundly disturbed by the apparently insoluble problems confronting mankind.

What a lively Communist corpse!

Within the United States, racism, hedonism, illegitimacy, family breakdown, drug indulgence, crime, and political cynicism remain the order of the day and provide fertile soil for the seeds of totalitarianism.

It remains true that "The price of liberty is eternal vigilance."

46

....

The Family

But if any man provide not for his own, and specially
for those of his own house, he hath denied the faith,
and is worse than an infidel.
—1 TIMOTHY 5:8

"Abolition of the Family! Even the most radical flare
up at this infamous proposal of the Communists.

On what foundation is the present family, the bourgeois family, based? On capital, on private gain. In its
completely developed form this family exists only among
the bourgeoisie. But this state of things finds its complement in the practical absence of the family among the
proletarians, and in public prostitution.

The bourgeois family will vanish as a matter of course
when its complement vanishes, and both will vanish
with the vanishing of capital."

This blunt statement was made by Marx and Engels in *The Communist Manifesto*. They reached this conclusion after examining the
progress of human society from primitive Communism, via barbarism and feudalism, to Capitalism.

Engels presents the historical evidence for this conclusion in his book, *The Origin of the Family, Private Property and the State,* which is regarded as one of the classics of marxism. Lenin boasted that he had read it many times. Reductionist arguments often appear logical and convincing. In such arguments the proponent isolates one of a number of factors that produce change and progress, and ignores others. He then predicts the developments that will logically ensue.

The eminent entomologist Harry Andersen, who is my personal friend and scientific adviser, has provided the following "reductionist" evidence that an environmental tragedy is about to engulf mankind in which we are all about to be drowned in a sea of fruit flies.

The reproductive powers of insects are often tremendous; most people do not realize just how great they are. The capacity of any animal to build up its numbers through reproduction depends on three characteristics of that animal—the number of fertile eggs laid by each female (which in insects may vary from one to many thousands), the length of a generation (which may vary from a few days to several years), and the proportion of each generation that is female and will produce the next generation (in some insects there are no males).

An example that might be cited to illustrate insects' reproductive powers is *Drosophila melanogaster,* the pomace fly that has been studied so much by geneticists. These flies develop rapidly and, under ideal conditions, may produce 25 generations in a year. Each female will lay up to 100 eggs, of which about half will develop into males and half into females. Now suppose we start with a pair of these flies and allow them to increase under ideal conditions, with no checks on increase (give them: all the room, food, oxygen they need, eliminate all predators, efficiently eliminate all waste products) for a year—with the original and each succeeding female laying 100 eggs before she dies and each egg hatching, growing to maturity, and reproducing again, at a 50:50

sex ratio. With two flies in the first generation, there would be 100 in the second, 5,000 in the third, and so on—with the twenty-fifth generation consisting of about 1.192×10^{41} flies. If this many flies were packed tightly together, 1,000 to a cubic inch, they would form a ball of flies 96,372,988 *miles in diameter*—or a ball whose diameter would approximate the distance from the earth to the sun!

Source of reference:
An Introduction to the Study of Insects, Fifth Edition,
(Saunders College Publishing, 1981
Donald J. Borror, Dwight M. DeLong and Charles A.
Triplehorn, all of the Ohio State University)

Please pardon our failure to mention such limiting factors as nutrition, predation, excretion, space, and numerous metabolic essentials.

Marxist arguments are frequently convincing. The element Marx selected as the cause of change and progress is the mode of production. Engels affirms this in his preface to the 1888 English edition:

> *The Manifesto* being our joint production, I consider myself bound to state that the fundamental proposition, which forms its nucleus, belongs to Marx. The proposition is: that in every historical epoch, the prevailing mode of economic production and exchange, and the social organization necessarily following from it, form the basis upon which is built up, and from which alone can be explained, the political and intellectual history of that epoch. . . .

I was aware that by presenting the Marxist arguments clearly I was taking a risk. The following anecdote illustrates this.

During a school of anti-Communism in Dallas, I was halfway through the presentation of the Marxist doctrine of the family when we paused for a break and a Baptist preacher said, "You have us all convinced. How do you unconvince us?"

Reductionist arguments may be logical but they lead to false conclusions. Actual events have shown that the predictions of Marx and Engels about the role and fate of the family were as fallacious as their companion conclusion in *The Manifesto* that "National differences and antagonisms between peoples are daily more and more vanishing." What nonsense!

The Marxist doctrine on the origin and role of the family may be summarized as follows:

The earliest forms of human society were roving bands of hunters and gatherers seeking food. Fatherhood was unknown and unknowable. A form of group marriage existed in which many women were available sexually to many men. Maternity and fraternity were knowable and known, but not paternity. Consequently, the mothers' brothers were considered the fathers of the children while potential fathers were called uncles.

Progress in the mode of production led to the creation of tools. These tools became the private property of the leader of the band—the chief or king. He became emotionally attached to them and wished to retain ownership when his brief life ended.

In order to continue ownership he must have an heir who was "bone of his bone and flesh of his flesh." He must be able to say, "This is my son." To assure this, a number of women must be set aside for his exclusive sexual use. Thus group marriage evolved into polygamy.

As Capitalist production progressed and the number owning private property increased, polygamy evolved into monogamy. The role of women in this process was to serve as instruments of production. Their products were children and food.

Thus marriage was a bourgeois creation. This conviction led to the statement in *The Manifesto*:

> The Bourgeois clap-trap about the family and education, about the hallowed co-relation of parent and child, becomes all the more disgusting, the more, by the action of Modern Industry, all family ties among the proletarians are torn asunder, and their children transformed into simple articles of commerce and instruments of labor.

Seldom has a bigger insult been given to working-class parents. They love their children and sacrifice to improve their lives. A personal illustration is my own upbringing. While my parents were proletarian—my father served as a laborer on the waterfront and in many other humble jobs—nevertheless they loved and nurtured each one of their eleven children with selfless devotion.

The Marxist doctrine of the family stands in stark contrast to the family responsibility described by St. Paul in his letter to Timothy: "But if any provide not for his own, and specially for those of his own house, he hath denied the faith, and is worse than an infidel." (1 Timothy 5:8)

Do I believe that women should be professionals? Of course I do. My wife Lillian is the most professional woman I know. Her talents are innumerable. The poet Wordsworth could have had a vision of her when he wrote:

A perfect woman, nobly planned
To warn, to comfort and command.

Lillian is a loving wife, a devoted mother, grandmother, and great-grandmother, a superlative homemaker, a proficient bookkeeper and accountant, a great chef, a splendid nurse, an understanding counselor and psychologist, a household plumber and handyman, and a wonderful friend. The idea that she needed the feminists to liberate her would surprise and amuse her.

What are riches? Money alone can never make anyone truly rich. Jesus taught this when he told the parable of the rich man who was perplexed because he had too much worldly wealth. This man decided to build bigger barns, and said to himself, "I will say to my soul, 'Thou hast much goods laid up for many years; take thine ease, eat, drink and be merry.' " Jesus rebuked him: "Thou fool, this night thy soul shall be required of thee: then whose shall these things be?"

Money, like air, is essential for life, but too much can be a handicap. Excessive breathing can induce hyperventilation and cause loss of consciousness.

To possess a loving family is to possess true riches. Judged by this standard Lillian and I are rich indeed.

On January 11, 1990, Lillian and I celebrated fifty years of married life. The celebration took place in the ballroom of the Beverly Wilshire Hotel in Los Angeles. Almost every member of the family was present—our children, their spouses, and our grandchildren. They adorned the stage and made our hearts rejoice. How proud we were.

I was eager that they should see and hear the nature and harvest of the message that had caused my absence from Australia for most of their lives. They heard messages from President Reagan, members of the U.S. Congress, and numerous others whose minds had been informed and whose lives have been influenced by my message.

Our friends also saw and heard members of our family tell their story. I spoke too, but many thought the major message was given by our red-haired eight-year-old grandson, Ben Schwarz Esler, who had insisted on preparing his own speech.

Our family is a tribute to God's love and to its expression in the nurturing life of our family mother, Lillian, whom I still affectionately call "Mummy" and whom the grandchildren call "Gar."

Two books that have added to my understanding and appreciation of family values are *Sexual Suicide* and *Man and Marriage,* both by George Gilder. They have enlightened me on how the pathway from barbarism to civilization has been built by the nature and work of women.

The existence of the human race is a miracle. A human baby is one of the most helpless and vulnerable of living things. Unless it receives constant daily attention from someone during the first years of life it will surely die. The continued existence of the human race proves that millions gave the necessary attention. Who were and are these people?

The obvious answer is the mothers of the babies. Throughout history it has rarely been the father. His identity was often unknown and unknowable. His contribution was fulfilled by the act of insemination.

In primitive societies the care of the baby must have been extremely burdensome. Consider a tribe moving from one location to another in the quest for food and water. Stragglers were often left behind to die. Carrying and feeding the baby tended to make nursing mothers stragglers. The urge to discard the burden must have been strong.

Since the human race has survived in inhospitable regions many, if not most, mothers must have resisted the urge to discard their burden. Motherhood has proved stronger than self-protection.

The mother instinct has enabled the human race to survive. Mothers are born with an inner imperative to care for the child to whom they have given birth. If this were not so, the human race would have become extinct long ago.

This motherhood instinct is present in the females of most higher animals. On one occasion Lillian and I watched its manifestation in a cow.

We visited a ranch in Emerald, a western town in the Australian State of Queensland. Cattle there are subject to infestation with ticks, and they need periodic spraying with a pesticide. We sat on the top rail of a fence and watched the spraying.

A mob of about two hundred cows and calves had been gathered. A group of about fifty was separated from the main herd and sprayed en masse. This group was then driven about a mile away to forage, while another fifty were corralled for spraying.

We watched as a large cow separated herself from the first foraging group and wandered back to where the spraying was taking place. She looked lonely and forlorn. Lillian said, "I'll bet you she is looking for her calf."

We watched as the second fifty were escorted away after spraying, and saw among them the mother cow accompanied by her calf, about half her size, hardly a newborn.

What brought her back? It was the mother instinct.

Human mothers are born with an inner need to care for their baby. This instinct is independent of culture and morality. It is basic.

To deny a woman the right to care for her baby is not to liberate but to enslave her. America needs more mothers at home caring for their babies, rather than more child-care centers. Radical feminism has been the enemy of femininity.

As babies grow they need food in addition to mother's milk. This is imperative, especially if a second or third child is born. Agriculture developed in order to fulfill this need. Seeds were planted, crops were grown, and essential food was harvested and used to feed the growing children.

To grow and harvest food it was necessary to remain in the areas where the crops were grown. This created settlements that gave rise to villages. Civilization commenced.

In order to secure the food for the children, the women became the tillers of the ground. Constant mobility yielded place to stability.

Thus female nature had the qualities that were essential for the nurturing of children, while primitive male nature retained the qualities which made for efficient hunting. Women were harvesters, while men remained predators.

A family came into existence when masculine nature became subordinate to female nature. The predatory mobility of the male yielded to the nurturing stability of the female. Predation was transformed into sustenation, and the family was formed.

Life in the family tamed the violent tendencies of the male who shared responsibility for the care of the children. Fatherhood added a dimension of responsibility and dignity to male nature; thus the family became the foundation of civilization.

The unattached male tended to retain the nature of the predator.

As the children were nurtured and reared in the joint care of the mother and father, they developed family and social qualities which reduced the dominance of predation.

The breakdown of the family released the predatory impulses of the men who were freed from the responsibility to care for the children. It also inhibited the development of responsibility and unselfishness in the children, especially the male children.

Gilder points out that unattached males in modern society often become the practitioners and victims of social pathology. The unattached male is more likely than the husband and father to be involved in poverty, crime, drug addiction, mental illness, homicide, and suicide. Gangs which foster violence and predation are substituted for nurturing families.

He points out that most programs to rehabilitate criminals have ended in failure despite the investment of large sums of money. Success has been achieved when a released prisoner has been grafted into stable family life.

Thus legislation, however well-intended, which breaks down family unity, becomes a source of predatory violence.

This is the primary cause for the deplorable conditions that exist in the communities of the inner cities of the United States. The gangs become substitutes for nurturing families. The communities become hotbeds of crime, sexual violence, physical insecurity, and frequent death. Predation rules. Periodic riots break out such as the one that engulfed Los Angeles after the verdict of "not guilty" was given in the original trial of the police who assaulted Rodney King.

It has been wisely said that "Whosoever fails in his family responsibilities fails in life."

FAMILY TESTIMONY

In over fifty-five years of married life, Lillian and I have never had angry words over the care of our children. Lillian returned to Australia in 1953 because she believed that was in the best interests of the children. I agreed, and events have proved that our decision was right. Though I have been absent most of each year, our family has remained a close and loving unit. Lillian and I have kept in close communication and have grown closer, if possible, as the years have passed. During the early years we wrote and mailed our letters daily and now we fax daily. I hurry to the office early each morning, eager to read Lillian's faxed love letter. I have returned to Australia twice each year and have spent a wonderful month or more with Lillian each time. It has always been as though I had not been absent a day.

As our family has grown it has continued to bring abundant pride and joy. The medical tradition has been well maintained, as four of our children are now medical doctors and four grandchildren are in medical school. The family also contains four nurses and one pharmacist. Lillian and I are not only in love, but are also proud of each one of our children and grandchildren. We enjoy the services of a personal physician, our son John. Fortunately, he has inherited many of his mother's qualities. Like his mother, he is a good listener.

Lillian and I feel as responsible about the needs of our family now as we did on the day they were born. Love never dies.

Shakespeare wrote the tragic story of a king in his famous play *Macbeth*. As the end of his life draws near, Macbeth laments:

> My way of life
> Is fall'n into the sere, the yellow leaf;
> And that which should accompany old age,
> As honor, love, obedience, troops of friends,
> I must not look to have; but in their stead,
> Curses, not loud but deep.
>
> (Act V, Sc 1, Line 22)

Our experience is a total contrast. As Jesus promised, we have received all the things that Macbeth lacked in "good measure, pressed down and shaken together and running over." (Luke 6:38)

Every day we thank God for our family and its values.

47

....

Faith and Sanity

Faith is the substance of things hoped for.
—HEBREWS 11:1

DURING MY LATE TEENAGE YEARS, when I was studying Physics at the University of Queensland in Australia, one of my heroes was the great British scientist Sir Arthur Eddington.

His scientific credentials were impeccable. He was Plumian Professor of Astronomy at Cambridge University in England and a close associate of Albert Einstein. And he was the author of numerous books which were way beyond my comprehension. One such that I remember was *The Internal Structure of the Stars*. I simply gazed at it in awe as I wondered how he found out.

He possessed literary as well as mathematical gifts and was able to translate scientific jargon into language that a layman could understand.

One story about him interested and intrigued me. On one occasion he was seated beside Albert Einstein at a banquet. At that time Einstein did not speak English and Eddington did not speak German. After a few minutes one of them, I forget who, turned the menu over and wrote a mathematical formula. The other replied

483

with a related mathematical formula. In this way they spent a pleasant evening conversing in the universal language of science-mathematics.

Eddington wrote books for ordinary people as well as fellow scientists. My favorite among these was titled *The Nature of the Physical World,* and my life has been guided by a statement from it that I memorized. I quote from memory after over sixty years so it may be partially paraphrased.

> As a scientific man I stand on the threshold of a room about to pass through a door. It's a complicated process.
>
> First, I have to step from one plank onto another moving at 20 miles per second round the sun. A second early or late, and the plank will be miles away.
>
> Secondly, stepping onto the plank will not be stepping on to something solid but more like stepping onto a swarm of flies. The probability is that sufficient of the flies will hit me under the soles of my feet and make my progress into the room approximately horizontal, but if not enough hit me and I fall through to the basement, or too many hit me and I am boosted to the ceiling, it would not be a violation of the laws of nature but merely an extraordinary coincidence.
>
> Thirdly, all this has to be done while hanging head outwards from a planet whirling round in space with a wind of ether rushing at nobody knows how many miles an hour through every interstice of my body.
>
> Fourthly, I must calculate the direction in which the entropy of the universe is increasing so as to be sure that my passage into the room is an entrance and not an exit.
>
> Surely it is easier for a camel to pass through the eye of a needle than for a scientific man to pass through a door, but whether the door be barn door or church door, it is better to lay aside scientific scruples, and walk in like an ordinary man rather than wait till all the difficulties involved in a scientific ingress are settled.

During my life I have tried to find answers to life's mysteries as an ordinary man.

Every thoughtful person has been perplexed by the question asked in the biblical book *Job:* "But man dies and wastes away; yea, man gives up the ghost and where is he?"

Religion exists to answer this universal question.

After I had spoken at a meeting in St. Louis, a young bright-faced Catholic priest rose and said, "The church has been too negative. We must be more positive."

I asked: "I wonder if I understand you. Do you mean that the church has been concentrating too much on the life to come and not enough on this life?"

He said, "That's exactly what I mean."

I said, "Why do we need a church? Scores of organizations such as governments, universities, hospitals, and civic clubs are attempting to solve the material problems of this life. None of them provides answers to such questions as, 'What is the purpose and meaning of life, and is there continuity of life after death?' These are questions that perplex most ordinary people. This accounts for the almost universal interest in the supernatural. If the church ignores these questions it betrays the reason for its existence."

The young priest said enthusiastically, "You're right! You're right!"

Security and happiness in life depend in considerable measure upon the answers to these questions. They can be answered only by the exercise of faith and choice.

FAITH

The cynic defines faith as "believing what is not true," but it is an essential element of life.

The Bible says, "The just shall live by faith," and this could be extended to "the sane shall live by faith." We exercise faith unconsciously scores of times every day. Consider reading a newspaper. When we read a news item concerning happenings in distant lands, or even nearby localities, we generally accept that the events reported are true. We do this by faith. We know that someone must have selected the items reported. We also know that partial information, however factual, may lead to deception. But, in most instances we exercise faith and believe that the motives of the reporter and editor are to inform rather than deceive. Faith is essential for sanity.

I believe many things which I cannot understand and which seem to defy reason. Hypothesis and experimentation are the doors to empirical knowledge. Others postulate the hypotheses and perform the experiments, and we ordinary people accept their reports by faith.

Consider the existence of genes. The body is made up of more than one trillion cells. Each cell is so small that it can be seen only under a microscope.

A small portion of each cell consists of a nucleus. Within that minute nucleus, there is a genome that contains 46 chromosomes. Within those chromosomes are approximately 100,000 genes. I cannot imagine how minute a gene must be.

Every living cell in the body contains the genome. When a scientist reports that a specific gene with an important function has been found, that means that one trillion models of that gene exist in the human body. The activities of that trillion must be coordinated. I cannot understand it, but I believe it by faith and cannot contain my admiration for those geneticists who discovered the genes and who can rearrange them by some arcane procedures.

Truly, as the Psalmist says, "I am fearfully and wonderfully made." (Psalm 139:14) I lack sufficient faith to be an atheist. I cannot believe that this infinitely complex jigsaw puzzle was assembled by accident.

CHOICE

We have freedom to choose what we believe. It is wise and rational to believe that which ministers health and happiness.

As a youth I chose to believe that "God so loved the world that He gave His only begotten Son that whosoever believed on Him should not perish but have everlasting life." (John 3:16) It is an act of faith that I have never regretted. It has added immeasurably to my health and happiness and to my serenity throughout life.

Atheism answers the question, "Does life continue after death" with a categorical No! Agnosticism is less dogmatic; it doesn't know. I prefer the answer of the poet Robert Browning in his poem "Prospice"—

> For sudden the worst turns the best to the brave,
> The black minute's at end,
> And the elements' rage, the fiend-voices that rave,
> Shall dwindle, shall blend,
> Shall change, shall become first a peace out of pain,
> Then a light, then thy breast,
> O thou soul of my soul! I shall clasp thee again,
> And with God be the rest!

Throughout the ages the poets have have voiced and lamented the despair that so often accompanies the realization of the inevitability of death.

In his magnificent poem, "The Everlasting Mercy," the Poet Laureate of England, John Masefield, recounts the inebriated meditation of his central character Saul Kane:

> And then I thought, "I wish I'd seen
> The many towns this town has been:
> I wish I knew if they'd a-got
> A kind of summat we've a-not,
> If them as built the church so fair
> Were half the chaps folk say they were;
> For they'd the skill to draw their plan,
> And skill's a joy to any man;
> And they'd the strength, not skill alone,
> To build it beautiful in stone,
> And strength and skill together thus . . .
> O, they were happier men than us.

> But if they were, they had to die
> The same as every one and I.
> And no one lives again, but dies,

And all the bright goes out of eyes,
And all the skill goes out of hands,
And all the wise brain understands,
And all the beauty, all the power
Is cut down like a withered flower.
In all the show from birth to rest
I give the poor dumb cattle best.

How Saul's mind changes after his embrace of God's mercy:

O glory of the lighted mind.
How dead I'd been, how dumb, how blind.
The station brook, to my new eyes,
Was babbling out of Paradise;
The waters rushing from the rain
Were singing Christ has risen again.
I thought all earthly creatures knelt
From rapture of the joy I felt.
The narrow station-wall's brick ledge,
The wild hop withering in the hedge,
The lights in huntsman's upper storey
Were parts of an eternal glory,
Where God's eternal garden flowers.
I stood in bliss at this for hours.

In his classical poem "Elegy Written in a Country Churchyard," Thomas Gray writes,

The boast of heraldry, the pomp of pow'r,
And all that beauty, all that wealth e'er gave,
Await alike the inevitable hour,
The paths of glory lead but to the grave.

St. Paul sums it up when he states, "If in this life only we have hope in Christ, we are of all men most miserable," and he follows this with a conclusion reached by many: "What does it profit me if the dead rise not? Let us eat and drink, for tomorrow we die." (1 Corinthians 15:19, 32)

My life has been joyful, and joy has been due in large measure to my faith that a happy continuing life is the sequel to death.

At the University of Texas in Austin, I debated Greg Calvert, one of the founders of Students for a Democratic Society. Greg favored anarchy and the sensualism of Herbert Marcuse rather than orthodox Marxism–Leninism, and the debate was remarkably free from acrimony.

After our formal presentations, each of us was entitled to ask the other two questions. Greg asked me, "Do you believe in the resurrection of the body?"

I understood that Greg was really asking me about my opinion on the teachings of such men as Herbert Marcuse, that the biblical teaching advocating mortification of the lusts of the flesh had killed the body. St. Paul had advocated this mortification in his letter to the Colossians.

> Mortify therefore your members which are upon the earth; fornication, uncleanness, inordinate affection, evil concupiscence, and covetousness, which is idolatry.

The Random House Dictionary gives this definition of the word "mortify"—"to subjugate [the body, passions etc.] by abstinence, ascetic discipline or self-inflicted suffering." *Webster* defines it—"to kill, to destroy."

The idea that Christian culture had eliminated enjoyment of most bodily pleasures seemed ludicrous to me. Most human activity has been devoted to the gratifying the senses of the human body. Consider the arts. They have been primarily concerned with pleasing sight and hearing through such media as painting, films and color television, and music. Taste has been served by cultivating and cooking foods of almost infinite variety. Smell has not been neglected, as the profusion of perfumes testifies. Temperature control has also ministered to bodily comfort.

Modern civilization has certainly nourished most of the senses of the human body. Nevertheless, Marcuse wished to resurrect the body through polymorphous sexuality. The phrase "resurrection of the body" was actually a prescription for sexual license and drug experimentation.

However, I chose to interpret the question in a literal sense and answered it with a simple Yes. I later amplified my answer by quoting the exultant words of St. Paul.

> Now if we be dead with Christ, we believe that we shall also live with Him: Knowing that Christ being raised from the dead, dieth no more. Death hath no more dominion over Him. For in that He died, He died unto sin once: but in that He liveth, He liveth unto God. (Romans 6:8–10)

> The last enemy that shall be destroyed is death. (Verse 26)

> Thanks be to God, which giveth us the victory through our Lord Jesus Christ. (Verse 57)

> O death, where is thy sting? O grave, where is thy victory?
> (1 Corinthians 15:26, 57, 55)

In the conflict between despair and hope I joined the side of hope. If this choice seems pragmatic so be it.

My Christian faith has illumined my pathway through life. It has guided me as I made major decisions. It led to Lillian and thereby flooded my life with happiness. It protected me from the seductive allure of the false Communist promises and enabled me to diagnose accurately the pathological horrors to which Communist doctrines must ineluctably lead. It comforted me by the assurance of forgiveness when my conduct was mistaken or sinful.

I can now rejoice with the Psalmist when he says, "Yea, though I walk through the valley of the shadow of death, I will fear no evil; for Thou art with me," and share the sentiments of Robert Browning expressed in his poem "Prospice."

> Fear death? to feel the fog in my throat,
>   The mist in my face,
> When the snows begin, and the blasts denote
>   I am nearing the place,

The power of the night, the press of the storm,
    The post of the foe;
Where he stands, the Arch Fear in a visible form,
    Yet the strong man must go:
For the journey is done and the summit attained,
    And the barriers fall,
Though a battle's to fight ere the guerdon be gained,
    The reward of it all.

I was ever a fighter, so—one fight more,
    The best and the last!
I would hate that death bandaged my eyes, and forbore,
    And bade me creep past.
No! let me taste the whole of it, fare like my peers
    The heroes of old,
Bear the brunt, in a minute pay glad life's arrears
    Of pain, darkness and cold.
For sudden the worst turns the best to the brave,
    The black minute's at end,
And the elements' rage, the fiend-voices that rave,
    Shall dwindle, shall blend,
Shall change, shall become first a peace out of pain,
    Then a light, then thy breast,
O thou soul of my soul! I shall clasp thee again,
    And with God be the rest!

I have a tremendous respect for human reason and its mighty achievements but I also recognize its limitations.

When I spoke at Anti-Communism Schools and Anti-Subversive Seminars I endeavored to be as factual and as logical as possible, but I was well aware that reason is often a thin veneer that conceals a mixture of presuppositions, prejudices, and hopes.

Knowledge may be attained intuitively as well as empirically. I knew that my manner and personality might create a barrier to my message in the minds of some, so I would often conclude a school or seminar by quoting this poem that expressed so well my hope:

Not only in the words you say,
Not only in your thoughts expressed;
But in the most unconscious way
Is Christ confessed.
To me 'twas not the truth you taught,
To you so clear, to me still dim;
But when you came to me you brought
 a sense of Him.
And from your eyes He beckons me,
And from your heart His love is shed;
Till I lose sight of you and see
 the Christ instead.

48

....

Joyful and Triumphant

Within my earthly temple there's a crowd.
There's one of us that's humble; one that's proud.
There's one that's broken-hearted for his sins,
And one who, unrepentant, sits and grins.
There's one who loves his neighbor as himself,
And one who cares for naught but fame and pelf.
From much corroding care would I be free
If once I could determine which is me.
EDWARD SANDFORD MARTIN, 1856–1939 (MIXED)

AWARE THAT HIS EARTHLY PILGRIMAGE was reaching its destination, Saint Paul wrote to his protege, Timothy:

I have fought a good fight, I have finished my course,
I have kept the faith: Henceforth there is laid up for me
a crown of righteousness, which the Lord, the righteous
judge, shall give me at that day. (2 Timothy 4:7–8)

This was the same man who had written:

493

> I am carnal, sold under sin. For that which I do I
> allow not: for what I would, that I do not; but what I
> hate, that I do. . . . For the good that I would I do not:
> but the evil which I would not, that I do. (Romans 7:14,
> 15, 19)

The finest life is a battle between good and evil; between love and hate; between selfishness and service.

All my life I have been conscious of this inner struggle. How often I have thought, as I observed the tragic failure and punishment of some brother, "There, but for the grace of God, go I."

One manifestation of God's grace was the parents He gave me. They produced eleven children and loved and nurtured every one of them.

Though my father had little formal education, he willingly sacrificed to provide the best possible education for me.

He was endowed with a good mind but this was often unrecognized because of his foreign accent. During my teenage years, this sometimes embarrassed me and I was not always kind and gracious to him.

He was the living essence of generosity. Whatever he had, he shared with all people in need. He would often arrive home with some unfortunate who was to be welcomed, warmed, and fed. Wherever there was an appeal for funds to help someone in need he was the first to respond.

I look like him. I have often wished that I had inherited his nondiscriminating loving heart as well as his physical appearance.

He died at the age of eighty-seven. Several years before his death he suffered a stroke. As death neared he became increasingly gentle and sweet-tempered.

My mother was gentle and loving. A superficial onlooker might think she was dominated by Dad, but within that gentleness there was a core of strength, and in many ways she dominated him. Her family was her world. She lived to be ninety-four. Both Mum and Dad remained in the care of the family until their deaths.

They left me a fine heritage. One great gift was an immunity against the potential ravages of alcohol. We were taught by precept and example to shun alcoholic beverages. The rationale for this attitude was the biblical teaching, "If eating meat causes my brother to stumble, I will eat no more meat."

Since the evidence of the stumbling caused by drinking alcohol was all around us, it was considered a Christian duty to abstain from alcoholic beverages. This did not extend to the medicinal use of the drug.

I did not need an alcoholic stimulus to remain cheerful. My Christian faith was a source of great enthusiasm and happiness. I was regarded as an eccentric by many of my peers but I was recognized as a happy eccentric. As a consequence I have avoided the alcoholic pitfall which has caused the destruction of so much health and happiness.

Social pressures to drink are powerful. I have spoken at many meetings that were preceded by a cocktail hour. Since I have always believed that a good offense is preferable to defense, I usually announced audibly that I do not drink alcohol and asked for a Coke. I was often surprised by the number of people who joined me.

I have had no need to pursue happiness; it has pursued me. I love the poem of Francis Thompson, "The Hound of Heaven," which tells of God's pursuit of suffering man. I have partaken of the "joy unspeakable and full of glory." (1 Peter 1:8)

During the time that remains, I have much to do and to enjoy.

I want the remainder of my life to be in tune with this poem:

An old man going a lone highway,
Came, in the evening cold and gray,
To a chasm vast and deep and wide.
The old man crossed in the twilight dim,
The sullen stream had no fear for him;
But he turned when safe on the other side
And built a bridge to span the tide.

"Old man," said a fellow pilgrim near,
"You are wasting your strength with building here,
Your journey will end with the ending day,
You never again will pass this way;

You've crossed the chasm, deep and wide,
Why build this bridge at evening tide?"

The builder lifted his old gray head;
"Good friend, in the path I have come," he said
"There followeth after me to-day
A youth whose feet must pass this way.
This chasm that has been as naught to me
To that fair-haired youth may a pitfall be;
He, too, must cross in the twilight dim;
Good friend, I am building this bridge for
him!"
(Anonymous)

Appendix I

....

The Liberty to Argue Freely Letters and Responses

Come now, and let us reason together.
—ISAIAH 1:1

EACH YEAR I HAVE RECEIVED thousands of letters. I have tried to read all and to answer as many as possible.

The letters can be divided into several categories—commendation, information, criticism, and abuse.

Most of the letters expressed appreciation and commendation. I accepted their message gratefully and responded appropriately.

Many correspondents wanted information, and whenever possible I provided it. When I did not have the information, I said, "I don't know."

Though often asked to pass judgment on other organizations and individuals, I always hesitated. In many instances I agreed with some things and disagreed with others, so a verdict of good or bad was difficult.

During the 1960s I was frequently asked, "What do you think of the John Birch Society?" My "Meet the Press" interview, recorded in chapter 1, shows how I attempted to answer.

I have always been impressed by what Jesus said when He was asked to adjudicate a quarrel between two brothers: "Who made me a judge or divider over you!" (Luke 12:13)

Many letters criticized my message, the results of my message, or my motives. Some of the criticisms were justified. I tried to answer them objectively and honestly. I often published a critical letter along with my reply in our monthly newsletter.

In my replies I tried to be guided by these principles:

> (1) Be fair in presenting my critic's views. Don't take statements out of context. To ensure this, I usually printed the letter in its entirety.
>
> (2) Do not engage in ad hominem attacks. I attempted to answer the arguments and not attack the writer personally. Abuse is no substitute for reason. I relied upon evidence instead of dogmatic assertion.

Since the critics often accused me of misrepresenting the doctrines and deeds of Communist leaders, I endeavored to rebut the accusation by direct quotation of the written or spoken words of those leaders. I relied upon their own words and not the accusations of their opponents.

The Bible tells us, "A soft answer turns away wrath." Such softness is not natural for me. I have an inborn tendency to be forceful, dogmatic, and sarcastic in an argument, so I made a conscious effort to restrain these urges. I am well aware that it is possible to win an argument and to lose a friend, and that if you "convince a man against his will he's of the same opinion still." I nevertheless hoped a manifestly truthful objective response, without invective, might encourage my critic to reconsider.

I consigned abusive letters to their appropriate destiny—the garbage disposal.

Here are a few samples of critical letters and my replies.

THE MIND OF MARX

The following letter reveals the mindset of a substantial number of *educated* people, those who believe that the doctrines of Marx are benign, and that Lenin, Stalin, Mao, and Pol Pot have distorted them.

Dear Dr. Schwarz,

I recently read an issue of the CACC (April 1). I find it hard to believe that your paper is so manipulative in your usage of the English language. You have twisted words and ideas beyond recognition. Anyone not familiar with the works of Karl Marx would believe he stood for the ideas of Communism now followed by much of the world's people. Marx's vision of a perfect society is not the twisted version you have portrayed. I suggest that you advise your readers to educate themselves about Marx's Communism and let them choose for themselves what his words were.

The regurgitation of facts by people such as yourself oftentimes come out looking much different than when it went in, and it is representation of this nature which has attributed to the state our country is in today. You've heard the term "brain washing", I'm sure. Why not spend your energy encouraging the development of people's power as individuals, and their ability to learn, as opposed to trying to create a bunch of blankless followers? People are confused enough in this world and it is this mass blank-mind which contributes to wars, famine and ecological destruction.

We must all have a cause and mine is to cause the greatest commotion I can to get people out of the social mind-state and into their own brains and ideas. I seriously doubt that your crusade would be as large as it is today if this were the case.

I hope peace of mind is yours and not piece of minds.

     To the Beautiful earth, Rebecca Smith

Dear Rebecca Smith,

 You make a serious charge when you affirm categorically that I have *"twisted words beyond recognition"*, and that, *"my usage of the English language is manipulative."* You also state that, *"Marx's vision of a perfect society is not the twisted version you have portrayed."* Unfortunately, you don't give any indication of what you believe, "*Marx's vision of a perfect society,*" is. Apparently you believe that you possess certain "unearthly" powers which enable you to know what is going on in the mind and emotions of another. I make no claim to possession of such powers. I am limited to reading what an individual writes, listening to what he says, and observing how he acts. I have endeavored to follow these procedures in my study of Karl Marx.

When I read your charges, I was foolish enough to think that you would provide some evidence to justify them. Having read your letter several times, I fail to find a trace of any such evidence. Your own unsupported affirmations do not constitute evidence, except possibly in your own mind.

I assume that you acknowledge that Karl Marx, with his co-worker, Frederick Engels, wrote the *Manifesto of the Communist Party,* and that it expresses some of his ideas. I submit for your consideration these statements in the *Manifesto* on the following important subjects: (1) The origin of ideas; (2) The role of force; (3) The elimination of the middle-class owners of property, often known as "*The liquidation of the Bourgeoisie;* (4) Nationalism; (5) The family.

The following quotations are taken from the 1973 printing of *The Manifesto of the Communist Party,* published by Progress Publishers, Moscow:

1. *Origin of Ideas:*

"*Your very ideas are but the outgrowth of the conditions of your bourgeois production and bourgeois property, just as your jurisprudence is but the will of your class made into a law for all, a will, whose essential character and direction are determined by the economical conditions of existence of your class.*" (page 67)

2. *The Role of Force:*

"*The Communists disdain to conceal their views and aims. They openly declare that their ends can be attained only by the* forcible overthrow *of all existing social conditions. Let the ruling classes tremble at a Communistic revolution. The proletarians have nothing to lose but their chains. They have a world to win." (page 96)*

3. *The liquidation of the bourgeoisie or the elimination of the middle-class owners of property:*

"You must, therefore, confess that by 'individual' you mean no other person than the bourgeois, than the middle-class owner of property. This person must, indeed, be swept out of the way, and made impossible." (page 66)

4. *Nationalism:*

"The Communists are further reproached with desiring to abolish countries and nationality.

"The working men have no country. We cannot take from them what they have not got. Since the proletariat must first of all acquire political supremacy, must rise to be the leading class of the nation, must constitute itself the nation, it is so far, itself national, though not in the bourgeois sense of the word.

"National differences and antagonisms between peoples are daily more and more vanishing, owing to the development of the bourgeoisie, to freedom of commerce, to the world market, to uniformity in the mode of production and in the conditions of life corresponding thereto.

"The supremacy of the proletariat will cause them to vanish still faster. United action, of the leading civilised countries at least, is one of the first conditions for the emancipation of the proletariat." (pages 71, 72)

5. *The Family:*

"Abolition of the family! Even the most radical flare up at this infamous proposal of the Communists.

"On what foundation is the present family, the bourgeois family, based? On capital, on private gain. In its completely developed form this family exists only among the bourgeoisie. But this state of things finds its complement in the practical absence of the family among the proletarians, and in public prostitution.

"The bourgeois family will vanish as a matter of course when its complement vanishes and both will vanish with the vanishing of capital." (page 68)

"The bourgeois clap-trap about the family and educa-tion, about the hallowed co-relation of parent and child, becomes all the more disgusting, the more, by the action of Modern Industry, all family ties among the proletari-ans are torn asunder, and their children transformed into simple articles of commerce and instruments of labour." (page 70)

The meaning of these statements of Marx seems to be fairly clear to me. While the meaning is clear, the state-ments are false. History has provided overwhelming evi-dence of this. Consider the statement about nationalism, for example. The Soviet empire is presently being torn to fragments by the nationalistic passions of the workers in its colonies. As this is being written, the focus of atten-tion is on Lithuania, but similar nationalistic passions are prevalent in Latvia, Estonia, Moldavia, the Ukraine, Georgia, Armenia, Azerbaijan, and the remaining Moslem republics. How Gorbachev must wish that the delusions of Karl Marx were reality, and that national-ism did not exist among the workers.

The ideas of Marx about the family are not only his-torically false, they are most insulting to the workers. Millions of workers throughout the world love their chil-dren passionately, and work selflessly to make a better life for them. The charge that they regard their children merely as *"articles of commerce and instruments of labor"* is so contrary to the evidence that it approaches insanity.

The Marxist teaching that the middle-class owner of property *"must be swept out of the way and made impossible"* has resulted in the agonizing deaths of mil-lions of victims. The latest example is the classicide of the Khmer Rouge in Cambodia. Karl Marx may not have meant that all who were not manual laborers should be killed, but Pol Pot, and the other leaders of the Khmer Rouge believed that this was what Marx had meant and proceeded to kill all Cambodians who were literate. Even the possession of a pair of glasses was regarded as conclusive evidence that the individual belonged to the bourgeois class, and that his or her destruction was obligatory.

I am puzzled, and even amused, by your suggestion that I advise my readers *"to educate themselves about Marxist Communism and let them choose for themselves what his words were."* Is it delusional to believe that the way to discover what the words of Marx were, is to read the books he has written, such as the *Manifesto of the Communist Party* and *Das Capital?* I have always accepted the responsibility of presenting the actual words of those I venture to criticize. May I suggest that you adopt this plan also? I could not discover one word of Marx in your critical letter.

I invite you to join me and confess that your knowledge of the vision and teaching of Marx is incomplete and that continuing study and thought is needed. Increased knowledge may result in increased understanding and wisdom, and lessen the power of those ugly twins—ignorance and intellectual arrogance.

THE "CHRISTIAN" ATTITUDE
TO COMMUNISM

The following letter by Daniel R. Miller of the History Department of Calvin College, Grand Rapids, Michigan was published in the February 21 edition of *Calvinist Contact,* 99 Niagara Street, St. Catherines, Ontario, Canada L2R 4L3, under the caption "Anti-Communist Zealotry as Dangerous as Communism":

THE LONGER LETTER
ANTI-COMMUNIST ZEALOTRY AS DANGEROUS
AS COMMUNISM

Fred Schwarz's letter ("Dialogue with a potential communist recruit") came to my attention on the same day that I received a letter from his organization describing his anti-communist crusade in Central America. They both exhibit a blindness to which the evangelical Christians in the United States have been consistently prone. He is naively uncritical about the goals and methods of his own nation's foreign policy.

Silent on U.S. sins

Mr. Schwarz is understandably appalled by the inhuman practices of the Soviet Union and other Marxist dictatorships, but he is virtually silent about the inhumanities that are practiced in the name of anti-communism and the American nationalism.

He refuses to take seriously the charge that the United States has been "imperialistic" in its relations with the Philippines. Has he never heard of the "Filipino Insurrection" (1899–1902) when over 100,000 Filipinos died resisting the U.S. conquest of their homeland? The whole bloody enterprise was justified as an act of charity ("The White Man's Burden"). Evidently other people besides Marxists know how to justify killing as an act of love.

In Central America, where Mr. Schwarz crusades against communism, it is the anti-communist reactionaries who have most consistently violated human rights and persecuted the Church. The Guatemalan military has killed between 30,000 and 50,000 peasants in a "counter-insurgency" campaign that is so free-wheeling it has forced many missionaries to flee the country.

Somoza, the Nicaraguan dictator, killed 50,000 of his fellow citizens, many of them non-combatants, in a vain effort to avoid being overthrown by the Sandinistas.

The present U.S.-backed government of El Salvador has killed a like number of people including many priests and nuns in its own war against "the left" (defined loosely enough to include almost anyone who criticizes the government openly).

The anti-communist FDN "Contras" who are trying to overthrow the Sandinista-dominated government of Nicaragua have employed kidnapping, torture, and assassination in a brutal war of attrition that has resulted in 10,000 deaths, mostly civilians. One need not be an apologist for the Sandinistas to conclude that nothing they have done justifies the use of such tactics against them.

CIA booklet recommends blackmail

It would be comforting to believe that the United States government which decries terrorism and lauds freedom and democracy has nothing to do with these brutal activities but the truth is far otherwise. The heavy-handed Guatemalan dictatorship was virtually installed by the U.S. Central Intelligence Agency in a covert action which overthrew the constitutionally-elected president. The air-war being waged against Salvadorean peasants (some guerrillas, some just non-combatants caught in the free fire zone) is financed, equipped and directed by the U.S. military.

The worst example of U.S. government complicity with right-wing terrorism comes from the 1984 "CIA Manual" which was an instructional booklet for Contra guerrillas. Some of the tactics it recommended were blackmailing people into joining the movement, provoking violence at public rallies so that innocent people would be killed and turned into "martyrs," and assassinating public officials.

Embarrassed by the public disclosure of this material, the Reagan administration purportedly withdrew the booklet from circulation, but Edgar Chomorro, who until recently served as Public Relations Director for the FDN, testified that the only thing which changed is that now the U.S. advisors refrain from writing anything down; the tactics they recommend are unchanged.

Need for prophetic word

My point is this. Anti-communist zealotry and uncriti-cal nationalism (patriotism) can be just as dangerous to human life and just as distant from true Christian concern as revolutionary Marxism. (Marxism gave us the gulag; anti-communist nationalism gave us two world wars.)

Yet Fred Schwarz, and the evangelical church in America as a whole, see only the sins of communism. They have closed their eyes and ears (and hearts?) to the victims of American national ambition.

Such hypocrisy weakens the witness of the church and ill-serves a nation which desperately needs a prophetic word of warning if it is to escape judgment for its sins.

The mindset of Daniel Miller is shared by a significant number of evangelical Christian academics and undoubtedly influences their students. I wrote the following letter to the editor of *Calvinist Contact*.

The Editor:

THE LONGER LETTER, written by Daniel R. Miller, and captioned "Anti-Communist Zealotry as Dangerous as Communism" has been drawn to my attention. Since this letter is critical of my message and ministry, I believe I am entitled to reply to it.

I reread the article carefully in an effort to find any reference to anything I had said, written or done that justified the warning that my ministry "can be just as dangerous to human life and just as distant from true Christian concern as revolutionary Marxism." My efforts were fruitless.

Mr. Miller does not specify one statement I have written which is false or un-Christian. My "fault" seems to be that I have not coupled my criticism of communism with a comparable criticism of the crimes which the U.S.A. has committed throughout history and continues to commit.

This attitude is familiar to me. I am, by profession, a medical doctor and aware that many fine doctors devote themselves to the diagnosis and treatment of one disease. The most brilliant surgeon is not expected to be an expert in the diagnosis and treatment of heart disease. One who claims to specialize in the treatment of all diseases is usually regarded as a "quack." To criticize an article on cancer in a medical journal because it did not also discuss the ravages caused by arthritis would be considered ludicrous.

I am founder and president of the Christian Anti-Communism Crusade, and my specialty is "Communism." Is it surprising that my concentration is upon the false doctrines, hideous history, present crimes and future objectives of the communists?

I try to follow the principle that I provide evidence for controversial statements that I make. Mr. Miller makes repeated questionable affirmations, without any evidence to support them. One example is "anti-communist nationalism gave us two world wars." This is the first time I have heard there was a substantial anti-communist element in the causation of the First World War.

Moral Equivalence

Mr. Miller represents those who believe and teach that there is a "moral equivalence" between the Soviet Union and the United States. They seize upon any historic injustice perpetrated by the U.S.A., however far in the past, and use it to excuse the recent and present conduct of the Soviet Union and associated communists.

The poet, Robert Burns, says: "Man's inhumanity to man makes countless thousands mourn," and examples of such inhumanity can be found in the history of all countries, including the U.S.A. However, the recent histories of the U.S.A. and the Soviet Union are very different. Ask Andrei Sakharov; ask the Jews who want to emigrate from Russia; ask the millions of refugees from communist countries scattered throughout the world; ask the Boat People of Vietnam; ask the survivors of the holocaust in Cambodia; ask the Poles; and ask the millions who are clamoring for admission and sanctuary in the U.S.A. There is no equivalence.

American treatment of the blacks, during the period when Hitler was ruling Germany before the Second World War, left much to be desired. Would it, therefore, have been un-Christian to expose the falsity of Hitler's anti-Semitic doctrines and to condemn his treatment of the Jews without simultaneously condemning the U.S.A. for its treatment of blacks?

Atheism

Mr. Miller works for a Christian institution and expresses concern for the witness of the Church. It is reasonable to expect him to show some concern for the basic doctrines of Christianity, especially the doctrine that God lives. Without this doctrine, there is no reason for the existence of the Church.

Communism states categorically that God does not exist. The communists are proudly and unashamedly atheistic. Karl Marx affirmed that "Religion is the opiate of the masses," and Lenin stressed repeatedly that atheism is a natural and inseparable portion of Marxism; while Khrushchev affirmed that one must be an atheist to be a communist but that "some of the comrades are atheists in the Party and believers at home." Is the atheism of communism of no concern to Christians?

Freedom of Religious Worship

It is true that the Soviet Constitution grants "freedom of religious worship, and freedom of anti-religious propaganda." This is applied in practice by allowing a few churches to remain open so that adult believers can worship. No church activities are permitted outside church buildings; no Sunday schools, no youth groups; no women's societies; no cottage meetings. Even church benevolences for the poor are illegal.

Spiritual Infanticide

The plight of the children is deplorable. Every child must attend school, where he or she is taught atheism from kindergarten on. Any child who professes belief in God is penalized educationally, socially, and, ultimately, economically. Any parents who lead a child to become a convinced and committed Christian, risk having the State take the child from them.

Jesus said: "Whosoever shall offend one of these little ones which believe in Me, it were better for him that a millstone were hanged about his neck, and that he were drowned in the depth of the sea." (Matthew 18:6)

The Soviet Union practices spiritual infanticide. Is this not a Christian concern, Mr. Miller?

The communist policy for the church is threefold: (1) Enslavement, (2) Utilization, and (3) Destruction. Should Christians excuse this because worship is allowed during the period of utilization? Did not Christ give a Great Commission?

I have spent much of my last 36 years in the U.S.A. I have traveled extensively, spoken to many churches, universities, colleges, high schools, and business groups, and conversed freely with thousands. I have never heard one American of any political persuasion express any anticipation or intention that the United States would or should conquer the world. I have never read any document advocating world conquest though I have read a few undocumented affirmations that such advocacy has been made.

On the other hand, it is difficult to read any theoretical communist document without confronting the statement that the "worldwide victory of socialism (defined as the first stage of communism) is inevitable."

Communist practice is guided by this doctrine of the inevitability of world conquest. Surely Mr. Miller is aware of the Brezhnev Doctrine and its consequences in Czechoslovakia, Afghanistan and Poland.

"Why Communism Kills"

I suggest that Mr. Miller gives each member of any class which he teaches, a copy of my booklet *Why Communism Kills*. The Crusade will gladly provide copies at no cost. After the students have read it, he can then point out any misstatements of fact or any logical fallacies which the message contains. He may be critical of the message because I do not discuss the tortures of the inquisition and the carnage of the Civil War, in addition to the classicide of communism. I respect the intelligence of his students and am content to let them judge the relevance of that charge.

My objective is to reveal the errors of Marxist doctrines and to prevent the casualties that will result from the application of those doctrines if the communists succeed in attaining their announced objective—the conquest of the U.S.A.

Every Christian has a God-given duty to expose and oppose the atheism of communism and the classicide to which it leads.

Dr. Fred Schwarz
President
Christian Anti-Communism Crusade

DIALOGUE WITH A POTENTIAL COMMUNIST RECRUIT

It is a rare day when the mail does not contain at least ten letters from Third World countries. Most of these letters are from individuals who are concerned about the danger created by the activities of the communists in their local area and who seek advice and help in combatting them. However, a number of letters come from

Communists and Communist sympathizers who seem genuinely puzzled by our opposition to Communism. Some of the letters come from individuals who consider themselves to be both Christian and Communist.

The following letter is from such a person. It touches my heart and simultaneously stirs anger. My heart goes out to the idealistic young student who has been victimized and seduced by the Communists; my anger is directed towards those who have deceived and exploited him so cruelly.

This young man is typical of thousands who are being deceived and recruited by the communists. We must reach them and tell them the truth.

Dear Dr. Schwarz,

It is a great privilege for me to introduce myself to you. I am [name withheld], 23 years old, and an eager student of the Bible, but a communist sympathizer.

I got your address from my friend here. I am writing you to know your motive and purpose. Why are you against communism? Communism is a very good term and has a good meaning. Their purpose is very constructive and their objective is to help people to have a responsible and happy life.

Here in our country the government claims to be democratic, but it can be condemned because the people are fighting each other and corruption and murder are rife. The people who are doing these immoral acts are the very ones who boast about democracy. Today we are close to civil war. This is also true in other countries under the banner of the so-called champion of government and freedom, democracy.

These countries are victimized by the imperialists like the USA who want to control our nation. The USA offers its so-called help to other developing countries, but this is a fraud because they are doing it for their own personal interest. They want to destroy our independence and freedom. For me this kind of government has no appeal because we are oppressed by the military under it. Under communism there is equality and fairness of wealth.

One day we will obtain victory because we have strength and are ready to fight for our freedom and liberty. We can and will overthrow this corrupt government and all oppressors, especially those who have practiced injustice towards their fellow man.

At this time, killing is justified for the sake of creating a more moral society. God commanded his people in the Old Testament to kill the enemy which would like to destroy them. This principle is from the Bible and can be applied in all ages. Here is the real meaning of 'love your enemy.' The proof of love is killing. God loved people in Old Testament times; that is why he killed them by his people.

We are not afraid to die if the cause is justice and for the goodness of mankind, so we are justified to kill people who contradict the moral law which we have adopted.

The USA always seeks ways to control other nations for personal and imperialistic motives. Why does the USA enjoy interfering in the affairs of other countries such as Nicaragua?

Anyway, I am not narrow-minded. I am still searching for the best way. I am open to receive your reply. The stronger argument will give us the verdict. Thank you.

I replied as follows:

Dear [Name Withheld],

I thank you for writing so frankly and honestly, and for presenting so eloquently the arguments and promises which have attracted you to Communism. I rejoice in your assurance that your mind is still open and that you can be convinced by reasoned arguments which are based upon truthful facts.

You desire to know my motive and purpose for being against Communism. I have published my reasons in a booklet entitled *Why I Am Against Communism* and I will send you a copy.

You present your arguments for favoring communism very well. I will try to state them and to answer them briefly:

1. *The name "Communism" indicates a noble purpose:*

Surely you must be aware that no political party or system can be judged by the name it chooses. The name is simply an identification tag. You illustrate your knowledge that this is so by your claim that, while your government is called democratic, this does not mean it practices democracy.

All parties and systems must be judged by their doctrines and practices, not their names. The doctrines of communism, known as Marxism–Leninism, teach inequality, due to the class nature of society, class war, and class dictatorship. The practices of communism create poverty, regimentation and fear.

Can you be entirely unaware of the conditions the Communists have created once they have seized power? Do you know nothing of the Boat People who have come from Vietnam? Have you seen the boats in which they crossed the ocean? How terrible their life must have been to compel them to risk death, storm, hunger, thirst, and pirates in such open boats, and to face a future of homeless exile.

Consider what percentage of the people flee once Communist dictatorship is established. Does this not give an objective measurement of the unbearability of the tyranny?

2. *The present regime in your country is unjust and oppressive:*

I do not doubt that many of your criticisms are justified. As a believer in the Bible, you will believe that human nature is sinful and that all systems designed and executed by sinful people have undesirable characteristics. This does not mean that all governments are equally sinful. Some are worse than others. In the history of mankind, communism can be justly condemned as being among the worst. It is the most efficient system of tyrannical control yet designed and executed by man.

Consider what your own situation would be if the communists were fully in power in your country. You would be under constant surveillance by a "Committee for the Defense of the Revolution." Any expression of hostility to the regime would be noted and punished by withholding your ration card which is necessary to obtain food. You would be in constant danger of arrest and possible execution. You would certainly not be able to write a letter such as the one you wrote to me.

This is based on the assumption that you were not one of those who exercised the surveillance, distributed the ration cards and carried out the arrests.

3. *The U.S.A. is an Imperialistic Power seeking to deceive, control, and exploit your country:*

Has not the U.S.A. conferred many benefits upon your people? Did it not grant independence to your country voluntarily? Did it not sacrifice many lives liberating your country from the military forces of Japan? Have not medicines discovered in the U.S.A. cured many of the diseases that blighted and shortened the lives of many Filipinos, thereby prolonging the expectation of life of your citizens?

4. *Killing the enemy is an expression of love:*

Frankly, this argument is what troubles me most about your letter. You do not affirm that killing may be a regrettable necessity at times in this sinful world but exalt it as a positive virtue and expression of compassion. I suspect you have learned this in some class teaching "Liberation Theology."

It is doctrines such as this that have led to the killing of masses of people such as was practiced in Russia by

Stalin, in Germany by Hitler, in China by Mao, and in Cambodia by the Khmer Rouge. I ask you to read the message, "Why Communism Kills" which I am sending to you.

In conclusion, I commend your desire to bring to pass a system of increased justice, health and happiness for the people of your country. I regret that the system you have chosen will result in the exact opposite. Communism is a cause, not a cure for hunger, oppression, and fear. If it conquers your country, the future state will be much worse than the present.

As a Christian you must believe in the existence of God. Communism affirms that there is no God. It is aggressively atheistic. One of the first acts of a communist government is to create an educational system that teaches all children that there is no God. This is spiritual infanticide.

As a medical doctor, I am devoted to life. Communism is a disease that destroys life. It is a physical disease because it kills massively; it is a mental disease because it is associated with systematized delusions, not susceptible to rational arguments; and it is a spiritual disease because it denies God and reduces man to a mere evolutionary animal. As a doctor, as a devotee of reason, and as a Christian believer, I am against it.

THE INTERNAL VERSUS THE EXTERNAL COMMUNIST DANGER

Asking whether the internal or external Communist threat is the greater danger is like asking whether the length or breadth contributes more to the area of a rectangle. The total danger is the product, not the sum of the internal and external communist menace.

It is foolishness to measure the significance of the Communist movement within the United States by the number of votes it secures for the candidacy in a national election. It must be recognized as the bridgehead of the Communist party of the Soviet Union.

AUGUST 1, 1993, NEWSLETTER
A BETRAYAL OF THE CONGRESS
OF THE UNITED STATES

The Crusade newsletter has been sent regularly to the members of the Congress of the United States during the past thirty years. During this time I have often wondered how much attention it receives, but have been encouraged by an occasional statement by a congressman that refers to an item that appeared in the newsletter. A sustaining hope has been that members of the congressional staff will read the newsletter, even if the congressman—or congresswoman—cannot find the time to do so.

I recently received a jolt which proves that someone in a congressional office is paying attention to the newsletter. The proof comes in the form of a cowardly, anonymous, poison-pen letter, on the letterhead of the Congress of the United States. This letter is photographically reproduced herewith, in its entirety. You will note that it is unsigned and that the name of the congressman has been carefully excised:

Congress of the United States
House of Representatives
Washington, D. C.

You would be doing a fine service by taking all the money you put into mailing and printing of your "newsletter" and giving the proceeds to the homeless or poverty-stricken.

Your newsletters are ignored, go into recycling bins or are passed around during lunchtime for ENTERTAINMENT. We get a lot of laughs from your publication.

And specifically in regards to AIDS, how you can write these articles is beyond our comprehension!!

DIDN'T YOU LEARN IN SUNDAY SCHOOL THAT *GOD LOVES EVERYONE!*

How AIDS is contracted has absolutely nothing to do with the fact that GOD LOVES EVERYONE including those with AIDS. It's no different than CANCER.

And, in case you didn't know, what two people do in the confines of their bedroom or home is ABSOLUTELY NO ONES BUSINESS BUT THEIR OWN!!

GET REAL! Stop wasting money. Do something PRODUCTIVE. PLEASE *STOP SENDING THESE NEWSLETTERS TO CONGRESS.* IT'S A TERRIBLE WASTE!!

And—read your Bible again. We think you have missed the messages behind the words. But the great thing is, about God, is that He loves everyone, including the *totally ignorant* like yourselves.

I cherish the hope that the writer may read this reply as I have no way of contacting him, or her, directly:

Dear Mr. (or Miss) Anonymous,

I cannot thank you for your letter since its anonymous and malicious nature casts a shadow over each member of the House of Representatives of the Congress of the United States and his or her staff. Is this not a despicable thing to do? Why do you lack the courage of your convictions, which would have enabled you to sign your name?

ARROGANCE

You write as though you are speaking on behalf of the entire U.S. Congress. Is this not unspeakable arrogance?

LOVE AND TRUTH

You state twice that "God loves everyone." Your implication is that the contents of the newsletter demonstrate lack of love, but no evidence for this is provided.

Words can be used to reveal, or to conceal, truth. My conviction is that truth and love walk hand in hand. The newsletters present truth, which is unpalatable, concerning the deadly diseases, Communism, and, more recently, AIDS. Does the description of the pathology of the disease processes demonstrate lack of love?

When a doctor informs a patient that the cancerous lump, which he has diagnosed, will probably kill the patient if it is not excised, is this unloving? If a mother informs her child that it is dangerous to play on a busy street, does this demonstrate lack of love? Are those who warn that smoking cigarettes may lead to cancer or other diseases motivated by hate?

Recent events in the Soviet Union and Eastern Europe have proved that the information on Communism, which the newsletter has provided during many years, has been accurate, truthful, and loving.

CAN PRIVATE CONDUCT HARM OTHERS?

You state categorically that "what two people do in the confines of their bedroom or home is absolutely no one's business but their own."

Is this so? Cannot private, voluntary activities produce deadly consequences for many other people? If two people make a personal, private decision to burn down the home which they own, is it not possible that the fire, which they start, may spread and burn other homes?

Consider the AIDS epidemic in the United States. How did it start? It was started by voluntary conduct of people in the privacy of their own bedrooms.

I refer you to the book, *And the Band Played On*, by Randy Shiltz. The author is a responsible journalist, who is a homosexual, and who has researched the origins of the AIDS epidemic. Sadly he has now contracted the AIDS disease himself. He traces the origin of the AIDS epidemic to the activities of a French Canadian, Gaetan Dugas, who became known as Patient Zero.

The original name for AIDS was "GRID" (Gay Related Immuno-Deficiency Disease). Shiltz states:

Of the first nineteen cases of GRID in Los Angeles, four had had sex with Gaetan Dugas. Another four cases meanwhile, had gone to bed with people who had had sex with Dugas, establishing sexual links between nine of the nineteen Los Angeles cases. (page 130)

He also states:

From just one tryst with Gaetan, therefore, eleven GRID cases could be connected. Altogether, Gaetan could be connected to nine of the first nineteen cases of GRID in Los Angeles, twenty-two in New York City, and nine patients in eight other North American cities. The Los Angeles Cluster Study, as it became known, offered powerful evidence that GRID not only was transmissible but was the work of a single infectious agent. (page 147)

Shiltz concludes:

A CDC statistician calculated the odds on whether it could be coincidental that 40 of the first 248 gay men to get GRID might all have had sex either with the same man or with men sexually linked to him. The statistician figured that the chance did not approach zero—it was zero. (page 147)

How can you contend that the homosexual coupling of Dugas and his voluntary partners did not have deadly consequences for countless other people?

THE TRAGEDY OF THE HEMOPHILIACS

The July 10 edition of the *Los Angeles Times* states that "An estimated half of the nation's 20,000 hemophiliacs are HIV infected and more than 2,700 have been diagnosed with full-blown AIDS."

These infections are the results of the use of blood products which were contaminated with the HIV virus. In the early days of the AIDS epidemic, blood banks collected blood from homosexuals. This was contaminated with HIV virus due to the voluntary conduct of Dugas and his associates in sodomy.

Private actions may indeed have public and deadly consequences.

CHILD OR FOOL

You classify me and other Crusade members as "totally ignorant." I am well aware of the limitations of my knowledge and understanding, and seek to improve them by constant study. As the Bible says: "If any man thinks he knows anything, he knows nothing yet as he ought to know." Our need for the guidance and wisdom of God is unlimited.

Your attitude reminds me of part of an ancient Arabic proverb: "He who knows not and knows he knows not, is a child, teach him; but he who knows not, and knows not that he knows not, is a fool. Shun him."

HELPING THE HOMELESS
AND POVERTY-STRICKEN

You urge us to give for the support of the "homeless or poverty-stricken." Your advice is welcome but belated. In 1956 we cooperated in the formation of the Indian Christian orphanages in Andhra State, India, and have provided a home for many homeless, and food for many poverty-stricken since then. Education, clothing, health care, and Christian training are also provided. At present, these orphanages feed, cloth, shelter, and nurture over 350 through the support garnered by the Crusade.

We also support over 300 Christian evangelists and their families in India, and many other truth workers in countries throughout the world.

More than 1,000 individuals are receiving their daily sustenance through the ministry of the Crusade.

I don't know if this letter will come to your attention, but I hope it does, and that you will read it with an open mind and loving heart.

With Christian love,
Fred Schwarz
President
Christian Anti-Communism Crusade

THE WORLD FEDERALISTS ATTACK

I was the guest of Bill Wardle on Radio Station WTAQ of Chicago on May 9. I discussed the possible motives of Mao Tse-tung for his new policy towards the United States, paying particular attention to his published thoughts and personal history, and answered questions phoned in by the audience.

The following day a delegation of World Federalists, led by Everett Millard, appeared on the same program. Questions asked by the audience appear to have disturbed Mr. Millard, and he wrote the following letter to Bill Wardle which contained these paragraphs:

WORLD ASSOCIATION OF WORLD FEDERALISTS
MOUVEMENT UNIVERSEL POUR UNE
FEDERATION MONDIALE

TASK FORCE "SUN" ("STRENGTHEN THE UNITED NATIONS")

SECRETARIAT: 4030 IRVING PARK ROAD
CHICAGO, ILLINOIS 60641, U.S.A.
PHONE 312-777-4030

Mr. Bill Ward   17 May 1972
Radio Station WTAQ
9355 West Joliet Road
LaGrange, Illinois 60525

Dear Mr. Ward:

It was a valuable experience and one which I personally enjoyed to take part in your program on May 9. I am sure that Bob Clark and Alva Tompkins join me in expressing our appreciation of the opportunity which you gave us to explain the relevance of world federalist goals to contemporary history.

It disturbs me, nevertheless, that your audience, to judge by the phone calls, showed themselves so uninformed and so hostile, and that your personal espousal of an "authority" of the nature of Dr. Schwartz seems to exploit these characteristics of the public you reach. I think you will agree that if Fred Schwartz's views of China's present role are indeed paranoid and without a foundation in fact, it is a disservice to our nation and to man's future to give them the currency which they have on your program.

You seem to be a pretty reasonable guy. You disclaim the "fanaticism" of some of your fellow-thinkers. Therefore, I believe you should re-examine what Schwartz says about China, if it is as you represent it to be. I have queried some of my knowledgeable friends about Chinese attitudes. No one I know seems to feel there is any objective evidence of a Chinese ambition to rule the world. Schwartz should put up or shut up. And if he can't prove his case, I think it would be most un-American of you to continue to air his ideas to people who rely upon your integrity.

With best wishes
Everett L. Millard, Secretary

On June 7, 1972, I mailed the following letter to Mr. Millard:

Dear Mr. Millard:

William H. Wardle of Radio Station WTAQ has forwarded to me a copy of your letter to him. In it you challenge me to "put up or shut up." I will try to do exactly that.

The major source of information we have concerning China comes from the Communist rulers of China. The ignorance of external "experts" is illustrated by the fact that not one of them can tell us what has happened to Lin Piao, who until recently was heir apparent to Mao Tse-tung.

The Chinese people are indoctrinated with the thoughts of Mao Tse-tung. The Chinese Communists have published the little red book *Quotations from Chairman Mao Tse-tung* and have distributed hundreds of millions of copies. I will give a few specific quotations from Chairman Mao.

War is the highest form of struggle for resolving contradictions, when they have developed to a certain stage, between classes, nations, states, or political groups, and it has existed ever since the emergence of private property and of classes. (page 58)

History shows that wars are divided into two kinds, just and unjust. All wars that are progressive are just, and all wars that impede progress are unjust. We Communists oppose all unjust wars that impede progress, but we do not oppose progressive, just wars. Not only do we Communists not oppose just wars, we actively participate in them. (page 59)

Revolutionary war is an antitoxin which not only eliminates the enemy's poison but also purges us of our own filth. (page 60)

Every Communist must grasp the truth, "Political power grows out of the barrel of a gun." (page 6)

From this it appears clear that Mao Tse-tung regards war as an acceptable if not a desirable means of attaining political power. He also believes in the inevitable triumph of world socialism which to him means world Communist dictatorship. He states this specifically in these words:

The socialist system will eventually replace the capitalist system; this is an objective law independent of man's will. However much the reactionaries try to hold back the wheel of history, sooner or later revolution will take place and will inevitably triumph. (page 24)

Mao has frequently classified the atomic bomb as a paper tiger. One specific quotation is:

I have said that all the reputedly powerful reactionaries are merely paper tigers. The reason is that they are divorced from the people. Look! Was not Hitler a paper tiger? Was Hitler not overthrown? I also said that the

tsar of Russia, the emperor of China and Japanese imperialism were all paper tigers. As we know, they were all
overthrown. U.S. imperialism has not yet been overthrown and it has the atom bomb. I believe it also will
be overthrown. It, too, is a paper tiger. (page 75)

Khrushchev tells us in the book *Khrushchev Remembers* that Mao Tse-tung in 1954 tried to persuade him to
provoke war with the United States. Khrushchev's precise words are:

I remember once in Peking, Mao and I were lying
next to the swimming pool in our bathing trunk discussing the problems of war and peace. Mao Tse-tung said
to me "Comrade Khrushchev, what do you think? If we
compare the military might of the capitalist world with
that of the socialist world, you'll see that we obviously
have the advantage over our enemies. Think of how
many divisions China, the USSR, and the other socialist
countries could raise."

I said, "Comrade Mao Tse-tung, nowadays that sort
of thinking is out of date. You can no longer calculate
the alignment of forces on the basis of who has the most
men. Back in the days when a dispute was settled with
fists or bayonets, it made a difference who had the most
men and the most bayonets on each side. Then when the
machine gun appeared, the side with more troops no
longer necessarily had the advantage. And now with the
atomic bomb, the number of troops on each side makes
practically no difference to the alignment of real power
and the outcome of a war. The more troops on a side,
the more bomb fodder."

Mao replied by trying to assure me that the atomic
bomb itself was a paper tiger! "Listen Comrade
Khrushchev," he said. "All you have to do is provoke
the Americans into military action, and I'll give you as
many divisions as you need to crush them—a hundred,
two hundred, one thousand divisions." I tried to explain
to him that one or two missiles could turn all the divi-

sions in China to dust. But he wouldn't even listen to my arguments and obviously regarded me as a coward. (pages 469, 470)

We may assume that Mao Tse-tung is possibly (1) a hypocrite; (2) a liar; (3) a mad man; or (4) a clever, patient, sincere, dedicated Communist.

In the light of his life's record of achievement, the evidence would suggest that we regard him as a dedicated Communist doing what he is convinced is his Communist duty. At present he needs protection against a possible preemptive Soviet strike to destroy his thermonuclear factories. It would be wise to consider what his doctrines would direct him to do once he has thermonuclear parity and adequate economic and military strength.

Hitler told us clearly his beliefs and his objectives in his book *Mein Kampf*. The world paid a terrible price for refusing to take him seriously. It will be a greater tragedy if we choose to ignore the history and doctrines of Mao Tse-tung.

With prayer for true peace,
Fred Schwarz

I suggest it is now the responsibility of Mr. Millard to "put up or shut up." No reply has yet been received.

WORLD FEDERALISM

I have received a letter from Everett L. Millard, secretary of the World Association of World Federalists Task Force "Sun" (Strengthen the United Nations) in reply to my letter to him which was published in the Crusade newsletter on July 1, 1972. So that his letter may be read in perspective, I will outline the events which preceded it.

I was the guest of Bill Wardle on Radio Station WTAQ of Chicago on May 9, 1972. I discussed the possible motives of Mao Tse-tung for his new policy towards the U.S.A. paying particular attention to his published thoughts and personal history, and I answered questions phoned in by the audience. The following day, Mr. Everett Millard, as part of a delegation of the World Federalists, appeared on the same program. Listeners, who phoned in questions, informed him of some of the things I had stated.

Mr. Millard was perturbed and wrote a letter to Bill Wardle suggesting that my views on China's role were paranoid and without foundation in fact and that it had been a disservice to the nation and to man's future to have me appear on the program.

I wrote Mr. Millard giving quotations from Mao Tse-tung which praised war and which stated that political objectives should be obtained by war. Mr. Millard has now sent me the following letter which I publish in full:

WORLD ASSOCIATION OF WORLD FEDERALISTS
MOUVEMENT UNIVERSEL POUR UNE
FEDERATION MONDIALE

TASK FORCE "SUN" ("STRENGTHEN THE
UNITED NATIONS")

SECRETARIAT: 4030 IRVING PARK ROAD
CHICAGO, ILLINOIS 60641, U.S.A.
PHONE 312-777-4030

Dr. Fred Schwarz
Christian Anti-Communism Crusade
P.O. Box 890
124 East First Street
Long Beach, California 90801

Dear Dr. Schwarz:
    Your reply to the question I raised in a letter to Mr. Bill Ward of Wardle of Radio Station WTAQ in LaGrange, Illinois, is courteous and informative. But the footnote which you appended to this correspondence in your publication of July 1, stating that I in turn should "put up or

shut up," seems irrelevant. It is you, not I who makes the assertion that China aspires to world conquest. It is up to you, not me, to prove it. And you have not done so.

Most of your "evidence" consists of quotations from Chairman Mao on the nobility of war, which are interesting enough but do not prove your point. Any impartial student of history can recognize Mao's views on war as a reaction to a century-and-a-half of injuries and insults to China by foreign aggressors including Europeans, Japanese and Americans. Your other "evidence" is a narration by Khrushchev that Mao, in a conversation beside a swimming pool, tried to con him into attacking the United States. This may well be so, and it tells us something, but it does not support your point.

Your claims to expertise on China seem illusory. You make no reference to China's restraint on the Indian frontier, which is one of the known facts we have to go on, nor to the folly of American intervention in Indo-China, a fact which a thousand times outweighs a swimming-pool conversation. To psychiatrists, an unreasoning fear of hostile conspiracies by "unseen forces" is a symptom of paranoia. Though you may be perfectly rational as an individual, your public viewpoint with respect to China expresses irrational fear and hostility which afflict many citizens both of China, Russia and our own country in this troubled era.

Fear may serve a useful purpose. But it is suicidal when it destroys our judgment. If we panic, destruction will be sure. Those who believe that only the sword will conquer Communism are doomed to advance it instead. Only a condition of public irrationality could have got us into the disastrous Viet-Nam war, which has made more Communists than it has cured. It will be a formidable enough task to cope rationally with the immense problems of our world of today. Any reasonable solution must seek the common denominator of humanity among people of contrasting beliefs.

Those Christians who are terrified of Communism are men of little faith. Those Americans who fear Communism will overwhelm freedom have little confidence in their own institutions of democracy. There is a better way, if I may suggest so. There is a more Christian way than hatred of Communism, and a more American way than war. It is self-government. The creation of a self-government of man is the greatest challenge we have ever faced. We cannot succeed if we ascribe inhumanity to everyone we consider infidels. We must think man is worth saving. We must think life is worth living. And we must put respect for other people before hatred.

World federalists believe that man is capable of governing his affairs. We believe that strengthening the United Nations is more hopeful for our future than a balance of terror. We believe that Americans were right in devising the Constitution of the United States, and that American institutions are a better model for all humanity than those of Marx or Mao. What our government is, the United Nations can become. The world needs not hatred or fear, not tyranny or terror, but the international institutions necessary for the government of those matters which no single nation can control by the exercise of its domestic sovereignty.

81 nations have joined to demand a debate in the General Assembly on a review of the United Nations Charter. Russia and China and the United States, the present wielders of great power, are dragging their feet on reforms of the United Nations. The less powerful nations, most of humanity, hope to strengthen the international institutions of peaceful decision. In this way people who are truly Christians, who are truly Americans, who truly believe in democracy, have the best chance to assure the survival of freedom. All of us should work by such means for the triumph of democracy over tyranny.

Under separate cover I am sending to you and several of your readers who have written to me a complimentary copy of the Fifth Edition of *Freedom in a Federal*

World. It is a report of studies now in their 20th year, which I have directed, on world law and world government among more than a thousand scholars of world affairs. You may find it of considerable interest, including a chapter on China and Russia. Others of your readers may wish to purchase it from us at $2.50 in paperback postpaid.

To be fair, I ask that you publish this letter to you in full, in your publication in the same manner you published my letter to Bill Ward or Wardle. I also ask that you furnish to me a copy of the publication in which it appears, which you have failed to do, perhaps by oversight, on the previous occasion. If you have 50,000 readers, as you claim, I believe that many of them will welcome a rational approach, rather than an irrational one, to the solution of the enormous problems which confront the human race in our age.

Sincerely yours
Everett L. Millard

cc.: Ward or Wardle
Correspondents
Everett L. Millard
Secretary, WAWF Task Force "SUN"

I sent the following reply to Mr. Millard:

7 August, 1972

Mr. Everett L. Millard
Secretary, WAWF Task Force "Sun"
World Association of World Federalists
4030 Irving Park Road
Chicago, Illinois 60641

Dear Mr. Millard:

I received your letter on August 15, and I have read it several times striving to lay aside prejudice and to con-

sider the points you raise, with all the objectivity of which
I am capable. Before discussing the major points of difference between us, I would like to make a few observations.

Frankly, I am somewhat disturbed because it seems to
me that you have reached your conclusions in advance
of consideration of the evidence. If this is the case, discussion between us is obviously an exercise in futility. I
have gained this impression by your statement in the
final paragraph of your letter, that your approach is
rational whereas mine is irrational and your persistent
suggestion that I am a victim of paranoia. I perceive little advantage in attaching pejorative terms to each other.
I prefer to state the facts and present evidence logically
and allow the readers to reach their conclusions concerning our relative rationality and sanity.

In order for our discussions to be fruitful, it is essential that there exists a common ground of agreement
from which we can depart. I find several points in your
letter with which I am in agreement. I agree that Americans were right in devising the Constitution of the
United States and that American institutions are a better
model for all humanity than those of Marx and Mao. I
also agree that the world does not need hatred or fear,
tyranny or terror. I would, however, qualify this latter
statement by stating there are some forms of fear which
are essential for survival. The prospects for the survival
of a child who did not learn to fear height and fire
would be dim; fear of cancer may cause an individual to
submit to a medical examination which may save his
life. Similarly, fear of the probable future conduct of an
ideologue whose doctrine would direct him to exercise
tyranny if he obtained power could lead to intelligent
democratic action to prevent his rise to power.

You state, "To psychiatrists, an unreasoning fear of
hostile conspiracies by 'unseen forces' is a symptom of
paranoia."

This is true but quite irrelevant to the discussion of
the danger presented by Communism. Communism is

not an "unseen force." It is a most massive, visible force. It has captured and controls more than one billion of the population of the earth; it has huge military and economic might; it has a vast worldwide propaganda campaign which it carries on by the printed and spoken word; it has a clearly enunciated doctrine which states that the victory of Communism throughout the world is inevitable. It has a history which indicates that it is actively cooperating with the "forces of history" which are "ordained" to bring about world Communism.

To illustrate, I quote Mao Tse-tung: "The socialist system will eventually replace the capitalist system; this is an objective law independent of man's will." (*Quotations from Chairman Mao Tse-tung,* page 24) Mao states he is a Communist and defines socialism as the "first phase" of Communism.

You state, "Your claims to expertise on China seem illusory." I have made no such claim. I doubt whether any true experts on China exist. Thousands of unbiased observers would need freedom of movement throughout China while freedom of speech prevailed there, before any comprehensive picture of the true situation could be obtained. Obviously this is not the case at present.

I do claim to have read the published writings of Mao Tse-tung and to have studied something of his history. I take his statements seriously. I believe he has earned the right to have his statements taken seriously. This statement by a writer in the Black Panther newspaper of April 15, 1972, expresses the situation well:

For some 50 years, Mao Tse-tung has worked diligently and unremittingly for the Chinese revolution; theorizing about its many stages and eventually carrying them through to completion, with the period of socialist construction still in progress. It's been said that in the 30s and late 20s (the lean years of the Chinese revolution), Chairman Mao was right when most others were wrong, invariably advancing along the correct path, depending upon the specific historical conditions in

China at a particular period in time. After half a century of struggle, a man like Chairman Mao does not abrogate his principles overnight.

In 1945, Mao Tse-tung went to Chungking, sat, talked, and toasted with Chiang Kai-shek. Did Chairman Mao betray the revolution when he did this? Certainly not. He simply realized logically that the People's Liberation Army was not yet strong enough to defeat Chiang. So he sat and talked and stalled for time. Four years later he talked with a gun and seized the time. Chairman Mao knew exactly what to do and when to do it. He moved with the ebb and flow of the struggle. He won; Chiang lost.

The writings and example of Mao have inspired many thousands throughout the world to "take up the gun." To dismiss Mao's teachings on war as "a reaction to a century-and-a-half of injuries and insults to China by foreign aggressors" seems to belittle his intelligence, his sincerity and his achievements. While his thoughts were doubtless influenced by the experiences of China, they also owe much to the writings of Marx and Lenin and many other factors.

The major area of disagreement between us seems to be concerning the role of doctrine in the motivation of human conduct. It is my conviction that ideas, which are sincerely believed, influence conduct to a considerable degree. If this is true, it follows that the only way to predict the future conduct of an individual or an organization is through giving due consideration to the ideas that motivate them. This is not to affirm that ideas are the soul determinants of human activity. Other factors must also be considered. However, it is rational to attempt to anticipate the future and to decide present conduct in the light of future probabilities. The ability to do this is one of the major differentials between man and beast.

Would it have been "paranoid" or "rational" for the Jews of Germany and enlightened people everywhere to have studied the published literature of the Nazis on anti-Semitism and to predict the course of action to which it could ultimately lead? If an individual had done this, would he have not run the risk of being accused of harboring an unreasoning fear of hostile conspiracy by "unseen forces"?

Your faith in the United Nations is touching, but I cannot share it. I agree with the Russian author, Alexander Solzehnitsyn, who described the United Nations in his essay which he wrote to the Nobel Foundation when he accepted the Nobel prize for literature. He classified the United Nations as an immoral organization in an immoral world. He stated:

It is not a United Nations organization, but a united governments organization, where all governments stand equal—those which are freely elected, those imposed forcibly and those which have seized power with weapons.

Relying on the mercenary partiality of the majority, the United Nations jealously guards the freedom of some nations and neglects the freedom of others. (*Sydney Morning Herald,* Friday, August 25, 1972)

I agree with your statement, "Those who believe that only the sword will conquer Communism are doomed to advance it instead." Communism attains power by deception and retains power by force. The best weapon against deception is knowledge. This knowledge can only be obtained through study of the doctrines and history of communism. For this reason the Christian Anti-Communism Crusade advocates a consistent program of education through which the Communist techniques of deception are exposed to the light of knowledge and reason. If the majority of people know the true nature of Communism, its techniques of deception, its rule by dictatorial tyranny, and its general objectives, they will spurn it.

Those who oppose this program are in effect waiting until Communism is established and is ruling through force. Thus, objectively, they are the supporters of violence.

Christianity should not ignore the anguish of those who are suffering the tortures of tyranny. To present a Christianity which is indifferent to the fate of those who suffer under Communism is a travesty of the love of Christ. Solzehnitsyn makes this very clear. He writes:

Prison sentences of 25 years, isolation cells where the walls are covered in ice and the prisoners stripped to their underclothes, lunatic asylums for the sane, and countless unreasonable people who for some reason will keep running away, shot on the frontiers—all this is common and accepted.

I hope we can shun both the complacency of a loveless faith and a trust in violence. I am praying that God will bring about the deliverance of those who live under Communist tyranny. In the meantime, I am working as intelligently, compassionately, and energetically as I can to prevent Communist capture of more people. I invite you to join me in this endeavor.

With Christian love,
Fred Schwarz
President
Christian Anti-Communism Crusade

FROM JULY 1, 1978, NEWSLETTER
DON ROSEWALL

Dear Friend,

A great friend and regular supporter of the Crusade, Don Rosewall of Rosewall Organic Gardens, 3675 Campus Drive, Oceanside, California, has sent me the following letter:

After reading your letter of May 15, I thought it was to the point and the best you have written in a long time. So I gave it to the pastor of the church we attend and asked him to read it and let me know of his reaction. His thoughts are on the enclosed envelope.

How true today your quote of Jesus, "You can discern the face of the sky, but can you not discern the signs of the times?"

The comments of the pastor were:

1. I think it is a very clever, professionally-produced mailing for funds, covering all bases.

2. I think it contains some truth, but a lot of innuendo and scare-stuff.

3. Schwarz raises enormous sums of money but gives no accounting to donors.

4. The big assumption: If you don't give to Schwarz you are not fighting communism; If you give ($1,000!) you are. I do not agree.

Many serious charges are contained in these comments. These include:

1. I publish much innuendo.

2. I raise enormous sums of money.

3. No accounting is given to the donors.

4. I assume that those who do not contribute financially to the Crusade are not fighting communism.

These charges are false, but the pastor probably believes they are true. With the hope that his mind, and other minds which have been similarly misinformed, are open to the truth, I submit:

1. I scorn innuendo. When I have a statement to make, I try to select words that are lucid and precise and to be as unambiguous as possible. I take seriously the instruction by Jesus, "Let your communication be 'Yea, yea; Nay, nay'."

2. Considering the work done, the Crusade income is very moderate indeed. It costs $50,000 each month to run the Crusade, and this is a substantial sum. However, here are some of the things achieved by it:

(a) Research into the statements and activities of the communists is conducted consistently, and a newsletter prepared which contains accurate, up-to-date, documented information about the doctrines, activities, plans and objectives of communism and which has a standard worthy of any university in the world. This newsletter is sent to the president, members of the cabinet, Justices, members of Congress, all governors, and many state legislators; newspaper editors and columnists; news directors of radio and T.V. stations; all college libraries and many high school libraries; and all citizens who wish to receive it, at no charge.

(b) Seminars, lectures and debates are conducted.

(c) Orphanages which care for the physical, mental, and spiritual well-being of 120 boys and girls are supported in Andhra State, India as well as 100 National Christian Anti-Communism workers.

(d) Literature, including the book *You Can Trust the Communists (to be Communists)* is translated, published and distributed in many nations threatened by Communist takeover.

(e) Multitudes of national leaders, Christian leaders, educators and citizens have been educated by the Crusade and are applying this knowledge and understanding in their work. The formula for Communist conquest, which I discovered and presented: "External encirclement, plus internal demoralization, plus thermonuclear blackmail, equals progressive surrender," is entering into the national consciousness.

(f) Many anticommunist organizations have been formed and are active throughout the world as a result of the Crusade work.

Let us place the Crusade's income in perspective. Many individual churches have a bigger income. The World Vision Mercy Ship which will offer relief—not rescue—to some of the pitiful refugees from Communism in Vietnam and Cambodia, will cost as much to run as the Crusade. This work is most commendable, and I urge support for it, but surely it is wise to spend as much to try to prevent Communist conquest as to give temporary comfort to a minute percentage of the victims of Communist conquest.

3. The auditing firm, Brown Lloyd and Stevenson, prepares an annual audit of the Crusade, and supporters are invited to inspect this audit. In addition the Crusade has been audited several times by the Internal Revenue Service.

4. There is no assumption that those who do not support the Crusade financially are not fighting Communism. I write many letters assuring individuals that they can serve the cause of freedom in many ways that are as effective as giving money. These include: (1) Learning the truth about Communism and teaching it to family, friends, and neighbors; (2) Conducting study groups; (3) Writing to the president, senators, congressmen, governors, and state legislators; (4) Distributing literature; 5) Writing letters to newspaper editors; 6) Calling radio and T.V. talk shows.

Nevertheless, the Crusade needs and merits support. I consider the Crusade friends and supporters the finest, most generous, most compassionate, most patriotic and most sacrificial group in the nation. I did ask for individual gifts of $1,000 but this was not the test of whether they were against Communism. Actually, we did not receive a single gift of $1,000 in response to that appeal, but many gave lesser sums generously and sacrificially. I am confident that our present great needs will be met.

Do false accusations such as those made by the pastor hurt? Yes, they do. I am devoted to the truth, and I feel pain when truth is violated. I am also hurt that professed Christian leaders show a spirit so contrary to the spirit of Christ. The damage done to the cause of freedom is most distressing. However, in the spirit of St. Paul, who, after listing his sufferings said he considered them nothing compared to the glories that were his in Christ, I consider these attacks nothing compared to the love and trust which have been showered upon me in such abundance.

With Christian love,
Fred Schwarz

HOAX OR CAUSE FOR ALARM?
What do you make of the following letter?

Dr. Fred Schwarz,

I am writing this letter to you asking you to please refrain from sending me these anti-Communism Crusade newsletters, since as of Dec. 28, 1992, I have become a full-fledged member of the Communist party. Dr. Schwarz, I suggest that instead of being so intent on destroying our Party, you should take a look at the benefits Communism holds for all the people. At this point in time, Communism is the only solution for our decaying country. One day this nation will be great again, but only under the power of Communism!

Maybe one day before you leave this world you will see the advantages of Communism. Until then, you will be blind to the only way.

Boston College, MA
(Name available on request)

On reading it, three possibilities occurred to me:

1. It's a hoax;

2. It reports an unusual but unsurprising attitude of an immature young student;

3. The writer is typical of many students who are disillusioned with the prevailing situation in the United States, and who are susceptible to the deceitful promises of the Communists.

This third possibility will doubtless surprise many. It is widely believed that the renunciation of Communism by the people of Eastern Europe, and the disintegration of the Soviet Union, have revealed the emptiness of Communist promises and destroyed the seductive appeal of Marxism–Leninism to student intellectuals. This belief is delusional. Marxism and its offspring, Marxism-Leninism, still appeal to many on U.S. campuses.

The following parable of Jesus deserves close attention today:

When the unclean spirit is gone out of a man, he walketh through dry places, seeking rest, and findeth none. Then he saith, I will return into my house from whence I came out; and when he is come, he findeth it empty, swept, and garnished. Then goeth he, and taketh with himself seven other spirits more wicked than himself, and they enter in and dwell there: and the last state of that man is worse than the first. Even so shall it be also unto this wicked generation." (Matthew 12:43–45)

This is not the appropriate time for complacency. The disintegration of the Soviet Union seems to have reinvigorated the U.S. Communist party. As Gus Hall said recently to a journalist's question, "Is Communism dead?"—"It's the liveliest corpse I've seen."

Like a malignant virus, the doctrines of Marxism-Leninism may be dormant for a time, and then strike with deadly force.

THE STUDENT MIND
SEPTEMBER 1, 1987, NEWSLETTER

The distribution of my pamphlet, *Why Communism Kills*, to nearly a million students and faculty members of universities, colleges, seminaries, and Bible schools, stimulated numerous letters. Some were critical and some were laudatory. Consider the following four letters selected from a folder containing hundreds.

IRRATIONAL ABUSE

> *Ignorant, rabid fools like you kill, not books or "isms". I don't know what you are a Doctor of, but it is surely an embarrassment to your colleagues. I give you my sincerest wishes that your intellectual atrophy is reversible. (University of Minnesota)*

Many people will be surprised to learn that Hitler's racism did not lead to killings.

MISDIRECTED IDEALISM

> *I am a student at the University of Michigan, majoring in Russian Language & Literature and Russian & East European Studies, and I hope to study at Leningrad*

State University next year. I am also an extremely active member of the United Church of Christ, and I have considered the possibility of becoming an ordained minister . . .

I consider your pamphlet a piece of propaganda that is no different than propaganda issued by the Soviet Union. You are using fear tactics to back your own ideology. I am not mindless. Why should I accept your ideas more readily than I would accept those of Marx? The truth is that I accept neither. The Soviet Union is not a good example of a just and peaceful human society; the United States is not such an example either. Capitalism also kills. Why don't you justify to me the vast and obscene range of material wealth in America? People are dying on the streets of our cities while others drive by in ten thousand dollar cars. Why don't you tell me what the Bible says about this??? (University of Michigan)

What I am asking is that he pay attention to the published ideas of Karl Marx.

CHRISTIAN COMMENDATION

I have worked in the area of campus ministry for six years. I am convinced that alternative perspectives are desperately needed on college campuses which are dominated by non-Christian, liberal-leftist (if not outright Marxist) viewpoints.

For this reason, I enthusiastically support the further distribution of Why Communism Kills. *It simply, accurately, and tellingly unmasks the true face of Communism.*

Certainly, you will continue to receive "hate mail" concerning it. One booklet cannot undo the countless hours of indoctrination given at the university. Nevertheless, you will get through to many who are open to a reasonable presentation. (Campus Ministry)

A HOME RUN

I am nineteen years old. I graduated from High School in 1986. Since graduation, I have attended the University of Alabama. I would like to thank you for being the first to explain communism to me. I took all the World History classes in High School, as well as in college. Not one teacher took the time or the effort to explain to me or my classmates the basis of communism. Oh sure, we were taught to believe it was 'bad and of the devil' as we were growing up, but never why. I would like to know why. (University of Alabama)

The truth about Communism will prevent the deception and ensnarement of youthful idealists.

Do you think that the author of this next letter displays a trace of arrogance in his description of a former generation of youth? "You live in a 50s fantasy world, in which the nation's youth are naive, unworldly, unaware, apathetic, and easily swayed." He states this in response to my offer to him, as a "National Merit Scholar" semifinalist, to send him the Crusade newsletter.

I sincerely thank you for your generous words of praise and the kind offer of your newsletter. Indeed, as you state, my "intellectual talents nourished by accurate information will be needed by [my] country during the dangerous days that lie ahead." It will require considerable determination and skill on the part of myself and members of my generation to counter the self-destructive, xenophobic efforts of people like you.

It seems to me somewhat ironic that you attempt to recruit into your organization National Merit Scholars, for we are theoretically the nation's most educable youth—and therefore the least susceptible to your closed-minded drivel. Evidently, Dr. Schwarz, you live in a 50s fantasy world, in which the nation's youth are naive, unworldly, unaware, apathetic, and easily swayed.

Of course, your newsletter would be incapable of swaying even the easily swayed, given its remarkable transparency. It amazes me that you call it "accurate" and "up-to-date," but it amazes me even further that you call it "controversial." Your profuse vocabulary in your explanation of dialectical materialism in the Mar. 15 issue is astounding, in that it almost conceals the fact that you have nothing new to say. And your analysis of foreign affairs in that issue brings new meaning to the word "accurate"—your "prominent black African leader" is the chief minister of KwaZulu, a South African homeland (i.e., puppet state); you stoop to calling the Khmer Rouge a Communist revolution when in reality they bore a much closer resemblance to the genocidal policies of Hitler. And your recommendation of compulsory testing and "humane" quarantine for carriers of the HIV virus certainly contradicts your cover statement that "this newsletter is written without rancor and without malice."

It also seems ironic that you regard your particular breed of capitalism as something that will lead to "the maintenance of peace, the control of toxic pollution . . . a society of harmony and freedom." Capitalism is an economic system based on "competition" and therefore "exploitation." Exploitation does not create "harmony and freedom." When the interests of multi-national corporations are challenged overseas, peace is not maintained. When corporations cut corners to save money, the environment suffers. It both amazes and sickens me that someone as articulate and cogent as you cannot realize that untempered capitalism is destroying the world.

You might defend your viewpoint in the name of patriotism. Of the two of us, I consider myself to be the true patriot. I love this country. I probably love this

country more than you do, for at least I am able to weep
for the state we are in today and to not only want but to
plan to do something about it.

I am deeply resentful of and offended by your efforts
to recruit me into your Children's Crusade, not only
because I know I am now on the mailing list of every
lunatic or zealot who thinks he has a cause, but also
because you have grievously underestimated today's
youth. Not only do we care about the world we live in,
but we want to improve on it instead of regressing. You
are wasting your time with us, Dr. Schwarz.

I replied:

I am most impressed by your letter. You demonstrate
intelligence, knowledge, conviction, and a remarkable
ability to express your ideas clearly and forcibly.

When conclusions are all predetermined, dialogue and
debate easily degenerate into mutual abuse. Can we
agree that a desirable attitude includes these two
assumptions? (1) It is possible that some of my conclusions may be wrong; and (2) Maybe I can learn something from my opponent.

Some of your conclusions are controversial. Consider,
for example: *"You stoop to calling the Khmer Rouge a*
Communist revolution when, in reality, they bore a much
closer resemblance to the genocidal policies of Hitler."

Do you not acknowledge that the leaders of the
Khmer Rouge claimed to be Communists? They were
converted to Communism while students in France and
considered themselves to be disciples of Marx and
Lenin. As Prince Sihanouk stated, *"They wished to be*
the best Communists in the world."

I agree, however, with your statement that their policies bore a close resemblance to the policies of Hitler.
Hitler practiced "genocide" while the Khmer Rouge
practiced "classicide." Could this resemblance be due to

the resemblance between the evil race doctrines of
Nazism and the evil class doctrines of Marx?

I suggest you read "Haing Ngor, A Cambodian
Odyssey" and consider why the Khmer Rouge were
determined to exterminate all who had been doctors in
pre-revolutionary Cambodia, and why they went to
extraordinary lengths to track them down. Could the
answer relate to the statement by Karl Marx in the *Manifesto of the Communist Party*—"by 'individual' you
mean none other than the bourgeois, than the middleclass owner of property. This person must, indeed, be
swept out of the way and made impossible."

Should we ignore the history of the world Communist
movement entirely? Hitler was not the only mass murderer of this century. There was another, known as
Stalin. In the current edition of *Pravda International,*
Vol. 3, No. 4, the dissident Soviet historian, Roy
Medvedev, estimates the number of victims of Stalin to
have been *"in the region of 40 million people."* It was
not a right-wing extremist who said, *"Those who cannot
remember the past are condemned to repeat it."* If a new
German leader were to arise, who criticized the practices
of Hitler, while he continued to believe Hitler's racist
doctrines, would you be fully reassured?

Maybe your criticism of capitalism should be directed
to Mikhail Gorbachev, Deng Xiaoping, and the other
Communist leaders who are now embracing capitalist
practices.

I can reassure you on one score. You have no need to
fear that you are now on the mailing list of every zealot
who thinks he has a cause. I will not add your name to
our mailing list unless you consent that I do so. Also,
our mailing list is confidential and not for sale. However, I know I have much to learn, and I believe you
have also. I hope we can learn from each other.

With Christian love,
Fred Schwarz

STUDENT AND FACULTY RESPONSE TO
"WHY COMMUNISM KILLS"

Consider this letter:

> *Thank you for the pamphlet, "Why Communism Kills." In it you outline some undisputed or rather indisputable points in the grave flaws of communist systems as practiced so far.*
>
> *As a human rights activist (Amnesty International) struggling to save lives in both extreme Eastern (Soviet Block) and extreme Western (Latin American) regimes, the question comes inevitably to mind, 'Why Capitalism Kills?' Within the U.S. we enjoy a great degree of freedom. Unfortunately, history has demonstrated that our system often does not respect the freedoms of other nations in the name of "free enterprise." A classic example is our government's condoning and encouraging the brutal death, torture and "disappearance" of hundreds of thousands of individuals in Chile. As you probably well know, in order to maintain great profits in the copper industry (Kennecott, ITT, Anaconda) the U.S. orchestrated one of the most brutal, bloody "coups" in this hemisphere. For fourteen years now the Chileans have been deprived of basic human freedoms which they formerly knew, and, most gravely, deprived of many scores of lives. I may point out that one of the 'death squad' organizations in the country acts in the name of "anti-communism."*
>
> *As Christian, thinking human beings concerned about the plight of our fellow men on this planet, we must question all systems.*
>
> (Ph.D., Wisconsin)

Overlooking controversial statements, I replied as follows:

Dear Doctor,
    I thank you for your thoughtful response to the message, "Why Communism Kills".

I am encouraged by your affirmation that it contains some indisputable points revealing the grave flaws of communist systems as practiced so far. I agree with your contention that the conduct of the U.S.A. has not always been commendable and that much can and should be criticized.

Maybe I misunderstand you, but I gain the impression that you are urging that I give equal attention to the evils of capitalism as I have done to those of communism. Frankly, I don't believe this is possible, and I doubt if it is desirable. May I use a medical analogy: There are many diseases that destroy health and life. The day when one individual could be an expert on all diseases has passed. Specialization in the diagnosis and treatment of one disease, or one group of diseases, is now recognized as the desirable norm.

All diseases are undesirable, but all are not equivalent in the suffering and loss of life which they cause. At one time syphilis was the most deadly venereal disease. It has now been outstripped in horror by AIDS.

I do not believe that there is moral equivalence between communism and capitalism or between the Soviet Union and the U.S.A. While millions try to flee from the Soviet empire, other millions try to flee into the U.S.A. Sometimes actions speak louder than words.

During 37 years in the U.S.A., I have never heard anyone claim that capitalism was destined to conquer the world. In contrast, the communist leaders routinely claim that the conquest of the entire world by "socialism", which will lead ultimately to "communism", is inevitable. The proclamation and practice of the Brezhnev Doctrine proves that the Soviet Communists are working to assure this conquest.

I believe that communism poses the greatest threat, both doctrinally and historically, to the "human rights" of the people of the United States and the world, so I am concentrating on its diagnosis and treatment.

With Christian love,
Dr. Fred Schwarz

COMPASSION AND CONFUSION

Some letters reveal emotional compassion but intellectual imma-
turity. The result is confusion and apparent excessive self-assurance.
Consider:

> *One of, if not the greatest, freedom we have as citi-
> zens of this country (the United States of America) is
> the freedom to formulate, verbally express, and if we
> have the financial means, publish our own personal
> opinions about other people's opinions. This is why I
> appreciate the pamphlet I received in the mail from
> your organization today. That you care enough about
> my welfare to attempt to persuade me against the threat
> of what you sincerely believe to be an evil system of
> beliefs, well, that just convinces me more of what a dear
> and wonderful potential this nation contains within its
> essence.*
>
> *But Sir, I beg to differ, not so much with your opin-
> ion, as with what I perceive to be the motivation behind
> your's and other people's seemingly 'scapegoat' attitude
> towards Communism.*
>
> *First of all, speaking first as a human being, second as
> a citizen of America, I am concerned that so few people
> seem to acknowledge the fact that the problems of the
> world—murder, rape, theft, political and military ambi-
> tions—stem not so much from systems of thought (you,
> sir, I feel sure, will admit that mass murder scourged the
> human race long before the birth and intellectual flower-
> ing of Karl Marx) as from some unidentified blight on
> the human (individual) consciousness. Now whether
> that blight is a necessary condition of human existence
> or not—and I feel sure that as a 'Christian' organization,
> you posses ample terminology with which to refer to the
> condition—is not the point, it seems to me. Rather, we
> should look at means and ends.*
>
> *Your pamphlet clearly says 'Communism kills.' Now
> from a 'Christian' organization, I would expect, not*

more, but certainly as much as I would from any human community in the world, and certainly you feel strongly enough about human suffering that you wouldn't risk selling your love out for results, or more clearly, the means for the ends. In other words, surely you realize that 'Communism' never killed anybody; a man killed somebody. A woman killed somebody. But after all, Communism is not even a real thing. It's an idea, the same as Christianity. Or Democracy. Or Islam. Or Hinduism. Or Nihilism. They all stemmed from the human consciousness, so they should be dealt with as such, not as Evil Entities, come from hell to destroy the race. I would suggest you read up on the history of the 'Christian Church'; it has had its share of scandal: witch-hunts, purges, persecutions to call its own.

What I want to express to you, sirs, is that humanity has from the dawn of history attempted to project individual fears, prejudices, and phobias onto something big and abstract. We have always seemed to have needed a story with which to express the meaning of our existence in this world, and any other story we have resisted to the point of being more brutal than the ones who tell the story we so despise. The thing to do, I sincerely believe with my most rational faculties, is to examine our individual motivations, and ask ourselves an honest 'why am I doing what I am doing right now?', and encourage our brothers and sisters to do the same, so that we may someday truly live in peace, and enjoy the spectacular, too wondrous for words, beauty and richness of this earth.

To close, I will leave you with a letter I once received from a Japanese friend of mine in response to the question posed to her, 'How do you feel about war?'

Dear Susie: The question you ask us is very difficult, also very valuable. Why our governments want to do wars? They are crazy! They know they killed many people, each other, but still they do. I am very sad. We want to friendship by meeting, and now you and I are good

friends. This is good. Someday perhaps there will be no war, if we continue to friendship. I hope so. Love, your friend, Yuko. (With hearts drawn to the side)
                                        Sincerely yours, Susie

Dear Susie,

Your letter reveals a tender heart and a genuine concern for human suffering.

Nevertheless, I am bewildered by your major theme, "Communism never killed anybody. A man killed somebody. A woman killed somebody." This seems to illustrate the statement by the poet, Tennyson:

> A lie which is half a truth
> Is the wickedest lie of all.

Human hands often pull the trigger of the gun, but the hand is directed by the human brain, and the direction often proceeds from ideas which are enshrined in the human mind and brain. Would you say: "Hatred never killed anyone; racism never killed anyone; anti-semitism never killed anyone; delusions never killed anyone." I remember a man I treated when I was a medical student. It was during the Second World War, and Brisbane, Australia, was host to the American troops. This man told me the American soldiers intended to kill him. Motivated by his delusion, he secured a gun in order to defend himself and proceeded to shoot and kill two U.S. servicemen.

Does not your letter illustrate action resulting from an idea? Did not the procedure that led to the typing, stamping and mailing of your letter commence with an idea in your mind? The idea led to the act.

Ideas have consequences. Deranged ideas lead to deadly deeds. Surely you would not contend that the ideas concerning the Jews, which festered in the mind of Adolph Hitler, did not contribute to the slaughter of the holocaust?

The communist idea that humans are merely soulless animals, who can be improved and perfected by being reared in a coercive socialist environment, and who can be liquidated if necessary, has already resulted in the death of millions and will certainly lead to the death of many more millions.

We agree that human nature is flawed and, as a Christian, I believe it can be transformed and regenerated by the power of God. This is cause for hope.

With Christian love,
Dr. Fred Schwarz

A BONUS

I will conclude on a positive note. This letter made me rejoice:

I have just read your booklet Why Communism Kills *which you had sent to one of my student sons at the U. of Wisconsin, Oshkosh. I found it to be the clearest and most accurate description of what communism really is that I have ever read. When I was a student at the U. of Chicago in the late forties, I was a fan of Marx and was convinced of the perfectibility of human nature. But over the years, after much thought and reading, my opinions about communism changed. After thinking about the Cambodian genocide and Afghanistan, I came to the same conclusions you expound. Because of all this thought and concern on the subject by me over the years, your booklet really "hits home." But my 4 sons who have never read Marx and thus never really thought seriously about communism, although they completely agree with your booklet, are not emotionally aroused by the booklet. And this is sad because an idea that is not taken into the heart is an idea whose time has not yet come.*

Since it is teachers who can do so much to put "heart" into ideas, it is the teachers that we should reach first. So enclosed is $10 for which please send me 5 copies of your booklet along with instructions for ordering more copies, and I will pass them out to my teacher friends whom I know will be very receptive. (Wisconsin)

I ask for your support so that our distribution of *Why Communism Kills* to the teachers and students the Universities and Colleges can continue.

COMMUNIST PROPAGANDA IN U.S. SCHOOLS

The Communists are active both without and within the United States. Internally their program is most successful in the prestigious schools of the United States. This morning I received this letter from a student at one of the most prestigious Ivy League Academies. I refrain from publishing the name of the student as his letter may prove a source of embarrassment to him when he matures. Here is his letter:

> *I first asked to receive your CACC newsletter some months ago because I was curious about the "lunatic fringe" of the militant, war-mongering right. You sign your letters, "With Christian love," but I think that I, an agnostic, have a better understanding of this term than you do. Jesus did not tell people to kill, to spy, to oppress, to exploit. He told them to be just, kind, and nonviolent. Are you unaware that the United States, in order to guard the freedoms you cherish and the wealth you enjoy, has for years and probably will for years take advantage of the poor in this country and abroad? Is this justice? The oppressed of the world look for equality. This should not surprise you, since we ourselves began as revolutionaries. Yet when they look to the US, which should support those who seek basic rights, they find that the CIA and the Department of "Defense" are poised for a conflict in Vietnam, in El Salvador, in Chile, in Korea, yes, perhaps even in South Africa. So these people look to the USSR and find what they need: moral, economic, and military support. When the oppressed people of Biafra tried to win their independence, they were all killed. Where was the US? We remained "neutral", while our NATO allies gave vast amounts of mili-*

*tary aid to the genocidal government forces. The people
of Cuba are today not free by our standards, but they are
happy in the prosperity, health, and literacy brought by
Castro. The people of Poland have found that they like
socialism, which was initially forced on them by the
USSR, but that they want to revise certain aspects of it.
In effect, they want freedom. Where do they turn? To
their own power as nonviolent protesters. They feel that
Caspar Weinberger with his extravagant remarks is hurt-
ing their cause, not helping it.*

*So where does this leave me? I cannot endorse the
extremes of Communist repression, but neither can I
endorse your "hawkish" stance. I believe that the
answer lies not in institutions but in individuals. The
CIA and the army are not going to do me any good
with their bloated budgets, their abuses of power, and
their eagerness to kill. They cannot serve justice. Justice
must come from within me, in my own decision not to
serve the ends of war and of hatred. Thus, I will, I
believe, join the great tradition of agnostic Quakers. I
will oppose the draft, the arms race intervention, and
all the other remnants of man's sad history of warfare.
I will support whoever supports freedom and equality
and non-violence through activities such as those sponsored by Amnesty International. While you urge those
younger and poorer than yourself to kill and die, I will
do the only thing a person really can do: refuse to contribute, by my own actions, to injustice. Please cancel
my subscription to your Newsletter; it is not Christian.*

The ideas of this student are not unusual. They are shared by
thousands of the most privileged youth.

I replied to him as follows:

I read your letter with great interest, and I thank you
for writing to me. You are obviously intelligent and idealistic. I ask you to use your intelligence to criticize

yourself and your letter with the same honesty and perceptiveness that you would use when criticizing the letter of an opponent.

Does not your letter reveal: (1) Prejudice? (2) Confusion? (3) Evidence that you have been duped by communist propaganda? 4) Arrogance? Consider the evidence:

1. *Prejudice:* You state that you asked to receive the Crusade newsletter to satisfy your curiosity about "the lunatic fringe of the militant, war-mongering right." Does this not indicate that you had judged the Crusade prior to studying the evidence?

2. *Confusion:* You berate the United States for interference in the internal affairs of other countries and also for failing to interfere in the civil war in Nigeria during which Biafra sought independence. How can you have it both ways? What you are actually saying is: "The United States should interfere if I approve but only if I approve.

3. *Evidence that you have been duped by Communist propaganda:* You state: "The United States, in order to guard the freedom you cherish and the wealth you enjoy, has for years and probably will for years take advantage of the poor in this country and abroad."

This is a repetition of the slander of the United States which is a main theme of the communist propaganda. The accusation that the United States is taking advantage of the poor abroad is one of the themes of the Leninist doctrine of Imperialism. With regard to the poor within, the United States has taken extraordinary measures to improve their well-being. The percentage of the U.S. population classified as poor has diminished spectacularly during the past generation.

You also state that the oppressed of the world receive what they need from the Soviet Union. Is Afghanistan an example of this?

4. *Arrogance:* By what extraordinary process do you know what the people of Cuba and Poland think and

feel? You make the categorical statements that the people of Cuba are happy in the prosperity, health, and literacy brought about by Castro and that the people of Poland have found that they like socialism.

You and I do share one conviction. I agree with your statement: "I believe that the answer lies not in institutions, but in individuals." I pray that the grace of humility may be added to your positive qualities of intelligence, idealism, and compassion. I also ask God for His gift of humility.

We must not surrender young, intelligent and idealistic minds to the communists. Increasing efforts must be made to reach the students in colleges and high schools with the liberating truth. Mass distribution of the booklet, *Why I am Against Communism,* can, with your help, be commenced immediately.

Actions speak louder than words. Please send your best sacrificial gift to inform me of your agreement with the Crusade message and ministry and your determination that the communists shall not succeed in conquering this country and administering treatment similar to that given to the people of Cambodia.

With Christian love,
Fred Schwarz
Editor

A YOUNG AFRICAN INTELLECTUAL ASKS

My heart goes out to the young Nigerian man who writes the following letter. I believe he is seriously seeking the truth, and that he is bewildered by some of the delusions concerning Communism that are widespread among the educated of most countries in the world, including the U.S.A. He writes:

> *I have two of your slim booklets from my brother. They are titled:* Why I Am Against Communism *and* Why Communism Kills. *These booklets are your propaganda machine to discredit Communism as an evil ideol-*

ogy. But is Communism the only evil on earth? What about Apartheid, Capitalism, Colonialism and neo-Colonialism? These are the questions my close friends always ask after they have read these books. But I always ask, 'What is wrong with the facts and evidence presented in these books?'

My Friends claim that your motive in painting Communism black is to serve the agents of the Capitalist west, who seek to kill the souls of the poor of society; that the Capitalist states are the guardians and supporters of Apartheid; that the Capitalist world is the cause of the problems of the third world nations; that the Marcoses are responsible for the Communist rebels in the Philippines; that the Somozas created the Sandinistas; and that the Cambodian youths, who had been trained in France and who hated Capitalism, came back home to purge the evil Cambodian society. They claim that in a Communist or Marxist system, care is taken of all social strata.

Impressionable minds can easily cave in to these assertions; but, personally, I am keeping a foot in both camps until I understand each camp well.

I hope I will hear from you and receive more information so that I will know enough about Capitalism and Communism to make my choice and to stand firmly by it.

Yours sincerely,
[Name Withheld]

Dear [Name Withheld],

I congratulate you upon your fine letter and your desire to learn all you can about Capitalism and Communism so that you can make an informed and wise judgment concerning them. I ask you to consider the following:

1. Communism is certainly not the only evil in the world. Evil existed long before Marx and Lenin invented the modern Communist system. History is largely the record of man's inhumanity to man.

There are many evil systems in the world, and I certainly agree that Apartheid and colonialism are among them. I cannot agree, however, when you list Capitalism, without qualification, as essentially evil. I will discuss this later.

Because an individual chooses to use most of his talents and energy fighting one evil, it does not mean that he approves of the others.

May I use a medical analogy? There are many diseases that threaten the health and life of men and women. These diseases must be fought one by one. Because one individual specializes in the fight against cancer, it does not mean that he supports malaria. Because I concentrate upon exposing and opposing Communism, it does not mean that I support or am indifferent to the other evils you mention. I do know Communism has killed many millions and that it is therefore a major disease threatening mankind.

2. Because a disease is bad, it does not follow that a treatment advocated for the disease must be good. There are many known instances where the treatment is worse than the disease. Because some of the criticisms made by Communists and others against the actions of some Capitalists are justified, it does not necessarily follow that the cure they recommend is good.

3. Because an individual or a movement claims to have a good goal, it does not follow that the program advocated will bring that goal to fulfillment. Most tyrants in history have advocated a good goal. The goal is often a mirage that will never be reached. Much human misery has been caused by people who sincerely believed they were seeking a good goal. The end does not always justify the means.

4. Communism must be judged by its present activities, not its professed goals. Its professed goal of a society of perfect human beings, with an abundance of all material goods, so that government will be unnecessary and everyone will be able to take whatever is needed

from the overflowing storehouse, without payment, will never come to pass. That promise is the imaginary pot of gold at the foot of the rainbow. Communism must be judged by its present programs of dictatorship, economic and political monopoly, food shortages, human inequality due to class divisions, class extermination, military might, compulsory atheism, and imperialist expansion.

CAPITALISM

5. Capitalism and Communism are not comparable, and they are not always in opposition to each other. Capitalism is essentially a system in which people are motivated to produce goods to exchange in order to receive a profit. It can coexist with any form of government including Communism. For example, Lenin restored capitalism in Russia in 1921 when he introduced the New Economic Policy. He stated at that time:

"Can the Soviet State, the Dictatorship of the Proletariat, be combined, united with state Capitalism? Are they compatible?

"Of course they are." (V.I. Lenin, *Selected Works*, Vol. 2-Part II, 1952 edition, Moscow, page 544)

Capitalist economics is also compatible with a democratic system of government in which two or more political parties compete for political power. They have freedom to hold rallies at which they speak without restraint, and access to newspapers, radio and television.

The power of the elected government is temporary, limited by a constitution and an independent judiciary, and reversible by elections held from time to time.

COMMUNIST POWER

The essence of Communist rule is that the Communist party holds a monopoly of political and economic power. The Party controls the gun. It controls the Army and the Police Force, aided by an extensive internal espionage mechanism. This is usually a Secret Police organization, aided by local "Committees for the Defense of the Revolution", defined as "the eyes and ears of the revolution". The Communist Party is the only political organization allowed to nominate candidates for elections when they are held.

As Mao Tse-tung stated, "Political power grows out of the barrel of a gun."

CONTROL OF FOOD

Communist rule by the gun is supplemented by control of the food supply of each individual. When the Communists seize power, a food scarcity usually develops and ration cards are issued. These cards are distributed by Communist agents such as the heads of the Committees for the Defense of the Revolution. It takes a brave man to risk offending the individual and Party which give him the wherewithal to secure the food required by his wife and children.

ATHEISM

Capitalism has no doctrine concerning God, but Communism affirms categorically that there is no God, and proceeds to teach atheism to every child in school. The Communist policy towards whatever church exists when the Party seizes power is: (1) Enslavement, (2) Utilization, and (3) Destruction. During the phase of utilization, a modified freedom of worship may be permitted in order to impress tourists from unconquered countries.

When democracy and capitalism go hand in hand, a variety of religious groups are allowed to worship and compete freely.

THE BLESSINGS OF PROFIT

The quest for profit by the individual capitalist may appear purely selfish, but there are numerous examples of the quest for personal profit, by the few, having conferred great benefits upon the many. Consider, for example, the discovery and manufacture of the life-saving drugs.

I am confident that you agree that health is preferable to sickness. A mere 50 or so years ago, many millions of young people died from infectious diseases such as lobar pneumonia, tuberculosis, poliomyelitis, meningitis and malaria. In the last 50 years, more than 100 life-saving drugs have been discovered and have become available worldwide. Most of the diseases caused by bacteria have been defeated in large measure.

Every one of these drugs has been discovered and developed in the capitalist world, and many have been discovered and produced by pharmaceutical companies in their quest for profit.

As long as the Communists retain a monopoly of military might, they can permit any economic system to operate temporarily because they can reverse it at will. The utilization of capitalist incentives by Communist rulers does not indicate any change of heart or renunciation of belief; it is an application of Communist "dialectical science."

Your letter shows that you are an intelligent and compassionate young man. I am confident that you will choose freedom over tyranny and that you will be protected from the deception and seduction of Communism by acquiring knowledge of the real nature of Communism as revealed by its doctrines, history and current activities.

I hope and pray that your future life will be enriched by understanding, service to mankind, and personal happiness. I look forward to friendship and cooperation as we seek to preserve and extend human freedom.

With Christian love,
Fred Schwarz

P.S. I will send you our current newsletter, and a copy of the book, *You Can Trust the Communists (to be*

Communists). I will gladly provide further literature if you request it.

It is much better to prevent the recruitment of youthful idealists into the ranks of the communists than to spend blood and treasure fighting them after recruitment.

Accurate information concerning the nature of Communism and its record of deception, enslavement, mass murder, and impoverishment will prevent such recruitment.

Appendix II

·······················

Potpourri and
Newsletter Clippings

Variety is the mother of enjoyment.
—BENJAMIN DISRAELI

HUMOR BEHIND THE IRON CURTAIN

People in the Soviet Union and its Eastern European satellites
often express their anger and frustration in humor.
Told in Moscow:

What are we living under now, Daddy?
Under Communism, my son.
And what did we live under before?
Under Socialism.
What is the difference between Communism and Socialism?
Well, under Socialism, for example, we often had to stand
 in queues to buy meat.
What is meat, Daddy?

(Munich, Radio Free Europe—
Chicago Daily News Foreign Service)

561

In Poland:

>CUSTOMER: "Have you any beef?"
>SHOP MANAGER: "No, madam."
>CUSTOMER: "Any mutton?"
>SHOP MANAGER: "Sorry, none."
>CUSTOMER: "Any other kind of meat?"
>SHOP MANAGER: "No, none at all."

After the customer leaves the shop, the manager says to his assistant: "Good heavens, what an extraordinary memory that woman has!"

Heard on a Moscow street:

>MOTHER: "I don't understand this *perestroika*. What is it?"
>SON: "It's very simple. I will show you."

He points to two buckets standing side-by-side. One is empty, and the other is full of stones. He tips the stones from the full one into the empty one and turns to his mother and asks: "Now do you understand, Mother?"

MOTHER: "No, I don't. There doesn't seem to be any change. There is still one empty bucket and one full of stones."

SON: "But, Mother dear, didn't you hear the noise?"

Pat challenges Mike, who has recently embraced Socialism:

PAT: "Now that you are a Socialist, do you believe in sharing?"

MIKE: "I certainly do."

PAT: "If you had a million dollars, would you give me half?"

MIKE: "I certainly would."

PAT: "If you had a thousand dollars, would you give me half?"

MIKE: "Don't be insulting, I told you I would share willingly."

PAT: "If you had ten dollars, would you give me half?"

MIKE: "What are you trying to do? Trick me? You know I have ten dollars."

A political joke in Hungary describes an imaginary visit by President Carter to a Budapest factory where the workers have been carefully briefed to tell him that they enjoy a high standard of living:

PRESIDENT CARTER (speaking to a worker): "Do you own a house?"

WORKER: "Yes, Mr. President, I have a big one in a town and a smaller one in the country, where I go on a weekend."

PRESIDENT CARTER: "How much do you earn?"

WORKER: "A very large wage, so much indeed that I am able to save quite a bit. My bank balance is getting bigger every month."

PRESIDENT CARTER: "Are you saving to buy something you particularly want?"

WORKER: "Oh yes, Mr. President, a pair of shoes."

An anecdote told on Moscow's street shows that appreciation there of Gorbachev may not be as warm as the Western media reports:

GORBACHEV asks STALIN: "What should I do about this *perestroika* business? It's causing no end of problems."

STALIN: "It's simple. First, shoot 80 percent of your officials; second, rename the White Sea the Black Sea and the other way around."

GORBACHEV: "I don't get it. Why do I need to rename the Black and White seas?"

STALIN: "Mikhail Sergeyevich, I'm delighted. I knew I could rely on you not to raise difficulties over the first proposal."

(Gorbachev is not only a disciple of the later Lenin, he is also similar in many ways to the early Stalin.)

Trying to understand Communist intentions when their actions are in conflict with their words is difficult. It is reminiscent of the story of the man who backed away in alarm when his friend's dog rushed at him, barking furiously and wagging its tail. His friend reassured him:

"Don't be frightened. Can't you see he's wagging his tail?"

"Yes," came the reply, "but I don't know which end to believe!"

PEOPLE'S OWNERSHIP?

We had a slogan in Queensland, the state in Australia where I was born: "Use the railways, you own them." But when you went to get on them, you had to buy a ticket at a high price. In my earlier days they were poorly run and usually late. Slogans mean nothing. It is content that counts.

The difference between Communist and American ownership is well illustrated by a story about a man who visited a factory in Russia. He asked the workers:

> "Who owns this factory?"
> "We do."
> "Who owns the land on which it is built?"
> "We do."
> "Who owns the factory's products?"
> "We do."

Noticing three cars in the adjacent lot, the visitor asked:

> "Who owns those cars?"
> "We do! We own them but one is used by the factory manager, one by the political commissar, and one by the representative of the secret police."

Later, the same man visited a great automobile factory in America. He asked the workers:

> "Who owns this factory?"
> "Henry Ford."
> "Who owns the land on which it is built?"
> "Henry Ford."

Alongside the factory thousands of modern cars filled a vast car park. He asked:

> "Who owns those cars?"
> "We do."

Would you sooner have nominal ownership of the factory where you work and slave for very little, or own the products of the factory in which you work, and use and dispose of them as you will? Personally, I'll choose the second type of ownership.

> (Excerpt from a debate with Roger McAfee)

JANE FONDA QUOTED

Actress Jane Fonda told two thousand students at Michigan State University, "I would think that if you understood what Communism was, you would hope, you would pray on your knees that we would someday become Communist." (*Detroit Free Press,* November 22, 1970)

Miss Fonda's beneficent attitude toward Communism is probably extracted from the meaning of the word "Communism." It ignores the history of the last hundred years, the doctrines of Marx and Lenin, the deeds of Lenin and Stalin, and the plight of the International Communist Movement. It ignores millions of corpses, millions of refugees, and the agony of hundreds of millions who have to be forcibly prevented from fleeing the Communist "paradise."

Communism declares there is no God. Should we then "pray on our knees that we would someday become Communist"? (See chapter 16)

A VIETNAMESE QUOTED

"The Chinese ruled us for a thousand years; we did not flee. The French ruled us for one hundred years; we did not flee. The Americans showered us with napalm, bombs, and bullets; we did not flee. The Communists rule; now we flee."

JUANITA CASTRO QUOTED

"Fidel will never be satisfied with merely being the dictator of Cuba. He hopes to dominate every country in the Americas. His ambition is ridiculous; it knows no bounds. To satisfy his ambition he is capable of using, indiscriminately, an armament given to him by Communist Imperialism which, in turn, uses him as a tool of its subversionist and interventionist policy.

"Before Cuba fell prey to Communist Imperialism, the Cuban people, who were not and are not Communists, did not have the experience necessary to understand what those intellectuals, politicians, students, and labor leaders who followed Communist ideology were capable of doing. These deceivers masqueraded, as they do everywhere, as defenders of freedom, democracy, and peace.

"This was our first mistake. We neither studied nor observed what the Communists had been doing since they took over the first country. We forgot their history of treason. And so, we were deceived.

"Those Communists who demand 'freedom,' tomorrow will refuse us that freedom.

"Those Communists who demand respect for human life, tomorrow will be firing at us when we stand before the 'wall.' Those Communists who are allowed to use the law for protection, tomorrow will destroy that very same law, so that we are deprived of its protection.

"I have seen how families, who made their fortune by means of honest, productive work, or inherited it legally, were dispossessed. These families were not anti-Communists. They didn't even know what Communism was. However, they were on the Communist's black list; they were considered enemies, and thus deprived of their properties.

"Now, they have no means of support. Many have committed suicide. Others are dying slowly, consuming meager food rations allowed them by the regime.

"I have seen parents and children jailed in inhuman political prisons and in concentration or hard labor camps, and I have heard personal witness accounts of thousands of executions before the 'wall.' "

(Fidel Castro's sister Juanita. A speech before the World Anti-Communist League and Asian People's Anti-Communist League, held in Tokyo, Kyoto, Japan, September 15–20, 1970.)

FIDEL CASTRO QUOTED

"I have been a Marxist–Leninist since my student days, but I hid it; for had I not done so, I could not have brought the revolution to a successful conclusion."

THE VERDICT OF HISTORY

Castro is concerned with the verdict of history. After the attack on the Mancada Army Barracks in 1953, Castro wrote, "History will absolve me."

History has a way of dealing with tyrants. The futility of human pride in empire building was well described in the following poem by Percy Bysshe Shelley, nearly two hundred years ago.

OZYMANDIAS

I met a traveler from an antique land
Who said: Two vast and trunkless legs of stone
Stand in the desert. Near them, on the sand,
Half sunk, a shattered visage lies, whose frown,
And wrinkled lip, and sneer of cold command,
Tell that its sculptor well those passions read
Which yet survive, stamped on these lifeless things,
The hand that mocked them and the heart that fed;
And on the pedestal these words appear:
"My name is Ozymandias, king of kings:
Look on my works, ye Mighty, and despair!"
Nothing beside remains. Round the decay
Of that colossal wreck, boundless and bare,
The lone and level sands stretch far away.

SVETLANA, STALIN'S DAUGHTER, QUOTED

In a letter to Malcolm Muggeridge: "Christ is alive, he is with me every day of my existence. He is with me in my room, in my house. He was with me even in Russia."

She was also seen in a BBC-TV interview with the Muggeridges at their home in Sussex when she spoke further about her faith. She described how she began to turn to Christianity:

"It was when my two aunts came back from six years, solitary confinement for doing nothing, that I talked to them about life and faith and I began to read the Bible. I read it very simply, and every time when I read my Bible it says something, reveals something.

Light comes. It was at that time I began to know that life is a gift of God. Then my life began to seem valuable. Every moment was valuable."

Asked if there were other people in the Soviet Union thinking that way she replied:

"Of course. Millions of people then and today vaguely feel this way, dissatisfied with the materialistic view of life through their experience of a godless, terrible, depressing life. In the Soviet Union there are millions of the 250 millions there who have never lost faith. It is the state which declares itself atheistic. But millions don't care what the state says."

Svetlana told how her grandmother, Stalin's mother, who lived in Tbilisi, Georgia, was pious and almost illiterate. When she was dying and he went to visit her she said:

"What a pity that you didn't become a priest." She cared nothing about his achievements as a great leader of a big country. To the last she lamented that he hadn't become a priest.

"I see my poor, hard-working grandmothers and grandfathers as more important than my father. It's more important to go back and see how they lived, a simple family life, life of faith, life of love."

She described the muddled incompetence when her father had the stroke from which he died.

(*CACC Newsletter,* September 15, 1982)

JOHN WAYNE

John Wayne was a personal friend and Crusade supporter. He did not waver in his support of the Crusade when the storm of slander was at its peak in the 1960s and some celebrities thought it the better part of valor to remain mute. When anti-Communism became unfashionable, he spurned fashion. He even did a little spontaneous fund-raising for the Crusade in unlikely places, as shown in his letter.

John Wayne received many honors in life and more since his death. Knowing him, I am confident he would have taken particular pride in the "eulogy" that appeared in the June 16, 1979, edition of the *Daily World,* published by the U.S. Communist Party. Under the caption, "Just whose hero was John Wayne?" the article begins by classifying him as a "warmongering, racist, anti-union millionaire" and goes on with trenchant criticism because he was one of the founders of the Motion Picture Alliance for the Preservation of American Ideals, formed to oppose the attempt of the Communists to control Hollywood. I can see his smile had he been able to read the attack in the *Daily World* and hear his wry comment, "So the Commies are running true to form. What else is new?"

JOHN WAYNE

5451 Marathon Street
Hollywood, Calif. 90038
January 13, 1970

Dr. Fred C. Schwarz
124 East First Street
Long Beach, Calif. 90801

Dear Dr. Schwarz:

I opened my big, fat mouth at our Annual
Bull Sale in Arizona, and look what I got
for you.

Sincerely,

John Wayne

Enc
($500.00 check)

JW:ms

DETENTE DELIRIUM

CACC newsletter, July 1, 1978:

When the manufacturers of a product print "poison" on the bottle in which the product is contained, but the users refuse to believe the label and insist on regarding the product as nourishing and harmless, who is to blame?

The Soviet Union has clearly labeled its product, "detente," as poison for the non-Communist world. Detente is designed to cause the death of political freedom, and the Communists have stated this consistently. The authorities in America, influenced by the liberal political commentators, the academic experts, the foundation pundits, and their natural desire to believe that which is pleasant, have just as consistently refused to believe them.

President Carter has now belatedly discovered that the Soviet Union is involved in offensive operations in Africa (using their Cuban dependents as surrogates), threatens Europe, possesses vast and increasing military might far beyond any requirements for defense, has a navy which can operate in any area of the world and which is backed by a large and growing merchant marine which can undercut and bankrupt the merchant marine of non-Communist countries, and he complains that this Communist conduct is contrary to the "code" of detente—a code that exists only in the liberal American mind.

In a speech to the graduating class of the U.S. Naval Academy on June 7, 1978, he called on the Soviets to accept "cooperation through a detente that increasingly involves similar restraints on both sides." (*The Los Angeles Times,* June 8, 1978)

This is asking Communism to renounce its doctrines, its history, and itself.

MURDER OF A GENTLE LAND

Familiar as I am with the history of Communist cruelty which has resulted from their doctrine of the guilt and decadence of the bourgeois class, I found it difficult to sleep after reading the story *Murder of a Gentle Land,* which appeared in the February 1977 edition of the *Reader's Digest.* It is a report of what happened in Cambodia following the Communist conquest of that country.

The authors are John Barron, a senior editor of the *Reader's Digest* and author of *The KGB: The Secret Work of Soviet Agents,* and Anthony Paul, an Australian and editor of the *Digest*'s Asia edition. Assisted by a team of experienced workers, they interviewed survivors from the Cambodia slaughter living in refugee camps in Thailand.

Emptying the Cities

The story tells how, after taking over in April 1975, the Communists launched a pitiless campaign of terror that "emptied the cities and turned the villages, fields, and jungles into charnel houses where unburied corpses lie putrefying in the sun." This was done because the new regime was determined to obliterate every vestige of past Cambodian civilization in order to create its own society.

As soon as the Communists had secured control of Cambodia, they ordered the evacuation of Phnom Penh, a city of three million inhabitants. No exceptions. This report states:

> Hundreds of men, women, and children in pajamas limped, hobbled, struggled out into the streets, where the midday sun had raised the temperature to well over 100 degrees. Relatives or friends pushed the beds of patients too enfeebled to walk, some holding aloft infu-

sion bottles dripping plasma into the bodies of loved
ones. One man carried his son whose legs had just been
amputated. The bandages on both stumps were red with
blood, and the son, who appeared to be about 22, was
screaming, "You can't take me like this! Kill me! Please
kill me!"

Murder of a Gentle Land, 231

Phnom Penh was purged of all printed matter as well as people.
Historically, burning books and burning people have gone hand in
hand:

Tens of thousands, perhaps hundreds of thousands of
books were thrown into the Mekong River or burned on
its banks. Untold others were burned at a dump, and the
libraries of Phnom Penh and Buddhist universities went
up in flames.

More Than a Million Dead

The authors estimate that, at a minimum, 1.2 million men,
women, and children died in Cambodia between April 17, 1975,
and December 1976 in the Communist purge. The population of
Cambodia, seven million before the war, has been reduced to five
million.

There has been remarkably little protest about this massive
slaughter. Instead the press of the world has been busy detailing the
crimes of Chile, Israel, Rhodesia, and South Africa. When one of the
authors of the Cambodian classicide, Leng Sary, appeared at the
United Nations, delegates from around the world *applauded* him.

Joseph Stalin showed insight into human nature when he said,
"The death of one man is a tragedy; the death of a million is a
statistic."

The Cause

There is a danger that those reading the story will be overwhelmed with horror but will fail to learn the right lessons. The

roots of the tragedy reside in Communist doctrine. Those who conceived and organized the operation were sincere believers in this doctrine. It taught them that man is a material machine and is formed in the mold of his environment; man is perfectible by creating a perfecting environment.

The doctrine also teaches that the Capitalist environment has produced a diseased and depraved nature. If mankind is to be perfected, this environment must be totally destroyed. The Communist leaders proceeded to do this with ruthless efficiency.

Since men and women are evolutionary animals, devoid of divine essence, without soul or spirit, and renewable, it is legitimate to dispose of them when this is necessary for the success of the project to perfect human nature scientifically. One Cambodian Communist leader is reported to have stated that one million survivors would be adequate for their purposes.

The objective is to create a new environment in which everyone works for others rather than for themselves. This will allegedly eliminate selfishness from human nature. When everyone works voluntarily for others, society will be perfected.

This program is delusional, but the rationale is clear. The roots are atheism, scientific materialism, and human pride; the antidote is faith in God, compassion, and humility.

(*CACC Newsletter,* February 15, 1977)

VIETNAM PERSPECTIVE

One common accusation is that America is intervening in what is essentially a civil war.

On this subject, the words of Nikita Khrushchev merit consideration: "There is more at stake in this war than just the future of the Vietnamese people. The Vietnamese are shedding their blood and laying down their lives for the sake of the World Communist Movement." (*Khrushchev Remembers,* 487)

The so-called "peace agitation" which is so prevalent in the United States, is regarded by the Communists of Vietnam as part of their war action.

(Xuan Thuy in "World Magazine" of the *Daily World,*
March 13, 1971)

COMMUNISM, OPIATE OF ATHEISTS

The apostle Paul (Romans 1:25) knew well that atheistic man's search for an opiate leads him to the crassest sort of idolatry, as we can judge from this typical *Pravda* poem of the 1930s:

> O great Stalin, O leader of the peoples,
> Thou who broughtest man to birth,
> Thou who purifiest the earth,
> Thou who restorest the centuries,
> Thou, who makest bloom the spring . . .
> Thou, splendor of my spring, O Thou
> Sun reflected in millions of hearts.
>
> (*Communism and Christ*, Charles W. Lowry, 51)

COMMUNIST PEACE

Wherever you find a Communist, you find an advocate of peace. "Peace" is one of the golden words of their vocabulary. They have "peace" movements of every kind; they have peace campaigns, peace prizes, peace conferences, peace processions. Every Communist is a devotee of peace.

Most people watching the military preparations of the Communists, noting the enormous percentage of their budget devoted to military objectives, observing their ruthless, brutal repression of any attempt by their captive nations to secure freedom, classify the Communists as blatant hypocrites. This is far from the truth. The Communists are not hypocrites. They are sincerely and genuinely dedicated to peace. If you gave a mature Communist a lie detector test and asked him if he desired peace with all his heart, he would pass with flying colors. They live for peace; they long for peace; they would willingly die for peace.

What is this peace which they desire? . . . To them, peace is that golden consummation when the progressive force of Communism totally overwhelms American Imperialism and climaxes in Communist world conquest. By definition, "peace" is Communist world conquest. Since this is true, any action that advances Communist conquest is a "peaceful" action.

(*You Can Trust the Communists (to be Communists*, pp. 6–8,
and *CACC Newsletter,* February 15, 1970)

THE FREEDOM PARADOX

Many have willingly surrendered their freedom to choose:

To kill whales;
To kill elephants;
To kill dolphins;
To kill deer out of season;
To kill eagles;
To kill buzzards, such as the Californian condor;
To kill little fish known as the snail darter;
To kill baby seals;
To kill many other animals. (How many can you name?)

But oh! How passionately they fight for the freedom to choose to
kill unborn babies.

(*CACC Newsletter,* January 1, 1990)

CUSTODIANS

Whether rich or poor, we are custodians of the resources God has
entrusted to us. We should spurn the conduct that earns God's
rebuke, "*YOU FOOL . . . ,*" and follow the advice of William
Cullen Bryant, who wrote:

So live that when thy summons comes to join
The innumerable caravan that moves
To that mysterious realm, where each shall take
His chamber in the silent halls of death,
Thou go not, like the quarry-slave at night
Scourged to his dungeon, but sustained and soothed
By an unfaltering trust, approach thy grave
Like one who wraps the drapery of his couch
About him, and lies down to pleasant dreams.

(*CACC Newsletter,* February 1, 1985)

ANTI-SEMITISM?

In her letter to me in October 1967, Eleanor Sternberg wrote:

My husband and I are not Christians; we are Jews. We have been attending your meetings and contributing to the Crusade for several years now, mainly because we know of no Jewish group so active in attempting to educate the public on what Communism is all about.

We are truly appreciative of the work you are trying to do. We respect and admire you as an individual and have never found anything about you or any of those connected with the Crusade to indicate to us that you are anything but honorable and devoted people in your fight against Communism. We only wish that more Jewish people would help you fight against this evil force and we may someday see the day when you shall see fit to change your name to "The Judeo-Christian Anti-Communism Crusade."

You have my permission to read this letter to any group.

COMMUNIST REGENERATION OF CHILDREN

The Communists attempt to justify their "Gulag Archipelago" by claiming they are creating new and regenerate people.

The processes used for such regenerative purposes are described in the *Samizdat Bulletin,* No. 81, January 1980:

For the maintenance of children, both those taken away from religious parents by the court and those left without parents when the latter are arrested, there exists a number of children's homes of the boarding school type.

Conditions in such schools are described by Vyacheslav Volobuyev who was raised in one:

The years passed, I grew more mature and, in the environment, I became a sadist and a criminal. I had already learned how to steal from the store, how to open a lock, how to break glass noiselessly, how to hit a person in order to knock him senseless.

When I became the "oldest" pupil, some power came to me. I became a detachment commander which gave me power over 200 pupils. I began to take revenge for all the old insults and taunts. I would beat pupils for no reason, degrade them and steal from them. This was my entertainment; I did not know any other. Everything was permissible to me because I kept order in the detachment.

Samizdat Bulletin, 4
(*CACC Newsletter,* April 15, 1980)

Knowing my love of poetry, Crusade friends send me poems. I quoted this poem in our newsletter.

YOU MUSTN'T QUIT

When things go wrong, as they sometimes will,
When the road you're trudging seems all uphill,
When funds are low and the debts are high,
And you want to smile but you have to sigh,
When troubles are pressing you down a bit,
Rest if you must, but don't you quit.

Success is failure turned inside out,
The silver tint of the clouds of doubt.
You can never tell how close you are,
It may be near when it seems afar;
So stay in the fight when you're hardest hit,
It's when things seem worst that you mustn't quit.
(Anonymous)

Epilogue

....

President Clinton
Makes History

IT LOOKED LIKE A PRIVATE, personal letter. The envelope was small and white, my name was handwritten, and the letter was hand-stamped. I opened it expectantly and was surprised to discover that it came from none other than Bill Clinton, the President of the United States.

Whoever wrote the letter—I doubt it was President Clinton—was laboring under certain delusions.

The signature is "Bill Clinton," apparently handwritten in blue ink.

I am not so naive that I believe that the president wrote and sent this letter himself. What puzzles me is how those responsible have such assurance that I have been, and am, a loyal and dedicated Democrat. What is the source of this delusion? I am Australian citizen who has never engaged in partisan political activity in the United States of America, and I am not legally entitled to do so.

I subscribe to a number of liberal left-wing publications. The Democratic fund-raisers possibly gained access to a list of subscribers to one of the magazines and assumed that all on the list were loyal and dedicated Democrats. Was this, in their minds, "virtue by association"?

Imagine the effect this letter could have on history. Any historian, after reading it, could report that he has documentary proof, from

A3F ABGG83

BILL CLINTON

Fred Schwartz
P.O. Box 890
Long Beach, CA 90801-0890

Dear Fred,

Over the next few weeks, I will begin my reelection campaign in the state of California.

And before beginning my campaign in your state, I want to invite you to become a member of the California Citizens for Clinton/Gore Committee.

Membership on this important committee is an honorary position. It is my way of saying thanks for your loyal support as a Democrat. And it is also my way of asking you to join me in this historic campaign. By joining, you will be making a statement of support that will mean a lot to me personally.

All members of the committee will receive updates on the progress of the campaign. You will have an opportunity to provide my campaign team with written input about the political situation in your area. You will also receive a certificate recognizing your membership. But no meetings or formal duties are required.

I have enclosed a reply card for you to indicate whether or not you accept this invitation. Whatever your answer, please respond soon so that I will know your decision, and we can finalize the committee's membership roster.

Time is short. Election day will be here sooner than we think.

And as you consider your decision, I hope you will consider the importance of this historic election. We are involved in a political struggle that will determine the future course of our nation as we enter a new century, and a new millennium.

P.O. Box 19827, Washington, DC 20036
Paid for by Clinton/Gore '96 GELAC

Will we continue my efforts to restore the American Dream, to grow the middle class and shrink the underclass? Or will America pursue a different vision which reduces government to an entity without room for helping children, community responsibility or sensible regulation to protect ordinary Americans?

You understand the importance of the task ahead. My message to you is that I need your partnership to succeed in the most challenging campaign I have ever faced.

The outcome will be decided not by political strategists or newscasters or powerful special interests. This election will be decided by individual citizens who become involved and give of themselves for the candidate of their choice.

Please let me know that I will have your support in the campaign ahead. With the commitment of dedicated Democrats such as you, I know we can win an important victory for the values we share.

Thank you in advance for your help and support.

Sincerely,

Bill Clinton

P.S. One of our important challenges is raising funds for the campaign ahead. Membership on the Citizens for Clinton/Gore Committee does not require a contribution of any kind. However, if you can afford to send a gift, I will be greatly appreciative of any help you can provide. Please respond today!

the President of the United States himself, that I had been a "loyal and dedicated Democrat."

This trifling incident illustrates how many delusions concerning the message of Fred Schwarz and the ministry of the Christian Anti-Communism Crusade have been accepted as historic truth in much of academia and the news media.

One purpose of writing the autobiographical history of the Christian Anti-Communism Crusade, *Beating the Unbeatable Foe,* is to remove truth from the scaffold and place it on the throne.

Index